# 中国文化概论

An Outline of Chinese Culture

（中英双语版）

赵春娥　达娃央宗　著

（美）狄志良（Keith Randall Sean Dede）　达娃央宗　译

·广州·

## 版权所有　翻印必究

**图书在版编目（CIP）数据**

中国文化概论：中英双语版/赵春娥，达娃央宗著；（美）狄志良（Keith Randall Sean Dede），达娃央宗译. —广州：中山大学出版社，2023.1
ISBN 978-7-306-07663-2

Ⅰ. ①中… Ⅱ. ①赵… ②达… ③狄… Ⅲ. ①中华文化—汉、英 Ⅳ. ①K203

中国版本图书馆 CIP 数据核字（2022）第 239739 号

ZHONGGUO WENHUA GAILUN

| | |
|---|---|
| 出 版 人： | 王天琪 |
| 策划编辑： | 金继伟 |
| 责任编辑： | 熊锡源 |
| 封面设计： | 曾 婷 |
| 责任校对： | 麦颖晖 |
| 责任技编： | 靳晓虹 |
| 出版发行： | 中山大学出版社 |
| 电　　话： | 编辑部 020-84110283，84113349，84111997，84110779，84110776 |
| | 发行部 020-84111998，84111981，84111160 |
| 地　　址： | 广州市新港西路 135 号 |
| 邮　　编： | 510275　　传　真：020-84036565 |
| 网　　址： | http://www.zsup.com.cn　　E-mail: zdcbs@mail.sysu.edu.cn |
| 印 刷 者： | 佛山市浩文彩色印刷有限公司 |
| 规　　格： | 787mm×1092mm　1/16　26.75 印张　607 千字 |
| 版次印次： | 2023 年 1 月第 1 版　2023 年 1 月第 1 次印刷 |
| 定　　价： | 68.00 元 |

如发现本书因印装质量影响阅读，请与出版社发行部联系调换

# 本书编委会

### 著者
赵春娥　达娃央宗

### 译者
狄志良（Keith Randall Sean Dede）
达娃央宗

### 编委
杨华　梁霞　夏丽梅　白雪梅

### 作者单位

赵春娥　青海师范大学历史学院教授
达娃央宗　美国佛罗里达大学博士研究生
狄志良　美国俄勒冈州路易斯克拉克大学外国语言文学系汉语言教授
杨　华　武汉大学历史学院教授
梁　霞　青海师范大学学报编辑部副教授
夏丽梅　青海师范大学历史学院副教授
白雪梅　青海师范大学历史学院副教授

# 序　言

诸君案头的这部《中国文化概论（中英双语版）》，是青海藏族学者赵春娥、达娃央宗为母语非汉语的大学生编撰的通识读本。赵教授等从中国文化生成环境考察入手，探求中国文化的基本精神，纵议中国文化的历史进程，横述中国文化形下之器与形上之道诸侧面。本书立基于文化史学的固有认知，又吸纳某些前沿成果，论析简洁明快、深入浅出、精练有趣，且图文并茂，可望成为雅俗共赏的文化学佳品。

冯天瑜<br>
2018 年 6 月 7 日<br>
于武汉大学

# Preface

This book, *An Outline of Chinese Culture* (*Chinese – English Edition*), was compiled by Qinghai Tibetan scholars Zhao Chun-E and Dawayangzong for college students whose native language is not Chinese. Prof. Zhao and other scholars started by examining the environment in which Chinese culture was created, explored the fundamental spirit of Chinese culture, discussed the historical process of Chinese culture, and described the aspects of Chinese culture in terms of its material and spiritual ways. This book is based on the inherent knowledge of cultural history but also draws on some cutting-edge achievements. It is concise and clear in its analysis, in-depth, concise and interesting, and illustrated—this book is expected to be a great work of cultural studies which suits both refined and popular tastes.

Feng Tianyu<br>
in Wuhan University<br>
on June 7, 2018.

# 目 录

导 论
**Introduction** ·················································································· **1**
  一、文化
    Culture ················································································ 1
  二、文明
    Civilization ············································································ 4
  三、中国・华夏・中华
    Three Names for China：*Zhongguo*, *Hua-Xia*, and *Zhonghua* ············ 5

第一章　中国文化的生态环境
**The Ecology of Chinese Culture** ··········································· **11**
  一、地理环境
    Geographic Environment ························································ 11
  二、经济形态
    Economic Patterns ································································ 13
  三、社会结构
    Social Structure ···································································· 14
  四、中西生态环境对文化的影响比较
    Comparing the Influence of Ecology on Culture Between China and the West ··· 21

第二章　中国文化的历史演进
**The Historical Evolution of Chinese Culture** ···················· **24**
  一、中国文化的起源
    The Origin of Chinese Culture ················································· 24
  二、文明奠基：夏、商、西周
    Foundation of Civilization：Xia, Shang, and Western Zhou ··············· 24

三、百家争鸣与元典创制：春秋战国时期
　　Contention among a Hundred Schools of Thought and Creation of the Primary Canon (Axial Age)：The Spring-Autumn (770-481 B.C.) and Warring States (481-221 B.C.) ·················· 30

四、政治一统和文化整合：秦、汉时期
　　Political Unification and Cultural Integration：The Qin-Han Period ·············· 40

五、胡汉、中印文化融合：魏晋至唐中叶
　　The Mix of Cultures from Han and non-Han, and Between China and India：From Wei-Jin to Mid-Tang Period ·················· 41

六、近古文化定型：唐中叶至明中叶
　　Finalization of the Near-Ancient Culture：Mid-Tang to Mid-Ming Period ········ 46

七、文化专制与西学东渐：明清时期
　　Cultural Dictatorship and Western Learning's Eastern Flow：Ming-Qing Period ·················· 51

## 第三章　中国的汉字
**Chinese Characters** ·················· **64**

一、汉字的起源
　　Origin of Chinese Characters ·················· 64

二、汉字的字体演变
　　Evolution of Calligraphic Styles ·················· 65

三、汉字的结构
　　The Structure of Chinese Characters ·················· 70

四、汉字的笔画
　　The Strokes of Chinese Characters ·················· 72

五、汉字的数量
　　The Number of Chinese Characters ·················· 75

六、汉语词汇的扩展（一）
　　——汉译佛教词语
　　The Expansion of Chinese Vocabulary：Chinese Translations of Buddhist Terms ·················· 76

七、汉语词汇的扩展（二）
　　——近代日制汉语新词
　　The Expansion of Chinese Vocabulary：Near-Modern Japanese-made Chinese Neologisms ·················· 84

八、汉语词汇的扩展（三）
　　——近代音译英文词语
　　The Expansion of Chinese Vocabulary: Transliterated Words from English …… 88
九、汉字改革
　　Chinese Character Reform …………………………………………………… 91
十、汉字文化圈
　　Sphere of Cultural Influence of Chinese Characters ………………………… 93

**第四章　中国儒家思想**
**China's Ru-ist（Confucian）Thought** ……………………………………… **95**
一、儒家思想的形成及核心内容
　　The Formation of the Ru-ist School and the Core Content ………………… 95
二、儒家的发展阶段
　　The Growth Stage of Ru-ism ………………………………………………… 101
三、儒学是不是宗教的争论
　　The Debate over Whether Ru-ism Is a Religion …………………………… 102
四、儒家语录
　　Ru-ist Quotations …………………………………………………………… 105

**第五章　中国古代的佛教、道教**
**Chinese Buddhism and Daoism** …………………………………………… **109**
一、佛教
　　Buddhism ……………………………………………………………………… 109
二、道教
　　Daoism ………………………………………………………………………… 115
三、中西宗教比较
　　Comparison of Chinese and Western Religions …………………………… 118

**第六章　中国古代教育**
**Ancient Chinese Education** ………………………………………………… **123**
一、古代教育制度
　　Ancient Educational System ………………………………………………… 123
二、选官制度的演变
　　The Evolution of the Official Selection System …………………………… 126
三、科举考试制度
　　The Imperial Examination System …………………………………………… 128

四、科举制度的影响
　　Impact of the Examination System ················ 133
五、中西教育比较
　　Comparison of Chinese and Western Education ················ 134

## 第七章　中国古代文学
## Chinese Ancient Literature ················ **136**

一、中国古代文学发展进程简述
　　Summary of the Growth of Ancient Chinese Literature ················ 136
二、中国古代文学成就
　　Literary Accomplishments of Ancient China ················ 138
三、中西文学比较
　　Comparison of Chinese and Western Literature ················ 170

## 第八章　中国古代书法、绘画
## Ancient Chinese Calligraphy and Painting ················ **174**

一、书法
　　Calligraphy ················ 174
二、绘画
　　Chinese Painting ················ 192
三、如何欣赏中国画
　　How to Appreciate Chinese Painting ················ 202
四、中国画与西方画的比较
　　Comparison of Chinese Painting and Western Painting ················ 204
五、中西对待雕塑的不同态度
　　Different Attitudes Toward Sculpture in China and the West
　　················ 207

## 第九章　中国古代音乐、戏曲
## Ancient Chinese Music and Opera ················ **214**

一、中国古代代表性乐器
　　Representative Instruments of Ancient Chinese Music ················ 215
二、十大古典名曲
　　Ten Famous Classical Songs ················ 233
三、中国古典音乐的特点
　　Characteristics of Chinese Classical Music ················ 236

四、中国戏曲的种类
　　Types of Chinese Opera ················ 237

五、中国戏曲的特点
　　Characteristics of Chinese Opera ················ 244

## 第十章　中国建筑
## Chinese Architecture ················ 247

一、中国建筑类型
　　Types of Chinese Architecture ················ 247

二、中国古代建筑的主要特点
　　Main Traits of Ancient Chinese Architecture ················ 259

三、长城及其他代表性建筑
　　The Great Wall and Other Representative Buildings ················ 263

## 第十一章　中国古代科技——四大发明
## Ancient Chinese Science and Technology—Four Great Inventions ······ 272

一、造纸术
　　Papermaking Technology ················ 273

二、印刷术
　　Printing Technology ················ 274

三、指南针
　　Compass ················ 277

四、火药
　　Gunpowder ················ 278

五、近代中国科技不发达的原因
　　Reasons for the Lack of Growth in Chinese Science and Technology in Modern Times ················ 279

## 第十二章　中国医学
## Chinese Medicine ················ 282

一、中医的起源
　　Origin of Chinese Medicine ················ 282

二、中医药理论
　　Theory of Chinese Medicine ················ 283

三、中医疗法
　　Chinese Medical Therapy ················ 286

### 四、古代名医
Famous Ancient Doctors ·················· 289

### 五、中医主要典籍
The Main Classics of Chinese Medicine ·················· 291

## 第十三章　中国古代服饰
**Ancient Chinese Apparel** ·················· **294**

### 一、传统汉服
Traditional Han Chinese Apparel ·················· 294

### 二、五行与着装
The Five-Phases Theory and Clothing ·················· 298

### 三、服饰中的文化观念
Cultural Notions in Apparel ·················· 299

## 第十四章　中国饮食
**Chinese Food and Drink** ·················· **302**

### 一、饮食原料和特点
Materials and Characteristics of Food and Drink ·················· 302

### 二、素食
Vegetarian Food ·················· 304

### 三、药膳
Medicinal Cuisine ·················· 304

### 四、八大菜系
Eight Great Regional Cuisines ·················· 305

### 五、茶
Tea ·················· 311

### 六、酒
Alcohol ·················· 330

## 第十五章　中国武术
**Chinese Martial Arts** ·················· **340**

### 一、武术的起源
The Origin of Martial Arts ·················· 340

### 二、武术流派的划分
Classification of Schools of Martial Arts ·················· 340

三、武术的主要派别
　　Main Schools of Martial Arts ·················································· 342

## 第十六章　中国传统节日
## Traditional Chinese Festivals ·················································· 348
一、主要的传统节日
　　The Main Traditional Festivals ··············································· 349
二、中国节日的特征
　　Characteristics of Chinese Festivals ········································· 368

## 第十七章　中国文化的基本精神
## The Basic Spirit of Chinese Culture ·········································· 370
一、自强不息
　　Constantly Strive to Become Stronger ····································· 371
二、天人合一
　　Oneness of Heaven and Humanity ·········································· 372
三、以人为本
　　Humans Are Principal ·························································· 373
四、中庸尚和
　　Doctrine of the Mean and Esteemed Harmony ·························· 375

## 第十八章　中国文化的特点
## Characteristics of Chinese Culture ············································ 378
一、重实际、求稳定的农业文化心态
　　The Agrarian Cultural Attitude of Valuing Practice and Seeking Stability ······ 379
二、重血缘、重家族的宗法观念
　　Patriarchal Notions of Valuing Blood Relations and the Clan ······ 381
三、重伦理、倡道德至上
　　Valuing Ethics and Advocating Morality above All Else ············· 383
四、专制主义、民本主义共存
　　The Co-existence of Absolutism and People-rooted Ideology (Democracy) ······ 385
五、绵延韧性、长期存在的生命力
　　Vitality from Continuous Tenacity and Long-term Survival ········ 387

## 第十九章　中国文化的近代转型及中西文化交会：晚清迄现代
## The Sino-Western Encounter and the Modern Transformation: Late Qing to the Present ······ 391

一、开眼看世界
　　Widen Horizons and View the World ······ 391

二、文化教育革新
　　Innovation in Cultural Education ······ 393

三、"维新"与"革命"
　　"Reform" and "Revolution" ······ 397

四、"德、赛两先生"
　　"Mr. Science and Mr. Democracy" ······ 400

五、传统习俗转化
　　Transformation of Traditional Customs ······ 402

六、中国文化的四次转折
　　The Four Shifts in Chinese Culture ······ 402

七、现代的中国
　　Modern China ······ 404

## 附录一　中国历史朝代顺序
## Appendix A　The Order of Chinese Dynasties ······ 406

## 附录二　中国历史朝代表
## Appendix B　The List of Dynasties in Chinese History ······ 407

## 后　记
## Epilogue ······ 412

# 导 论
# Introduction

## 一、文化
## Culture

### 1. 文化的定义
### Definition of Culture

"文化"一词,语义非常广泛。因为东西方各学派观点不一致,其定义各有不同;同时,因为历史时代的演变,其定义也在不断更新。据统计,古今中外关于文化的定义有二百多种。

The meaning of the term culture is extraordinarily broad. There are differences in defining the term due to the lack of unity in various schools of thought and between western and eastern points of view. It has also evolved over time in accord with changing historical eras. By some counts, there are over 200 different definitions in the world, in ancient times and modern.

中华先民很早就有对于"文化"的认识。战国时期(前475—前221)的《易传》中记载:

> 刚柔交错,天文也。文明以止,人文也。观乎天文,以察时变。观乎人文,以化成天下。

Ancient people in China recognized the idea of "culture". The *Book of Changes* from the Warring States Period (475 – 221 B. C.) records the following:

> The hard and soft intermingle and mix, this is the *wén* of Heaven. Pattern and light are used as the basis, this is the *wén* of humans. Observing the *wén* of Heaven is used to examine the season's transformations; observing the *wén* of humans is used to change the

whole world.

"文"的本义，指的是纹理、纹饰、文采、文章，可以引申为包括文字在内的各种象征符号，再引申为典籍、制度；"化"的本义，指的是变易、生成、造化，可以引申为教化、教行、培育；"天文"指天道自然规律，"人文"指人伦秩序，以"人文""化成天下"，使天然世界变成人文世界。

The basic meaning of *wén* refers to "patterns in the grain of wood or marble", "adornments", and "rich and bright colors", which can be extended to all kinds of symbolic markings including writing, and further extended to "canonical records" and "ordered system". The basic meaning of *huà* is "to change", "to generate", and "Nature", which can be extended to "to enlighten", "to teach" and "to train". The "*wén* of Heaven" refers to the natural rules of the heavens. The "wen of humans" refers to the social order among human relationships. To use "the *wén* of humans" to "change the whole world" means to cause the natural world to transform into the world of human affairs.

这段话的意思是说，刚美与柔美交相错杂，这是天的文采；文章灿烂止于礼仪，这是人类的文采。观察天的文采，可以知道四季变更的规律；观察人类的文采，可以推行教化以促成天下光明。这便是中国古人赋予"文化"的内涵，它注重的是文治、教化，与武力、暴虐相对。已经包含有"以文教化"为主要含义的"文化"一词的基本内涵。

The connotation the ancient people of China ascribed to "culture" emphasized "to enlighten", and "civilized rule", as opposed to military force and tyranny. It contains the basic meaning of the word "culture" that is primarily "to enlighten by means of patterns".

英语中 culture 一词源于拉丁文，指人类为满足生存需要而对土壤进行耕作栽培，它强调的是人征服自然、改造自然的过程。

The English term "culture" comes from Latin and refers to humankind carrying out planting and cultivation with regards to the soil so as to fulfill the needs of survival. What it emphasizes is the process of humans conquering and transforming nature.

世界上被视作经典的"文化"的定义是英国人类学家泰勒（Edward Burnett Tylor）在《原始文化》（1871）一书中对"文化"的定义：文化是一个复杂的总体，包括知识、信仰、艺术、道德、法律、风俗，以及人类在社会生活里所得的一切能力与习惯。

What is generally regarded as the classic definition of "culture" is in Edward Burnett Tylor's book *Primitive Culture* (1871), in which culture is defined as a complex whole that includes knowledge, beliefs, art, morals, law, customs, and all the abilities and habits humans acquire in social life.

本书所采用的"文化"概念,其本质含义是"人类化""自然的人化",它是人的价值观念在社会实践中对象化的过程与结果。例如,一块天然的石头,这不是文化,可是经过人类加工以后,成为石器,这是石器文化(见图1)。

The conception of culture we use in this book is basically "humanized" or "natural humanization". It is the process and result of human values instantiated in social practice. For example, a natural stone is not culture, but after humans work on it and it becomes a stone tool, it represents stone-tool culture (see Figure 1).

钻孔石斧　　　　纺轮　　　　二鱼纹彩陶盆
Stone Ax with Drilled Hole; Weaving Wheel; Clay Bowl with Two Fish Design.

图1　新石器时代石器及彩陶盆,距今10000～5000年左右,陕西西安半坡遗址出土
Figure 1　Stone tools and painted pottery from the Neolithic Era, around 10000 – 5000 years old, unearthed in the Banpo ruins in Xi'an, Shaanxi

## 2. 文化的结构
**Structure of Culture**

文化的结构,大体上可以分为四个层次:物质文化层、制度文化层、行为文化层、心态文化层。

The structure of culture can basically be divided into four layers: material culture, systemic culture, behavioral culture, and mental culture.

物质文化层即物态文化层,是由人类加工自然创制的各种器物构成。它是人的物质生产活动方式和产品的总和,是可触知的具有物质实体的文化事物,构成整个文化创造的物质基础。

The material cultural layer is made up of all sorts of utensils humans create by working on nature. It is the products and manner of human activities that produce materials, i. e., the cultural material that is palpably made up of material substance, and which creates the material basis of all cultural creation.

制度文化层是人类在社会实践中建构的各种社会规范、典章制度，如国家模式、法律体系、赋税制度等。

The systemic culture layer is all kinds of social norms and codified systems that humans construct in social practice, such as national models, legal systems, tax systems, etc.

行为文化层是人类在社会交往中约定俗成的习惯定式，以礼俗、民俗、风俗形态出现的行为模式，如婚丧嫁娶、礼尚往来等。

The behavioral culture layer is the habitual mindset humans establish by popular usage in their social interactions; the behavioral patterns that appear as forms of etiquette, popular customs and social customs, such as marriages, funerals, and returning politeness for politeness, etc.

心态文化层是人类在社会实践和意识活动中培育出来的价值取向、审美情趣、思维方式，凝聚为文化的精神内核。

The mental culture layer is the value orientation, aesthetic inclination and thought patterns humans cultivate in their social practice and conscious activity.

上述物质、制度、行为、心态四个层面的文化内涵，都是本书所要探究的内容。

The implications of the aforementioned four layers of culture, i.e., material, systemic, behavioral, and mental, is the contents that this book will investigate.

## 二、文明
## Civilization

### 1. 文明的定义
### Definition of Civilization

与"文化"含义相近的古典词是"文明"。"文明"的含义是：从人类的物质生产（尤其是对火的利用）引申到精神的光明普照大地。

"文明"是人类进步的状态，是文化发展到特定阶段的产物，人类在进入文明阶段之前，已经走过了漫长的原始文化时期。

"Civilization" (*wénmíng*) is an ancient term with a meaning close to that of "culture". "Civilization" means the radiance that illuminates the earth from humans' material production (especially that of fire) and extending to spiritual production.

"Civilization" is the condition of human improvement, the product of a culture developing to a certain stage. Before entering the stage of civilization, the human being has already passed through a long period of primitive culture.

### 2. 文明的标志
### Markers of Civilization

世界上大多数学者以文字的出现、金属工具的使用、城市国家的建立、宗教场所的建成为文明出现的标志。

Most scholars throughout the world regard the appearance of writing, the use of metal tools, the establishment of city-states and the establishment of religious places as the standard markers of the appearance of civilization.

"文明"的西文语源也来自拉丁语,但与 culture 的词根带着农耕的意思大为不同,civilization 一词则源于城市,表示城镇社会生活的秩序和原则,是市民世界的产物。

The roots of the English word "civilization" are from Latin, but they are much different than those of "culture" which carries the meaning of cultivation. The word "civilization" originates in the word "city", expressing the order and principles of urban social life. It is the product of the world of city people.

从今天习用的汉语语义看来,具有文化烙印的行为不一定就是文明的行为,例如社会中的粗野、丑恶、犯罪现象,可以视作特定的文化现象,但与"文明"相对立,被视为"不文明"或"非文明"。

In modern common Chinese usage of the word "civilized", behavior that has the imprint of culture is not necessarily civilized behavior. For example, the crude, ugly and criminal phenomena in society may be regarded as a special cultural phenomenon, but as it is opposed to "civilization" it is regarded as "uncivil" or "non-civilized".

## 三、中国·华夏·中华
## Three Names for China: *Zhongguo*, *Hua-Xia*, and *Zhonghua*

### 1. 中国
### *Zhongguo*

从地域概念来说,"中国"是一个历史的范畴,随着时代的演进,其范围在不断拓展。先秦时期,"中国"或指周王朝的京师所在,用来和"四方"(周边)对称;或指黄河中下游文明早成的地带,与落后的"四夷"对称,其范围十分有限。

As a territorial concept, *Zhongguo* or China, is a historical category whose scope expands following changing times. In the Pre-Qin era, it either refers to the location of the capital city of the Zhou Kingdom, in contrast to the "four directions" (surrounding areas); or, it refers to the region in the middle or lower stretch of the Yellow River where civilization developed early, in contrast to the backward "foreigners". As such, its scope was quite limited.

秦汉以后,"中国"指定都中原的大一统王朝及其所管辖的版图,原来先秦时期的夷、狄、戎、蛮等民族早已成为中国的主体部分了。中国的范围扩大了,更远的未知区域便被称为"四夷"。雄踞东亚大陆的元帝国自称其统治区域为"中国",称其邻国为"外夷",如日本、高丽(朝鲜)、安南(越南)、缅甸等地。明清亦沿袭此说。

After the Qin-Han era, *Zhongguo* referred to the territory of the great unified kingdoms in the Central Plains and the lands they governed. The Yi, Di, Rong and Man ethnic groups of the Pre-Qin period had become a central part of China. The scope of China had expanded, so even farther unknown territories were regarded as "foreign". The Yuan Empire that occupied the entire East Asian mainland regarded their governed territory as *Zhongguo*, and called their neighbors, such as Japan, Gaoli (Korea), Annan (Vietnam) and Myanmar, "foreigners". The Ming and Qing eras continued this designation.

历史上,清朝的面积最大,清乾隆二十四年(1759年)大体确立了中国领土范围:北起萨彦岭,南至南海诸岛,西起帕米尔高原,东至库页岛,约1260万平方公里。今日中国国土面积960万平方公里,仅次于俄罗斯、加拿大而居世界第三。

The Qing Empire was historically the largest. The 24th year of Qianlong (1759) largely established the scope of China's territory: in the north up to the Sayan Mountains, south to the islands of the South China Sea, west to the Pamir Plateau, and east to Sakhalin Island, around 12.6 million square kilometers. The area of modern China is 9.6 million square kilometers, third largest in the world after Russia and Canada.

"中国"作为一个近代国体意义上的主权国家概念,只是近三百年来的事情,是欧洲外交模式的产物。1689年签订的《中俄尼布楚条约》,在开头以满文写明外交使臣的身份是:"中国大皇帝钦差分界大臣领侍卫大臣议政大臣索额图……"在外交上使用汉文"中国"一词,首见于1842年8月29日签订的《中英南京条约》。在随后的近百年间,清王朝以"中国"的名义与列强签订了一系列丧权辱国的不平等条约。1911年10月11日,武昌起义次日,革命军议定的十三条方针中,第二条即称中国为"中华民国"。

The concept of *Zhongguo* as a sovereign state with significance in the modern state system is something that has only been around for the last 300 years, and was the product of European diplomatic models. At the beginning of the *Treaty of Nerchinsk between Qing China and Russia* signed in 1689, the identity of the diplomatic envoy is clearly written in Manchu as: "The Divine Emperor of China, having appointed as Imperial Border-Defining Commissioner Songgotu, Commander of the Imperial Body Guard, Grand Secretary, and Councilor of State". As for using the Chinese word *Zhongguo* in diplomacy, it first appeared in the *Treaty of Nanjing*, signed between Great Britain and China on August 29, 1842. During the subsequent 100 years, the Qing regime used the name *Zhongguo* to sign a series of humiliating, unequal treaties with other powers. On October 11, 1911, the day after the Wuchang Uprising, in the second of their thirteen guidelines that the revolutionary army agreed upon, China is referred to as the "Republic of China" (*Zhonghua Minguo*).

## 2. 华夏
### *Hua-Xia*

"华夏",是汉族先民的古称,他们居住在黄河中下游地区,据说黄帝和炎帝是他们的部族首领和祖先神。在春秋时期,"华夏"是中原人民的自称,以区别于胡、楚等居住在周边的其他民族。

经过几千年的民族融合,生活在中国境内的华夏——汉族及55个少数民族,共同组成中华民族。中国文化不是由华夏——汉族单独创造的,而是由中华民族共同创造的。

*Hua-Xia* is an ancient name of the ancestors of the ethnically Han people. They lived in the middle and lower reaches of the Yellow River drainage area, and according to legend, the Yellow Emperor and the Yan Emperor were the leaders of their tribe and ancestral spirit. *Hua-Xia* was a self-designation for the people of the Central Plains in the Spring-and-Autumn Period, differentiating them from other ethnic groups living around them, such as the Hu and Chu.

Through several thousands of years of ethnic mixing, the *Hua-Xia* living within the borders of China, the Han, have created the *Zhonghua* ethnicity together with the 55 minority ethnic nationalities.

中华民族的图腾、中国文化的象征——龙,就是这种共同性和综合性的体现。龙的崇拜起源很早,龙是古代神话传说中的神异动物,常用来象征祥瑞。在甲骨文、金文中已有"龖"字,时间在三千年以前。龙的初期还有其他实体的形象,但定形后的龙的形象却是牛头(或者马头)、鹿角、龟眼、蛇身、鱼鳞、鹰爪等。龙可以在水中游、云中飞、陆上走,所以,这是一个综合了多种部族符号的复合图腾,正是早期部族融合的生动写照。

The totem of the *Zhonghua* ethnicity and the symbol of Chinese culture, the dragon, is the manifestation of this commonality and synthesis. Dragon worship originated very early. It is a mystical animal of ancient myths and legends, often interpreted as an auspicious omen. The graph 龖 (*long*) appeared in the oracle-bone and bronze scripts, as long as 3000 years ago. The image of the dragon in the early period still included images of other entities, but the later fixed dragon image was bovine (or equine) head, deer antlers, turtle eyes, snake body, fish scales, and eagle talons. The dragon can swim in the water, fly through the air and walk on land. So it is a compound totem, amalgamating the symbols of many tribes; the vivid portrayal of early tribal fusion.

"中国"与"华夏"也是文化的概念。"中国"这一概念在古代虽然不断演化,但其主旨却始终守住一个"中"字——中国者,天下之中也。这既是一种地理学的中心意识(内部和外部的区别),更是一种文化学的中心意识(文明和野蛮的差异)。如同世界其他民族在进入整体文明观之前一样,居住在"中国"范围内的华夏——汉族曾坚持一种自我中心文化观,认为华夏文化比周边四夷的文化要优越得多。孔颖达(574—648)在《春秋左传正义》里说:

中国有礼义之大,故谓之夏;有服章之美,故谓之华。华夏一也。

华,美丽、光彩的意思;夏,中原人。意思是:正因为中原人有完备的礼仪,所以才叫作夏;有华丽的服饰,所以才叫作华;华与夏是一致的。

*Zhongguo* (China) and *Hua-Xia* are also cultural concepts. While the idea of *Zhongguo* evolved throughout ancient times, its gist always maintained the idea of "middle/center". Those of the middle are the center of the world. This is both a central geographic awareness (distinguishing internal from external), and a kind of cultural center awareness (separating cultured from barbarian). Just like other people in the world prior to their entering a unified cultural perspective, the *Hua-Xia* residents within the scope of *Zhongguo*, i. e., the Han, once held an egocentric cultural perspective, believing the culture of *Hua-Xia* was far superior to that of the surrounding barbarians. Kong Yingda (574 – 648), in his *Correct Meaning of the Zuo Commentary to the Spring and Autumn Annals* writes:

*Zhongguo* has the greatness of etiquette and ceremony, and thus is referred to as *Xia*; it has the beauty of clothing and medals, and thus it is referred as *Hua*; *Hua* and *Xia* are the same.

*Hua* means glorious, beautiful; *Xia* means people of the central plains. The meaning of the passage is: because the people of the central plains have complete ritual ceremony, they are called *Xia*; they have beautiful clothing and decorations, so they are called *Hua*. *Hua* and *Xia* are in accord.

这种有华美服饰、道德大国的文化优越感和文化中心意识,还表现在"中华"一词上。

This cultural superiority and egocentricity of a great, well-adorned moral country is also expressed in the word *Zhonghua*.

## 3. 中华
### *Zhonghua*

"中华"由"中国"和"华夏"二名复合而成,意思是居住在中心而文化优越的民族。中国古代的华夏族——汉族立国,大多把首都建立在黄河中下游的中原地区、周边的少数民族之中,后世因此称"中华":"中"即中心,"华"指文化繁盛。它也兼有地域观念和文化概念,但更强调文化概念。"中华"一词约出现于华夷大融合的魏晋南北朝时期,时间到了近代,中国人的中心意识逐渐淡化。

*Zhonghua* is made of a hybridization of the two names *Zhongguo* and *Hua-Xia*, meaning the ethnic group with the superior culture residing in the center. The ancient Chinese *Hua-Xia*, i.e., the Han, established the country and for the most part built their capital in the Central Plains in the middle and lower reaches of the Yellow River, among the surrounding minority nationalities, and therefore were called *Zhonghua* in later times. *Zhōng* means "center" and *huá* means "culturally thriving". The term *Zhonghua* first appeared in the period of disunity following the fall of the Han Dynasty, but as time progressed to the modern age, the consciousness of centrality has gradually waned.

中国、华夏、中华三词语的含义表明,地域、国家、民族、文化四者合为一体,这是中国文化区别于西方文化的一大特点。故中国文化的历史轨迹,便与地域上的开疆拓土、国家政权的改朝换代、民族之间的夷夏互动等有着直接关系。

The connotations of the terms *Zhongguo*, *Hua-Xia*, and *Zhonghua* indicate that the territory, nation, ethnicity and culture are joined in a single system, which is an important feature differentiating Chinese culture from western culture. Therefore, the historical track of Chinese culture is directly related to the geographic expansion of territory, the political changing of ruling houses, and the interaction of ethnicities.

**思考题**

1. 什么是文化？
2. "华夏"的概念可以代替"中国""中华"吗？

***Questions***

1. What is "culture"(*wenhua*)?
2. Can the idea of *Hua-Xia* replace *Zhongguo* or *Zhonghua*?

# 第一章  中国文化的生态环境
## The Ecology of Chinese Culture

自古以来，中国人之所以自认为处于世界中心，与中国传统文化的生态状况有关。

文化生态由自然场与社会场交织而成。"自然场"指人的生存与发展所依附的自然环境（又称地理环境）；"社会场"指人在生存与发展过程中结成的相互关系，分为经济层与社会层。考察中国文化的生成机制，应从地理环境、经济土壤、社会结构等方面综合考察。

Since ancient times, Chinese people's idea that they reside in the center of the world is related to the ecological circumstances of traditional Chinese culture.

Cultural ecology is formed by the interweaving of the natural scene and the social scene. By "natural scene" we mean the natural environment (or geographic circumstance) people rely on to survive and develop. By "social scene" we mean the mutual relationships, which can be sub-divided into economic and social layers, people form as they survive and develop. As we investigate the productive mechanism of Chinese culture, we need to comprehensively study such aspects as the geographic circumstances, economic soil, and social structure.

## 一、地理环境
## Geographic Environment

中国处于世界最大的大陆亚欧大陆的东部，东边面临大海，是古人难以逾越的太平洋；西北是茫茫戈壁；西部和西南耸立着世界屋脊——帕米尔高原、青藏高原以及纵贯南北的横断山脉。

China is positioned at the eastern end of the Eurasian Continent, the world's largest continent. On the east it overlooks the Pacific Ocean, which was difficult for ancient people to cross. In the northwest there is the boundless Gobi Desert. In the west and southwest rises the roof of the world, the Pamir Mountains, the Tibetan Plateau and the Crisscrossing Mountain Ranges.

大海、沙漠、高山将中国与外部世界相隔离，这种地理格局，成就了中国文化的独立发生，并使中国文化在以后的漫长岁月中少受外来文化冲击，从而保持一贯的发展。但是封闭隔绝的地理环境在客观上又增加了中国人突破自然屏障、向外开拓的难度，助长了自大自尊、自我中心的文化惰性。

Oceans, deserts and mountain ranges isolate China from the outside world. This geographic layout has brought about the independent birth of Chinese culture. Chinese culture has rarely suffered external cultural shocks over the subsequent ages, and therefore it has maintained a consistent development. However, objectively, this closed, isolated geographic circumstance has made it harder for Chinese people to break out of their natural barriers and open up to the outside, encouraging a cultural inertia of arrogant self-regard and self-centeredness.

中国地域辽阔，所跨纬度和经度远比希腊、埃及、印度等文明古国广大，其物产资源丰富多样，天地广袤开阔，当中原农业文明受到北方游牧文明的压迫时，中国的经济中心和文化中心能够向东向南实现大规模的迁徙转移。

Chinese territory is vast; the latitudes and longitudes it crosses are broader than those of other ancient civilizations, such as Greece, Egypt and India; its material resources are rich and varied; its field of activity is vast and open. When the agricultural civilization of the Central Plains suffered repression from northern nomadic civilization, China's economic and cultural centers were able to move and transform east and south on a large scale.

在东亚大陆的内部，地域广阔，地形和气候条件复杂多样，南北温差近摄氏50度，东西年降水量相差几千毫米，大河东西横贯，山系纵横，种种自然特点，把中国分割成大大小小的"国中之国"，从而造成中国文化多样发展，各区域文化间差异极大，所谓"百里不同风，千里不同俗"。

The interior of the East Asian continent is vast. The topography and climate is complicated and varied; temperature differences between north and south are as much as 50° Celsius, and the rainfall differential between east and west is several thousand millimeters; large rivers flow west to east and mountain ranges are woven throughout. All these natural features carve China into large and small "countries within a country", and therefore have created the diverse growth of Chinese culture. The differences between the cultures of each territory are enormous, so that, as the saying goes, "Every three miles is a different climate, and every thirty miles is a different custom" (*Han Shu*: "Wang Ji Zhuan").

中国地形西高东低，山脉、河流因而多东西走向；大部分地区属温带，最南部伸入热带，最北部伸入亚寒带；完备的气候带提供了农业经济多样发展的地理基础；东部农耕区，西部畜牧区；南部水田农业区，北部旱地农业区。中华文化的南北差异、东西之别，正是基于这种与地理环境有密切关系的经济生活。

The topography of China is high in the west and low in the east, so most rivers and mountain ranges run west to east. Most of the region is in the temperate zone, though the far south is in the tropical zone and the far north extends to the sub-polar zone. A complete climatic zone has supplied China with a geographic basis for the agricultural economy's diverse growth. The east is the farming area, the west is the animal husbandry region, the south is the paddy agricultural area, and the north is the dry-field agricultural area. Chinese cultural differences between north-south and east-west are precisely due to the differences in economic livelihoods which are closely related to the geography.

## 二、经济形态
## Economic Patterns

地理环境影响文化发展，是通过人类的物质生产实践得以实现的。

中国文化大体植根于农耕与游牧这样两种经济生活的土壤之中。以年降水量400毫米线为界，中国大体上分为温润的东南和干寒的西北两大区域。自然条件的差异，使温润的东南被人们开辟为农耕区，养育出一种以定居农业做基石的，礼制法规齐备、文化昌盛的农耕文化；干寒的西北则成为游牧区，盛行以游牧为生、全民善骑善战的游牧文化。恰巧万里长城东起海滨，西到大漠，大体上与这条年降水量400毫米线重合，这也是农耕文化与游牧文化的边界线。中国历史上的许多大剧就是在这里演出的。

Geographic circumstances influence cultural development as realized through human's material productive practice.

Chinese culture for the most part has taken root in the soil of two kinds of economic life, farming and animal husbandry. There is a 400 mm/year rainfall boundary that basically separates China into a wet, warm southeast and a dry, cold northwest. The differences in natural conditions have caused humans to develop the wet southeast into farmland, fostering a farming culture founded on settled agriculture, a complete set of rites and statutes and a prosperous culture. The arid northwest has become an area of animal husbandry, rife with a nomadic culture based on animal husbandry in which every individual is practiced at riding and warfare. By coincidence, the Great Wall of China, rising from the seashore in the east and extending into the desert in the west, basically coincides with this 400 mm/year rainfall boundary, the dividing line between farming culture and nomadic animal husbandry culture. Many of Chinese history's great dramas have played out on this stage.

古代中国农业经济长期存在。自春秋、战国开始，以男耕女织的生产方式为主，小农业自然经济构成主体。但中国南部亚热带山地民族（如苗、彝、黎、高山等族），直到近古甚至近代，仍然刀耕火种。自秦汉以后的两千年间，中国社会的基础是小农业与家庭手工业相结合的自然经济。

The ancient Chinese agricultural economy survived for a long time. Since the Spring-and-Autumn and Warring States periods, the natural economy of small-scale farming formed the main thread, taking the productive pattern of males cultivating and women weaving as its basis. However, the peoples of China's sub-tropical south (such as the Miao, Yi, Li, Gao shan, etc.) still practiced slash-and-burn agriculture up until the medieval and even modern times. In the two thousand years since the Qin-Han period, the basis of Chinese society was the natural economy joining small-scale farming with household handicraft.

自给自足的小农经济土壤还决定了中国文化深层次的许多特点，例如注重经验、务实、中庸的思维模式，重农抑商的社会结构，尊君重民、集权专制的国家体制，等等。这种格局一直延续到清中期。随着西方资本主义文化的大规模东来，中国的自然经济逐步解体，日益加入世界统一市场，以商品经济为动力的新的经济结构开始形成，从而为中国文化的发展提供一种更新的土壤。

Self-sufficient, small-scale agriculture economic soil also determined many deep-seated features of Chinese culture, such as patterns of thinking that favor experience, pragmatism and the "golden mean"; social structure that emphasizes agriculture and restrains trade; and, a national system of respecting the ruler, valuing the people and concentrating power in an autocracy. This pattern lasted up to the middle of the Qing Dynasty, when following the large scale eastern movement of western capitalist culture, China's natural economy gradually disintegrated and day by day entered into the global market. It began to form a new economic structure motivated by a commodity economy, which, in turn, provided a new kind of soil for the development of Chinese culture.

## 三、社会结构
## Social Structure

中国的社会结构中，长期存在着以血缘为纽带的宗法制度。

宗法制度开始于商代，定型于西周，是把血缘纽带同政治关系结合起来的一种制度。宗法制度通过血缘的亲疏，确立起一整套土地、财产和政治地位的分配与继承制度。嫡长子继承制、分封制、宗庙祭祀制度，共同构成宗法制度的基本内容。

The structure of Chinese society takes as its characteristic the long-standing patriarchal clan system tied to bloodlines.

The patriarchal system began in the Shang Dynasty and finalized its design in the Western

Zhou. It is a system in which familial blood ties are combined with political relationships. The patriarchal clan system instituted the complete set of distributions of land, wealth and political position, and it ensured succession through blood ties. The systems of primogeniture, enfeoffment, and sacrifices at ancestral shrines jointly form the basic content of the patriarchal system.

## 1. 嫡长子继承制
### The System of Primogeniture

嫡长子继承制是宗法制度的核心。先秦统治者实行一夫多妻制,多妻中有一个正妻,即"嫡妻",其子为嫡子;其他妻子为"庶妻",其子为庶子。继承王位的必须是嫡妻长子,至于这位嫡长子是否贤与不肖,不在考虑之内。如果嫡妻无子,则立庶妻中级别最高的贵妾之子,至于被立者是否为庶子中最年长者,也不在考虑之内,即所谓"立嫡以长不以贤,立子以贵不以长"的王位继承制度。嫡长子是土地、财产和权力的主要继承者,有主祭祖先的特权,地位最尊贵,故嫡长子也被称为宗子。

Primogeniture is the core of the patriarchal system. The ancient rulers practiced polygamy, in which the son of the first wife was known as *dizi*, and sons of secondary wives were known as *shuzi*. The one to inherit the ruler's position had to be the eldest son of the primary wife. Whether this eldest son was worthy or degenerate was never under consideration. If the primary wife had no sons, then the son of the highest ranking noblewoman among the secondary wives was chosen. Whether the one who was chosen was the oldest among the *shuzi* was also never under consideration. This was the royal succession system known as, "In setting up the son of a primary wife, chose age over worthiness; in setting up the son of a secondary wife, chose nobility over age." The son of the primary wife inherited of the land, wealth and power. He had the special authority to perform sacrifices to ancestors and the position of greatest respect. The eldest son of the primary wife was also known as the "lineal son".

西周统治者划分为四个等级:天子、诸侯、卿大夫、士。不管哪个等级,位子的继承遵循的都是嫡长子继承制。天子的嫡长子继承天子之位为大宗,其余诸子被分封为诸侯,为小宗;诸侯的嫡长子继承诸侯之位,为大宗,其余诸子被封为大夫,为小宗;卿大夫之嫡长子继承卿大夫之位,为大宗,其余诸子成为士,为小宗。这样,周王朝通过分封诸侯国,保证了他们世世代代的宗族统治,万里江山遂成一家。

The Western Zhou rulers were divided into four ranks: son of heaven, noble lords, high ranking and senior officials, and members of the senior ministerial class. Regardless of rank, the eldest son of the primary wife inherited the position. The eldest son of the primary wife of the son of heaven inherited that position as the "great lineage"; the other sons were bestowed the title noble lords and lesser lineages. The eldest son of the primary wife of a noble lord inherited the position as the "great lineage"; the other *sons* were bestowed the title high ranking officials and lesser lineages. The eldest son of the primary wife of high ranking officials inherited the position as the "great lineage"; the other sons were bestowed the title minister and lesser lineages. Thus the Zhou Dynasty, by means of dividing and conferring vassal states, safeguarded generations of clan rule, so that eventually far and wide everyone was under a single family.

## 2. 封邦建国制
### The System of Conferring States and Establishing Countries

封邦建国，简称"封建"，即今人所说的分封制，由周人创立。分封就是分土封侯，是指天子按照血缘关系的亲疏，把同姓子弟分封到各地，把土地和土地上的居民分赐给诸侯，诸侯再把土地和人民分封给下一级的卿大夫，卿大夫再往下分，自天子、诸侯、卿大夫到士，逐级层层分封，从而建立起大小不等的诸侯国；分封制的目的是以血缘为纽带把周王室和地方邦国联系起来，从而使地方邦国成为保护周王室的有力屏障。

Known simply as "confer and establish", i.e., what is now known as the system of dividing and conferring was established by the Zhou people. "Divide and confer" is simply dividing land and conferring noble titles. The "son of heaven", according to the distance of blood relationships, divided land among the sons of the family and conferred titles on them. He gave the land and the residents on the land to the noble lord, who, in turn, divided the land and people and gave it to his high ranking officials, and so on down the line. From the ruler down to the lowest official, each level was divided and conferred with a title, and as a result larger and smaller vassal states were established. The goal of the system was to link the Zhou ruling house with the local states based on blood relationships, and make the local states into a powerful barrier protecting the Zhou royal household.

## 3. 宗庙祭祀制度
### The System of Ancestral Shrine Sacrifices

"宗"是个会意字，宗法的"宗"，"宀"为房顶，"示"为神，合起来指供奉神位的庙，《说文解字》将其解释为"宗，尊祖庙也"。这是"宗"的原始含义，本意就是祭祀祖先的场所，就是祖庙、宗庙，习惯上称为祠堂，是供奉祖先牌位、进行祭祀活动的场所，被视为宗族的象征。宗法制度以血缘的远近来辨别一个大家族里的尊卑等级关系，以维系宗族的团结，维护家族的凝聚力，故十分强调"尊祖敬宗"，表现形式就是隆重庄严的宗庙祭祀制度。

The character 宗 is an associative compound character, used for "patriarchy". The top part of the graph means "roof" and the bottom means "deity, spirit". When combined they indicate a shrine for worshipping spirit tablets. The *Shuowen Jiezi* explains it as "shrine for honoring the ancients". This is the primitive meaning of the term, which at root is a place for making sacrifices to ancestors, i.e., an ancestral temple. By custom it is known as the ancestral hall, the place for worshipping the ancestral tablet and carrying out sacrificial activities. It is considered to be emblematic of the clan. The patriarchal system discriminates levels of respect among clan members by means of the distance of their blood relationship. In order to maintain the unity of the clan and the cohesion of families, they strongly emphasize respecting the ancestors, and the outward form of that is the serious, solemn system of ancestral shrine sacrifices.

宗法制度下，君王是天下大宗，故君王主持的宗庙祭祀，意义重大，制度也极为严密。历代君王都很重视宗庙的修建，将祭祀祖先的宗庙和祭祀土地神的社稷坛并列，共同作为国家权力的象征。

Under the patriarchal system, the ruler is the patriarch of the world, and so the temple sacrifices over which the ruler presides are both serious in meaning and strict and well-organized. Rulers throughout the ages have attached great value to the construction of shrines, and placed shrines for making sacrifices to ancestors side by side with altars used for making sacrifices to the gods of earth and grain. They were equally regarded as emblematic of state power.

王宫的前面，左祖右社的制度一直沿袭到明清。"左祖"是宗法的标志，是把祖庙修建在宫殿的左前方；"右社"是国土的象征，是把社稷坛修建在宫殿的右前方。社是土地，稷是粮食，社稷坛就是帝王祭祀土地神、粮食神的地方。它们一起表明了王朝的血缘系统和对全国土地、百姓的占有。

In the front courts of ruling palaces, the system of "left ancestors, right deities" lasted until Ming-Qing times. "Left ancestors," the symbol of the patriarchy, refers to building the ancestral shrine on the left side of the front of the palace. "Right deities," emblematic of the state's territory, refers to building the altars for the gods of earth and grain on the left of the front of the palace. Together they indicate the lineal relationship of the ruling house and their possession of the state's land and people.

今天北京故宫的前面，左边的劳动人民文化宫（1950年改名）便是明清时期的太庙，右边的中山公园则是明清时期的社稷坛，即"左祖右社"格局。

In front of the Forbidden City in modern Beijing, to the left there is the Working People's Cultural Palace (named in 1950), which was the Imperial Ancestral Temple of the Ming-Qing era. Zhongshan Park on the right was the altar for the gods of the earth and grains in Ming-Qing times. This, then, is the "left ancestors, right deities" formation.

太庙（见图1-1），位于北京天安门东侧，是明清两代皇帝的宗庙。太庙是皇权世袭的重要标志，历朝历代都极为重视。太庙祭祀，是为大祀，即皇帝亲临祭拜。除夕为祫祭，皇帝亲自率领皇子、亲王行三跪九叩大礼。北京太庙修建于明朝初年，现存太庙为明朝嘉靖（1507—1566）皇帝重建，有大殿11间，规格与最高等级的紫禁城（故宫）太和殿建筑相似。

Imperial Ancestral Temple (see Fig. 1-1) locates on the east side of Tian'anmen in Beijing. It was the ancestral shrine for the emperors of the Ming and Qing Dynasties, an important symbol of imperial power highly valued by successive dynasties. The sacrificial ceremony of Imperial Ancestral Temple is the grand sacrifice, as the emperor worshipped in person. On the eve of the Lunar New Year is the *Xia* sacrifice. The emperor leads the heir-apparent and princes in carrying out the ritual of three full prostrations. The Imperial Ancestral Temple in Beijing was first built in the early years of the Ming Dynasty. The present building is the one rebuilt under the Jiajing (1507-1566) Emperor of the Ming. There are 11 halls and its specifications are comparable to the highest ranking building in the Forbidden City, the Hall of Supreme Harmony.

图1-1 太庙（明清）
Figure 1-1 Imperial Ancestral Temple (Ming and Qing dynasties)

## 4. 宗法制度对中国文化的影响
### Influence of the Patriarchal System on Chinese Culture

宗法制度长期存在的主要原因是小农经济生活方式的一直延续。

秦汉以后，分封制被郡县制取代，除了帝王系统继续由皇族的血缘确定之外，行政官员的选拔、任用，实行的是推荐、考试的制度。但是，宗法制度却长期影响中国社会。

The primary reason the patriarchal system survived for so long is the continuity of the small-scale agricultural economy.

After the Qin-Han era, the system of division and conferral was replaced by a system of prefectures and counties. Except for the imperial systems continuing to be determined by the ruling families' blood relationships, the selection, appointment and implantation of official administration was by a system of recommendation and examination. Nevertheless, the influence of the patriarchal system for a long time enveloped Chinese society.

首先，父系单系世系原则广泛实行。即在血缘家族世系的排列上，完全排斥女性成员的地位。男尊女卑观念盛行，女人只能服从，必须遵守"三从四德"："三从"指未嫁从父、出嫁从夫、夫死从子；"四德"指妇德、妇言、妇容、妇功。

在家族里，继承权完全由父系掌握，女性没有继承权利，从政治权利、经济财产，甚至在某些专业特种技艺方面，有"传媳不传女"的家规，媳妇是到本家族来，女儿是要到别人家去，"嫁出去的女儿泼出去的水"，女儿嫁人随丈夫，所以没有继承权。

First, the widespread implementation of the principle of single, patrilineal lineage. That is, on the arrangement of the consanguineous family lineage, the position of female members was completely excluded. The notion of regarding men as superior to women was prevalent, so that women could only obey and were compelled to abide by the "three obeys and four virtues": the "three obeys" were to obey one's father before marriage, obey one's husband in marriage, and obey one's son in widowhood; the "four virtues" were feminine morality, feminine speech, feminine countenance and feminine achievement.

Within a clan, rights of inheritance were entirely in the patrilineal line, so women had no rights of inheritance. In politics, economic capital, and even with some specialized technologies, there was the principle of "bequeath to the daughter-in-law not to the daughter". The daughter-in-law was within the family, but the daughter would be married into another family, as suggested by the saying, "a daughter that is married off is like water that is sloshed away". When the daughter marries, she must obey her husband, and so she had no rights of inheritance.

其次，家族制度长盛不衰。无论社会怎么变化，家族始终是构成中国社会的基石。维系家族制度的主要是三样东西：祠堂、家谱和族田。

Second, the long, flourishing survival of the clan system. No matter how society changed, from beginning to end the clan was the foundation for constructing Chinese society. There were primarily three things maintaining the clan system: ancestral halls, genealogies, and clan fields.

祠堂供奉祖先神位，每逢春秋祭祀，全族成员在祠堂集合隆重祭祀祖先。
Ancestral halls were for worshipping the ancestral tablets. Sacrifices were made every spring and autumn, and all of the clan's members gathered in the ancestral hall to solemnly make sacrifices to the ancestors.

家谱是家族的档案、法规，详细记载全族的世系源流、子嗣系统、婚配关系、祖宗墓地、祖产公田、族规家法。家谱的主要作用是防止血缘关系混乱，它还是解决族内纠纷等的文本依据。
Genealogies are the clan's archive and legislation, carefully recording the entire clan's lineal origin and development, system of heirs, marriage relationships, ancestral cemetery, ancestral wealth, clan rules and family laws. The primary purpose of the genealogies was to protect against the muddling of consanguine relationships, or serve as the textual support for resolving disputes within the clan.

族田是家族公共的田产，供族人困难时用。
Clan fields are the real estate held in common by the clan, providing for clan members in times of difficulty.

最后，家国同构的社会格局长期存在。国和家的结构一致，即家庭—家族—国家在组织结构方面的共同性。
Third, the long-term survival of the social pattern of family-state isomorphism. The structures of the family and the state were the same, i.e., the commonality of the organizational structure of the family-clan and the state.

历代统治者都把国家当作自己家看待，认为家是小国，国是大家，家和国的组织结构是一样的，皇帝就是一个大家长。无论家还是国，都是父家长制，宗法关系因此渗透到社会。这是中国社会区别于印度、欧洲的根本之点。
Rulers through the ages have treated the state as their own family, regarding the family as a small country and the state as a large family. The organizational structure of the family and the state were the same, so the emperor was the clan leader. Regardless of being the family or the state, they were both patriarchal and so patriarchal relations permeated society. This is a basic point in which Chinese society was different from that of India and Europe.

宗法制度一直深深地影响着中华民族的生活。历朝历代统治者都认为国家权力要牢牢掌握在自己家族手中,每一个朝代的统治史,就是一部家族统治史。家族统治的主要特点就是一姓家族统治一个朝代,只要这个朝代不灭亡,这个家族就一直统治下去。例如,杨氏的隋朝,李氏的唐朝,赵氏的宋朝,朱氏的明朝,爱新觉罗氏的清朝,等等。每一朝的统治者都要把自己家族的人分封到地方上做官,以保证家天下的延续。

The patriarchal clan system deeply influenced the life of the Chinese people. Dynastic rulers believed state power must be securely grasped within the hands of their clan. The history of the rulers of every dynasty is the history of clan rulership. The main characteristic of clan rulership is that a clan of a single surname rules a dynasty, and as long as the clan is not extinguished, this clan will continue to rule, as in the Yang family's Sui Dynasty, the Li family's Tang Dynasty, the Zhao family's Song Dynasty, the Zhu family's Ming Dynasty, and the Aisin Goro family's Qing Dynasty. The rulers of every dynasty must confer the people of their clan as officials in localities and thereby ensure the continuity of their familial world.

家族制度长盛不衰,以血缘为纽带的家族始终稳固。民间的大家族用族谱、族规、族训管理本家族,家族成员也许不知道国法,但是必须遵循族规生活。南方一些大的家族在很大程度上承担了地方政府的职能。

The clan system persisted, because from beginning to end, the clans based on blood relationships were stable. Large clans among the common people used clan genealogies, clan rules, and clan instructions to manage their clans. Clan members may not know the laws of the state, but they certainly lived in compliance with clan rules. Some large clans in the south, to a large extent, assumed the role of a local government.

## 四、中西生态环境对文化的影响比较
## Comparing the Influence of Ecology on Culture Between China and the West

中西文化生态环境的不同,导致了中西文化不同的发展路向。

首先,产生西方文明的自然地理条件与中国地理环境不同。如果说中国文化的产生地是在大陆,是大陆文明;西方文化的诞生地则是在海洋,是海洋文明。中国文明诞生在中原大地,欧洲文明的故乡是在爱琴海区域。

The difference between the cultural ecology of China and the West brought about the different developmental patterns in the cultures of China and the West.

First, there is the difference between the natural geography that produced western civilization and China's geographic circumstances. If the productive territory of Chinese culture is continental, then the birth of Western culture is on the seas. It is an ocean-going civilization.

The birth place of Chinese civilization is the Central Plains, while the native place of European civilization is the Aegean Sea.

其次,古希腊罗马的工商业文明孕育了欧洲工商业和航海业的发展,以及伴随发生的文艺复兴,近代西方资本主义由此发展。

Second, ancient Greco-Roman business civilization nurtured the development of European business and navigation, as well as accompanied the occurrence of the Renaissance. Modern Western capitalism developed out of these conditions.

再者,中国以血缘为纽带的传统社会里,宗族发达,父权地位崇高,皇帝也是以百姓之父的身份管理国家,集中所有权力于一身。从秦始皇于公元前221年建立皇帝制度开始,中央集权的专制政体就一直存在到了1912年,延续了两千多年。

Third, in traditional Chinese society where blood relationships were key, the clans developed, the patriarchal power was dominant, and the emperor managed the country by means of an identity as father of the people, concentrating all power in his person. Beginning with the establishment of the system of imperial power by Qin Shihuang in 221 B. C., the autocratic system of government that concentrated power in the center survived more than 2000 years until 1912.

欧洲文明在古希腊罗马时期,形成了以地缘为主的人群结合方式,血缘关系淡薄,创立了以城市为中心、以地区划分和财产差别为基础的城邦制度,人们更加注重契约关系,发展的结果是与之相应的民主政治体制的建立。

In contrast, European civilization in the ancient Greco-Roman era formed a pattern of joining communities based on territorial relationships, blood relationships were weak. They created a city-state system that regarded the city as center and regarded territorial divisions and differences in wealth as its foundation. People put more emphasis on contractual relationships, and correspondingly the developmental result was the establishment of a system of democratic government.

在以血缘为主的宗法社会,把皇帝当作最高的家长,社会成员划分成不同的等级,社会治理倡导的是以道德为主的"礼治"。西方社会则以制约王权为目标,实行的是"法治"。

In the patriarchal society based on bloodlines, the emperor was considered the highest patriarch, members of society were divided into different ranks, and "ethical rule" based on morality was promoted for social control. Western society implemented the "rule of law" with the goal of restricting monarchal power.

**思考题**

1. 地理环境对文化的形成有哪些方面的影响?
2. 宗法制度对中国传统社会产生了什么样的影响?
3. 中西文化为什么走上了不同的发展道路?

***Questions***

1. What influences does geography have on the formation of culture?
2. What influence on Chinese traditional society has the patriarchal system produced?
3. Why did China and the West take different developmental paths?

# 第二章　中国文化的历史演进
## The Historical Evolution of Chinese Culture

文化的生成、发展都具有阶段性,中国文化史大体上依据王朝系列,同时按文化自身演变的阶段性作出分期。

Both the generation and development of culture occur in stages. The periodization of the history of Chinese culture is largely based on the dynastic series, but at the same time, periodization is done according to steps in the evolution of the culture itself.

### 一、中国文化的起源
### The Origin of Chinese Culture

有了人,就开始有了历史,也开始有了文化。

中国境内最早的人类活动的依据是云南元谋人的发现。1965年5月,考古学者在云南元谋上那蚌村发现了距今170万年的猿人化石,定名为元谋猿人。据考证,元谋人已经能够制造和使用石器。

Once you have people, you begin to have history, and you begin to have culture.

The earliest human activity within China's borders is based on the discovery of Yuanmou Man in Yunnan. In Shangnabeng Village, Yuanmou County, Yunnan Province, archeologists discovered fossils of *homo erectus yuanmouensis* from 1.7 million years ago in May, 1965. According to their findings, Yuanmou Man was already capable of making and using stone tools.

### 二、文明奠基:夏、商、西周
### Foundation of Civilization: Xia, Shang, and Western Zhou

约公元前21世纪夏朝建立,标志着国家的诞生。夏朝之后的商朝和西周,都是中国早期古典文明的辉煌时期。

Around the 21st Century B.C., the Xia Dynasty was founded, symbolizing the birth of the country. The Shang and Western Zhou Dynasties that followed the Xia are the glorious period of the earliest classical civilization.

## 1. 文字的使用
### The Use of Writing

目前所见中国正式的古文字,是商代的甲骨文,因其刻于龟甲、兽骨上,故称甲骨文。(详见第三章"中国的汉字")

The earliest formal Chinese writing known to date is the oracle bone writing of the Shang Dynasty, so-called because it was written on tortoise shells and the bones of animals for oracular purposes (for more details see Chapter 3: Chinese Characters).

## 2. 青铜器的使用
### Use of Bronze Utensils

青铜是铜锡合金,呈青灰色。大量使用青铜器的夏、商、周被称为"青铜时代"。

Bronze is a copper-tin alloy that assumes a bluish-green color. The Xia, Shang, and Zhou eras in which there were a great number of bronze implements in use have been called the "Bronze Age".

至今世界上出土最大、最重,被称为镇国之宝的青铜礼器是后母戊鼎(原称司母戊鼎,见图2-1)。鼎呈长方形,口长112厘米、口宽79.2厘米、壁厚6厘米,连耳高133厘米,重达832.84公斤。1939年3月在河南安阳出土,是商王祖庚或祖甲为祭祀其母戊所制。后母戊鼎是用陶范法铸造而成的,在商后期铸造后母戊鼎至少需要1000公斤的原料,且要在二三百名工匠的密切配合下才能完成,经测定,鼎含铜84.77%、锡11.64%、铅2.79%,与古文献记载制鼎的铜锡比例基本相符。

The largest, heaviest bronze ritual implement excavated in the world so far, known as the Treasure that Guards the Country, is the Houmu Wu Ding (though originally called the Simu Wu Ding (see Figure 2-1). The *ding* (a large cooking cauldron on three or four legs) is rectangular, with an opening 112 centimeters long and 79.2 centimeters wide, with walls 6 centimeters thick, standing 133 centimeters tall at the ears, and weighing 832.84 kilograms. It was excavated in Anyang, Henan Province, in March 1939. It was made by the Shang king Zu Geng or Zu Jia for making sacrifices to his mother Wu. It was cast using the Pottery-Mold Method during the latter period of the Shang Dynasty, requiring at least 1000 kilograms of material and the closely coordinated work of two to three hundred craftsmen. Upon analysis, it was revealed to be composed of 84.77% copper, 11.64% tin, and 2.79% lead, basically matching the ratios of copper and tin found in ancient documents for the manufacture of *ding* (see Fig. 2-1).

图2-1 后母戊鼎（原称司母戊鼎）
Figure 2-1 Houmu Wu Ding

青铜器主要有以下几类：
食器，如鼎、鬲、簋、俎、豆等。
酒器和水器，如爵、壶、鉴、缶等。
兵器，如戈、矛、刀、剑等。
生产工具，如耒、耜、锄等。
乐器，如钟、鼓等。
Types of bronze utensils:
Eating utensils, such as *ding*, *li*, *gui*, *zu*, *dou* (standing cup), etc.
Wine and water utensils, such as *jue* (three-legged pot with a hoop handle), pots, mirrors, and *fou* (covered jar), etc.
Weapons, suchas spears, lances, knives, swords, etc.
Tools, suchas plows, plowshares, hoes, etc.
Musical instruments, suchas bells, drums, etc.

商周时期的青铜器主要用于祭祀和战争。这是因为，当时的"国之大事，在祀与戎"[①]，即国家最重要的事情是祭祀和战争。所以，制作的大量青铜器是用来敬天、尊祖和作战。

---

① 《左传·成公十三年》。

Bronze implements of the Shang and Zhou period were primarily used for ancestral sacrifices and warfare. This is because "the most important business of the country is located in sacrifices and military affairs". So, the majority of these manufactured bronze implements were used to venerate heaven, pay respects to ancestors, and make war.

青铜器的纹饰：商周青铜器的主体纹饰是虚拟的动物纹——饕餮纹（饕餮 tao tie，传说中一种贪吃的猛兽）（见图 2-2 和图 2-3）。饕餮纹也叫兽面纹，凶猛威严、制作精巧，代表着神秘和权力。统治者想用猛兽的纹饰寄托他们的威严和希望，并渴望借助动物与神灵沟通，得到神的保佑。

Bronze decorative motif: The main decorative motif on Shang and Zhou bronze implements is an abstract animal design—the *taotie* motif (*taotie*, according to legend, was a kind of voracious, fierce animal) (see Figure 2-2 and Figure 2-3). The *taotie* motif is also called the "animal face design". It is fierce, imposing and its manufacture is elaborate, representing mystery and authority. The rulers used the motif of a fierce animal to express their hopes for prestige, and wished to communicate with supernatural beings by means of the animal to attain spiritual blessings.

图 2-2　青铜器中的饕餮纹（商周）

Figure 2-2　*Taotie* design on a bronze implement (Shang and Zhou Dynasties)

图 2-3　饕餮纹，现通用的 20 元币面作为防伪纹使用

Figure 2-3　The *taotie* motif as reproduced on the face of the 20 *yuan* note

利簋：西周早期青铜器，用来盛放熟食或作为礼器（见图2-4）。利簋内底铸铭文4行32字，记载了甲子日清晨武王伐纣这一重大历史事件，因做器者名"利"，故称利簋。利簋采用上圆下方的形制，是西周初期铜簋的典型造型，同时体现了古人天圆地方的观念。该利簋出土于陕西省西安市临潼县，现收藏于中国国家博物馆。

Li Gui: Early Western Zhou bronze, used for filling with cooked food or as a sacrificial vessel (see Figure 2-4). There is an inscription on the bottom of the vessel, four lines and 32 characters long, recording the momentous historical event of King Wu conquering Zhou (the last Shang king) in the early morning of the *jiazi* day. It was excavated in Lintong County, Xi'an, Shaanxi Province, and is currently stored in the National Museum of China.

图2-4 利簋（西周）
Figure 2-4 Li Gui (Western Zhou)

总之，青铜作为当时最先进的材料，主要用来制造礼器和兵器，是国家政治权力的象征，拥有青铜器数量的多少，象征着其等级的高低和身份的贵贱。

In short, bronze, as the most advanced material of its time used primarily for manufacturing ritual vessels and weapons, was a symbol of the state's political authority. The number of bronze implements one possessed symbolized the height of one's rank and the nobility of one's identity.

## 3. 城市、国家的出现
### The Appearance of Cities and States

西方有学者把5000人的规模和高筑城墙作为城市的标志，而从考古发掘来看，宫殿基址、陵墓、居住及手工业遗址等则是中国古代城市的基本因素。早于殷墟的商代城址有偃师尸乡沟、郑州、湖北盘龙城等处。在公元前3000年至前2000年的黄河、长江流域及其他地区，都发现有用夯土或石头筑成的城市遗址，都是具有相当规模的雏形城市。①

Some western scholars consider the definition of a city to be a settlement on the scale of around 5000 people and the construction of high city walls. Yet from archeological excavations, the basic elements of Chinese ancient cities are palace foundations, tombs, relics of residences and handicraft industry. Shang Dynasty city ruins earlier than Yinxu are found in Shixianggou in Yanshi County (Henan Province), Zhengzhou (Henan Province), and Panlong City (in Hubei Province). City ruins that used rammed earth and stone construction have been found along the Yellow and Yangtze River valleys, and other places, dating 2000 – 3000 B.C., all of which are early-stage cities on a significant scale.

## 4. 宗教场所
### Religious Sites

祭祀活动在中国上古极为频繁，因而祭祀中心的出现也极早，在红山文化、良渚文化、齐家文化中都有发现，如红山文化牛河梁遗址中所见的女神庙、女神像，良渚文化反山、瑶山遗址中所见的堆土祭坛、玉制礼器等，都说明专门用来祭祀的宗教场所已经出现。

Sacrifices to gods and ancestors were extremely common in ancient China, and so centers for sacrifices appeared very early. They have been discovered in sites associated with Hongshan Culture (4700 – 2900 B.C., Inner Mongolia and Liaoning), Liangzhu Culture (3400 – 2250 B.C., lower Yangtze valley) and Qijia Culture (c. 2000 B.C., Gansu Corridor); for example, the goddess temple and goddess image seen at the Niuheliang Ruins of the Hongshan Culture, or the heaped-earth altar and jade ritual objects found in both the Fanshan and Yaoshan Ruins of the Liangzhu Culture. These findings are evidence that religious sites specifically used for sacrifices to gods and ancestors had already appeared by that time.

中国古代早期文明的典型是以河南安阳小屯殷墟为代表的商代文明。

商朝时期正式跨入文明门槛，商朝都城遗留下城市基址、宫殿、陵墓、宗庙、手工

---

① 李学勤主编：《中国古代文明与国家形成研究》，云南人民出版社1997年版。

业作坊、带字甲骨和大量青铜器，提供了一个完整的早期文明社会范本。

The prototype of early ancient Chinese civilization is the Shang civilization represented by the Yinxu site at Xiaotun, Anyang, Henan Province.

The Shang Dynasty formally crossed the threshold of civilization. The Shang capital left behind city foundations, palaces, tombs, ancestral shrines, craftsmen's workshops, oracle bones with writing on them, and a great number of bronze implements, providing a complete template of early civilization.

## 三、百家争鸣与元典创制：春秋战国时期
## Contention among a Hundred Schools of Thought and Creation of the Primary Canon (Axial Age): The Spring-Autumn (770 – 481 B. C.) and Warring States (481 – 221 B. C.)

公元前770年，周平王把都城向东迁移到了洛邑（今河南洛阳西），东周开始。东周的前段因鲁国史官编纂《春秋》记载而得名"春秋"（前770—前481），后段因为各个诸侯国之间战争不断而称"战国"（前481—前221）。春秋战国是中国历史上第一次发生重大的社会变革和文化转折时期。

In 770 B. C., King Ping of the Zhou moved the capital east to Luoyi (west of modern Luoyang, Henan Province) and thus began the Eastern Zhou Dynasty. The early part of the Eastern Zhou is known as the Spring-Autumn Period (770 – 481 B. C.), named after the records of the historians from State Lu family titled *Spring-Autumn* (or *Spring and Autumn Annals*). The later part is known as the Warring States Period (481 – 221 B. C.) because of the constant warfare between the various vassal states. These periods in Chinese history are one of the most important periods of social transformation and shift in cultural trends.

诸子百家和他们创立的思想体系，成为后来中国乃至整个东方文化的基本精神资源。如同古希腊罗马文化于西方文明、哈拉巴－雅利安文化于印度文明一样，这一时期也成为东方文明的元典时代。

The Hundred Schools and the systems of thought they created became the basic spiritual resource for later Chinese, and even all of East Asian, culture. Just as ancient Greco-Roman culture was to Western civilization, and Harappan-Aryan Culture was to Indian civilization, this period became the era of the primary canon (axial age) for East Asian civilization.

私学的兴起。文化教育从"学在官府"到"学在私门"。商周时期是"学在官

府"，贵族设学受教，垄断文化，平民没有接受教育的权利。春秋末年，私学出现，大批平民子弟开始有了接受教育的权利，许多士人收徒讲学，最有成就的是孔子，相传他"有教无类"，"以诗书礼乐教，弟子盖三千焉，身通六艺者七十有二人"①（教学内容是诗书礼乐，弟子有3000人，精通六艺的有72人）。

Rise of private schools: Cultural education moved from "learning in official residences" to "learning in private homes". In the Shang and Zhou periods, the aristocracy established schools for instruction and monopolized culture, and the common people had no right to receive an education. In the latter years of the Spring-Autumn period, private schools appeared and many *shi* (a status above commoner, but lowest ranking member of the aristocracy) took in students and lectured. The most famous of these was Confucius, who according to legend "educated everyone regardless of background", and "taught poetry, history, etiquette and music; his disciples and followers numbered around 3000, of whom there were 72 who were expert in the six arts".

士的兴起。私学带动了作为知识阶层的"士"的勃兴。士，在殷商西周时期属贵族的最低等级，士以下是平民和奴隶；春秋末期以后，士逐渐成为知识阶层的通称。先秦士子形成一个个杰出的群体，各种学术和流派形成了诸子百家争鸣的格局。

The rise of the *shi*: Private education spurred the growth of the *shi* as an intellectual class. *Shi* was the lowest level of the aristocracy in the Shang and Western Zhou period, below whom were commoners and slaves. Toward the end of the Spring-Autumn period *shi* gradually became the generic term for the intellectual class. The pre-Qin *shi* formed all kinds of outstanding communities, creating every kind of learning and school of thought, setting the pattern for the contention among a Hundred Schools of Thought.

诸子争鸣。各学派的创始人及主要思想家称"子"，诸子指的是孔子、老子、庄子、管子、墨子、荀子、孟子等，战国时期诸子正式形成。百家里著名的有儒家、墨家、道家、名家、法家、阴阳家、农家、纵横家、杂家、小说家等。主要的有以下几家。

Contention among a Hundred Schools: The founders of each school of thought, as well as the primary thinkers within it, were given the appellation *zi* attached to their family name, so the various *zi* refers to Confucius (Kongzi), Laozi, Zhuangzi, Guanzi, Mozi, Xunzi, Mencius (Mengzi), etc. The Hundred Schools were formed in the Warring States period, and included such schools as Ru-ists (also known as Confucian school), Mohists, Daoists, School of Logicians (also called the School of Names), Legalists, School of Yin-Yang, School of

---

① 《史记·孔子世家》。

Agriculture, School of Diplomacy, Miscellaneous School, and School of Minor-talks. Several of most important are described below.

## 1. 儒家："复礼"与"归仁"
## Ru-ists: "Restore the Rites" and "Return to Humanity"

儒家创始人为孔子（前551—前479），儒家学说记载于由其弟子及再传弟子整理的言论集《论语》中，其要旨在"礼"与"仁"。"礼"指宗法制度下的行为规范，孔子要求人们以礼约束自己，"非礼勿视、非礼勿听、非礼勿言、非礼勿动"，不符合"礼"的要求的，都不做。并自我克制，以达到礼的要求，此即"克己复礼"。如果说"礼"是外在规范，"仁"便是思想内核，只有"礼"的外形，而无"仁"的实质，则毫无意义，"人而不仁，如礼何？"（一个人没有仁爱之心，遵守礼仪有什么用？）"仁者爱人"等。孔子身后，儒家代表人为孟子、荀子。

The founder of Confucianism was Confucius (551 – 479 B. C.), whose theory was recorded in the *Lun Yu* (*Analects of Confucius*) which was a collection of his sayings gathered and arranged by his disciples and their disciples. The gist of the teachings was "rites" and "humanity". "Rites" refers to the rules of behavior under the patriarchal system. Confucius required that people restrict themselves by means of the rites; "if not in accord with the rites, do not look; if not in accord with the rites, do not listen; if not in accord with the rites, do not speak; if not in accord with the rites, do not act." Moreover, self control is required to attain the rites, so, "control oneself and restore the rites." If "rites" are the external rules, "humanity" is the core of the system of thought. If one only has "rites" on the outside, but lacks the substance of "humanity", it is all meaningless; "to not act in accord with humanity while being human, then what is there of the rites?" Or, "One who acts in accord with humanity cares for people." Following Confucius, the best known representatives of the Ru-ist school are Mencius and Xunzi.

孟子（约前371—前289），是儒家学派的第二号人物，他侧重发展孔子的仁学，政治上宣扬"仁政"理想，并以人性善作为仁政说的人性论基础。其学说载于《孟子》。

荀子（约前313—前238），主张通过礼与法规范社会，达到"一天下"的目的，人性恶则是其礼学的人性论基础。其学说载于《荀子》。

Mencius (371 – 289 B. C.) is the Ru-ist school's second most important person. He placed particular emphasis on developing Confucius' theory of humanity. In the realm of politics he proclaimed the ideal of "humanistic government" based on the theory that human nature is fundamentally good. His ideas are recorded in *Mencius*.

Xunzi (313 – 238 B. C.) advocated regulating society through the rites and the law, attaining the goal of a "unified world", and the theory of human nature that says humans are fundamentally evil, and so they need to study the rites. His ideas are recorded in *Xunzi*.

## 2. 墨家:"兼爱"与"尚同"
## Mohists: "Universal Love" and "Revere Convergence"

墨家的创始人是墨子(前478—前392),墨家学说载于《墨子》。墨家主要是小生产者的代表,故墨家学说强调物质生产劳动在社会生活中的地位,即"尚力";提倡以普遍的爱停止战乱取得太平,即"兼爱""非攻";要求平等地位,即"尚贤""尚同";生活上提倡简朴、实用,即"节葬""节用";同时尊崇天神,即"尊天"。

墨家在战国时是著名的学派之一,但在秦汉以后逐渐消失,直到近代才又开始出现。

The founder of Mohism was Mozi (478 – 392 B. C.), and the Mohists' ideas are recorded in *Mozi*. Mohists are primarily representative of small manufacturers, so Mohist theories emphasize material productive labor's position in social life, i.e., "revere effort". He promoted ending warfare and attaining peace by means of universal love, i.e., "universal love" and "condemn attacks". He sought equality of position, i.e., "revere the worthy" and "revere convergence". In life, he advocated simplicity and practicality, i.e., "frugal funeral" and "cost reduction". At the same time, he advocated respect and worship of heaven and spirits, i.e., "respect heaven".

The Mohists were a well known school during the Warring States period, but after the Qin-Han, they gradually disappeared until modern times when they again began to appear.

## 3. 道家:"无为"与"自然"
## Daoist: "Inaction" and "Nature"

道,本义是人走的道路,引申为规律、宇宙本源等意义。以"道"为学说核心内容的学派称"道家"。道家的基本方针,是主张以超脱的态度来对待尘世的纷争,认为人生在世,受到无数外在的束缚,例如功名利禄等,只有超然于这一切之上,才能领会到人生之真谛——道。

道家创始人老子(约前580—前500),其思想在战国时期被修订成《道德经》(后来又称《老子》)。老子主张"无为"(一切顺应自然,不过分人为),认为先要"无为"然后才可以"无不为"(有所作为)。道家以"自然"为最高范畴,"人法地,地法天,天法道,道法自然"。(法:效法,简言之,道的运作是以自然的规律为法则。)把道看作人生的唯一规律,提倡顺应天道,崇尚无为。

The basic meaning of *dao* is "a path" such as one might walk on, but has been extended to such meanings as "law of behavior" and "origin of the universe". The school that takes the theory of *dao* as its core content is called "Daoist". The Daoists' basic policy is to advocate for treating the mundane world's disputes with a transcendent attitude. They believe life in the world comes with suffering innumerable external restrictions, such as rank, fame, and fortune, and only when one transcends beyond all of these can one comprehend the real meaning of life—the *dao*.

The founder of Daoism was Laozi (c. 580 – 500 B. C.), whose ideas were revised in the Warring States period into the *Dao De Jing* (later also called *Laozi*). Laozi advocated "inaction" (everything in tune with nature, not too much human effort); he believed one first had to "do inaction" and only then could one "enact". Daoists consider "nature" to be the highest category; "humans imitate the earth, the earth imitates heaven, heaven imitates the *dao*, and the *dao* imitates nature." (Simply put, the workings of the *dao* take the patterns of nature as the law).

They regard the *dao* as life's sole rule of behavior. They advocate conforming to heaven's law and hold the doctrine of "inaction" in high esteem.

庄子（前369—前286）认为人的本性被外在的名、利、家族、事业等没有意义也没有价值的事物所掩盖、所伤害。只有超越这一切，才能回归人的自然本性。主张追求精神自由，超脱于世。其学说载于《庄子》。

Zhuangzi (369 – 286 B. C.) believed a person's inherent quality was obscured and harmed by such external, meaningless and valueless things as fame, profit, family and activity. Only by transcending these can a person return to their natural inherent quality. He advocated pursuing spiritual freedom and transcending the world. His ideas are recorded in the *Zhuangzi*.

儒家强调个人对家族、国家的责任，道家追求个人对社会的超脱。

但是，儒、道的一致之处在于：士大夫们在追求功名时，能够有超脱之心；位居高官时，也可以不为世俗所累。只有这样，士大夫们在志得意满的时候，都以治国平天下为己任，出将入相；而在心灰意冷之日，又可以追求老庄，隐入山林。《孟子·尽心上·忘势》说："穷则独善其身，达则兼善天下。"（一个人在不得志的时候修养个人品德，得意时惠泽普施于百姓。）道家的"出世"与儒家的"入世"共同构筑了中国式的人生态度，统治者既可用儒家学说求得文治武功，又可用道家学说确保休养生息。"儒道互补"组成了中国文化的基本框架。

Ru-ists emphasized the individual's duty to family and country, while Daoists pursue the individual transcendence of society. However, one point Ru-ists and Daoists have in common is that when scholar officials pursue fame and achievement, they can have a mind that stands aloof; when occupying a lofty position, they may not be wearied by the profane. In this way, when scholar officials are fully content with their achievements they take ruling the country and pacifying the world as their own duty, and are talented in all necessary skills. If discouraged, they may pursue Laozi/Zhuangzi Daoism and hide in a mountain forest. The Daoist "retreating from the world" and the Ru-ist "entering the world" jointly construct the Chinese-style attitude toward life. The ruler may use Ru-ist ideas to seek civilian and military achievements, and also use Daoist theories to recover or recuperate. The "Ru-Dao complementarity" constitutes the basic framework of Chinese culture.

### 4. 法家:"变法"与"专制"
### Legalists: "Political Reform" and "Autocracy"

韩非子(约前280—前233),是法家代表人物,提出以法为本,法(政令)、术(策略)、势(权势)三者结合的"南面术"作为帝王统治的主要工具。法家的"法"与儒家的"礼"同样为历代帝王所惯用。

Han Feizi (c. 280 – 233 B.C.) is the Legalists' representative. He proposed considering laws as most basic foundation of society. Laws (government decrees), methods (policies) and power blended into the "art of the one who faces south" (i.e., the ruler), the primary tools with which the monarch rules. Monarchs used the "laws" of the Legalists and the "rites" of the Ru-ists in similar ways through the ages.

两汉以后帝王的典型形象是:一手捧着儒家经典,宣扬教化;一手高举法家利剑,实行专制。

After the Han Dynasty, the typical image of the monarch portrays him in one hand holding the Ru-ist classics, symbolic of his civilizing role, while in the other hand holding high the sharp sword of the Legalists symbolizing his implemention of autocratic rule.

此外还有兵家,代表人物有孙武,著作《孙子兵法》。还有名家、阴阳家等学派。

创立诸子学派的孔子、墨子、老子等人,是中国文化史上的第一批百科全书式的学者,他们开创学派,编纂了中国文化的"元典"性著作,并对宇宙、社会、人生等问题广泛议论,使得中国文化精神的各个侧面得到充分的展开和升华。所以,有学者借用德国学者雅斯贝尔斯的概念,将春秋战国时期称为中国文化的"轴心时代"(Axial Age)。

Besides these, there was the School of the Military, represented by Sun Wu (c.500 B. C.), who authored *The Art of War*. Also, there were such schools as the School of Names, the Yin-Yang School, etc.

The founders of the various schools, Confucius, Mozi, Laozi, etc., were Chinese cultural history's first batch of encyclopedic style scholars. They initiated schools of thought and compiled writings that constitute the "primary canon" of Chinese culture. They broadly discussed the universe, society, life, etc., launching and spreading every aspect of Chinese culture. Therefore, some scholars borrow the German scholar Karl Jaspers' idea to refer to the Spring-Autumn and Warring States periods as Chinese culture's "Axial Age".

## 5. 轴心时代与元典创制
### "Axial Age" and Creation of the Primary Canon

德国学者雅斯贝尔斯在《历史的起源与目标》一书中认为，公元前800年到公元前200年间（尤其是公元前6世纪前后），是人类文明的"轴心时代"（Axial Age）。这一时期，在世界各国文化都进入创制基本民族精神的阶段，纷纷出现有专门知识的"圣贤"，例如中国的孔子、老子，印度的佛陀，波斯的琐罗亚士德，犹太的以赛亚，以及希腊的毕达哥拉斯等诸多人物，他们几乎生活在同一个时期。孔子比释迦牟尼小14岁；孔子死后10年，古希腊的苏格拉底诞生；古希腊哲学家亚里士多德比孟子大12岁，比庄子约大15岁。这些聪明的人思考的结果是"人类意识"首次觉醒，进入理性思维时期，所创制的精神文化范式，决定了其后各个民族的文化走向。

The German scholar Karl Jaspers, in his *The Origin and Goal of History* (New Haven, 1953), believed that between the 8$^{th}$ Century B.C. and the 2$^{nd}$ Century B.C. (but especially around the 6$^{th}$ Century B.C.) human civilization experienced an "axial age". In this period the various cultures of the world entered a stage in which they created the basic spirit of their people. "Wise and holy men" with specialized knowledge appeared repeatedly, as, for example, Confucius and Laozi in China, the Buddha in India, Zoroaster in Persia, the Jewish Isaiah, even Pythagoras in Greece. These important people all seemed to appear in the world in this one time period. Confucius is 14 years younger than Sakyamuni Buddha; ten years after Confucius died Socrates was born in Greece; the ancient Greek philosopher Aristotle is 12 years older than Mencius, and 15 years older than Zhuangzi. The result of these brilliant people's thoughts was the first awakening of "humankind's consciousness". Having entered into rational lines of thinking, the spiritual cultural paradigms they created determined the cultural direction of their later nationalities.

"轴心时代"的另一重要特征，是世界各主要文明民族在此一时段都创作出包含着该民族基本精神的文化元典，如印度的《吠陀》《佛经》，希伯来的《旧约全书》《新约全书》，希腊的《理想国》《形而上学》，波斯的《古圣书》等先哲典籍，所以这几百年间可以说是人类文明的"元典时代"。这一时期，世界上主要文明交相辉映。

Another important feature of the "axial age" is that in this time period the primary civilized peoples of the world created the cultural canon containing the basic spirit of their people, as, for example, the *Vedas* and Buddhist scripture in India, the *Old Testament* in Hebrew, Plato's *Republic* and Aristotle's *Metaphysics*, Persia's ancient sacred texts, and other classics.

So, these several hundred years may be said to be human civilizations "period of the primary canon".

中国的元典时代大约相当于西周和东周,中华文化元典——《诗》《书》《礼》《易》《春秋》等"六艺"诸经及其他诸子著作都在此间出现。这批典籍初步建立了中国人的价值取向、公理体系和思维模式,对两千多年的历史进程产生了深刻影响。

China's period of the primary canon is generally in line with the Western Zhou and the Eastern Zhou. The primary classics of China's culture, such as the *Book of Odes*, *Book of Documents*, *Book of Rites*, *Book of Changes*, and *Spring and Autumn Annals*, the "six arts" and various classic texts, and even the writings of the Hundred Schools, all appeared in this period. This batch of ancient texts established the value orientation of the Chinese people, their systems of axioms and their modes of thought. It had a profound influence on the more than 2000 years of subsequent history.

## 6. 先秦区域文化
## Pre-Qin Regional Cultures

中国地理环境的复杂性决定了中国文化面貌的多样性,春秋战国间主要有以下几种地域文化。

The complexity of China's geographical environment determined the diversity of Chinese culture. In the Spring-Autumn and Warring States periods there were primarily the following regional cultures.

### (1) 齐鲁文化
### *Qi-Lu Culture*

"齐鲁"之地范围与今天的山东省大概一致,故成为山东的代称。齐鲁文化实际是由齐、鲁两国文化共同构成的一个文化圈。春秋时期的鲁国,产生了以孔子为代表的儒家学说,齐国主要是当地的土著文化。两国文化稍有差异:齐文化尚功利,鲁文化重伦理;齐文化呈现华丽活泼、开放创新的风格;鲁文化质朴务实,尊重传统。齐鲁文化影响深远,成为中华文化的主要源头。这里出现了孔子、孟子、墨子、孙武、诸葛亮、李清照、辛弃疾、蒲松龄等杰出人物。

The geographic scope of "Qi-Lu" is generally the same as modern Shandong Province, so the term has become an alternative name for Shandong. In fact, Qi-Lu culture is a cultural sphere jointly composed of the two national cultures of Qi and Lu. The Lu state in the Spring-Autumn period produced the Ru-ist school as represented by Confucius. The Qi state was primarily the local culture of the area. There are slight differences between the two; Qi valued utility, while Lu valued ethics; Qi manifested a flowery, lively, open, creative style, while

Lu was simple, pragmatic, proper and conventional. Qi-Lu's cultural influence was deep and broad, and it became a main source for China's culture. Many outstanding historic figures emerged from this culture, including Confucius, Mencius, Mozi, Sun Wu, Zhuge Liang (181 – 234, military leader), Li Qingzhao (1084 – 1151, poet), Xin Qiji (1140 – 1207, poet), and Pu Songling (1640 – 1715, writer).

### (2) 三晋文化
#### Three Jin Culture

春秋时期的晋国到战国时分成韩、赵、魏三国，故称之为"三晋"，大致包括今天的山西省全境及河南中北部、河北中南部，故晋成为山西的代称。三晋位居中原，较早使用铁器，经济文化发达，是法家文化的发源地。

燕赵地区自古"多慷慨悲歌之士"。

The Jin state of the Spring-Autumn period was divided into the three states of Han, Zhao and Wei in the Warring States period, so they are known as the Three Jin, which were located in modern Shanxi Province, north and central Henan Province, and south and central Hebei Province. Jin has become an alternative name for Shanxi Province. The Three Jin were located in the Central Plains, and relatively early began using iron implements. Its economy was advanced, and it was the source of Legalist culture.

Since ancient times, the Yan and Zhao regions produced "many *shi* who were generous and elegiac".

### (3) 秦文化
#### Qin Culture

秦地以今天的陕西关中、汉中为核心，东起函谷关，西达甘肃中部。关中沃野千里，是中华文明的发源地。公元前221年，秦国统一六国，建立了中国历史上第一个统一的王朝，也是中国皇权专制社会的开始。秦王嬴政统一六国后，认为自己"德高三皇、功过五帝"，因此把古代传说中神和人最尊贵的三皇五帝的称号合二为一，号称"皇帝"。从此，"皇帝"便成为中国古代国家最高统治者的称号，一直用到最后一个皇帝——清朝宣统皇帝溥仪为止。秦朝采取的一系列统一措施，例如统一文字、货币、度量衡等，让中国成为一个统一的、多民族的国家。

The Qin lands are centered on modern Shaanxi Province's Guanzhong and Hanzhong, in the east rising from Hangu Pass and in the west stretching to the central part of Gansu Province. Guanzhong, with hundreds of miles of fertile land, is one of the birthplaces of China's culture. In 221 B.C. the Qin state unified the six states and established Chinese history's first unified dynasty, marking the beginning of China's imperial autocratic society. After the Qin emperor Ying Zheng unified the six states, he believed himself to be morally superior to the Three Sovereigns (*sānhuáng*) and more meritorious than the Five Emperors (*wǔdì*). He thus combined the titles of these respected figures from traditional legend and called himself "Emperor" (*huángdì*), and henceforth "emperor" became the title of the highest rulers of China's ancient states all the way up until the last emperor of the Qing Dynasty, Puyi, stepped down in 1912. The series of unifying measures the Qin adopted, such as unifying writing, currency, weights and measures, etc., allowed China to become a unified, multi-ethnic state.

秦王朝的建立，在我国古代历史上具有划时代的意义，从此开始的政治、经济制度在以后两千多年的皇权社会中有着极为深远的影响。所以，"秦人"同后来的"汉人""唐人"一样，成了世界各国对中国人的代称。

The establishment of the Qin Dynasty had epoch-making significance in ancient Chinese history. The political-economic system that began then had an extremely profound influence on the subsequent 2000 years of imperial-power society. Thus, "the people of Qin", just as "people of Han" and "people of Tang" in later times, became an alternative name for "Chinese people" for countries around the world.

### (4) 楚文化
### *Chu Culture*

东周时，楚地指今湖北、湖南以及河南、安徽、江西的部分地区。这里地处长江中游，土地肥沃、湖泊众多，是著名的"鱼米之乡"。楚地是道家的发祥地。楚文化精美的工艺，主要有青铜铸造、丝织和漆器，例如青铜编钟、素纱禅衣（长沙马王堆汉墓出土，重仅49克，西汉时期）等。出现了老子、屈原等杰出人物。

楚人信鬼好巫，善于幻想也成为楚文化一大特色。

In the time of the Eastern Zhou, the region of Chu referred to modern Hubei, Hunan and parts of Henan, Anhui, and Jiangxi. This area, located in the central Yangtze valley with its fertile land and numerous lakes, is the famous "land of fish and rice". It is the cradle of the Daoist School. The exquisite handicrafts of Chu culture are primarily their bronze casting, silkware, and laquerware, including sets of bronze bells and fine silk clothing *susha danyi* (the one unearthed at the Mawangdui tomb in Changsha weighed barely 49 grams). Such outstanding people as Laozi and Qu Yuan came from here.

The people of Chu believed in ghosts and were fond of wizards; being adept at creating fantasy also became a major characteristic of Chu culture.

晚周地域文化，富有特色的还有吴越文化、巴蜀文化、滇文化、燕文化等，它们与上述文化一起构成纷繁多姿的华夏文化。

The regional cultures of the late *Zhou* Dynasty also include characteristic *Wu Yue* culture,

*Ba Shu Dian* culture and *Yan* culture etc. Above all, these cultures constitue a variety of *Hua Xia* Culture.

## 四、政治一统和文化整合：秦、汉时期
## Political Unification and Cultural Integration: The Qin-Han Period

### 1. 大一统帝国模式
### The Great Unification Mode

秦汉时期，中国古代的大一统帝国模式形成。

"大一统"，所谓"大"，就是尊重、重视；所谓"一统"，即"万物之本皆归于一"，指普天之下在政治、文化等各方面的同化一致，全国实现统一格局。

China's imperial model of the great unification took shape in the Qin-Han period.

The "great" in "great unification" means "eminent" and "valued". The "unification", i.e., "the root of all things is affiliated with one", means everything in the world is consistent through the assimilation of politics and culture, the whole country implement nationalwide unification.

公元前3世纪末叶，秦王嬴政（前259—前210）建立中国历史上第一个君主专制的中央集权国家，实现了政治、文化上的统一。实行了书同文（统一文字）、车同轨（统一道路宽度）、度同制（统一货币、度量衡等）、行同伦（统一全国的文化心理）、地同域（开发边境、传播中原文化）、修秦律。采取一系列措施，以保证人们认同帝王统治。

In the latter years of the 3$^{rd}$ Century B.C., King Ying Zheng of Qin (259 – 210 B.C.) established Chinese history's first autocratic monarchical centralized state and achieved political and cultural unification. They put into practice a unified script, unified road system, unified currency, weights and measures, unified national culture, opened new lands to spread Central Plains culture, and cultivated the laws of Qin. By adopting this series of measures, they guaranteed the people would acknowledge the monarch's rule.

秦朝确立的大一统的帝国模式，即专制集权的国家制度和整齐划一的文化形态，为后世各朝所沿袭。西洋的"China"、东洋的"支那"，都是"秦"变音后的音译。

汉代完善了秦代创立的大一统帝国文化模式。其后两千多年，统治者大都追求政治和文化的大一统。

The unified imperial model the Qin established, that is, a state system of autocratic, centralized authority and a uniformly adjusted cultural form, was followed by all later dynasties. In Western so called "China", Oriental so called "Zhi Na," they are all transliteration of "Qin."

The Han Dynasty improved the unified imperial cultural model the Qin created. For the more than 2000 years that followed, rulers pursued political and cultural unification.

## 2. 文化整合
**Cultural Integration**

秦汉时期的文化大一统，还包括思想学术上的统一。汉朝推行"罢黜百家，独尊儒术"的文化政策，独奉儒家经典，此后，"经"专指儒家经典，主要有"五经"，即《诗》《书》《礼》《易》《春秋》。从此，经学被推尊为统一天下思想的官方哲学，正式成为大一统帝国的法定经典。

The Qin-Han great cultural unification also included unification of thinking and learning. The Han Dynasty put into effect the cultural policy of "dismiss the Hundred Schools, revere only the Ru-ists", and solely promoted the Ru-ist classics. Thereafter, the term "classic" specifically referred to the Ru-ist canon, primarily the "Five Classics", i. e., *The Book of Odes*, *The Book of Documents*, *The Book of Rites*, *The Book of Changes*, and *The Spring and Autumn Annals*. The study of the classics for their revered philosophy unified thinking in the world, and the texts officially became the statutory classics of the great unified empire.

# 五、胡汉、中印文化融合：魏晋至唐中叶
**The Mix of Cultures from Han and non-Han, and Between China and India: From Wei-Jin to Mid-Tang Period**

## 1. 魏晋玄学
**Wei-Jin *Xuan*-ology**

魏晋时期，经学受到冷落，玄学兴起，并成为一种新的文化思潮。"玄"有深奥、玄妙之意，玄是"众妙之门"（万物产生的根本），"玄"和"道""无"一样。道家的《老子》《庄子》和儒家的《周易》三部书被称为"三玄"，"玄学"则因为研究阐述这三部书而得名。

The study of the classics was pushed to the side during the Wei-Jin period. *Xuan*-ology rose up and became a new way of cultural thinking. *Xuan* means "profound and mysterious";

it is "the gate to the multitude of mysteries" (the basis producing all things), so it is like the *dao* and "nothingness". The Daoist's *Laozi* and *Zhuangzi* and the Ru-ist's *Book of Changes* became known as the "three *xuan*". *Xuan*-ology got its name because of the study and elaboration of these three texts.

玄学提倡崇尚自然，即崇尚道家的"无为"；又笃信名教，即笃信儒家的三纲五常。玄学家们轻视人事、崇尚自然的价值观深深地影响了士人，进而铸造了中国士人玄、远、清、虚的生活情趣。

*Xuan*-ology promoted reverence of nature, i. e., the Daoist idea of "inaction". They firmly believed in the Religion of Names, that is, the Ru-ist's idea of the three rules (ruler guides the minister, father guides the son, and husband guides the wife) and five constant virtues (humanity, justice, rites, wisdom, and trustworthiness). The *Xuan*-ologist's sytem of values, including disparaging worldly affairs and reverence for nature, profoundly influenced scholars. It also provided the basis for Chinese scholar's lively interest and inclination in the mysterious, the remote, the distinct, and the empty.

## 2. 胡汉交流与文化互补
### Han and non-Han Interaction and Cultural Complementarity

经过夏商周至秦汉约两千两百年，一个以华夏汉族为主体的多民族国家初步形成。魏晋南北朝369年间，则是继春秋战国以后又一次更大规模的民族迁移和民族融合高潮。少数民族先后进入中原，建立政权。

Through the 2200 years from the Xia-Shang-Zhou to the Qin-Han, a multi-ethnic state based on the Hua-Xia (Han) ethnicity began to take shape. But during the 369 years of the Wei-Jin and Northern and Southern Dynasties, there was an upsurge in large-scale migration and ethnic mixing, the first since the Spring-Autumn and Warring States period. Minority ethnicities entered the Central Plains in succession and established political power.

游牧或半农半牧民族的"胡"（指少数民族）文化与中原农耕人的"汉"文化长时间交会，在冲突中走向融合。和少数民族的交流融合，弥补了中原文化里的不足。这种各民族文化交流的结果，就是出现了绚丽多彩、盛极一时的隋唐文化。隋唐帝国达到中国古典文化的全盛佳境。

The nomadic and semi-nomadic "Hu" (meaning minority ethnic group) culture interacted for a long time with the Central Plain's "Han" culture, and tended toward mixing together amid conflicts. The interaction and mixture with minority peoples supplemented insufficiencies in Central Plain's culture and strengthened it. The result of this ethnic cultural exchange was the emergence of the grand, glorious Sui-Tang culture. The Sui and Tang Empires encompassed the most flourishing stage in ancient Chinese culture.

## 3. 隋唐的都城
### The Sui-Tang Capital

西安：古称长安，是中国五大古都之一，也是中国历史上建都时间最长、建都朝代最多、影响力最大的都城，历史上最为强盛的周、秦、汉、隋、唐等13个朝代均建都于此。隋朝兴建后称大兴城，唐代改名长安。唐长安以100多万人口、80多平方公里的面积，雄踞当时世界都会之首。

Xi'an: Known as Chang'an in the past, Xi'an was Chinese history's longest-serving capital city, serving the most dynasties, and with the most influence among capital cities of ancient China. Thirteen dynasties, including the rich and powerful Zhou, Qin, Han, Sui, and Tang built their capital here. After the Sui Dynasty arose, they called it the "Great-Rise City", but the Tang Dynasty changed it to Chang'an "Long Peace". Tang's Chang'an had more than one million residents, covered an area of more than 80 square kilometers and was preeminent among the world capitals of its day.

有人说人类历史上真正的文化中心有三个——公元7世纪的长安、19世纪的巴黎和今天的纽约。7世纪的长安城里，有许多亚欧国家的外交使团，有外国留学生，有阿拉伯、罗马、波斯等国的商人；长安已经是一个国际化的大都市。

Some people say there are only three true cultural centers in human history: 7th Century Chang'an, 19th Century Paris, and New York City in the present. In 7th Century Chang'an there were diplomatic missions from many Eurasian countries, foreign exchange students, and business people from Arabia, Rome, and Persia. Chang'an was already an internationalized metropolis.

长安城内的建筑按照住宅的等级身份展开：宫殿地势最高，政府机关次之，寺观和官僚住宅又次之，一般居民等而下之。唐代诗人白居易（772—846）如此描述长安："百千家似围棋局，十二街如种菜畦。"南北11条大街，东西14条大街，成直线纵横交错，将全城划分为108个坊和两个市，隋唐长安的平面构图，左右对称，区划整齐，方正如同棋盘（见图2-5、图2-6）。

东都洛阳：面积小于长安，由宫城、皇城和外郭城三重组成。

Buildings within the city unfolded according to the ranked status of the residence. The palace stood on the highest ground, with government buildings second to it, temples, monasteries, and bureaucratic residences were below that, and then finally the commoners' residences. The Tang poet Bai Juyi (772–846) described the city as, "Hundreds or thousands of homes arranged as a Go chess board, 12 streets lined up like rows in a vegetable garden."

There were 11 main streets running north-south, and 14 main streets running east-west, criss-crossing in straight lines, dividing the city into 108 districts and two fair towns. The city was symmetrically composed on an north-south axis, the subdivisions were neat and tidy, and the layout was as square as a chess board (see Figure 2 –5, Figure 2 –6).

Luoyang, the Eastern Capital, was smaller in area than Chang'an, with three sets of city walls surrounding a palace city, an imperial city and an outer city.

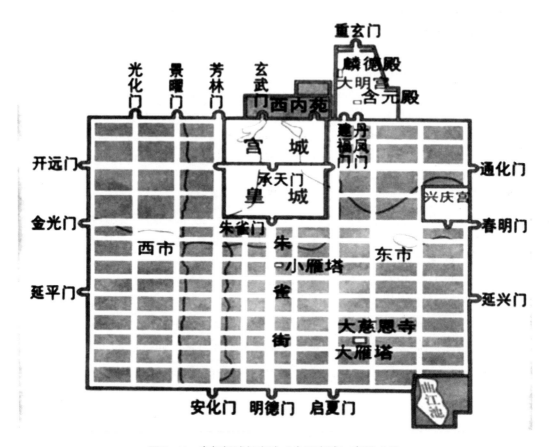

图 2 –5　唐朝都城长安城（今西安城）布局（1）
Figure 2 –5　Layout of the Tang capital Chang'an (modern Xi'an)

中国古代都城规模宏大，面积与人口都居世界前列，其中居第一位的是长安城，占地 84 平方公里，北魏（386—534）洛阳约 74 平方公里，元大都约 50 平方公里，明清北京约 60 平方公里。

The scale of China's ancient capitals was huge, among the leading cities in the world in terms of area and population. The first among them was Chang'an, covering 84 sq. kilometers. Luoyang under the Northern Wei (386 - 534) covered around 74 sq. km. Dadu

(i. e. modern Bejing) under the Yuan Dynasty covered around 50 sq. km. Beijing under the Ming and Qing Dynasties covered around 60 sq. km.

与多数国家拥有较稳定、单一的首都不同，中国的都城多次转移。中国古代先后出现过数以百计的都城，著称于世的中国古都有五个：西安、洛阳、开封、南京、北京。

Different from many other countries which had a single, relatively stable capital city, the capital of China moved several times. In fact, there appeared hundreds of capitals. There are five world-renowned ancient China capitals: Xi'an, Luoyang, Kaifeng, Nanjing, and Beijing.

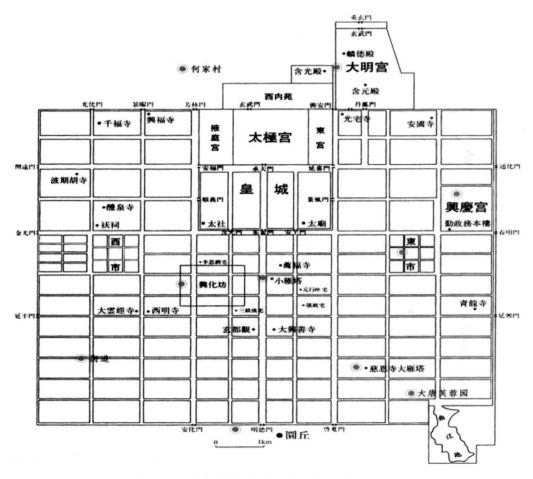

图 2-6　唐朝都城长安城（今西安城）布局（2）

Figure 2-6　Layout of the Tang capital Chang'an (modern Xi'an)

## 六、近古文化定型：唐中叶至明中叶
## Finalization of the Near-Ancient Culture: Mid-Tang to Mid-Ming Period

### 1. 唐朝历史前后转折的标志——"安史之乱"
### The Tang Dynasty's Historical Turning Point—The An-Shi Rebellion

唐朝的"安史之乱"历来被视为唐朝历史上前后转折的标志。公元755年冬天爆发的"安史之乱"，历时八年，给唐朝社会造成严重破坏，唐朝从此由强盛转入衰弱。唐朝灭亡后，相继出现五个王朝、十个国家，史称"五代十国"。直到赵匡胤（927—976）即宋太祖建立北宋并再度统一中国。

The An-Shi (An Lusha and Shi Siming) Rebellion has always been regarded as a symbol of the turning point in Tang history. The rebellion erupted in the winter of 755 and lasted eight years, causing serious damage to Tang society. The Tang went from being rich and strong to weak. After the Tang Dynasty collapsed, there was a series of five dynasties and ten kingdoms in succession, which became the name used to refer to the following period. The disunion lasted until Zhao Kuangyin (927 – 976), i.e., Song Taizu, founded the Northern Song and once again unified China.

### 2. 中国文化史上的第三次转型
### The Third Transformation in Chinese Cultural History

"安史之乱"后，唐代中叶（8世纪中叶至9世纪上半叶）出现一系列变化，成为中国文化史的转折点。

西方汉学家评论道：

> 在公元8世纪的唐朝，中国有过最辉煌的岁月，而到了公元12—13世纪，情势就发生了令人瞩目的扭转。在这4个世纪中，发生过急剧的变化。一个尚武、好战、坚固和组织严明的社会，已经为另一个活泼、享乐和腐化的社会所取代了。①

After the An-Shi Rebellion a series of changes took place in the middle of the Tang Dynasty (mid 8th Century to early 9th Century) and there was a turning point in Chinese cultural history.

---

① ［法］谢和耐著：《蒙元入侵前夜的中国日常生活》，刘东译，江苏人民出版社1995年版，第2页。

A Western Sinologist commented on it as follows:

8$^{th}$ Century Tang Dynasty had its most glorious years, but by the 12$^{th}$ – 13$^{th}$ centuries the situation had a startling reverse. Within these four centuries, rapid changes took place. A society that revered martial skill and was fond of warfare, stable and organizationally firm had been replaced by another society that was lively and decadent and enjoyed the pleasures of life ( Jacques Gernet *La Vie quotidienne en Chine a la veille de l" invasion mongole*, 1959).

中唐以后，中国的文化心理从隋唐帝国的自信活泼、宽松自由、积极向上的精神风貌，渐趋不振，由开拓转为内敛，由尚武转为尚文，国力大减，边患不断。

中国的经济、政治、文化重心开始从北向南迁移，表明了唐中期是历史的转折时期。

After the mid-Tang, China, in terms of cultural psychology, gradually changed from the Sui-Tang's confident liveliness, broad freedom and optimistic spiritual ethos, to one lacking vitality; from open to the outside to introverted, from esteeming martial skills to valuing arts and letters; the national power greatly decreased and the border suffered unceasing incursions.

China's economic, political, and cultural center started to move from the north to the south, indicating that the mid-Tang was a historical turning point.

## 3. 近古文化
**Near Ancient Culture**

从唐中期到宋中期的文化，可以称作近古文化，主要特点是从汉唐时期的宏大气势转向之后的精致内敛。例如，比较唐诗和宋词，唐诗大多气魄雄浑，宋词则更多倾向于内敛的哲理。

隋唐科举制度创立，宋代理学开创。

Culture from the mid-Tang to mid-Song may be referred to as the period of "near ancient" culture, the primary characteristics of which was delicate introversion, a change from the expansive vigor of the Han to Tang period. An example is revealed in the comparison of Tang poetry to Song lyric. Tang poetry was mostly bold and vigorous, while Song lyrics were mostly inclined toward an introverted philosophy.

The Sui-Tang established the imperial examination system. The Song Dynasty founded the Rationalist School (Neo-Confucianism).

理学，亦称为新儒学、道学或宋学。称为理学，是因为理学的思想体系的最高范畴是"理"，"理"即天理，是构成万事万物的本体存在。理学高度强调人们要自觉地遵从理，认识理的途径就是正心、诚意、修身、齐家、治国、平天下。儒家思想在理学体系中得到形而上的新的解释。理学的集大成者——朱熹（1130—1200），成为继孔子、孟子之后的又一圣人，是儒学正宗的继承者。

  The most important mark of Song culture was the founding of the Rationalist School, also called "Neo-Confucianism", "Confucian Study of Ethics", or "Song Learning". It is called Rationalism (*lǐ xué*) because the highest category in the system of thought is *lǐ* "reason", or "Heaven's Law". *Lǐ* is the main part of existence, the thing of itself, that forms all things and all living things. Rationalists stress that people must consciously comply with *lǐ*; the path of recognizing *lǐ* is rectifying the mind, sincerity, moral cultivation, and management of one's household, in order to rule the country and pacify the world. In the Rationalist School, Ru-ist thinking obtained a positive new interpretation. The school's great synthesizer, Zhu Xi (1130 – 1200), became a sage in the model of Confucius and Mencius and the successor of the Ru-ist orthodoxy.

  理学将中国重伦理、重道德的传统精神推到极致，对中国文化产生了深远影响。
  理学对中国文化最重要的影响，是使东汉以后被打破的礼治秩序得以重建。但是，它"存天理，灭人欲"，过分地限制人性，否认个体的独立存在。尤其把对女性的约束推向了极致，"饿死事小，失节事大"（宁可饿死，也不能失去贞洁），格外看重妇女的贞洁操守，残酷地压抑女性情感，给中国妇女的文化心理造成长久的重压。

  The Rationalist School pushed China's traditional spirit of attaching importance to ethics and morality to its peak, generating a deep influence on Chinese culture.

  Most importantly, it enabled a re-establishment of the rule of etiquette-based social order that had been broken after the Eastern Han. However, "preserve Heaven's Law, extinguish human desire" overly restricted human nature, denying the independent existence of the individual. It especially pushed restrictions on women to an extreme, as in the saying, "starving to death is a small matter, losing one's chastity is an important one". The particular regard paid to women's chastity and personal integrity, and the cruel repression of women's emotions resulted in a long-lasting burdon on Chinese women's cultural psychology.

  另一影响是理学提倡士人建立功业、积极研究社会实际问题，士人们要树立起道德自觉的理想人格。

  Another influence was the Rationalists advocacy for scholars establishing industry and actively investigating real social problems. They believed scholars must establish a morally self-conscious ideal integrity.

  在理学的影响下，中华民族文化性格中更加强调道德、社会责任、历史使命。高尚的君子应该做到：

> 为天地立心，为生民立命，为往圣继绝学，为万世开太平。
>
> ——［北宋］张载（1020—1077）

Under the influence of the Rationalist School, the Chinese people's cultural temperament even more stressed morality, social responsibility and historical mission. The enlightened gentleman should:

> Set one's mind for the sake of Heaven and Earth; set one's life for the sake of enlivening the people; continue lost learning for the sake of past sages; create the ultimate peace for all future generations.
>
> — ［Northern Song Dynasty］Zhang Zai（1020 – 1077）

## 4. 经济和文化重心南移
### The Political and Cultural Core Moves South

中国自上古以来就有南北之分，一般说来，北方主要指黄河流域，南方主要指长江流域，大致以秦岭—淮河一线为界。

秦汉时期，北方的经济和文化发展水平超过南方，中国的几个著名古都——长安、洛阳和开封等，皆在北方。宋代以来，除了政治中心尚在北方地区之外，经济和文化重心都转移到南方。

There have been divisions between north and south in China since ancient times. Generally speaking, the north refers to the Yellow River basin, and the south refers to the Yangtze River basin, with the Qinling Mountain and the Huai River serving as a general border.

In the Qin-Han period, the level of northern economic and cultural development surpassed that of the south. China's several famous capital cities, such as Chang'an, Luoyang, and Kaifeng, were all in the north. Starting in the Song Dynasty, with the exception of the political center remaining in the north, the economic and cultural centers shifted southward.

政治中心人物开始南方化，即政治上的代表性人物籍贯分布多在南方。唐代、北宋初期以前，中央政权基本上为北方人垄断。北宋中期以后，南方人当宰相的逐渐增多。南宋时期包括政治人才在内的各类人才分布，以两浙居全国首位，福建第二，江西第三，四川第四。

Central characters in politics began to southernize. That is, most representative characters on the political stage had their origins in the south. Prior to the Tang and early Song, central political authority was basically monopolized by northerners. After the middle of the Song, more southerners served as prime minister. In the Southern Song, Zhejiang was the primary place of origin of people of talent, including political talent, with Fujian in second, Jiangxi in third, and Sichuan in fourth.

学术中心南移。从南宋直至近代，南方地区各学派纷呈，宗师辈出，如王阳明（浙江人）、顾炎武（江苏人）、黄宗羲（浙江人）、王夫之（湖南人）等，引领着中国学术文化主潮，他们的所在地成为学术中心。尤其是苏南、浙北，不仅是财富重地，而且人才辈出，科举考试的进士人数历年均为全国之首。

Academic centers moved south. From the Southern Song to modern times, the various schools of thought flourished in the south. Eminent scholars appeared in great numbers there, such as Wang Yangming (1472 – 1529, from Zhejiang), Gu Yanwu (1613 – 1682, from Jiangsu), Huang Zongxi (1610 – 1695, from Zhejiang), and Wang Fuzhi (1619 – 1692 from Hunan). These scholars led the mainstream Chinese academic culture, and these places became centers of academic learning. Southern Jiangsu and northern Zhejiang, especially, were not only important areas of wealth, but also the source of a great deal of talented people, producing the most successful candidates for the imperial examination year after year.

## 5. 少数民族不断进入中原
### Minority Peoples' Continuous Migration into the Central Plains

自唐末五代始，西北游牧民族再次对中原农耕世界发动规模日益巨大的冲击。契丹、党项、女真相继建立政权，1206 年，成吉思汗建立起蒙古政权。

Beginning from the Tang and Five Dynasties era, nomadic peoples from the northwest once again launched increasingly large scale assaults on the Central Plain's agricultural world. The Khitan, Tangut, and Jurchen set up political power in succession, and in 1206 Genghis Khan established the Mongol authority.

## 6. 元朝与中西文化的沟通
### The Yuan Dynasty and Chinese-Western Cultural Communication

忽必烈（1215—1294）建立的元朝（1271—1368），是一个疆域空前辽阔的帝国，东西方的交往空前频繁，使节的往来、命令的传递、商队的贸易络绎不绝。大批中亚军卒、商贩、工匠来到中原汉地，成千上万蒙、汉及其他族人民从元朝迁往中亚各地。

The Yuan Dynasty (1271 – 1368) established by Khubilai Khan (1215 – 1294) was an unprecedentedly large empire. East-West communication became more frequent than ever before, with an endless stream of envoys, decrees, and trade caravans coming and going. A large number of Central Asian soldiers, traders and craftsmen came to the Han areas of the

Central Plains, and thousands of Mongols, Han, and other ethnic groups migrated to various places in Central Asia following the Yuan Dynasty.

威尼斯人马可·波罗（1254—1324）取道波斯，沿着古丝绸之路东行，翻越帕米尔高原，穿过河西走廊，经宁夏（银川）、天德军（今呼和浩特东），于1275年抵达大都（今北京），完成横贯欧亚大陆的旅行。在大都，忽必烈接见马可·波罗，马可·波罗叔侄二人被留在宫廷服务。

The Venetian Marco Polo (1254 – 1324) came east via Persia following the Silk Road, crossed the Pamir Mountains, traversed the Hexi Corridor, passed through Ningxia and modern Hohhot to arrive in the Yuan capital in 1275, completing his trip across the Eurasian continent. In the capital, he was granted an interview with Khubilai Khan, and he and his nephew were allowed to stay in the palace in his service.

亚欧大陆得以沟通，使节、商人、工匠、艺人、翻译、僧侣、俘虏等往来不断，东方和西方的相互了解有了不同于以往任何时代的新发展。

With the new ability to communicate across Eurasia, envoys, merchants, craftsmen, artists, translators, monks, and captives went back and forth uninterrupted, and mutual understanding between East and West experienced a new era of growth.

### 7. 科技成就
**Achievements in Science and Technology**

宋代科技为人类文明贡献出了指南针、活字印刷术和火药三项重大科技发明（参考第十一章）。

Song Dynasty science and technology gave humankind the compass, movable type block printing and gun powder, three important inventions and innovations in science and technology (see also Chapter Eleven).

## 七、文化专制与西学东渐：明清时期
## Cultural Dictatorship and Western Learning's Eastern Flow: Ming-Qing Period

明朝（1368—1644）是朱元璋（1328—1398）重新建立起的汉人当权的朝代。清朝（1644—1912）是满族建立的王朝，也是中国古代历史上最后一个朝代。

明清时期是专制集权高度发达的时代，是政治高压的时代，但又是一个市民文化的时代，是思想启蒙的时代。

The Ming Dynasty (1368 – 1644) is the ethnic Han Dynasty founded by Zhu Yuanzhang (1328 – 1398). The Qing Dynasty (1644 – 1912) is the dynasty established by the Manchus and the last ancient Chinese dynasty.

The Ming-Qing period is a time of highly-developed power centralization and intense political pressure, but also a time of urban cultural development and enlightened thinking.

## 1. 文化专制政策
### The Policy of Cultural Dictatorship

明清两朝,专制君主集权走向极端,并严厉实行禁忌主义的文化政策。

明太祖朱元璋废黜中书省和百官之长——丞相,分相权于吏、户、礼、兵、刑、工六部,使六部直属皇帝。这样,皇帝既是国家元首,又是政府首脑。

In the Ming-Qing period, the autocratic monarchy's centralization of power trended toward the extreme, and they implemented a cultural policy of strict taboo-ism.

The Taizu Emperor of the Ming Dynasty, Zhu Yuanzhang, discarded the Central Secretariat and the Prime Minister who was in charge of all officials. He divided authority between the Six Ministries: Ministry of Appointments (in charge of the bureaucracy), Ministry of Revenue, Ministry of Rites, Ministry of War, Ministry of Punishments, and Ministry of Works. Moreover, he made these six ministries report directly to the emperor. Thus, the emperor was both the head of state and the head of the government.

清朝基本沿袭明制,一直不设丞相,另外设置军机处,由皇帝直接掌握,而军机处也只有传达皇帝诏令的功能,一切政令都要听命于皇帝。

The Qing basically followed the Ming system and never appointed a prime minister, but they established an Office of Military and Political Affairs directly under the control of the emperor. Moreover, this office had the sole function of transmitting the emperor's imperial orders, so all government decrees had to come directly from the emperor.

明清两代实行严厉的文化专制政策。一方面,朝廷将儒学、宋明理学规定为官方哲学,并将科举制度进一步完善化;另一方面,对于在思想、文字上稍有越轨、反抗表现的士人,实行无情镇压。

明太祖朱元璋不放心文臣,以致演成挑剔字句,大开杀戒,大兴文字狱。朱元璋出身贫寒,青年时当过和尚,参加过农民起义,忌讳人们提起,一旦他认为受到冒犯,就要治罪。

The Ming and Qing implemented a strict policy of cultural dictatorship. On the one hand, the court made Ru-ist and Song-Ming Rationalist schools the official ideology, and they further improved the system of imperial examinations. On the other hand, they mercilessly suppressed scholars who even slightly stepped out of line or resisted in the fields of politics and culture.

Zhu Yuanzhang, the first Ming emperor, was not at ease with civilian court officials, even to the extent that he picked nits with their writing, openly admonished and killed some, and undertook a large-scale literary inquisition. Zhu Yuanzhang was born to a poor family, had been a Buddhist monk in his youth, and participated in peasant revolt. He made a taboo of people speaking up, and if he believed someone offended him in any way, he would punish them.

清朝康、雍、乾三朝文字狱仅见记载的就有108起之多,而且愈演愈烈。有一个康熙末年的进士,写的诗作中有这样两句:"明月有情远顾我,清风无意不留人",被人告发,说他思念明朝,依据大不敬的律法,被处以"斩立决",立即杀头,他的诗文稿全部被烧毁。

According to official record, under the Qing emperors Kangxi (1654 – 1722), Yongzheng (1678 – 1735) and Qianlong (1711 – 1799) there were as many as 108 cases in which officials persecuted intellectuals for their writing. Moreover, each was more severe than the last. One successful imperial examinee in the later years of the Kangxi reign wrote a poem that had these two lines: "The bright moon out of love, though distant, looks after me; the clear breeze, inadvertently, does not preserve the people" (note: "bright" is the same character as the name of the Ming Dynasty, and "clear" is the same character as the name of the Qing Dynasty). Somebody lodged an accusation against the writer, saying he was longing for the Ming Dynasty, and based on the statutes of disrespect, the poet was sentenced to "immediate decapitation." His head was immediately cut off and all his writings were burned.

明清时期的文字狱是君主专制制度发展到顶峰状态的产物,其目的是要在思想文化领域内树立起君主专制统治的绝对权威。这是中国文化史上黑暗、血腥的一页。

The literary inquisition of the Ming-Qing period was the ultimate endpoint of the monarchal autocratic system. The goal of the literary inquisition was to establish the absolute control of the monarch's autocratic rule in the sphere of thought and culture; it was a dark, bloody page in Chinese cultural history.

## 2. 八股文章
### The Eight-legged Essay

为了控制思想,明清统治者在科举考试中实行"八股"之法。所谓"八股文",是科举考试中答卷时写作的固定格式,即由破题、承题、起讲、入手、起股、中股、后股、束股等几部分组成,一共八股,故称"八股文"。八股文体格式刻板,禁忌颇多,内容空虚无物,最大效用在于控制士人思想,影响恶劣。八股文直到1905年推行学校教育、废除科举后方才退出历史舞台。

In order to control thought, Ming-Qing rulers implemented the "essay in eight parts" for the imperial examinations. The so-called "eight-legged essay" was the rigid form for writing answers in the imperial exam. It was composed of the following parts: opening (broach the topic), amplification (elaborate and clarify the theme), preliminary exposition (outline over-all conclusion), setting out, initial argument, central argument, latter argument, final argument. The literary form of the essay was rigid, there were numerous taboos, and the content was empty and meaningless. Its greatest utility was controlling the thinking of scholars, so its effect was abominable. It lasted until 1905 when education in schools was promoted and the imperial exams were abandoned.

### 3. 地理远航
### Distant Voyages

15—16世纪是一个地理大发现、海道大通的时代，意大利人哥伦布（约1451—1506）于1492年发现了美洲新大陆，葡萄牙人达·伽马（约1469—1524）于1498年绕过好望角开辟了到印度的东方新航路，葡萄牙人麦哲伦（1480—1521）绕过南美大陆的最南端（后被称为麦哲伦海峡）进入太平洋，到达菲律宾，后来其属下于1522年回到西班牙，完成了人类历史上的首次环球航行。

The $15^{th}$ – $16^{th}$ centuries were an age of geographic discovery and opening of sea routes. The Italian Christopher Columbus (c. 1451 – 1506) in 1492 first sailed to the new continent of America. The Portuguese Vasco da Gama (c. 1469 – 1524) in 1498 sailed around the Cape of Good Hope and established a new sea route to India. The Portuguese Ferdinand Magellan (1480 – 1521) sailed around the southern most point of South America (later named the Straits of Magellan) into the Pacific Ocean and later reached the Philippines. His subordinates returned to Spain in 1522, completing humankind's first circumnavigation of the globe.

与哥伦布和达·伽马等人相比，郑和（1371—1433）的远航不仅早一个世纪，而且次数和总里程都远远超过前者，其船队排水量和载重量也要大几十倍，并且拥有当时世界上最先进的罗盘技术、地图绘制技术和帆船技术等，但是郑和远航对未知海域的突破、对世界文明史的影响却无法与前者相比，只能算是一次以武力炫耀和朝贡贸易为主要内容的政治远航。

In comparison to Columbus and Da Gama, Zheng He (1371 – 1433) set out on distant voyages a century earlier, and the number of voyages and total distance travelled far surpassed those later navigators. The displacement of his fleet and their carrying capacity was also several tens of times greater than theirs. Moreover, he possessed most advanced compass technology, map-making technology, and sailing technology of his day. However, Zheng He's breakthroughs in charting new waters and his influence on the history of world civilization can not rightly be compared to the later navigators. His can only be counted as a one-time political voyage that primarily served as a display of military force and opened imperial tribute and trade.

## 4. 西学东渐
## Western Learning's Eastern Flow

### (1) 传教士来华
### *Missionaries Arrive in China*

明清之际，即 16—17 世纪，世界格局发生了重大变化，资本主义在欧洲各国迅速发展，文艺复兴已达到极盛时期，与此同时，一个反对罗马教廷的宗教改革运动蓬勃兴起；以扶助教皇为宗旨的耶稣会成立，继而与新教抗衡。地理大发现缩短了世界交通的距离，于是耶稣会十分注意培养博学的牧师，前往南美、非洲和亚洲。幅员广阔、人口众多的中国，自然成为耶稣会宗教扩张的重点目标，于是耶稣会士纷纷来华，其中著名的有意大利传教士利玛窦（Matteo Ricci，1552—1610）、龙华民（Niccolo Longobardi，1559—1654）、高一志（Alfonso Vagnone，1566—1640）、熊三拔（Sabbathinus de Ursis，1575—1620）、艾儒略（Julius Alenius，1582—1649）、毕方济（P. Francois Sambiasi，1582—1649）、罗雅谷（Jacques Rho，1593—1638）、葡萄牙传教士阳玛诺（Emmanuel Diaz，1574—1659）、傅汎际（Francisco Furtado，约1587—约1653）、德国传教士汤若望（Johann Adam Schall von Bell，1592—1666）、邓玉涵（Johann Schreck，1576—1630）、法国传教士金尼阁（Nicolas Trigault，1577—1628）。这是继唐代景教和元代也里可温教之后，基督教文化与中国文化的第三次大接触。

In the Ming-Qing transition, i. e., the 16$^{th}$ – 17$^{th}$ Centuries, large changes took place in structures around the world. Capitalism developed rapidly in European countries, the Renaissance in arts and literature had attained a period of flourishing growth, and a religious reform movement opposing the Church in Rome vigorously grew. The Jesuits (Society of Jesus) were established with the goal of assisting the Roman Catholic Pope and opposing Protestantism. Great geographic discoveries had shortened the distances for communication around the world, and so the Jesuit missionaries who cared deeply about nurturing erudition, left for South America, Africa and Asia. China, with its vast scale and large population naturally became an important goal for the Jesuits, and so they came to China in great numbers. Among the most famous of them were the Italian missionaries Matteo Ricci (1552 – 1610), Niccolo Longobardi (1559 – 1654), Alfonso Vagnone (1566 – 1640), Sabbathinus de Ursis (1575 – 1620), Julius Alenius (1582 – 1649), P. Francois Sambiasi (1582 – 1649), Jacques Rho (1583 – 1638), the Portuguese missionaries Emmanuel Diaz (1574 – 1659), Francisco Furtado (c. 1587 – c.1653), the German missionaries Johann Adam Schall Von Bell (1592 – 1666) and Johann Schreck (1576 – 1630), and the French missionary Nicolas Trigault (1577 – 1628).

This is the third contact between Christian culture and Chinese culture, following the Nestorians in the Tang Dynasty and Christian missionaries in the Yuan Dynasty.

西方文化进入中国内地时,走在最前列的是传教士。这批传教士来到中国,下功夫了解和学习中国的礼俗、社会和民情,努力顺应当地习俗,寻找基督教与儒学之间的共同点,同时又注意走上层路线,推行学术传教方针,取得了一定的成功。其中,对传播西方文化做出实质性贡献的是利玛窦。

When Western culture entered China, missionaries were at the forefront. They made efforts to understand and learn Chinese rites and customs, society, and popular sentiment. They strove to adjust to local culture, to find commonalities between Christianity and the Ru-ist School. At the same time, they took note to walk the path of the upper strata of society, and also established academic and missionary guidelines. They achieved a certain amount of success. Among them, Matteo Ricci made substantial contributions to the transmission of Western culture.

(2) 著名传教士利玛窦

*Matteo Ricci, the Famous Missionary*

利玛窦(Matteo Ricci,1552—1610)(见图2-7),意大利人,1583年来到中国,1610年在北京去世后,万历皇帝(1563—1620)在北京阜成门外赐地厚葬。中国学者梁启超(1873—1929)等人对利玛窦在中国的学术活动给予高度评价。

Matteo Ricci (1552 - 1610) (see Figure 2 - 7), Italian, came to China in 1583. He died in Beijing in 1610, and the Wanli Emperor (1563 - 1620) conferred land outside Beijing's Fuchengmen for a generous burial. The Chinese scholar Liang Qichao (1873 - 1929)

图2-7 利玛窦(Matteo Ricci,1552—1610)

Figure 2-7  Matteo Ricci (1552 - 1610)

evaluated the academic activities Ricci carried out in China quite positively.

利玛窦1583年由广东肇庆进入中国。刚到中国的时候，利玛窦一身和尚打扮，人们叫他"西僧"，后来他改穿儒服，读四书五经，就像是一个虔诚的孔子信徒。当时的中国排外，不允许外国人随便住在国内，不允许外国人到内地，为此，利玛窦采取了一些行之有效的方法。

Matteo Ricci in 1583 entered China through Zhaoqing, Guangdong Province. When he first arrived he was dressed from head to toe as a monk, so people called him the "Western Monk". Later he changed and wore traditional Han dress as a Ru-ist, read the "Four Books" and the "Five Classics" just as if he were a pious disciple of Confucius. China at the time was xenophobic, making it difficult for foreigners to reside in the country. Because he was not allowed to travel into the interior of the country, Matteo Ricci adopted a few effective methods.

(3) 利玛窦的传教策略
***Matteo Ricci's Strategy for Evangelization***

首先，利玛窦取得了官员、士大夫的支持。他广泛结交社会各层人士，尤其上层人士，包括皇室贵族、朝廷命臣、地方官员、学术精英，并以其宗教精神和广博见识赢得了当时士大夫的信任。

First, he acquired the support of local government officials and scholars. He broadly made friends with figures from every level of society, especially those of the upper levels, including nobility, court officials, local officials, and learned elite. His religiosity, wide-ranging learning, and experience won him the trust of contemporary scholars and officials.

其次，顺应中国习俗。他学习中国语言文字，穿着中国服装，读儒家书籍，熟悉中国文化习俗。为了使自己的名字像中国人的姓名，他把自己的意大利姓名玛泰奥·利奇（Matteo Ricci）叫成姓"利"名"玛窦"，以后就被中国士大夫呼为"利先生"或"利子"。

Second, he conformed to Chinese customs. He studied Chinese language and writing, wore Chinese clothes, read the Ru-ist classics and familiarized himself with Chinese cultural traditions. In order to make his name more like that of a Chinese person, he changed his Italian name "Matteo Ricci" to the Chinese Li Madou. Later, Chinese scholars and officials called him "Master Li" (*Lizǐ*).

再者，利用学术传教。学术传教就是通过介绍西方的科学技术和人文学的一些知识来征服、吸引中国的士大夫，然后在这个过程当中来传教。利玛窦把西方的科学、哲学、艺术介绍给中国士大夫，并和他们合作，翻译了大量的西方著作。如和徐光启

(1562—1633）合作，翻译了包括欧几里得的《几何原本》在内的一批西方学术著作。开始用汉字或汉字系统来翻译、介绍西方的学术术语，西方文化由此流传开来，并成为明末清初士大夫中间的时髦学问。

Third, he evangelizes through learning. This means that he planned to conquer and entice Chinese scholars and officials by means of introducing Western science and technology and some knowledge of western humanities. Later, in the course of this he would share religion. He introduced Western science, philosophy, and arts to Chinese scholars and officials and collaborated with them in translating a large number of western books. He collaborated with Xu Guangqi (1562 – 1633) and translated western academic works including Euclid's *Elements*. He started to use Chinese characters to translate and introduce western technical terminology, and in this way, western culture spread and became a fashionable field of study among scholar-officials of the late-Ming and early-Qing.

（4）西学的输入

### *The Import of Western Learning*

耶稣会传教士带到中国来的西方著作多达7000余部。除了文艺复兴时期的科技成就之外，还包括欧洲的古典哲学、逻辑学、艺术、神学等内容，特别是在数学、天文历算学、军火制造等方面的引入，对明清之际的经济文化有一定的促进作用，打开了一部分中国先进士人的眼界。

Jesuit missionaries brought to China as many as 7000 Western texts. Besides the science and technological achievements of the Renaissance, they also included European classical philosophy, logic, art, and theology. In particular, the introduction of mathematics, astronomical calendar calculations, and gun powder manufacture had the effect of boosting the Ming-Qing economy and broadening the horizons of China's advanced scholars.

从19世纪末到20世纪20年代，西方传教士纷纷在中国创办教会学校。在上海、北京、南京等地创办了一批大学、医学院等。南京大学、华中师范大学（武汉）、北京协和医院等的前身都是教会学校。

From the late 19th Century to the 1920s, Western missionaries set up church schools in China one after another. They started colleges, medical schools and other such institutions in Shanghai, Beijing, Nanjing and other large cities. The forerunners of such schools as Nanjing University, Central China Normal University (in Wuhan), and Peking Union Medical College and Hospital were all church schools.

天文历法

*Astronomy and Calendar Science*

在传教士输入的著作中，天文历法方面的著作达43种，其中有21种被收入著名的

《崇祯历书》。《崇祯历书》由徐光启等人编撰，基本上代表了传教士输入的西方天文历法的水平，至今仍然沿用的阴历就是这个历法。

Among the works missionaries imported, as many as 43 were on astronomy and calendar science, and among those, 21 were included in the famous *Chongzhen Almanac*. The *Chongzhen Almanac* was compiled by Xu Guangqi and others and basically represented the level of Western astronomy and calendar science the missionaries imported. The lunar calendar used to this day is based on this calendar science.

数学

*Mathematics*

西方数学对中国影响最大的是利玛窦、徐光启合译的《几何原本》（前6卷），该书介绍了古希腊数学家欧几里得的平面几何学，今天，汉语世界使用的数学术语，如点、线、面、直角、平行、体积、面积等，都是始于该书。

The Western mathematics that had the greatest influence on China was Matteo Ricci and Xu Guangqi's translation of Euclid's *Elements* (first six chapters). The book introduced the ancient Greek mathematician Euclid's plane geometry. The technical vocabulary the Chinese speaking world uses today, such as terms for "point", "line", "surface", "right angle", "parallel", "volume", and "area", all first appear in this book.

地理学

*Geography*

耶稣会士向中国学术界介绍的《坤舆万国全图》引进明确的地圆概念，并以经纬度划分球面，对于破除中国旧有的天圆地方或地平观念有着重要的意义。该图还介绍了五大洲、三大洋的概念，体现了地理大发现的成就。清代康熙朝的《皇舆全览图》和乾隆朝的《乾隆内府地图》，都是当时地理测绘工作的最新成就，是中西地理学者合作的结晶。

The *Great Universal Geographic Map* that the Jesuits introduced to Chinese academic circles introduced precise cartographic ideas. Using longitude and latitude to divide the earth's surface, it had great significance for getting rid of China's old ideas of circular heaven or a flat earth. It introduced the idea of five continents and three oceans, manifesting the achievements of geographic discovery. The Kangxi Emperor's *Imperial Panoramic Map* and the Qianlong Emperor's *Qianlong's Interior Palace Map* were the newest achievements of contemporary geographic mapping work, the crystallization of cooperation between Chinese and Western geographers.

物理学与机械工程学
*Physics and Mechanical Engineering*

传教士邓玉涵翻译的《奇器图说》(3卷)一书，介绍了重心、比重、杠杆、滑轮等物理学原理。

由熊三拔撰、徐光启译、李之藻订的《泰西水法》(6卷)，介绍了西方的水利机械。汤若望的《远镜说》，介绍了望远镜，是关于西方光学的著作。这些著作均引起人们的兴趣。

The missionary Johann Schreck translated the *Diagrams and Explanations of the Wonderful Machines of the Far West* (three chapters), and introduced such physical principles as center of gravity, specific gravity, lever, and block and tackle.

The *Taixi Laws of Hydrology* (six chapters) written by Sabatino de Ursis, translated by Xu Guangqi, and arranged by Li Zhizao, introduced Western irrigation machinery. Johann Adam Schall von Bell's *Discourse on Distance Mirrors* introducing telescopes, was an important work on Western optics. All of these attracted people's interest.

## 5. 中学西传
### Chinese Learning's Western Transmission

西方文化传入中国的同时，中国文化也经西方传教士的介绍，传到了欧洲。耶稣会士不自觉地成为欧亚大陆两大文明之间文化联系的桥梁。

罗明坚(Michele Ruggieri)是第一个用汉文发表传教书籍的传教士，也是第一个翻译"四书"的西方人。其后，金尼阁(Nicolas Trigault)发表利玛窦著作《基督教远征中国史》，揭示儒学的主要观念。1735年，耶稣会士杜赫德(Du Halde, 1674—1743)在巴黎刊印由耶稣会士在中国的考察资料汇总成的巨著《中华全志》。这部被誉为中国百科全书的大部头著作分为四卷，许多中国著作的译文如《古文观止》《赵氏孤儿》都被收入该书。传教士们把中国的政治制度、科举制度、风土人情等传递到西方，让西方人对中国有了更多的了解。

中国的茶、丝绸、绣品、瓷器和漆器等物品开始在17、18世纪的欧洲社会流行。

At the same time Western culture was entering China, Chinese culture was transmitted to Europe through the introduction of Western missionaries. The Jesuits unknowingly became the bridge connecting the cultures of two great Eurasian civilizations.

Michele Ruggieri was the first missionary to publish religious doctrine in Chinese, and the first Westerner to translate the "Four Books". Later, Nicolas Trigault published Matteo Ricci's great work *The History of Christianity in China* (Latin title: *Regni Chinensis Descriptio*), making known the primary ideas of the Ru-ists. In 1735, the Jesuit Jean-Baptiste Du Halde (1674 – 1743) in Paris set in print the monumental *Description géographique, historique, chronologique, politique, et physique de l'empire de la Chine et de la Tartarie chinoise*

(*Gazetteer for the Chinese Empire*) which compiled the research materials the Jesuits observed in China. This work, the first great encyclopedia of China, was divided into four volumes, and included many translations of important Chinese works, such as *Guwen Guanzhi* and *The Orphan of Zhao*. The missionaries passed onto the West China's political system, examination system, and local customs and conditions, allowing Westerners to gain a better understanding of China.

Chinese tea, silk, embroidery, porcelain and laquerware were very popular in 17th and 18th Century European society.

## 6. 中国礼仪之争
### Chinese Rites Controversy

17世纪，耶稣会内部及耶稣会与多明我会、方济各会之间，对利玛窦在中国采取的传教策略，例如"天""帝"的称号、祭祖祭孔仪式的合法性等产生了分歧，史称"中国礼仪之争"。1704年，罗马教皇派铎罗（Tournon，1668—1710）来到中国，颁布教令，明令禁止中国教徒祭祀祖先和孔子，引起康熙帝及中国朝野的愤怒。1707年，康熙帝下令将教皇派来的公使监禁于澳门，清廷与耶稣会关系趋于紧张。雍正元年（1723），在华传教士被全部驱逐。至此，持续百余年的中西文化交流中断，直到一百多年后才再次继续。

In the 17th Century, between Jesuits themselves and between the Jesuits, the Dominicans and the Franciscans divisions arose over the evangelical strategy Matteo Ricci adopted in China, such as the translations of "heaven" and "God", and the legality of ceremonies honoring ancestors and Confucius. This became known as the Chinese Rites Controversy. In 1704, the papal legate Charles-Thomas Maillard de Tournon (1668 – 1710) arrived in China and issued religious decrees ordering the Chinese faithful to stop making sacrifices to ancestors and Confucius, which angered the Kangxi Emperor and the Chinese court. In 1707, Kangxi ordered the papal legate envoy to be locked up in Macau, and the relations between the Qing court and the Jesuits grew increasingly tense. In 1723, the Yongzheng Emperor ordered all missionaries in China out of the country. This interrupted the more than 100 years of Sino-Western cultural exchange, and it lasted for more than 100 years.

明末清初，耶稣会士给中国带来了西方的学术和宗教精神，并将西方科学的实证精神与中国传统的经世思想做了融合，对当时以及后来的思想启蒙起了不小的促进作用。不管他们远渡重洋、来到中国的最初动机是什么，他们在欧亚两大文明交流中都是功不可没的。

At the end of the Ming and beginning of the Qing, the Jesuits brought to China western technology and religious spirit, and fused Western scientific empiricism with Chinese traditional experiential thinking, influencing contemporary and subsequent ideas. Regardless of their initial motivations for traversing the oceans to come to China, their contributions to communication between the two great civilizations of Eurasia cannot go unnoticed.

## 7. 学术集成
## Compendia of Learning

明清两朝调动人力物力，编纂《永乐大典》《古今图书集成》《四库全书》等类书、丛书。这些类书、丛书规模之宏大、编制之精密，不仅在中国是空前的，而且在世界文化史上亦屈指可数。

《永乐大典》是明清第一部巨型类书，《大不列颠百科全书》第15版曾特别指出，"《永乐大典》是世界上最大的百科全书"。

清初《古今图书集成》用铜活字排印，共10000卷，6117部，是我国现存最大的类书。

Both the Ming and Qing dynasties mobilized human and material resources to compile encyclopedias and book collections, such as the *Yongle Great Encyclopedia*, *Ancient and Modern Book Compendium*, and the *Siku Quanshu*. These encyclopedias and collections were on a grand scale and their editing was meticulous, not only unprecedented in China, but very rare in the cultural history of the world.

The *Yongle Great Encyclopedia* was the first giant encyclopedia of the Ming-Qing era. The 15th edition of *Encyclopedia Britannica* points out, "*Yongle Great Encyclopedia* is the world's largest encyclopedia."

The early Qing *Ancient and Modern Book Compendium* was printed in movable copper type, in 10000 chapters over 6117 volumes. It is the largest encyclopedia extant in China.

编纂于乾隆年间的《四库全书》，是一部大型丛书，它把多种著作整部编印在一起，其功能在于广泛网罗书籍。纂修20多年，任职于四库馆的共有360人，若加上担任缮写、装订的人数在内，最多时达到3800人。其历时之长、动员人力物力之巨，非安定、强盛的朝代无法实现。

上述这些书与18世纪中叶法国狄德罗（Denis Diderot，1713—1784）主编的著名的《百科全书》比较，可看到这三部书的规模。狄德罗《百科全书》2268万字。明《永乐大典》3.7亿字，清《古今图书集成》1.6亿字，清《四库全书》9.97亿字。若将《四库全书》的4000万页摊开，逐页相接，可以绕地球一周又1/3圈。自《四库全书》纂修迄今，无论中外，尚无一部书籍的规模可与之相比。

The *Siku Quanshu* is a book collection compiled in the Qianlong reign. It took many works and entirely reprinted them into one collection, the function of which is to bring under one umbrella a wide range of texts. The compilation went on for over twenty years, with 360 people on staff in the "four book depositories" office; if one were to add the number of people who served as copy-editors and binders, the number would reach 3800 people. The time it took was so long, and the human and material resources so vast, if it had not been a stable, rich, and powerful reign, it would not have been achieved.

Through comparison of these books with the French Denis Diderot's (1713 – 1784) mid 18th Century compilation *Encyclopédie*, we can see their scale. Diderot's *Encyclopédie* 22.68 million words; Ming *Yongle Great Encyclopedia* 370 million characters; Ming *Ancient and Modern Book Compendium* 160 million characters; Qing *Siku Quanshu* 997 million characters. If one spread out all 40 million pages of the *Siku Quanshu* and laid them end to end, they would go around the world 1 and 1/3 times. Since the publication of the *Siku Quanshu* there has not been a comparable large-scale book compilation in China or elsewhere.

中国文学发展到明清，在小说领域取得大丰收，明清小说仅目录就有1300余种。明清小说不仅是中外文学交流的载体，而且成为外国人认识中国社会、理解中国文化的一个窗口。

Literature flourished through the Ming-Qing period, with over 1300 titles published during this time. Ming-Qing fiction is not only a vehicle for Chinese and foreign literary communication, it has also become a window through which foreigners learn of Chinese society and understand Chinese culture.

**思考题**

1. 先秦区域文化有哪几种？它们有什么特点？
2. 简述明清之际以利玛窦为主的传教士采用的传教策略及西学输入的成果。

*Questions*

1. What kinds of regional cultures can be divided into in the Pre-Qin period? What are the characteristics of each of them?
2. Describe simply at the Ming-Qing juncture, what was the evangelical policy adopted by Matteo Ricci, and what were the results of input the western learning.

# 第三章 中国的汉字
## Chinese Characters

中国传统的语言学称为"小学","小学"在汉代时指称文字学,隋唐以后概念扩大,文字学、训诂学、音韵学都统称为"小学"。今天中国使用"小学"的概念,主要指的是进行初等教育的学校。

China's traditional study of language is known as *xiǎoxué* "minor learning". In the Han Dynasty, "minor learning" referred to philology or grammatology, the study of graphs. The idea expanded in the Sui-Tang era and later to include grammatology, interpretation and commentary on classical texts, and the study of sounds and rhymes. In modern China, the term *xiǎoxué* means primary school.

## 一、汉字的起源
### Origin of Chinese Characters

在文字被发明以前,中国人用结绳的方法记事。

结绳记事法:传说神农氏结绳而治,就是用一条单色绳子做主绳,用不同的细绳做副绳,可算到百万以上的数字。结绳记事法可能对汉字的产生有一定的影响,但是,文字是记录语言的符号,要具有形、音、义三个要素,所以,文字不可能从结绳记事直接产生出来。那么,文字的直接渊源是什么呢?

Prior to the invention of writing, Chinese people used knot-tying to keep records.

Knot-tying record keeping: According to legend, Shennong ruled having tied knots. Using a single-colored string as the main string, and using different smaller strings as subsidiary strings, one can calculate numbers over one million. This method of knot-tying probably had a certain influence on bringing about Chinese characters. But, writing is the symbolic recording of speech, and must have the three elements of form, sound and meaning. Therefore, writing cannot be directly produced from knot-tying. So, what was the immediate source of writing?

汉字的起源有两种传说:一是仓颉造字的传说,二是汉字出自八卦的传说。但是,都没有可靠的证据。一般认为,在原始社会出现在陶器、玉器上面的刻画符号是文字的直接来源之一,中国的汉字经历了从刻画符号到文字的过程。

There are two legends concerning the origin of Chinese characters. One is Changjie created writing, and the second is characters come from the eight tri-grams. However, there is no reliable evidence. It is generally believed that one direct source for writing was the occurrence of carved symbols on pottery and jade implements in primitive society. Chinese characters went through a course of events from carved symbols to writing.

## 二、汉字的字体演变
## Evolution of Calligraphic Styles

世界上最古老的文字有三种:一是5500年前两河流域苏美尔人创造的楔形文字,二是5000多年前尼罗河流域的古埃及人创造的圣书字,三是3300年前中国殷商时期的甲骨文字。前两种文字已经成为死文字,只有甲骨文演变为现代汉字。

There are three kinds of writing in the ancient world: First, the cuneiform writing created by the Sumerians in Mesopotamia 5500 years ago; second, the hieroglyphics created by ancient Egyptians in the Nile River basin 5000 years ago; finally, the oracle bone writing of the Shang period in China 3300 years ago. The first two types have become extinct, yet the oracle bone writing evolved into modern Chinese characters.

汉字的正式形体从甲骨文开始,汉字字体演变的过程可以概括为:甲骨文—金文—篆书—隶书—楷书。此外,还有两种辅助性字形,即草书和行书。

The formal writing of Chinese characters began with the oracle bones. The evolutionary process of the calligraphic styles of Chinese characters can be outlined as follows: Oracle bone writing—Bronze writing—seal script—official/clerical script—regular script. Also, there are two kinds of auxiliary forms of the characters, i.e., grass (or cursive) script and running script.

汉字字体类型上可分为篆书—隶书—楷书—草书—行书五大类(见图3-1)。

Divided in terms of types of calligraphic styles, there are five major categories: seal, official, regular, cursive, and running (see Figure 3-1).

### 1. 甲骨文
### Oracle Bone Writing

古汉字经历了由图画文字到表意文字的演变过程。目前所见中国正式的古文字,是商朝时期的甲骨文,因刻于龟甲、兽骨上,故称"甲骨文";甲骨文是殷商王室从事祭祀、征伐、田猎、农事等活动时进行占卜的记录,出土于河南安阳小屯村。

Chinese characters went through the process of evolving from pictographs to logographs.

| 篆书 | 隶书 | 楷书 | 草书 | 行书 |
| Seal script | Official script | Regular script | Cursive script | Running script |

图 3-1 汉字字体的五种类型

Figure 3-1 Five types of calligraphic styles

The earliest known formal Chinese writing is the oracle bone writing of the Shang period, so-called because they were carved on tortoise plastrons and animal bones for divination purposes. They are the records of divinations carried out when the Shang royal house undertook such matters as making sacrifices to ancestors, war, hunting and farming. They were excavated in Xiaotun, Anyang, Henan Province (see Figure 3-2、Figure 3-3).

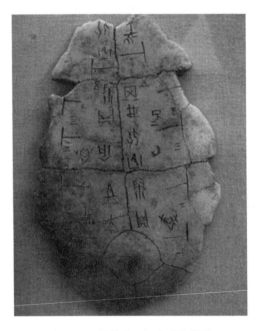

图 3-2 甲骨文，河南安阳殷墟

Figure 3-2 Oracle bone writing from the Yin ruins in Anyang, Henan

图 3-3 图中文字：第一行简体汉字——鸡、日、月、羊、鹿、山；第二行简体汉字——竹、目、鱼、龟、车、耳。

Figure 3-3 Pictographs: The first line, left-to-right are the characters for "chicken" "sun" "moon" "sheep" "deer" and "mountain". The second line are the charcters for "bamboo" "eyes" "fish" "tortoise" "cart" and "ear".

## 2. 金文
**Bronze Writing**

古代称铜为金，铸刻在铜器上的铭文即称"金文"。因这类文字大多铸刻在礼器"鼎"和乐器"钟"上，故又称"钟鼎文"，也叫籀文或大篆，最长的毛公鼎铭文，有498字。研究西周、春秋时代的历史，金文是最重要的资料。

In ancient times, bronze was called *jīn* "gold or metal", so the inscriptions cast and carved on bronze implements was called *jīn wén* "gold writing", what we call bronze inscriptions. Also, because much of this writing was cast on ritual vessels like cauldrons or musical instruments such as bells, it is also called "bell and cauldron writing". The longest of them, the inscription on the Duke Mao Tripod, is 498 characters long. It is also called seal writing or the great seal script. For research into the history of the Western Zhou and the Spring-Autumn period, bronze writing is the most important resource.

甲骨文是以刀镌刻于坚硬的甲骨上，所刻文字线条细瘦，字形方长；而金文多是在松软的模板上刻好再铸成，故而笔画线条粗壮，字形长圆。

Oracle bone writing was carved into solid bone and shell, and the characters had long, thin lines, and a square shape. But the bronze script was mostly carved onto a soft mold and then cast in bronze. So, the strokes are thick and solid, and the characters are long and rounded.

毛公鼎：西周晚期毛公所铸青铜器，鼎高53.8厘米，口径47.9厘米，鼎内铭文32行，长达498字，其内容是周王册命大臣毛公，要他忠心辅佐周王，并赐给他大量物品，毛公为感谢周王，特铸鼎记其事（见图3-4）。这是一篇完整的《册命书》，是研究西周晚年政治史的重要史料。书法是成熟的西周金文风格，字体方长。清道光二十三年（1843年）出土于陕西岐山（今宝鸡市岐山县），现收藏于台北故宫博物院。

图中文字前两行解读：

王若曰："父歆，丕显文武，皇天引厌厥德。"（周王这样说："父歆啊！伟大英明的文王和武王，皇天很满意他们的德行"。）

The Duke Mao Tripod, a bronze implement cast by Duke Mao in the latter Western Zhou, is 53.8 centimeters high, and the diameter of the opening is 47.9 centimeters. The inscription in the cauldron is 32 lines and 498 characters long, the content of it is that the Zhou king conferred the title chancellor the Duke of Mao, wanting him to faithfully assist the Zhou king, and he bestowed upon him a large amount of goods; Duke Mao specifically casts this *ding* and records the event as a show of gratitude to the Zhou king (See Fig. 3-4). It is a complete *Text of an Order Conferring a Title*, and an important historical resource for studying the political history of the late Western Zhou. The calligraphy is in the mature, Western Zhou bronze style, the characters are rectangular. It was excavated in Qishan, Shaanxi (modern Qishan, Baoji City, Shaanxi) in 1843, currently stored at the Palace Museum, Taipei.

The first two lines of characters read:

The Zhou king said thus: Father Yin! The great, wise King Wen and King Wu, august Heaven is pleased with their moral conduct.

图 3-4 毛公鼎（西周）
Figure 3-4 The Duke Mao Tripod (Western Zhou)

### 3. 小篆
**Small Seal Script**

秦始皇统一文字，小篆是法定的主要字体。到西汉末年，隶书取代小篆成为主要字体。小篆后来就逐渐成为主要用于刻印章的字体。

Small Seal Script: When Qin Shihuang unified writing, small seal was the official calligraphic style. Only at the end of the Western Han did clerical/official script replace small seal as the primary calligraphic style. Later, small seal script became primarily used for carving seals.

### 4. 隶书
**Official Script**

隶书在战国晚期秦国已经形成，到了汉代通行。隶书字体一般呈扁方形，横画长而竖画短。

Official or clerical Script: It had already been formed in the Qin state in the later years of the Warring States period, and by the Han Dynasty it was in common use. Official script characters are generally flat and square, the horizontal stroke is long and the vertical stroke is short.

## 5. 楷书
### Regular Script

汉末时期出现了楷书,笔画平直,字体方正,汉字成为"方块字"就完全定型了。楷书取代了各种字体而成为一种通行的汉字,自汉以来,一直通用至今,不仅在书写上,而且在书籍印刷上都普遍使用楷书。

Regular Script: It appeared in the end of the Han period. Strokes are level and the characters are square, so Chinese writing fully became "square characters". It replaced the various other forms and became the generally used form. Since the Han it has been in use to the present, not only for handwriting, but printers generally use it for printed materials.

## 6. 行书
### Running Script

行书是介于楷书和草书之间的字体,分行楷、行草两种,东汉时期形成。行书比楷书书写方便,比草书容易辨认,一直流行至今,成为人们日常使用的一种手写字体。

Running Script: Running script is an intermediary form between regular and cursive scripts, and can be divided into running regular and running cursive scripts, formed in the Eastern Han Dynasty. It is easier to write than regular script and easier to read than grass script. It has been in use up to the present, becoming a handwritten script people use daily.

## 7. 草书
### Cursive Script

草书具有结构简省、笔画连绵的特点。草书字体形式较多,主要有章草、今草和狂草三种。广义来说,不论时代,凡是写得潦草的书法都可以算草书。草书在汉代形成。草体字较难辨认,唐代以后的狂草,写出来很多人都不认识,也就不能广泛使用,因而成为一种仅仅用来欣赏的艺术。

Grass or Cursive Script: The stroke of cursive script has the characteristics being simple and concise, fluent and continuous. There are quite a lot calligraphic forms of grass script. The primary ones are "regulated grass", "modern grass", and "mad grass". Broadly speaking, regardless of the era, any calligraphy that is written illegibly can be considered grass script. It is formed in the Han Dynasty. Grass-script characters are relatively difficult to recognize. The "crazy grass" from after the Tang Dynasty is unrecognizable to many people, and so it cannot be widely used, in effect becoming an art form that can only be appreciated.

# 三、汉字的结构
# The Structure of Chinese Characters

以形示意是汉字的重要特点,六书是汉字结构的基本原理。
六书是指象形、指事、会意、形声、转注、假借。
Using form to express meaning is an important characteristic of Chinese characters. The six categories of Chinese characters include the basic principle.

The six categories are pictogram, ideogram, associative compound, semantic-phonetic compound, mutually explanatory, and phonetic loans. The first four of these are ways in which characters were constructed. Pictograms and ideograms constitute a small number of characters, while the associative and phonetic compounds constitute a large number of characters.

## 1. 象形
### Pictograms

象形是依照物体的外貌特征来描绘事物。如日、月、山、水四个字,最早就是描绘日、月、山、水的图案,后来逐渐演变成现在的字样。

Pictogram relies on the characteristics of the outer appearance of a body to describe a thing. The characters for sun, moon, mountain and water, for example, started as pictures of these things, and later gradually changed to the present form.

## 2. 指事
### Ideograms

指事是指表现抽象事物的方法,用象征的符号,或在象形字上加上符号来表示某个词。如人在其上写作"上",人在其下写作"下";"刃"在刀口上加一点,表示这里最锋利,这就是刀刃;等等。

Ideograms: a method to show abstract things using symbolic marks, or adding a mark on a pictogram to express some word. The characters for up, down, and sharp are examples of this type of character.

## 3. 形声
### Semantic-phonetic Compounds

形,指形旁,表示字的意义类属、意义范畴;声,指声旁,表示字的读音。由形旁、声旁构成的字,叫形声字。例如,"胡"字的构成,"月"为形旁,"古"为声旁,是一个形声字。"胡"又可作声旁,构成蝴、湖、葫、瑚、醐等字,而以同样的发音(也有的只有声母一样),表达不同的事物。形声是汉字里造字最多的方法。

Semantic-phonetic compounds: The semantic refers to the semantic part in Chinese characters. It represents the character has different types of meaning. The phonetic refers to the phonetic part of a character. It represents the sound of the character. Chinese characters formed by semantic and phonetic are called semantic-phonetic compounds. For instance, the combination of character "胡" *hú*, "月" *yuè* is the semantic part, "古" *gǔ* is the phonetic part. "胡" *hú* also can be an independent phonetic part to form a word, like 蝴, 湖, 葫, 瑚, 醐, etc. While using the same pronunciation (some have only the same initials), it can represents different things. The vast majority of Chinese characters are formed using this method.

## 4. 会意
### Associative Compounds

会意是用两个或几个字组成一个字,把这几个字的意思合成一个意义。如"日"和"月"组起来,就是日光加月光变成"明"。"人"字和"言"字合成"信"字,意思就是人过去所言有信,就是这个人很遵守自己说过的话。"休","人"和"木"合在一起,一个人靠在树上,表示休息。

Associative compounds use two or more elements and combine their meaning to indicate a new meaning. For example, the character for "sun" *rì* 日 combines with the character for "moon" *yuè* 月 to form the character 明 *míng*; both the sun and moon are light-producing objects, so the meaning of *míng* is "bright".

## 5. 转注
### Mutual Explanatory

转注是两个字互为注释,转注出来的字和本字属于同一个部首,意思相同,但是字形不同。例如,"考"和"老",古时"考"可作"长寿"讲,"老""考"意思相通,字形有所不同。

Mutual Explanatory: Experts disagree on exactly how this category works, but presumably, as the name suggests, these are characters that in some way explain each other. The two characters have similar shape, are close in meaning, and have similar sound values. The prototypical example of this category is the characters 考 *kǎo* and 老 *lǎo*, both of which can mean "old".

## 6. 假借
### Phonetic Loans

假借是借用一字,去表达别的事物。一般来说,有一个无法描述的新事物,就借用一个发音相同或相近的字根，来表达这个新事物。例如"又"，本来是指右手（最早见于甲骨文），但后来被假借当作"也是"的意思。又如"闻"，本意是用耳朵听的意思，后来被假借成嗅觉动词。

Phonetic Loans：to borrow one character to express something else. Generally, if there is something that cannot readily be described, then one can borrow a character with the same, or similar, sound value to express this new thing. For example, the character 又 *yòu* was originally a pictographic representation of a right hand (it occurs in oracle bone writing as such), meaning "right side, recto" (that graph later evolved into the modern graph 右 *yòu* "right"). The original character 又 was borrowed to write the word meaning "also" because it was pronounced the same.

## 四、汉字的笔画
## The Strokes of Chinese Characters

汉字笔画的故事。
A story about strokes in Chinese characters.

明代有一位文人名字叫徐渭，能诗善画，会写灯谜。当时绍兴有个开点心铺子的商人请他写一块牌匾，徐渭便写了"点心店"三个大字，但是，心字上面有一点没有写，因为徐渭是名家，商人也就没有在意。

There was a literary person named Xu Wei in the Ming Dynasty who was good at composing poetry and painting and was able to write riddles on lantern shades. At the time, there was a businessman in Shaoxing who opened a shop selling pastry. The businessman asked Xu Wei to make a sign for his shop, so Xu Wei wrote 点心店 "Pastry Shop" (but he left out the top dot on the central character 心 *xīn* "heart") in large characters. Because Xu Wei was a renowned expert, the shop owner did not mind that the second character was written incorrectly.

牌匾挂出后，人们看到中间的心字少了一点，谁也猜不出是什么意思。这件事情传出去后，有很多人就来看这块奇怪的牌匾。人们来了之后，自然会顺便在店里买一些点心，这样一来，点心店的生意一直很兴隆。

After the sign was hung, people noticed that the character in the middle was missing a dot, but nobody could figure out what it meant. After this news spread, many people came to see the strange sign. After the people arrived, they naturally picked up some pastry to eat. And so, the shop did a thriving business.

过了一段时间，商人觉得牌匾上有个错别字不太好，就把"心"字上面少写的一点填了上去，真正写成了"心"字了。可是从此以后，不知为何，顾客没有以前那么多了，生意也没有以前好了。商人只好去找徐渭，徐渭笑着说："你这个点'心'店是专门招呼饿肚人的店，人们空着肚子才来吃，现在你在人们肚子里装进了东西，人们不饿了，那谁还来吃点心呢。"商人听了才明白徐渭写心字的时候少写一点的原因。

After a while the shop owner figured it was a bad idea to have an incorrectly written character on his shop's sign, so he added the missing dot to the middle character. But afterward, for some unknown reason, customers stopped coming as frequently as before and his business suffered. All he could think to do was to go ask Xu Wei about it. Xu Wei laughed and said, "This pastry shop of yours is principally a shop for empty stomachs; people with empty stomachs go there to eat something. Now you've filled something into their stomachs, so they aren't hungry anymore; so who's going to come to eat pastry?" Upon hearing this the shop owner finally understood the reason Xu Wei left the dot off of the middle character.

汉字笔画的写法要准确，否则，字体相似，但是意思不同。例如，人、文、又、父、田、由、申、甲、中、主、王、丰、生等字，看似简单，但很容易混淆。

Writing the strokes of Chinese characters must be precise, or else characters of similar form but with different meanings will become confused. For example, the characters 人，文，又，父，田，由，申，甲，中 and 主，王，丰，生，etc., all have very different meanings. It may seem simple, but it is easy to mix them up.

汉字的笔画，就是构成汉字的书写线条。写字时，从落笔到起笔所写的线条，叫"一笔一画"。笔画也具有一定的含义，如横画（一），可表示地平线（如旦字，最下面的一横）等等。

The strokes of Chinese characters are the lines that construct it. When writing, the line written from the moment the pen touches the paper to the moment it is raised is called one stroke.

汉字的基本笔画有八种：
There are eight basic strokes：

点 丶
*Diǎn*：a dot，丶
横 一 由左往右写。
*Héng*：horizontal, written from left to write 一
竖 丨 由上往下写。竖也叫直。

*Shù*: vertical, written from top to bottom, also called *zhi* ｜

撇 丿 由右上往左下写。

*Piē*: written from upper right down toward left 丿

捺 ㇏ 由左上往右下写。

*Nà*: written from upper left down to the right ㇏

挑 ノ 由左下往右上写。挑也叫提。

*Tiāo*: writing from lower left up toward the right, also called *ti* ノ

折 ㇕ 横画的一端和竖画的一端相接。

*Zhé*: joins one end of a horizontal stroke to one end of a vertical stroke ㇕

钩 乚 收笔轻快挑出的笔画。

*Gōu*: the end a stroke in which the pen is quickly lifted up toward the right or the left 乚

笔画最少的汉字只有一画,例如"一"字。

笔画较多而且到现在还在使用的汉字有56划,是biang字(见图3-5),发音读第二声,指的是陕西地区的一种面条。biang字现在主要用在面食店的招牌上,很少其他的用途。

The character with the fewest strokes has only one stroke, for example, 一 *yī* "one".

The character with the most strokes has 56, *biáng* (see Figure 3-5), a kind of noodle in the Shaanxi area. The character is only used on signs advertising noodle and dumpling shops.

图 3-5 biang 字

Figure 3-5 The character for *biang*

关于biang字的写法，有一个字谜：

一点飞上天，黄河两道弯，八字大张口，言字在里面。

东一扭，西一扭，左一长，右一长，中间坐了个马大王。

心字底，月字旁，打个钩钩挂麻糖，推个车车逛咸阳。

A puzzle concerning the writing of the character for *biáng*：

One dot flies up to heaven, two turns in the Yellow River, the large mouth of the character for "eight" 八 *bā*, the character for "speech" 言 *yán* is inside. One turn to the east, one turn to the west, one 长 *zhǎng* (leader) on the left, one 长 on the right, and in the middle sits a horse king.

The heart character 心 *xīn* is on the bottom, the moon character 月 *yuè* is on the side, make a hook and hang hemp and sugar on it, push a cart, and it visits Xianyang.

## 五、汉字的数量
## The Number of Chinese Characters

秦代的《仓颉》《博学》《爱历》三篇共有3300字，汉代扬雄（前53—18）作《训纂篇》，有5340字，许慎（约58—约147）作《说文解字》有9353字。到清代《康熙字典》就有47000多字了。1915年欧阳博存等的《中华大字典》，有48000多字。1959年日本诸桥辙次（Morohashi Tetsuji 1883—1982）的《大汉和辞典》，收字49964个。1971年张其昀（1901—1985）主编的《中文大辞典》，有49888字。1994年冷玉龙（1954—　）等的《中华字海》，多达85000字，但绝大部分汉字是"死字"，日常使用的汉字不过六七千而已。

Three Qin Dynasty texts, the *Cangjie*, *Boxue*, and *Yuanli* (three early writing texts), altogether had 3300 charcters. Yang Xiong's (53 B.C. – 18 A.D.) *Xunzuan Pian* had 5340 characters. Xu Shen's (d. 147 A.D.) *Shuowen Jiezi* (China's first dictionary) had 9353 characters. The Qing Dynasty's *Kangxi Zidian* (The Kangxi Dictionary) had 47000 characters. In 1915 Ouyang Bocun and others compiled the *Zhonghua Da Zidian* (Great Character Dictionary of China) with 48000 characters. In 1959, Morohashi Tetsuji (1883 – 1982) compiled the *Dai Kan Wa Jiten* (Great Chinese-Japanese Dictionary) with 49964 characters. In 1971 Zhang Qiyun (1901 – 1985) compiled the *Zhongwen Da Cidian* (Great Dictionary of China) with 49888 characters. In 1994, Leng Yulong (b. 1954) and others compiled the *Zhonghua Zi Hai* (China's Sea of Characters) with more than 85000 characters. In fact, most of the characters in these collections are obsolete, and there are only about 6000 – 7000 characters in daily circulation.

## 六、汉语词汇的扩展（一）
### ——汉译佛教词语
### The Expansion of Chinese Vocabulary: Chinese Translations of Buddhist Terms

如果真要彻底摒弃佛教文化的话，恐怕他们连话都说不周全了。
——赵朴初（1907—2000）

If they truly wanted to thoroughly discard Buddhist culture, they probably would not even be able to speak complete sentences anymore. —Zhao Puchu (1907 – 2000)

佛教用语浸透了日本文化。
——［日本］《岩波佛教词典·凡例》，岩波书店出版

Buddhist phraseology has saturated Japanese culture— (Japan) *Iwami Dictionary of Buddhism: Notes to the Reader*, Iwanami Shoten Publishing House.

汉字里的新词语是汉字文化在外来文化刺激下的创造。

汉语词汇大量的扩展有两个来源，一是来自佛教词语，一是来自日制汉语新词。这是中国历史上大量引进外来词的两次浪潮。

汉译佛教词语的形成期相当于佛教典籍的汉语翻译期。佛教典籍大多用印度的梵文和巴利文写成，伴随着佛教文化的传入，佛教经典的汉文翻译主要在魏晋南北朝隋唐时期。

New words in Chinese characters are the creation of Chinese-writing culture under the stimulation of foreign cultures.

There are two sources for the bulk of the expansion of Chinese vocabulary: first, terms from Buddhism, and second new words coined in Japan. These are the two waves in Chinese history in which large numbers of foreign words were introduced.

The period of the formation of Chinese-translated Buddhist terms coincides with the period of Chinese translation of Buddhist texts. Buddhist texts and scripture were mostly written in Sanskrit and Pali. Accompanying the transmission of Buddhist teachings and culture, Chinese translation of Buddhist scriptures was primarily from the Wei-Jin periods to the Sui-Tang periods.

在中国和日本，汉译佛教词语构成宗教、伦理、哲学等领域的中坚概念，如佛性、天堂、地狱、宿命、悲观、觉悟、境界、唯心、世界、时间、现在、真实、真理、相

对、绝对等等；或者融入大众俗语，以至于百姓日用而不知其为佛教词语，如平等、眼光、刹那、缘起、手续、翻译、翻案、方便、大无畏、开眼界、门外汉、一刀两断、一丝不挂、一厢情愿、十字街头、清规戒律、少见多怪、吉祥如意、对牛弹琴、盲人摸象等等。汉译佛教词语不下一万数千条之多，相关成语即占汉语史上外来成语的90%以上。

外来音译词被汉语大批吸收，始自佛教典籍的翻译。

In China and Japan, the Chinese translation of Buddhist terms constituted the core concepts of the religious, ethical, and philosophical fields; such as, "Buddha-nature", "heaven/paradise", "hell", "karma", "pessimism", "enlightenment", "realm", "mind-only", "world", "time", "now", "real", "truth", "relatively", and "perfectly". Having fused into the masses common speech, people use Buddhist translated words every day without knowing they are Buddhist terms. These words include "equality", "vision", "instant", "origin", "procedure", "translation", "reverse a verdict", "convenient", "utterly fearless", "expand one's horizons", "layman", "to make a clean break", "not wearing a single thread (absolutely naked)", "one's own wishful thinking", "intersection", "monastic rules (convention)", "rarely seen, very strange (to express amazement due to lack of experience)", "Auspiciousness and as one wishes (a common New Years wish)", "play a lute to a cow (offer a treat to unappreciative audience)", and "blind person touches an elephant (unable to see the big picture)". Chinese-translated Buddhist terms number in the many thousands, and constitute more than 90% of the foreign-origin set phrases and idioms in Chinese.

Chinese has absorbed a large batch of foreign transliterated terms, beginning with the translation of Buddhist texts.

## 1. 佛教里的音译词
**Transliterated Words**

音译词也称"借词"，在这里是指汉语里把佛经母语——梵语中的词连音带义都接受过来。例如：

Transliterated words are also called loan words. The term refers to accepting both the sound and meaning of the original Sanskrit word in Chinese. For example：

梵文词 Sarīra，译词"舍利"；词义原指释迦牟尼遗体焚烧之后结成珠状的东西，后泛指德行较高的和尚死后烧剩的骨头。

Sanskrit – Sarīra "body" is translated as *shèlì*; originally referred to the crystals that resulted from burning the corpse of Siddhartha Gautama (563 – 485 B. C., founder of Buddhism). Later, it referred to the bones that remained after the cremation of a monk with particular high morality and conduct.

梵文词 Pārāmitā：彼岸、究竟

Sanskrit Pārāmitā "perfection, completeness" is translated as *bǐ'àn* "the other shore", or "to go to the bottom of the matter".

梵文词 Adibudaha：初觉者、第一觉者

Sanskrit Ādibudaha is translated as "the primordial enlightened one", "the first enlightened one".

梵文词 Bhikkhuni：比丘尼、女僧、尼姑

Sanskrit Bhikkhuni is translated as *bǐqiūní*, meaning female monk, nun.

梵文词 Yoga：思维

Sanskrit Yoga is translated as thinking.

梵文词 Bodhi：菩提

Sanskrit Bodhi is translated as *pútí*, meaning enlightenment.

## 2. 佛教里的半音半译词——梵汉合成词
## Half Transliterated Half Translated—Sanskrit-Chinese Compound Words

梵汉合成词即一个词由两部分组成，一半音译，一半意译。

例如，佛，梵文 Buddha，音译佛陀、浮图、浮头等。

梵汉合成词有下面三种情况：

Sanskrit-Chinese compound words are composed of two parts, one half is transliterated and one half is translated.

There are three kinds of Sanskrit-Chinese compounds.

### （1）音译加汉语语素构成双音词
### *Disyllabic Words Composed of a Sanskrit Transliterated Word and an Added Chinese Morpheme*

例如佛经、佛像、佛土、佛门、佛祖、佛事、佛身、佛法、佛骨等。

For example, Buddhist sutra, Buddha image, Buddha land, Buddhist, the Buddha, Buddhist ceremony, Buddha body, Buddhist doctrine, Buddha bone.

### （2）汉语语素加音译合成词
### *Compounds of a Chinese Morpheme with an Added Transliterated Word*

卧佛（偏正结构）：据说释迦牟尼佛临终时，右胁而卧，向弟子们嘱咐后事，然后涅槃。后来就有卧佛像。"卧"和"佛"在汉语构词法中是附加与被附加关系。

Reclining Buddha (attributive + nucleus construction): When the Buddha was moments before death, he reclined to his right and instructed his disciples on future events, and then passed to nirvana. Later, there was the image of the reclining Buddha. In Chinese morphology, "reclining Buddha" is an "annex and being annexed" relationship.

念佛（动宾结构）：思念佛的形象和功德，或念颂佛的名号。净土宗以为一心念佛可以不生情欲，有助于达到解脱或死后往生佛国西方极乐世界。"念佛"是汉语构词法中支配与被支配关系。

Pray to Buddha (verb + object construction): to think of the image of the Buddha and his virtue, or say aloud the name of the Buddha in praise. The Pure Land School believes praying to the Buddha can help not produce desire, and is an aid to attaining freedom from worldly concerns or being reborn in the Western Pure Land of Ultimate Bliss. Pray to the Buddha, in Chinese morphology, is a "dominate and being dominated" relationship.

欢喜佛（偏正结构）：藏传佛教密宗本尊神。即佛教中的欲天，爱神。作男、女二人裸身相抱之形。"欢喜佛"是汉语构词法中修饰限制与被修饰限制关系。

Happy Buddha (attributive + nucleus construction): Deity in the Tantric School of Tibetan Buddhism, i.e., Buddhist god of love. It is made in the image of a man and woman embracing each other. Happy Buddha is a modifier and modified relationship in Chinese morphology.

(3) 新造译字加汉语词汇。

***Newly Constructed Transliterated Morphemes Added to the Chinese Vocabulary***

汉语在吸收佛教文化的同时，不仅接受了许多音译借词，而且还改造或更新了许多佛教借词，使之汉语化，称为佛化汉字、佛化汉词。这种梵汉合成词成为汉语词汇的一部分。例如：

While absorbing Buddhist culture, the Chinese language both accepted a large number of transliterated loanwords, and also reformed or renovated a large number of Buddhist loan words, in effect sinicizing them. The results are Buddha-ized morphemes or Buddha-ized words. This kind of compound then became a part of the Chinese vocabulary. For example:

塔：梵文塔婆（stūpa）之节译，词义是宝塔、庙、坟。汉语中原来没有"塔"字，它是魏晋以后专门造出的。以"塔"为词根，再造了许多新的合成词，例如灯塔、水塔、石塔、木塔、砖塔、宝塔、金字塔、喇嘛塔、藏式塔、纪念塔、金刚宝塔、北海白塔、雷锋宝塔等。

塔 *tǎ*: a partial transliteration of Sanskrit *stūpa* "heap", the meaning of which is "pagoda, temple, tomb". Chinese originally did not have this character, rather it was specifically created. With this character as a root, the language created many compounds. For example, "lighthouse", "water tower", "stone tower", "wooden tower", "brick tower", "pagoda", "pyramid", "lama tower", "Tibetan-style tower", "commemorative tower", "vajra tower", "white stupa of Beihai Park", "Lei Feng Pagoda", etc.

僧：佛教名词，梵文 Samgha，音译作"僧迦"。简称"僧"，即僧团，一般4人以上方可称"僧迦"。在汉语中，由"僧"组成的新词不胜枚举，例如僧寺、僧户、僧房、僧宇、僧舍、僧院、僧衣、僧袍、僧鞋、僧袜、僧帽、僧巾、僧徒、僧侣、僧众、僧籍、僧家、僧团、僧王、僧主、僧统、僧官、僧纲、僧正等。

僧 *sēng*：Transliterated from Sanskrit *samgha* as 僧伽 *sēngjiā*, it means the community of monks. Generally a group of four or more monks can be referred to as *sēngjiā*. Words composed in Chinese using the element *sēng* are too numerous to mention individually. A few examples are "monk temple (Buddhist temple)", "monk portal", "monk house", "monk room", "monk residence", "monastery", "monk clothes", "monk robe", "monk shoes", "monk socks", "monk hat", "monk scarf", "monks", "group of monks", "monk registry", "community of monks", "monk king", "monk master", "monk ruler", "monk official", etc.

### 3. 佛教里的意译词
### Translation of Meaning Words

意译词，就是根据某种语言词语的意义译成另一种语言的词语；指抛开了外语词原有的语音形式，而用汉语的构词材料，据汉语的构词方法创造一个新词，以表示新的概念。佛教词语大多数是通过意译的途径产生的。例如有情、法宝、世界、天堂、地狱、真理等，其中一部分产生了引申义，成了汉语里的通用词。佛教中的佛（释迦牟尼）、法（佛教教义）、僧（出家修行的佛教徒）为"三宝"，三宝中的"法"就是法宝。我们常说"无事不登三宝殿"，意思是没事不随便去别人家。

These are words translated based on the meaning of the word in some language into a new language; they toss out the sound of the original foreign word and use Chinese morphological patterns to create a new word to express the concept. Most Buddhist vocabulary was created this way. For example, some have generated extended meanings and become commonly used in Chinese, such as, "sentient beings (to be in love)", "dharma jewel (talisman, specially effective device)", "world", "heaven", "hell", "truth". In Buddhism, the "three jewels" are Buddha, dharma, and samgha (Buddha, his laws, and the community of monks); among these the "dharma" is the "dharma jewel". We have a saying: "Without business one doesn't ascend the temple of the three jewels", meaning "If you don't have anything to do or discuss, don't drop in".

## 4. 成语佛源
## Buddhist Origins of Idiomatic Phrases

此类成语包括天女散花、小题大做、朝三暮四、大千世界、六根清净、神通广大、五体投地、无所不晓、一针见血、三生有幸、心花怒放、不可思议、三世有缘、一知半解、不二法门、三头六臂、不知不觉、心领神会、一刀两断、一丝不挂、一厢情愿、十字街头、清规戒律、少见多怪、吉祥如意、对牛弹琴、盲人摸象等。

A few examples are: "to cut in two with one stroke of knife—to make a clean break with something"（一刀两断）, "without a rug—naked"（一丝不挂）, "one's own wish"（一厢情愿）, "crisscross of the street"（十字街头）, "regulations and restrictions from religion perspective"（清规戒律）, "easily impressed because of one have not seen much of the world"（少见多怪）, "good fortune and best luck"（吉祥如意）, "play a lute to a cow—offer a treat to an unappreciative audience"（对牛弹琴）, "blind men feeling an elephant—to take a part for the whole"（盲人摸象）, etc.

### (1) 一尘不染
#### *Untainted by a Speck of Dust—Selfless and Incorruptible*

"尘"为梵语 Guna 之意译。佛教把色、声、香、味、触、法称为"六尘"，六尘产生于眼、耳、鼻、舌、身、意六根；即眼所对的是色，鼻所对的是香，耳所对的是声，舌所对的是味等，总称"六尘"。"六根"与"六尘"相接触，会引发许多迷妄与烦恼。佛教主张修道的人不被六尘所玷污，叫作"一尘不染"。后来成了汉语的成语，比喻十分清净，也比喻人的品格清新脱俗。

尘 *chén* "dust" is a translation of Sanskrit *guna* "quality". Buddhism refers to appearance, sound, scent, flavor, touch, and dharma as the six qualities, which arise in the six roots: eyes, ear, nose, tongue, body and consciousness. Mutual contact between the six qualities and the six roots will initiate many delusions and disturbances. Buddhism's position is that the cultivated person will not be tarnished by the six qualities, or "untainted by a speck of dust". It later became an idiomatic phrase in Chinese, a metaphor of being extremely clean, or a person who is aloof from politics and the material world and free from vulgarity.

### (2) 回头是岸
#### *If One only Turns His Head, There Is the Shore—Repent and Be Saved*

佛教的"苦海无边，回头是岸"一说，意思是有罪的人好像掉进苦海，只要回过头来，决心改悔，就能爬上岸来，获得再生。释迦牟尼说法之初，便讲"苦谛"，认为众生在生死轮回中遭受种种痛苦，生死之苦，茫茫无边，称为"苦海"，只有悟道才能解脱。后来比喻做坏事的人，只要彻底悔悟，就有出路。

In Buddhism there is the saying, "The bitter sea is boundless; if one turns his head, there is the shore". It means that a person who has sinned is like having fallen into an ocean of bitterness, but all he needs to do is turn his head back, resolutely mend one's ways, then one can climb onto shore and attain rebirth. When Siddhartha first expounded his teachings, he spoke of the truth of suffering, believing all living things in the cycle of birth and death endure many kinds of suffering. The suffering of life and death, boundless without border, is called "the bitter sea". One can get free of it only through grasping the truth. Later, this phrase became a metaphor for the way to salvation for people who thoroughly repent after doing something wrong.

(3) 味同嚼蜡
***Tastes like Chewing Wax-insipid, Tasteless***

味同嚼蜡，也作"味如嚼蜡"。指文章、说话枯燥无味，或对某事某物没有一点兴趣等。

This refers to writings or discussions that are tedious and dreary, or a complete lack of interest in some matter or thing.

汉译佛语在中日之间并非单向传播，而是双向互动。

汉译佛语由中国流出是随着中国化佛教传入朝鲜、日本。佛教在日本传播开以后，至奈良时代（710—794），《法华经》等汉译佛典被尊为"护国"经典。随着大批汉译佛典的传入，汉译佛教词语也在日本广为流行，构成日本汉字文化的重要组成部分。明治时代（1868—1912）的望月信亨（1869—1948）编纂的《佛教大辞典》收词35000条，大多是汉译佛教词语，展示了从魏晋南北朝到隋唐间的汉译佛教词语在日本语文中庞大的阵容。

Chinese-translated Buddhist terms did not experience a one-way transmission between Chinese and Japanese. Rather, it was a two-way interaction.

Chinese-translated Buddhist terms flowed out of China following Sinified Buddhism's importation into Korea and Japan. After Buddhism started to spread in Japan, up to the Nara Period (710 – 794), the *Lotus Sutra* and other Chinese translations of Buddhist works were regarded as "nation-protecting" scriptures. Following the import of large numbers of Chinese translations of Buddhist scriptures, Chinese-translated Buddhist terms became fashionable in Japan and constituted a major component of the Japanese *kanji* culture. Shinkō Mochizuki (1869 – 1948) of the Meiji Period (1868 – 1912) compiled the *Great Dictionary of Buddhism* with 35000 entries, most of which were Chinese-translated Buddhists words and phrases. This compilation revealed the tremendous array in the Japanese language of the Buddhist terms translated into Chinese in the Wei-Jin through Sui-Tang period.

汉译佛语由日本逆输入中国,则发生在近现代。明治维新以来,日本在翻译西方学术文化的过程中,用汉字佛语翻译西洋术语概念是方法之一,而这些以佛语翻译的西洋术语概念又传播到中国,成为中国现代语汇的组成部分。例如,唯心,原是汉译佛语,出自《华严经》,日本人借"唯心"一词作 Idealism 的意译,后被中国沿用,成为一个基本哲学概念。又例如"知识"一词,本来是汉译佛语,日本人借作 Knowledge 的意译,后逆输入中国,成为现代中国的重要词汇。有些汉译佛语创自中国,但未在中国普及,传入日本方得流行,再由日本传入中国。例如"手续"一词,产于中国,后来随着密宗传入日本,近代又由日本逆输入中国。

The importation from Japan into China of Chinese-translated Buddhist terms happened in the near-modern and modern era. Since the Meiji Restoration, in the process of translating Western academic culture, one of the methods Japan used was to use Chinese Buddhist terms to translate Western terms and concepts. These western terms and concepts translated with Buddhist terms again spread to China and became a component of the modern Chinese vocabulary. For example, the term "*wéixīn (only mind)*" was originally a Chinese-translated Buddhist term from *Garland Sutra*. The Japanese borrowed this term to translate "idealism", which later was continued in China and became a basic philosophical concept. Again, "*zhīshí (knowledge)*" was originally a Chinese-translated Buddhist term that the Japanese used to translate the English word "knowledge". It later was imported back to China and became an important vocabulary item in modern Chinese. Some terms had originally been created in China, but never spread widely there. They only became popular in Japan, and spread back to China from Japan. For example, the term "*shǒuxù (procedure)*" was created in China, later followed the Tantric School and spread to Japan, and in the near-modern era was again imported back into China from Japan.

汉译佛语主要完成于魏晋南北朝到隋唐,构成汉字文化圈的一大词汇来源,中国、日本都受惠无穷。

The Chinese-translated Buddhist terms that were primarily completed in the Wei-Jin to Sui-Tang era constitute a large source of vocabulary for the Chinese-character cultural area; both China and Japan have received endless benefits.

## 七、汉语词汇的扩展（二）
## ——近代日制汉语新词①
## The Expansion of Chinese Vocabulary: Near-Modern Japanese-made Chinese Neologisms

汉字在日本，简直像希腊文和拉丁文在西洋各国一样，它们可以被用来作为构成日语新词的基础。
——王力（1900—1986）：《汉语史稿》，北京：中华书局1980年版，第529页。

Chinese characters in Japan, like Greek and Latin in Western countries, can be used as a basis for the creation of new Japanese words.
Wang Li (1900 - 1986), *Hanyu Shi Gao*, Beijing: Zhonghua Shuju, 1980, pg. 529.

王力在注释中指出："唯一不同之点是，希腊语、拉丁语和现代西洋语言是同一来源，而汉语和日本语没有亲属关系。"

Wang Li points out in a note that, "The point of difference is: Greek and Latin are from the same source language as modern Western languages, but Japanese and Chinese do not have a genetic relationship."

日制汉语新词，是近代日本在翻译西方著作时，用汉字创制的一批新词。这些词汇在清末时传入中国，构成中国近代各个学科的核心概念词汇。

19世纪末叶以来，西方术语大量入华，其输入渠道有二：一是直接译自西书，二是以日译西书为中介。故中国近代新术语既是悠久的汉语词汇史发展到当下的表现，也是中、日、西三种语汇系统互动的产物。

New Chinese words made in Japan were a batch of new words made using Chinese characters when Japan was translating Western works in near-modern times. This vocabulary was imported into China toward the end of the Qing Dynasty and composed the core conceptual vocabulary of each branch of learning in China's near modern period.

Since the end of the 19th Century, a large number of Western terms entered China through one of two paths: 1) direct translation of Western books, 2) through the intermediary of Japanese translations. So, China's near-modern neologisms are both the manifestation of the long

---

① 冯天瑜：《中国元典文化十六讲》，郑州大学出版社2006年版，第132页。

development of Chinese vocabulary into the present age, and also the product of the interaction among the vocabularies of China, Japan and the West.

## 1. 中日汉字文化的双向"互动"
### Two-way Interaction Between Chinese and Japanese Chinese-Character Culture

汉字文化圈内的中日两国,以汉字为媒介,近两千年来展开了颇有广度和深度的文化交流,并且是至今仍然沿用汉字的两个主要国家。古代主要是从先进的中国流向日本,公元1—2世纪汉代的时候,汉字就已经传入日本,5—7世纪的时候,日本的史籍用汉字书写。后来日本人依据汉字创制了日本文字,至今日本使用的常用汉字有1945个,加上人名用汉字284个,总共有2229个。汉字词汇则为数众多,在日语系统中占到50%以上。沿用汉字语汇词义的也很多,如日本围绕天皇和皇室的一系列专用语,几乎全部套用中国汉字词,如玉音、玉座、玉体、圣体。汉字词汇在日本社会随处可见,例如日本三大名园——金泽的"兼六园",冈山的"后乐园",水户的"谐乐园",皆得名于中国古典。

到了近代,日本又成为中国学习西方文化的走廊。

China and Japan, two countries within the realm of Chinese-character culture, have carried out a broad and deep cultural interaction over the last 2000 years using Chinese characters as the intermediary. They remain in the present the two main countries that still use them. In ancient times, they mainly flowed from the more advanced China to Japan. In the $1^{st} - 2^{nd}$ centuries A. D., Chinese characters had already been imported to Japan, and in the $5^{th}$ and $7^{th}$ centuries, Japanese historical records were written in Chinese characters. Later, based on Chinese characters, Japanese people invented their own writing systems, but even today, there are 1945 commonly used Chinese characters in Japan, and adding another 284 used in names, the total is 2229. The vocabulary written with Chinese characters in the Japanese system is numerous, constituting more than 50%. There are also many terms that use only the meanings of the characters, such as the whole series of words surrounding the emperor and imperial court which is seemingly entirely based on Chinese characters, e. g., "imperial voice", "imperial throne", "imperial presence". Chinese character based words can be seen everywhere in Japanese society, such as the three famous parks, Kenroku-en in Kanazawa, Kōraku-en in Okayama, and Kairaku-en in Mito; all have names based on Chinese classics.

In the near-modern period, Japan became the corridor through which China learned Western culture.

## 2. 日本译介西洋术语的高潮
### The High Tide of Japanese Translations of Western Terms

日本从19世纪50年代起,尤其是明治维新以来,引进、吸纳外国文化的方向,已由中国转为欧美。学习欧美资本主义国家的科技、文教、学术思想、政治法律乃至生活方式。在这一形势之下,翻译和介绍反映欧美近代文明的新概念、新术语,成为明治时代日本新知识界的一项重要任务。日本出现了创制汉字新词以译介西洋术语的高潮。

Starting from the 1850s, especially during the Meiji Restoration, Japan's source for learning and absorbing foreign culture shifted from China to Europe and America. They studied the European and American capitalist countries' technology, religion, academic thought, politics, law and even lifestyles. Under this condition, the most important duty of the new Japanese intelligentsia of the Meiji Era became the translation and introduction of Western civilization's near-modern ideas and terminology. A high tide of creating new words based on Chinese characters to translate Western terminology arose in Japan.

## 3. 日制汉语新词大量涌入中国
### The Large Influx of Japanese-made Words into China

清末,中国开始学习日本,近代日本人创制的翻译介绍西学术语的汉字新词大量涌入中国。而这些日制汉字新词大多是按汉语语法构造的,容易被中国人接受,许多西学术语通过日制汉字新词传入中国,推动了汉语的大发展。

In the latter Qing period, China started to learn from Japan, and the new words based on Chinese characters the Japanese people made to translate and introduce Western terminology flowed into China. Moreover, these new words were largely constructed according to Chinese morphological principles, so they were easily accepted by Chinese people, and many Western words were imported to China through these Japanese-made Chinese character neologisms, spurring the development of the Chinese language.

在日制汉字新词入华的同时,中国学人也在创制译介西学术语的新词汇,从事翻译介绍西学的工作,如用"理学"翻译哲学,"玄学"翻译形而上学,"格致学"翻译自然科学,"平准学"翻译经济学,"名学"翻译逻辑学,等等。而此时日制汉字新词一般都经过了几十年的选择、提炼而趋于定型,入华后往往取代了还处在游移状态的中国自制翻译的词。例如用日制汉字新词"哲学"取代"理学","形而上学"取代"玄学",等等。还有一些中国人音译的西洋术语,也被日制汉字意译词所代替,如"葛郎玛"改为"文法","德律风"变为"电话",等等。日制汉字新词在中国"短命"的,也不在少数。如"写真""切手""放送"等日制新词曾一度传入中国,却被中国人自创的汉译词"照相""邮票""广播"所代替,因为后者更清楚易懂,自然被民众所接纳。19世纪末、20世纪初,两国共创、同享的汉译西洋术语,作为宝贵的历史遗产,是中日两国与西洋文化互动的不朽铭记。

At the same time Japanese-made Chinese-character neologisms that translated Western terminology were entering China, Chinese scholars were also busy working on translating and introducing the new vocabulary of Western learning. For example, the term for the Rationalist (Neo-Confucian) School was used to translate "philosophy"; *xuánxué* was used to translate "metaphysics", "form-manage study" was used to translate "natural science", "even-grant study" was used to translate "economics", the term for the School of Names *míngxué* was used to translate "logic", etc. But the Japanese-made neologisms generally went through several decades of selection and refinement before being settled on, so after these words entered China, they always replaced the newly made Chinese words, which were still in a state of wavering and vacillation. For example, the word for philosophy became the Japanese made *zhéxué* rather than the word for the Rationalist school. Also, there were some Western terms that were transliterated in Chinese which were also replaced by the Japanese made neologisms. For example, the word "grammar" was transliterated as *gélángmǎ*, but that word was replaced by the Japanese made word *wénfǎ*. There were also quite a few Japanese made neologisms that had a short life in China. For example, the Japanese-made words for "photograph" (*shasin* 写真), "stamp" (*kitte* 切手), and "broadcast" (*hoso* 放送) were replaced by the neologisms Chinese people created (*zhàoxiàng* 照相, *yóupiào* 邮票, and *guǎngbō* 广播, respectively). The Chinese made terms were clearer and easier to understand to Chinese readers, so they were readily accepted by the populace. The translations of Western terminology bilaterally created and mutually shared is a precious historical legacy from the late 19th and early 20th century, the lasting memorial to Chinese and Japanese interaction with Western culture.

日制汉字新词还有文化、文明、文学、法律、革命、自由、权利、阶级、共和、社会、进步、手段、世界、选举、主席、服务、物质、代表、断交、独裁、独占、新闻、特务、概念、法学、批评、自治、改良、目的、政府、政治、伦理、消费、物理、经济、民主、哲学、抽象、客观、主观、否定、民族、动员、动产、命题、干部、取缔、游学、化学、美学、心理学、杂志、工业、建筑、概念、理想、保健、身份、背景、独占、互惠、交流、解放、供给、说明、动员、方针、交通、浪人、认可、市场、想象、要素、体验、作物、电报、电话、电子、电车、茶道、上告、上诉、代理、保释、公诉、拘留、教唆、法人、破产、不动产、所有权、优先权、违约金、生产力、入场券、游击战、传染病、大本营、武士道、归纳法、可能性、信教自由、形而上学、文明开化等等。

Japanese neologisms made from Chinese characters include contemporary Chinese words for such terms as culture, civilization, literature, law, revolution, freedom, authority, class, republic, society, progress, method, world, election, chairman, serve, material, represent, break diplomatic ties, dictatorship, monopolize, news, spy, concept, legal studies, criticism, self-determination, reform, goal, government, politics, ethics, consume, physics, economy, democracy, philosophy, abstract, objective, subjective, negate, nationality/ethnicity, mobilize, personal property, proposition, cadre, to suppress, study tour, chemistry, aesthetics, psychology, magazine, industry, architecture, concept, ideal, health protection, identity, background, monopoly, mutual benefit, communication, liberation, to provide, explain, mobilize, policy, transportation, vagrant, to approve, market, imagination, essential factor, to experience for oneself, crop, telegram, telephone, electronic, trolleybus, tea culture, to appeal (a case in court), surrogate, release on bail, public charges, to detain (a prisoner), to instigate, legal person, bankruptcy, real estate, property rights, rights of precedence, penalty, productivity, admission ticket, guerrilla warfare, infectious disease, headquarters, Bushido (Warrior's way), induction (in logic), possibility, religious freedom, metaphysics, and open civilization, etc.

## 八、汉语词汇的扩展（三）
## ——近代音译英文词语
## The Expansion of Chinese Vocabulary: Transliterated Words from English

汉语的外来词里，英语词汇有很多，这里列举一些汉语翻译比较成功的词语。这些英语词汇本来一般，翻译成汉字后，却变得含义深刻又有趣。

There are a lot of English words among China's foreign loanwords. The following are a few of the more successful examples. While these English words are originally quite plain, once translated into Chinese characters their connotations change in really interesting ways.

托福：英语 TOEFL 的音译。是美国的一种外国学生英语水平考试，中国人称为考"托福"。"托福"一词是中国人的一个日常口头语，含义吉利，考托福不管是托谁的福，就是希望顺利通过考试。

TOEFL：托福 tuōfú (entrust luck), an American test for English proficiency for foreign students. The term has come into daily use for Chinese people; its connotations are lucky. In "taking the TOEFL exam", it doesn't matter to whom one will "entrust" their "luck", one hopes one will smoothly pass the exam.

可口可乐：英语 coca-cola 的音译。世界著名饮料，英语原文并无深意，翻译成汉语"可口可乐"后，一下变得有意思了。

Coca-Cola：可口可乐 *kěkǒukělè*（palatable fun），the world famous soft drink does not have much of a deep meaning in the original English, but translated into Chinese it becomes fun.

雪碧：英语Sprite的音译，原意为妖怪、精灵。雪，有寒意；碧，清澈碧蓝。在夏天，这样的饮料名，听着就想喝。

Sprite：雪碧 *xuěbì*（snow blue），the English meaning is a fairy or elf. In Chinese, the "snow" implies cold, and the "blue" implies a clear, dark blue, so on a hot day, just hearing the sound of this soft drink makes one want to drink it.

雷达：英语radar的音译，无线电波探测装置，也叫"千里眼"。雷，联想到的是闪电雷鸣，突出了一个快字，雷达的"千里眼"的作用也就更加突出。

Radar：雷达 *léidá*（thunder reach），a wireless electric wave detection device. The first character is associated with the sound of thunder after lightning, giving prominence to the notion of "fast", the utility of radar is then even more apparent.

迷你裙：英语miniskirt的翻译，"迷你"是音译，裙是意译，原意是超短裙，翻译为"迷你裙"，含有了穿迷你裙迷人的想象。这也是把英语里mini作为"微型"前缀的最早的翻译，后来汉语里就把一系列的微型产品，都翻译为"迷你"，例如"迷你相机"等。

Miniskirt：迷你裙 *mínǐqún*（charm-you-skirt）. The first two syllables *mínǐ* transliterate the English "mini" while the last *qún* translates "skirt". The Chinese term connotes the idea that wearing one will charm people. This is the earliest translation of English "mini". Later a whole series of miniature products were translated into Chinese using this collocation, for example, minicamera, etc.

香波：英语Shampoo的音译，原意为洗头膏，使用的时候既起泡沫又有香味，听着就想用。

Shampoo：香波 *xiāngbō*（fragrant wave）. When used there are both a lot of bubbles and a nice smell; just hearing the term, one wants to use it.

维他命（现多作维生素）：英语Vitamin的音译，是人体不可缺少的化学物质。维他命，维护、维持他的生命。一听就像是一种很要紧的救命药。

Vitamin：维他命 *wéitāmìng*（safeguard his life）; just hearing the Chinese word makes one imagine it is an incredibly important life-saving medicine.

敌杀死：英语 Decis 的音译，一种杀虫农药。汉语的含义深刻而形象。
Decis：敌杀死 díshāsǐ（enemy kill dead），is a pesticide, but the Chinese word is deep and vivid.

马拉松：英语 marathon 的音译，是42公里的赛跑。马拉松，有"即使是马拉着跑也该松软了，何况是人呢"之意，突出了赛跑的长距离。
此外，"霹雳舞""披头士（乐队）""盖世太保""嬉皮士"等译名也译得精彩。
Marathon：马拉松 mǎlāsōng（horse drag loose），has the connotation that, if a horse dragged it and ran, the horse should be spongy/tired, even more so if a human did it. The term highlights the long distance of the race.
There are also the Chinese translations for "break dance", "the Beatles", "the Gestapo", and "hippy", which are also quite on target.

其他还有一些音译比较好的词语。
阿司匹林：英语 aspirin 的音译，是解热镇痛的药物。
奥斯卡：英语 Oscar 的音译，美国电影界的金像奖。
芭蕾（舞）：英语 ballet 的音译，一种起源于意大利的舞剧。
白兰地：英语 brandy 的音译，酒名。
百事可乐：英语 Pepsi-Cola 的音译，一种饮料品牌，英文原无深意，译为汉语后，有趣多了。
保龄球：英语 bowling 的音译，一种室内体育运动项目。
奔驰：英语 Benz 的音译，德国汽车品牌，译为汉语后显得更为生动形象，更适合用作汽车品牌的名字。
比基尼：英语 bikini 的音译，女式泳装。
考拉：英语 koala 的音译，树袋熊（澳洲产，树栖无尾动物）。
克隆：英语 clone 或"cloning"的音译，指无性繁殖。
伦巴舞：英语 rumba 的音译，一种交际舞，原为古巴的黑人舞。
罗曼蒂克：英语 romantic 的音译，浪漫。
吗啡：英语 morphine 的音译，由鸦片制成的白色结晶粉末。
马赛克：英语 mosaic 的音译，一种视觉效果。
麦克风：英语 microphone 的音译，话筒、扩音器。
模特：英语 model 的音译，展示服装的人或模型。
尼古丁：英语 nicotin 的音译，烟碱、烟草素，一种有毒的生物碱。
尼龙：英语 nylon 的音译，一种合成纤维。
诺贝尔：英语 Nobel 的音译，瑞典科学家名，后作为一种奖项的名称，为诺贝尔奖。

恰恰（舞）：英语 cha-cha 的音译，一种起源于拉丁美洲的节奏明快的现代交际舞。
巧克力：英语 chocolate 的音译，以可可粉等为原料制成的食品。
色拉：英语 salad 的音译，西餐中的一种凉拌菜。
苏打：英语 soda 的音译，纯碱，学名碳酸钠，一种重要的化工基本原料。
坦克：英语 tank 的音译，一种军用车辆。
踢踏舞：英语 tittup 的音译，一种以皮鞋击地作声的舞蹈。
乌托邦：英语 utopia 的音译，指理想中的社会。
席梦思：英语 simmons 的音译，一种有弹簧装置的床垫。
雪茄：英语 cigar 的音译，用烟叶卷成的烟，比一般香烟粗、长。

## 九、汉字改革
## Chinese Character Reform

### 1. 汉字的弊端
**Disadvantages of Chinese Characters**

随着西方文明的传入，汉字的许多弊端也渐渐显露出来。

其一，汉字的笔画繁多，结构复杂，不易书写。《康熙字典》的 214 个部首中，5 笔以下的只有 118 个，多的达 17 笔，未简化之前的汉字，平均笔画为 11～12 画。

Following the importation of Western civilization, the many disadvantages of Chinese characters have gradually come out into the open.

First, the number of strokes is too many, the structure is complicated and they are not easy to write. Among the 214 components identified in the *Kangxi Zidian*, only 118 have five or less strokes, while several have as many as 17. Prior to simplification, the average stroke count for characters was 11 – 12.

其二，汉字的数量太多，极难掌握。东汉的《说文解字》收字 9353 个，金代的《五音集韵》收字 53523 个，清代的《康熙字典》收字 47030 个，后来又出现不少生造的新字怪字，汉字的数目越来越庞大。

Second, there are too many overall characters, making it difficult to master the system. The *Shuowen Jiezi* of the Eastern Han had 9353 characters; the *Wuyin Jiyun* of the Jin Dynasty (1115 – 1234) had 53523, and the Qing Dynasty's *Kangxi Zidian* had 47030. Later, even more newly created characters and oddities arose, so the number of characters has gotten greater and greater.

其三,汉字的读音与字形之间差距太大,尽管汉字中的绝大多数是形声字,但是声符太多,读音无定,同音字数目惊人,文化交流极不方便。

因此,清末民初时,一些有识之士开始着手进行汉字改革的探索。

Third, the distance between the form of the character and its pronunciation has become too big. Even though many characters are phonetic compounds, there are too many phonetic components, their pronunciation is not fixed, and the number of homophonous characters is staggering, making cultural interactions extremely inconvenient.

So, in the latter part of the Qing and beginning of the Republican period, some learned people set their hands to carrying out Chinese character reform.

## 2. 汉字改革的内容
### Tasks of the Chinese Character Reform

一百多年来,汉字在简化、拼音化以及推行普通话等方面的变化主要有以下几项。

汉字简化包括两个方面,一是精简字形笔画,二是精简字数。1964年公布了《简化字总表》,一共收简化字2236个。此后,简化的汉字便成为现代通用汉字的规范。需要说明的是,台湾和香港、澳门使用的汉字依旧是繁体字;日文里使用的两千左右的汉字也大多是繁体字。

One hundred years later, the primary changes in character simplification, alphabetization, and even promoting Standard Mandarin have had the following tasks.

Simplification includes two aspects: 1) simplify strokes, and 2) reduce the number. In 1964, *the Complete Table of Simplified Characters* was published, which included 2236 simplified characters. Afterward, simplified characters became the standard for modern commonly used characters. Taiwan, Hong Kong and Macau still use the traditional forms of the characters, and the roughly 2000 characters used in Japanese are also mostly traditional forms, or simplified in different ways.

字数的精简:始于20世纪50年代,80年代出版的《现代汉语常用字表》共收汉字3500个,其中常用字2500个,次常用字1000个。而国家对外汉语教学和汉语水平考试所用的《汉语水平语汇与汉语等级大纲》(简称《汉字等级大纲》),只收汉字2864个。1988年公布的《现代汉语通用字表》,共收汉字7000个。目前通用汉字的总量基本控制在6000多个,常用汉字的总量基本控制在3000多个的范围内。

Reduction started in the 1950s, and in the 1980s the *List of Common Characters in Modern Chinese* was edited and published, containing 3500 characters, among which 2500 are commonly used characters and 1000 are less commonly used characters. And, the *Outline of Chinese Language Standard Vocabulary and Chinese Language Ranking* (simplified as *Outline Chinese Character Ranking*) used for teaching Chinese to foreigners and for the Chinese proficiency test, only collected 2864 characters. The *List of Common Characters in Modern Chinese* published in 1988 altogether collected 7000 characters. At present, the amount of commonly used characters is basically controlled at around 6000, while the amount of frequently used characters is controlled at around 3000.

推广普通话：从20世纪50年代起，开始进行普通话的推广工作。几十年来，全国各行业、各阶层人士，包括海外、港澳的华人都学习和使用普通话（台湾省也普及了被称作"国语"的普通话），普通话基本上已经成为全球性的汉语通用语。
汉字是世界上使用时间最长、使用人数最多的一种文字，也是世界各古文明中唯一仅存的意音文字。

Promoting Standard Mandarin: starting in the 1950s, the work of promoting Standard Mandarin was begun. In the several decades since, Chinese people in all industries in the country, at every social class, including those living abroad and in Hong Kong and Macau learn and use Standard Mandarin (Taiwan also popularized Standard Mandarin which they call the "National Language"). It has basically become a world-wide common Chinese.

Chinese characters are a kind of writing used for the longest time in the world and by the most people in the world, and also the only semantic-phonetic writing system still in use from among all the ancient civilizations of the world.

## 十、汉字文化圈
## Sphere of Cultural Influence of Chinese Characters

日本语言学家河野六郎于1963年首次提出"汉字文化圈"的概念。1988年，日本语言学家野村雅昭给"汉字文化圈"下定义：

> 在东亚位置上，由于中国的政治、文化影响，形成过去使用汉字，或现在仍然使用汉字的地域，总称为"汉字文化圈"。
> ——［日］野村雅昭：《汉字の未来》，筑摩书房1998年版，第219页。

The Japanese linguist Rokurō Kōno (1912 – 1998) in 1963 first raised the idea of the "sphere of cultural influence of Chinese characters". In 1988, the Japanese linguist Masaaki Nomura (b. 1939) provided the following definition for the term:

> In East Asia, owing to the political and cultural influence of China, there has formed a territory that either in the past used Chinese characters, or in modern times con-

tinues to use them, which may generally be referred to as "the sphere of the cultural influence of Chinese characters". (Japan) Masaaki Nomura, *Kanji no mirai*, Chikumashobō, 1998, p.219.

以中国、朝鲜、日本、越南组成"汉字文化圈"或称"东亚文化圈"的东亚民族及国家,并无共同语言,除中国内地(大陆)和香港、澳门、台湾的汉人,以及新加坡等东南亚华人以汉语为母语外,其他如中国的若干少数民族及越南人、朝鲜人、日本人等,都各有语言,却曾经或至今仍在使用汉字或汉字型文字,并且长时期以汉文、儒学、华化佛教、中国式律令等汉字文化要素作为自己传统的重要组成部分,人们读写汉字,根据汉字的书写格式和文法进行思想文化交流。例如,中国人与日本人在语言不通的情况下,可用汉字、汉文进行"笔语",达成一定程度的沟通。

The "cultural sphere" composed of China, Korea, Japan and Vietnam, also known as the people and countries of the "East Asian Cultural Sphere", all lack a common language. Except for the common Chinese language of the Chinese people of mainland China, Hong Kong, Macau, and Taiwan, and the Chinese people of Singapore and other Southeast Asian Chinese people, the others, such as some ethnic minorities of China, Vietnamese, Koreans, and Japanese, all have their own language. Yet, they have at some time used, or currently still do use, Chinese characters or writing formed on Chinese characters. Moreover, for a long time, they used the Chinese written language, Ru-ism, Sinified Buddhism, Chinese-style law and titles, and other Chinese-character cultural elements as an important component of their own tradition. The people read and write Chinese characters, and based on the written form of Chinese characters and their grammar undertake the interchange of ideas and culture. For example, Chinese and Japanese people, in a situation in which their languages do not make sense, can use Chinese characters as a kind of "writing language" and achieve a certain degree of communication.

**思考题**

1. 简述构成中国汉字字体的"六书"。
2. 举出几个源自佛语的成语。
3. 举出几个近代日制汉语新词。

***Questions***

1. Describe simply the six categories of Chinese characters.
2. Point out several idioms that originate in Buddhist terminology.
3. Point out several near-modern Japanese-made Chinese neologisms.

# 第四章  中国儒家思想
## China's Ru-ist (Confucian) Thought

儒家思想是中国传统文化的核心,要了解中国传统文化,首先就要了解儒学。

Ru-ist (what is sometimes called "Confucian") thought is the core of traditional Chinese culture. To understand traditional Chinese culture, one must first understand Ru-ism.

## 一、儒家思想的形成及核心内容
## The Formation of the Ru-ist School and the Core Content

### 1. 孔子创立儒家学说
### Confucius Establishes Ru-ist Doctrine

孔子(前551—前479年),名丘,字仲尼,鲁国人。父亲做过鲁国的下级武官。孔子幼年丧父,生活贫穷,一生在政治上也不顺利。青年时做过会计和牛羊管理人,51岁时出任过鲁国的中都宰,后升任司空、司寇,但都时间不长,后来被迫离职流放,离开鲁国,带着弟子周游列国,推行自己的学术思想和政治主张,想寻找一个采用他主张的国君,却遭冷遇。68岁时回到鲁国,边整理古代文献,边从事教学。见图4-1。

Confucius (551 – 479 B.C.), named Qiu, formal name Zhongni, was a native of the Lu State, and his father had been a low-level military official. He buried his father at a young age, and lived a life of poverty, unable to find a good job in government. In his youth he had been an accountant and livestock manager. At the age of 51 he worked as the chief Executive of a middle-sized city in the Lu State (modern Wenshang County of Shandong), and advanced up the bureaucracy to minister of public works and minister of criminal justice, but held none of these posts for long, and was later forced to leave them and go into exile. He left Lu with his disciples and roamed among the various states promoting his own academic thought and political positions, hoping to find a ruler who would adopt his ideas. But he only got the cold shoulder. At the age of 68 he returned to Lu, carrying on his teaching while he sorted out ancient documents. See Figure 4 – 1.

图 4-1 先师孔子行教像（唐朝吴道子）
Figure 4-1 Image of the First Teacher, Confucius, Educating (Wu Daozi, Tang Dynasty)

## 2. 孔子的政治主张
**Ru-ist's Political Position**

孔子主张实行"德治"，强调用道德治理国家，反对武力征伐，崇德尚文。孟子继承了孔子"仁"的思想，提出"仁政"学说，主张统治者宽厚地对待百姓，争取民心，以使统治长久。儒家的政治思想成为几千年来历朝治理国家的主要思想体系。

Confucius advocated implementing "moral rule", stressing the use of virtue and morality to govern the country and opposing military force for punitive expeditions; he raised morality high and esteemed culture. Mencius succeeded Confucius' ideas about "humanness", and put forth the theory of "government by humanness", which advocated the ruler's magnanimous treatment of the common people; to win the hearts of the people will make the regime last a long time. Ru-ist political thought became the main political ideology of the several thousand years of dynastic control of the country.

## 3. 孔子的教育思想
### Ru-ist's Ideas about Education

孔子是私人办学的开创者，创办了第一所私塾学校，发展了教育理论，积累了丰富的教育经验，是中国古代教育思想和实践的奠基人。他认为教育应该"有教无类"，接受来自不同阶层的学生，打破了贵族垄断教育的局面。教学内容方面，重视政治与伦理教育，主要课程为礼、乐、射、御、书、数。学习上提倡勤奋好学、不耻下问的学习态度。总结出"学而时习之""温故而知新"等学习方法，主张学生不仅要向书本学习，也要向周围的人学习，"三人行，必有我师"。

孔子有弟子3000多名，其中优秀的有72人。

Confucius was the founder of private education, founding the first private school. He developed educational theory and amassed bountiful educational experience. He was the pioneer of China's ancient educational theory and practice. He believed education should be for everyone; one should accept students from different social classes and smash the aristocracy's monopolization of education. He valued political and ethical education. The primary curriculum was etiquette (rites), music, archery, chariot driving, calligraphy and numeracy. He promoted an attitude of diligent studiousness and not being afraid to learn from subordinates. In general, he came out with such methods as "to study and review frequently", and "review the old and know the new". He stood for the idea that one not only learns from books, but also from the people around oneself; "If three people walk together, my teacher is inevitably among them" (you have something to learn from everyone).

Confucius had 3000 disciples, of whom 72 were outstanding.

## 4. 孔子言论集——《论语》
### Collection of the Sayings of Confucius—*The Analects*

《论语》并不是孔子自己写成，而是他的弟子和再传弟子整理的老师的言行录，记载了孔子对弟子的教诲以及与弟子之间的谈话内容，是后人研究孔子的基本资料。

儒家的经典著作是四书五经。四书是《大学》《中庸》《论语》《孟子》，五经是《诗》《书》《礼》《易》《春秋》。儒学经典后来发展为十三部，即"十三经"，是科举考试的主要内容。两千多年来，宣言儒家思想的著作浩如烟海，约有两万多卷。

*The Analects* was not compiled by Confucius himself. Rather, it is the record of his sayings tidied up by his disciples and their disciples. It recorded Confucius' instruction to his disciples together with the content of conversations between Confucius and his disciples. It is the basic resource for which later people researched Confucius.

The classic works of the Ru-ist School are the "Four Books" and "Five Classics". The "Four Books" are the *Great Learning*, *Doctrine of the Mean*, *Analects*, and *Mencius*; the

"Five Classics" are the *Book of Odes*, *Book of Documents*, *Book of Rites*, *Book of Changes*, and *Spring and Autumn Annals*. Later it grew to include thirteen texts, the so-called "Thirteen Classics", which were the primary content for the imperial examinations. Over more than 2000 years, works propounding on Ru-ist thought are as vast as the open sea, by some estimates more than 20,000 volumes.

## 5. 儒家思想的核心
### The Core of Ru-ist Thought

儒家思想的核心可以概括为以下三点。

The core of Ru-ist thought can be outlined in the following three points.

### (1) 以礼为行为规范
#### *Regard "Etiquette" as the Norm for Behavior*

春秋时代，社会混乱，孔子要求用周代的礼来约束人们的一切行动："非礼勿视，非礼勿听，非礼勿言，非礼勿动。"一切非礼的视、听、言、动都必须加以克制，每个人做到这一步，社会的矛盾就可以缓和；强调社会的等级秩序，每个人要明白自己在社会、家庭中的位置，严格遵守相应的责任、义务，这样，社会就会安定。

Society was chaotic in the Spring and Autumn Period. Confucius demanded to use the "etiquette" of the Zhou Dynasty to constrain all human actions: "If it isn't etiquette, don't look at it, if it isn't etiquette, don't listen to it, if it isn't etiquette, don't speak it, and if it isn't etiquette, don't touch it." All non-etiquette things must be controlled. Emphasizing ranked social order, every person had to be clear about their own position in the household and in society and strictly comply with the corresponding duties and obligations. If everyone is able to do this, contradictions among society could be alleviated, and society will be stable.

### (2) 以仁为思想核心
#### *Regard "Humanness" as the Ideological Core*

孔子的学生问他，什么是"仁"？孔子回答："仁者，爱人。"（仁就是爱人。）"克己复礼为仁。"（克制自己，使自己的行为符合礼的规范。）"己所不欲，勿施于人。"（不要把自己不喜欢的强加给别人。）"刚、毅、木、讷近仁。"（刚强、坚毅、质朴、讷言这四点接近仁。）这都是仁的伦理体现。仁是人的本性的最高表现，是人的美德的最高概括。

Confucius' student asked him, "What is 'humanness'?" Confucius answered, "One who has humanness loves people." "Subdue the self and observe etiquette, and it becomes humanness." "What you don't want done to yourself, don't enact on others." "Firmness, persistence, simplicity and speaking carefully draw near to humanness." These are all the ethical incarnations of humanness. Humanness is the highest expression of human's basic nature, the highest generalization of human virtue.

### （3）以义为价值准绳
### *Regard Justice as the Yardstick of Worth*

如何确定人的行为是否符合"礼"的规范、"仁"的精神，儒家提出必须以"义"为价值准绳。孔子以义为立身之本，一生不问事情有利无利，只问合义不合义。合义，就是真、善、美；不合义，就是伪、恶、丑。"舍生取义"就成了人生价值的最高实现。

How is one sure that a person's behavior is in accord with the standards of "etiquette" and spirit of "humanness"? The Ru-ists propose that one must use justice as the yardstick of worth. Confucius regarded justice as the root for self-conduct. Throughout one's life, one doesn't ask whether something is beneficial or not, one asks whether it fits with justice or not. That which fits with justice is true, good, and beautiful; that which does not is false, evil and ugly. Mencius said, "Give up one's life for justice," which became the highest realization of life's worth.

## 6. 儒家思想中的"三纲五常"
## Three Principles and Five Virtues

儒家思想主要通过"三纲五常"来维护社会的伦理道德教化。从孔子讲君君臣臣、父父子子的伦理观开始，孟子进一步提出"父子有亲，君臣有义，夫妇有别，长幼有序，朋友有信"的"五伦"道德规范，到汉代董仲舒按照他的大道"贵阳而贱阴"的阳尊阴卑理论，对儒家伦理观念做了进一步的发挥，提出了三纲原理和五常之道，即儒家"三纲五常"的伦理思想。

Ru-ist thought primarily upholds social, ethical, moral enlightenment through the "three principles and five virtues." Starting from Confucius' teaching that "a ruler acts as a ruler, a minister acts as a minister, a father acts as a father, and a son acts as a son", Mencius went one step further to propose the moral standard of the "five cardinal relationships"; "between father and son there is intimacy, between ruler and minister there is justice, between husband and wife there is difference, between older and younger there is succession, and between friends there is trust." In the Han Dynasty, Dong Zhongshu (179 – 105 B. C.) made a further development in Ru-ist ethical thought in accordance with his theory of "value the Yang and abase the Yin". He put forward the Ru-ist ethical theory of the three guiding principles and five constant virtues.

"三纲"，即君为臣纲，父为子纲，夫为妻纲，是讲人和人之间的伦理关系。董仲舒认为，在人伦关系中，君臣、父子、夫妻三种关系是最主要的，而这三种关系存在着天定的、永恒不变的主从关系：君为主、臣为从；父为主，子为从；夫为主，妻为从。三纲皆取于阴阳之道。具体地说，君、父、夫体现了天的"阳"面，臣、子、妻体现了天的"阴"面；阳永远处于主宰、尊贵的地位，阴永远处于服从、卑贱的地位。董仲舒以此确立了君权、父权、夫权的统治地位，把皇权社会的等级制度、政治秩序神圣化为宇宙的根本法则。

The "three guiding principles" are that the leader is the guide for the minister, the father guides the son, and the husband guides the wife. It is about the ethical relationship between people. Dong Zhongshu believed that in human relationships, the ruler-minister, father-son and husband-wife were the most important, and that there exists a primary-secondary relationship in them that is determined by heaven and is never-changing: the ruler is primary, the minister is secondary; the father is primary, the son is secondary; the husband is primary, the wife is secondary. The three guiding principles are all selected from the theory of Yin-Yang. In concrete terms, the lords, fathers, and husbands manifest heaven's Yang side, and ministers, sons, and wives manifest heaven's Yin side. Yang is always in the dominant, respected position, and Yin is always in the deferential, lowly position. With this theory, Dong Zhongshu instituted the position of the regime as having monarchal power, patriarchal authority and authority over the household, sanctifying the imperial social hierarchy and political order as based in universal code.

"五常"，即仁、义、礼、智、信，是处理君臣、父子、夫妻、上下尊卑关系的基本法则，主要是个人道德。"五常"是"三纲"的具体化。儒家认为只有遵守三纲五常，才能维持社会的稳定和人际关系的和谐。后经历代统治者强调，成为皇权社会的教条。

The theory of the five constant virtues, i. e., humanity, justice, etiquette, wisdom, and trust, all deal with the basic code of senior-junior relationship between ruler and minister, father and son, husband and wife, and between superior and inferior. It is mainly about the personal ethics. The "five constant virtues" are the concretization of the "three guiding principles." Ru-ists believe that only by complying with the "three guiding principles and five virtues" can social stability and harmony in human relationships be maintained. Later, through repeated emphasis from generations of rulers, it became the doctrine for all imperial society.

## 二、儒家的发展阶段
## The Growth Stage of Ru-ism

儒家创立的春秋战国时代，是社会大变革的时代，人们对当时社会大变革中的许多问题，表明自己的态度，提出自己的主张，形成了很多学派，总称为"诸子百家"。各派各家都著书宣传自己的观点，既互相批判，又互相影响，在学术思想领域内出现了"百家争鸣"的局面。参加争鸣的主要有儒家、墨家、道家、法家、兵家等。这些思想成为以后中国思想文化的主要源头。

The Spring-Autumn and Warring States periods in which Ru-ism was founded was an era of great social transformation. People made known their own attitudes and proposed their own positions with regard to the many problems of the contemporary social transformation, in turn forming numerous schools of thought, which were called "The Hundred Schools of Thought". Each sect and each school wrote books to spread their ideas, both criticizing each other and influencing each other, and the "hundred schools of thought contend" situation arose in the sphere of learned ideas. Those participating in the contention were primarily Ru-ists, Mohists, Daoists, Legalists, the School of Military, and others. These ideas became the main fountainhead of Chinese ideological culture.

儒家的发展大致有三个重要阶段。

一是两汉时期"罢黜百家，独尊儒术"的提出，百家变为一家，儒学独尊地位从此确立，孔子成为圣人，不再是普通人。汉武帝时把儒学提升为国家意识形态。

There are more or less three main stages in the growth of Ru-ism.

The first stage is in Han Dynasty, When Dong Zhongshu put forward the "dismiss the hundred schools, only revere Ru-ist arts". The hundred schools became a single one, and the sole reverence for Ru-ism was established. Confucius became a "sage", no longer an ordinary person. The Wu Emperor (141 – 87 B.C.) of the Han promoted it to the national ideology.

二是宋代儒学又被称为"理学"，吸收了佛教、道教的思辨方法，丰富了儒学，使儒学哲学化，儒学得到了进一步发展。经过和佛教、道教的激烈争夺之后，再一次提升儒学为国家正统的地位。

The second was in the Song Dynasty when Ru-ism evolved into the "Rationalist School." Having absorbed the Buddhist and Daoist methods of thinking and differentiating, enriching Ru-ism and making it more philosophical, it gained another stage of growth. After having experienced the fierce contention with Buddhism and Daoism, once again Ru-ism was instituted as the national orthodoxy.

三是产生于20世纪20年代的现代新儒学，吸纳融合西方文化，关心如何在道德主体的"本"之上，开创民主制度的新，以复兴儒学。新儒学以融合中西方文化为主要目的。

The third is the modern, new Ru-ism emerging in the 1920s, which accepted Western culture and mixed with it. It became concerned with how to initiate a democratic system on the main "root" of morality, and thereby rejuvenated Ru-ism. The main goal of the new Ru-ism is the fusion of Chinese and Western culture.

自从孔子创立儒家，到汉代"独尊儒术"，再到宋代吸收佛教、道教思想后，以"理学"形态丰富了儒家内容，儒家思想全方位深远地影响了中国人，渗透到了中国文化的各个方面，达到了"百姓日用而不知"的程度。

From Confucius' founding Ru-ism, to the Han Dynasty's "only revere Ru-ist arts," and then to when it absorbed Buddhist and Daoist ideas in the Song Dynasty in the form of the "Rationalist School", Ru-ism has been repeatedly enriched. Ru-ist ideology deeply and holistically influenced the Chinese people, penetrating every aspect of the culture, to the point that "the common people unknowingly use it every day".

## 三、儒学是不是宗教的争论
## The Debate over Whether Ru-ism Is a Religion

儒学是不是宗教问题的争论，始于明末清初利玛窦入华传教，他明确否定儒学是宗教。第二次争论由康有为等人引发。1866年，康有为提出孔教与佛教是世界两大真正的宗教，后与陈焕章等人创立孔教会。他们关于儒学是宗教的观点遭到梁启超、蔡元培、章太炎、陈独秀等人的批判。第三次争论是由台湾、香港及海外华裔学者发起。1958年，唐君毅、牟宗三、张君劢、徐复观等人联名发表"中国文化与当今世界"宣言，强调儒学的宗教性，赞同者有杜维明、刘述先等人。第四次是1978年底，任继愈重提"儒学是宗教"的说法，以汉代儒学独尊为宗教化开端，以宋明理学的形成为宗教化完成，详述儒教的形成及特征作用等，赞同者有其弟子李申及何光沪、张立文等，但遭到了冯友兰、张岱年、牟钟鉴、李国权、成中英等人反对。这一问题的争论波及海内外，直至今日仍在延续。

The debate over whether Ru-ism is a religion began in the late Ming and early Qing when Matteo Ricci entered China as a missionary. He clearly rejected the idea that Ru-ism was a religion. The second debate was initiated by Kang Youwei and others. In 1866, Kang Youwei proposed that Confucianism and Buddhism are two real worldwide religions, and later founded the Confucian Church with Chen Huanzhang and others. Liang Qichao, Cai Yuanpei, Zhang Taiyan, Chen Duxiu and others criticized their view that Confucianism is a religion. The third debate was initiated by Chinese scholars from Taiwan, Hong Kong and overseas Chinese scholars. In 1958, Tang Junyi, Mou Zongsan, Zhang Junli, Xu Fuguan and others jointly made the declaration about the "Chinese Culture and Today's World." They emphasized the religious nature of the Confucianism, and Du Weiming, Liu Shuxian and others agreed. The fourth debate was at the end of 1978, when Ren Jiyu restated that "Confucianism is religion," which started with the religiousization of Confucianism in the Han Dynasty, finished by the religiousization of Song and Ming Neo-confucianism. It detailed the formation and characteristics of Confucianism. There are his disciples Li Shen and He Guanglu, Zhang Liwen, etc. However, they were opposed by Feng Youlan, Zhang Dainian, Mou Zhongjian, Li Guoquan, Cheng Zhongying and others. The controversy of this issue was spread overseas, and it continues until today.

20 世纪 70 年代末，任继愈（1916—2009）重提儒学是宗教的说法，先后发表一系列文章，以汉代"罢黜百家、独尊儒术"为儒教宗教化过程的开端，以宋明理学的形成为儒学宗教化过程的完成，详细论述了儒教的形成、变化、宗教特征，以及儒教在中国历史上的地位与作用等问题，认为儒学就是宗教。他的弟子李申于 1999 年出版《中国儒教史》（上、下）一书，力证老师观点，再次引发对这个问题的讨论，全国较有名望的大学者几乎全部参与到这一次的讨论之中，基本形成以下三种观点，论辩主要围绕以下三种观点展开。

In the end of the 1970s, Ren Jiyu (1916 – 2009) raised the topic again with the theory that Ru-ism is a religion. In a series of articles, he took the "dismiss the hundred schools and revere only Ru-ist arts" of the Han Dynasty as the starting point of the process of making Ru-ism a religion, and the Song-Ming formation of the "Rationalist School" as the completion of the process. He makes a detailed exposition of Ru-ism's formation, transformation and religious characteristics, including its role and position in Chinese history. His student, Li Shen, in 1999 published *The History of China's Ru-ist Religion*, in two volumes, forcefully arguing for his teacher's position, and again triggering a discussion of the question. Prestigious scholars from around the country seemingly all entered into the discussion, basically forming the following three positions. The debate mainly focuses on the following three perspectives.

### 1. 儒学是宗教
### Ru-ism Is a Religion

儒学是宗教。持这一观点者认为儒学具备了基本的宗教因素：人格化了的神、经典、礼仪、孔庙等，有宗教的实践活动。

代表性观点——赖永海："否认儒学是宗教就等于拦腰砍断了儒家学说的上半截，就无法全面地认识中国传统文化。"①

Ru-ism is religion. Those holding to this position believe Ru-ism to be equipped with the basic religious elements: anthropomorphized deity, scripture, rituals, temples, etc. And, there are religious practices.

Lai Yonghai, representative of this position, wrote, "To deny that Ru-ism is a religion is equivalent to slicing across the waist and chopping off the upper half of Ru-ist theory, in which case there is no way to be comprehensively cognizant of traditional Chinese culture" (Lai Yonghai, 1992, *Foxue yu Ruxue*).

## 2. 儒学不是宗教
**Ru-ism Is Not a Religion**

儒学不是宗教。持这一观点者认为儒教之教，不是宗教之教，是教化之教。认为传统宗教追求来世，是出世的；儒教追求入世，是现实的。冯天瑜认为，中国人追求的是在现实世界做圣贤，"以求得人生的'三不朽'（立德、立功、立言），这正是中国传统文化的主潮——儒学不是宗教的根本原因"。②

Ru-ism is not religion. This faction believes the "teaching" in "Ru-ist Teaching" is not the "teaching" in "religious teaching", but rather it refers to "enlighten, civilize". They believe traditional religion is in pursuit of the coming world and leaving this world. Ru-ism seeks to engage in this world; it is realistic. Feng Tianyu (b.1942) believes what Chinese people pursue is being wise and worthy in the real world and "to try to obtain the "Three Immortal Deeds" (set one's virtue, set one's merit, expound one's ideas in writing) in a lifetime. This is really the main tide in Chinese traditional culture, and the fundamental reason Ru-ism is not a religion" (Feng Tianyu, He Xiaoming, Zhou Jiming, 2006, *Zhonghua Wenhua Shi*).

利玛窦也认为：儒家不承认自己属于一个教派，他们宣称他们这个阶层或社会集团倒更是一个学术团体，是为了恰当地治理国家和国家的普遍利益而组织起来的。因为儒家没有教规，没有宗教仪式，没有宗教场所，不具备一般宗教的基本属性。

代表性观点——梁漱溟：儒学不信鬼神，不讲来世，所以不是宗教。

Matteo Ricci also believed it was not a religion. Ru-ists do not acknowledge that they themselves belong to a sect. They assert that this stratum of theirs or this social group is an ac-

---

① 赖永海：《佛学与儒学》，浙江人民出版社1992年版。还可以参考任继愈《论儒教的形成》（《中国社会科学》1980年第1期第67－74页）等文章；李申：《中国儒教史》上下卷，上海人民出版社1999年版。
② 冯天瑜、何晓明、周积明：《中华文化史》第2版，上海人民出版社2006年版。

ademic group, organized for appropriately managing the state and for the general interest of the state. Because Ru-ism does not have religious rules, or religious ceremony, or religious locations, it is not equipped with the basic attributes of a religion.

A representative advocate for this position was Liang Shuming who argued that Ru-ism does not believe in ghosts and spirits, and does not discuss the coming world, so it is not a religion.

### 3. 儒学不是宗教，但是有宗教的作用
### Ru-ism Is not a Religion, But It Has the Effect of a Religion

儒学不是宗教，但是有宗教的作用。持这一观点者认为儒学虽然不是宗教，但是从儒家思想对中国文化产生的深远影响来说，起到了宗教的作用。蔡尚思等人认为儒学之教是教育教化，所起作用比宗教还大。

代表性观点——李泽厚（1930—2021）：儒学不是宗教，却起了比某些宗教还要大的作用。

Ru-ism is not religion, but has religious function. Those that hold this position believe that although Ru-ism is not a religion, yet, from the perspective of the deep, broad influence Ru-ist thought has had on the production of Chinese culture, it has played the role of a religion. Cai Shangsi and others believed that the Ru-ism's teaching is education, and its role has greater impact than religion.

A representative of this position is Li Zehou (1930 – 2021): Ru-ism is not a religion, but it has played a bigger role than some religions.

## 四、儒家语录
## Ru-ist Quotations

（1）仁者爱人。
One who has humanness loves people.
（2）克己复礼为仁。
Restraining oneself and returning to etiquette constitutes humanness.
（3）智者不惑，仁者不忧，勇者不惧。
One who is wise is not muddled, one who has humanness is not anxious, one who is brave is not fearful.
（4）富贵不能淫，贫贱不能移，威武不能屈，此之谓大丈夫。
Not able to be corrupted in the face of wealth and riches, not able to be shaken in the face of need and destitution, not able to be bent in the face of formidable might: this is what is

referred to as a man of character.

（5）己所不欲，勿施于人。

That which you do not wish upon yourself, do not enact upon others.

（6）玉不琢，不成器，人不学，不知道。

Jade, but not cut, does not attain the status of an implement; human, but does not study, does not know the *dao*.

（7）不学礼，无以立。

Not studying etiquette, one lacks the means to stand.

（8）学而不厌，诲人不倦。

To study and not feel satiated; to instruct others and not feel weary.

（9）穷则独善其身，达则兼济天下。

If at one's end, then improve yourself alone; if one attains success, then share it throughout the world.

（10）人之初，性本善，性相近，习相远。

A person at the beginning has a nature that at root is good. While their natures are close to each other, their practice is far from each other.

（11）食不语，寝不言。

When eating one does not speak, when sleeping one does not talk.

（12）礼之用，和为贵。

The utility of etiquette is that harmony becomes valued.

（13）吾十有五而志于学，三十而立，四十而不惑，五十而知天命，六十而耳顺，七十而从心所欲，不逾矩。

At fifteen years old, I set my ambition on study; at thirty, I was established; at forty I was without doubt; at fifty, I was aware of heaven's mandate; at sixty, my ear was tuned; at seventy, I followed that which my heart desired and did not exceed the rules.

（14）温故而知新。

Review the old, and know of the new.

（15）见贤思齐焉，见不贤而内自省也。

On seeing a worthy person, I think to be equal to him; upon seeing an unworthy person, I inwardly reflect on my shortcomings.

（16）君子欲讷于言而敏于行。

The gentleman desires to be agile in actions while being slow in speech.

（17）知之者不如好之者，好之者不如乐之者。

One who knows of it is not as good as one who is fond of it; one who is fond of it is not as good as one who rejoices in it.

（18）知者乐水，仁者乐山。知者动，仁者静。知者乐，仁者寿。

One who knows enjoys water; one who has humanness enjoys mountains. One who knows, moves; one who has humanness, is still. One who knows is happy; one who has humanness lives long.

（19）三人行，必有我师。

If three people walk together, my teacher is inevitably among them.

（20）非礼勿视，非礼勿听，非礼勿言，非礼勿动。

If not in accord with the rites, do not look; if not in accord with the rites, do not listen; if not in accord with the rites, do not speak; if not in accord with the rites, do not act.

（21）名不正，则言不顺；言不顺，则事不成。

If the names are not upright, then the speech is not in the same direction; if the speech is not in the same direction, then affairs will not be achieved.

（22）君子和而不同，小人同而不和。

The gentleman is not the same while being harmonious; the petty man is not harmonious while being the same.

（23）君子喻于义，小人喻于利。

The gentleman opens the mind to justice; the petty man opens the mind to profit.

（24）人无远虑，必有近忧。

A person without far-sighted thinking inevitably has near-by troubles.

（25）小不忍，则乱大谋。

If one does not endure small slights, then one would never achieve great things.

（26）道不同不相为谋。

Those who walk a different path do not make plans together.

（27）学而优则仕。

If one is successful upon having studied, then they can serve as an official.

（28）有朋自远方来，不亦乐乎？

Isn't it delight to have a friend who came from far away to visit you?

今天我们能够继续用汉语朗诵孔子在2500年前说过的话，又从另外一个方面注解了第十八章里提到的中国文化的特点，即中国文化有着绵延韧性和长期存在的生命力。

That today we are able to continue to use the Chinese language to recite those sayings that Confucius uttered 2500 years ago, explains to a certain extent the characteristic of Chinese culture mentioned in Chapter Eighteen; the characteristic that, in sum, Chinese culture has a vitality that is continuously tenacious and capable of long-term survival.

**思考题**

1. 你认为儒学是宗教吗？为什么？
2. 说出三条你喜欢的儒家语录，并解释其含义。

***Questions***

1. Do you believe Ru-ism is a religion? Why?
2. Tell us three Ru-ist sayings that you particularly like and explain their implications.

# 第五章　中国古代的佛教、道教
## Chinese Buddhism and Daoism

## 一、佛教
## Buddhism

### 1. 佛教的传播
### The Importation of Buddhism

佛教创始人乔达摩·悉达多（约前565—约前485年），约与孔子同时期，比孔子大14岁，原为迦毗罗卫国（今尼泊尔南部）净饭王的太子，觉悟成道后，信徒尊称他为"释迦牟尼"（释迦族的圣人）或"佛"（觉悟者）。印度孔雀王朝阿育王时期（前273—前232年在位）立佛教为国教，并派遣高僧到中亚、西亚传播佛教，使之扩展成为一种世界性宗教。

The founder of Buddhism, Siddhārtha Gautama (565 – 485 B.C.), roughly contemporary with Confucius though older by 14 years, was originally the heir apparent to the king Śuddhodana of Kapilavastu (modern southern Nepal). After attaining enlightenment, his followers called him "Sakyamuni" (sage of the Sakya clan), or "Buddha" (the enlightened one). Buddhism was established as the state religion in the Ashoka period (273 – 232 B.C.) of the Maurya Dynasty (324 – 187 B.C.) in India, and they sent monks to spread Buddhism to Central and West Asia expanding its influence and making it a world religion.

### 2. 佛教的教义
### Buddhist Doctrine

释迦牟尼成佛后开始宣扬他觉悟出来的"佛法"，主要内容是"四谛说"和"十二因缘"，这也是原始佛教的基本教义。

After becoming the Buddha, he began to make known his "Dharma" (teachings of the Buddha, or Buddhist doctrine) that he had become enlightened to. The primary content of them was the "Four Noble Truths" and "The Twelve Principle and Secondary Causes". This is the basic doctrine of primitive Buddhism.

"四谛说",即苦谛(人生是痛苦的)、集谛(人生痛苦的原因)、灭谛(灭除痛苦)、道谛(灭除痛苦的方法)。

The Four Noble Truths are: 1) the truth of suffering (human life is suffering), 2) the truth of the cause (the reasons for human suffering), 3) the truth of extinguishing (extinguishing suffering), and 4) the truth of the path (the methods for extinguishing suffering).

十二因缘,是人生过程中十二个彼此互为条件或因果的环节,是佛教轮回说的理论基础。十二因缘又分为三个阶段,就是过去世、现在世和未来世;三个阶段中的因果:过去因是现在果,现在因是未来果。所以,十二个环节,因果相随,三世相续而无间断,使人流转于生死轮回的大海,只有修行解脱才能脱离苦海;佛教修行要达到的最高目的就是"涅槃",即进入不生不灭的状态。

The Twelve Principle and Secondary Causes are the twelve links that mutually act as conditions, or causes-and-effects, in the course of a person's life; they are the foundation of Buddhism's theory of reincarnation. The Twelve Causes are again divided into three periods: past age, present age, and future age. The cause-and-effect among the three periods: the past causes lead to the present's effects; the present's causes lead to the future's effects. So, the twelve links, cause-and-effect follow each other, the three ages succeed each other, and there is no break, which causes people to wander in the sea of reincarnation between life and death. Only through the religious practice to free oneself of worldly worries can one be allowed to escape the abyss of suffering. The highest goal the Buddhist practitioner wants to attain is "nirvana", i.e., to enter the state of non-birth and non-extinguishing.

### 3. 大乘佛教、小乘佛教
### Mahayana Buddhism and Hinayana Buddhism

佛教对外传播的路线有两条:向北传播到中国、朝鲜、日本、越南等国家,向南传播到斯里兰卡、缅甸、泰国、柬埔寨、老挝等国家。

There were two paths over which Buddhism spread: north into China, Korea, Japan, Vietnam and other countries, and south into Sri Lanka, Burma, Thailand, Cambodia, Laos and other countries.

北传以大乘佛教为主,追求"普渡众生";南传以小乘佛教为主,追求"自我解脱"。南传佛教流行在今天云南傣族地区。

The northern spread was based on Mahayana (Great Wheel) Buddhism, seeking to "deliver all living creatures from suffering".

The southern spread was based on Hinayana (Lesser Wheel) Buddhism, seeking "self liberation". This form is popular in the Dai regions of modern Yunnan Province.

秦汉之际，佛教开始在中亚各国流行；两汉之际，佛教传入中国。
今天中国的佛教分为汉传佛教、藏传佛教两种，都属于大乘佛教。

Buddhism became popular in the various countries of Central Asia in the period around the Qin-Han transition, and spread to China in the period around the Western Han-Eastern Han transition.

Buddhism in China today may be divided into Han-Chinese Buddhism and Tibetan Buddhism, both of which belong to Mahayana Buddhism.

## 4. 汉传佛教
### Chinese Buddhism

汉传佛教主要流行于中原内地汉族人群。

佛教在两汉之际传入中国以后，不断发展壮大，到隋唐进入鼎盛时期。寺院、僧尼、教派众多，佛教逐渐中国化。

中国化佛教宗派中，禅宗流传时间最长，至今仍有影响。

Chinese Buddhism is mainly popular among the Han communities of the Central Plains and interior parts of the country.

After Buddhism came to China in the Han Dynasty, it continuously grew and expanded, and by the Sui-Tang period it entered its golden age. There were numerous monasteries, monks and nuns, and sects. Buddhism gradually became Sinicized.

Chan (i.e. Zen) Buddhism was transmitted for the longest time among sinicized Buddhist sects, and even today it still has influence.

禅宗，因为主张修习禅定（即打坐，佛教的一种修行方法）而得名。创始人是菩提达摩（？—约536），曾经在少林寺修行。禅宗经典是《金刚经》，提倡心性本净，佛性本有，见性成佛。所以，可以一悟即悟，放下屠刀，立地成佛。

Chan Buddhism gets its name from advocating for the practice of meditation (that is, to sit in meditation, a religious practice in Buddhism). The founder was Bodhidharma (?—536), who once practiced at the Shaolin Temple. The scripture of Chan is the *Diamond Sutra*, which advocates that one's nature is pure at the root, i.e., the Buddha nature is present at the root. So, if one sees one's true nature one becomes enlightened. Thus, one can become enlightened all of a sudden. As the saying goes, "Lay down the butcher's knife, and become a Buddha on the spot."

到了五祖弘忍（601—675）的时候，他为了选拔继承人，要求大家各做一首偈。

神秀（？—706）写了一首偈：

身是菩提树，心如明镜台，时时勤拂拭，莫使有尘埃。

At the time of the 5<sup>th</sup> Patriarch, Hongren (601 – 675), in order to choose his successor, he asked everyone to each compose a Buddhist hymn. Shenxiu (？ – 706) wrote one as follows：

The body is a Bodhi tree, the mind is like a bright mirror stand; diligently dust and wipe it constantly, do not allow dust on it.

慧能（638—713）回了一偈：

菩提本无树，明镜亦非台，本来无一物，何处惹尘埃。

Huineng (638 – 713) responded with one as follows：

Bodhi originally had no trees, the bright mirror is not a stand; originally there is no one thing, wherein is the dust provoked?

五祖弘忍就把世代相传的法衣交给了慧能，正式传慧能为禅宗六祖。
The 5<sup>th</sup> Patriarch Hongren then turned over the ceremonial garments to Huineng and formally transferred to Huineng the role of 6<sup>th</sup> Patriarch of Chan Buddhism.

汉传佛教戒律的特点：
Characteristics of Chinese Buddhism and religious discipline：

汉族僧人遵行的戒律基本上保持印度传统，但是也有一些自己的特点。
出家僧徒一律以"释"为姓；僧人必须吃素；僧人受菩萨戒，燃顶，就是在头顶烧香疤；僧人可以从事农业劳动养活自己等。
The monastic disciplines obeyed by Chinese monks basically preserve the Indian tradition, but there are a few of their own traditions. Monks uniformally take the surname *Shi* 释; monks must eat vegetariandiet; monks endure the Buddha discipline and "burn the top", i. e., burn incense scars onto the top of their heads; monks may engage in agricultural labor to support themselves.

## 5. 藏传佛教
**Tibetan Buddhism**

藏传佛教主要流行于西北地区藏族以及蒙古族、土族等。在 7 世纪松赞干布时期传入西藏。

藏传佛教主要分为四大派别：格鲁派、噶举派、萨迦派、宁玛派。

Tibetan Buddhism is mainly popular in the northwest region among Tibetans, as well as Mongolians, Monguors, etc. Buddhism came to Tibet in the time of Songtsen Gampo (617 – 650).

It is mainly divided into four major denominations: Gelugpa, Kagyu, Sakya, and Nyingma.

格鲁派：意为善规，因为该派僧人严守戒律；又因为此派僧人戴黄色僧帽，故又称为黄教。格鲁派创始人为宗喀巴（1357—1419），出生于青海省湟中鲁沙尔（见图 5 – 1）。宗喀巴在西藏修建甘丹寺是格鲁派正式形成的标志。后来随着势力扩大，又修建了哲蚌寺、色拉寺、扎什伦布寺等。清代以来，西藏以外修建甘肃拉卜楞寺（见图 5 – 2）、青海塔尔寺等寺院，北京雍和宫也是格鲁派寺院。清代格鲁派形成达赖、班禅、章嘉（内蒙古）、哲布尊丹巴（外蒙古，今蒙古国）四大活佛转世系统。

Gelugpa means good at the rules, because the monks of this sect strictly maintain monastic discipline. Because the monks of this sect wear yellow monk hats, they are also called Yellow Hat. The founder was Tsongkhapa (1357 – 1419), born in Lusha'er (see Figure 5 – 1), Huangzhong County, Qinghai Province. That Tsongkhapa constructed the Gandan monastery in Tibet is the mark of the formal formation of the Gelugpa sect. Later, following the expansion of their influence, they constructed Drepung, Sera, and Tashi Lhunpo monasteries. Starting in the Qing Dynasty, outside of Tibet, they constructed Labuleng Temple in Gansu Province (see Figure 5 – 2), Ta'er Monastery in Qinghai Province, and others. Even the Yonghe Temple in Beijing is a Gelugpa temple. In the Qing Dynasty, the Gelugpa created the four great Living Buddha transmigration systems of the Dalai Lama, the Panchen Lama, the Janggya (Inner Mongolia), and the Jetsun Dampa Living Buddha (Outer Mongolia, the present Mongolia).

噶举派："噶举"，藏语意为"口授传承"，创立者先后有两人。一是琼布朗觉巴，一是玛尔巴。因该派僧人按印度教的传统穿白色僧衣，故称为白教，支派最多，有塔布噶举和香巴噶举两大传承。主要寺院有西藏墨竹工卡的止贡寺、四川德格的八邦寺等。

Kagyu means "transmit the word" in Tibetan. There were two founders; one was Khyung-po rnal-'byor (990 – 1140), and one was Marpa Lotsawa (1012 – 1097). Because monks of this sect wear white monks' robes in accordance with the Indian religious tradition,

图 5-1　宗喀巴（1357—1419）
Figure 5-1　Zongkaba (1357-1419)

图 5-2　拉卜楞寺（格鲁派），位于甘肃省夏河县
Figure 5-2　Labuleng Temple (Gelugpa), Located in Xiahe city, Gansu Province

they are called the White Religion. There are numerous branch sects; the two big traditions are Dakpo Kagyu and Shangpa Kagyu. The main monasteries are Bri gung mthil in Maizhokunggar County, Tibet, and Palpung Monastery in Dege County, Sichuan Province.

　　萨迦派：藏语意为灰白色的土地，因为主寺——萨迦寺所在地的土地是灰白色而得名。萨迦派寺院围墙涂有象征文殊、观音和金刚菩萨的红、白、黑三色花条，故又称花教。主要寺院有四川德格的贡钦寺、青海玉树的结古寺、西藏林周的那烂陀寺，今锡金境内的结蔡寺等。1550 年在四川德格贡钦寺设立的德格印经院，是藏区最著名的印经院。

Sakya in Tibetan means ash-grey earth, because the dirt at the main monastery, the Sakya Monastery, is ash-grey colored. Daubed on the walls surrounding Sakya monasteries there are red, white, and black flower strips which symbolize Manjushri, Avolokiteśvara, and Vajrapani Boddhisatva, and so it is also called the Flower Religion. Their main monasteries are Gonchen Monastery in Dege, Sichuan, Geygu Monastery in Yushu, Qinghai, Nalanda in Linzhou County, Tibet, and Sa-Ngor-Chotshog within the borders of modern Sikkim. In 1550, the Dege printing house was established in Gonchen Monastery in Dege, Sichuan, becoming the most famous sutra printing academy in Tibetan areas.

宁玛派："宁玛"藏语意为"古旧"，是藏传佛教最古老的一个派别。因为宁玛派僧人戴红色僧帽，因而又称红教。主要寺院有西藏的多吉扎寺、敏珠林寺，四川的噶托、竹庆寺等。现在不丹、尼泊尔、印度、比利时、希腊、法国、美国等地都建有宁玛派寺院。

Nyingma in Tibetan means "ancient," and it is one of the oldest sects in Tibetan Buddhism. Because monks of this sect wear red monk hats, so they are called the Red Religion. Their main monasteries are Dorjidak Gompa and Mindrolling monasteries in Tibet, and Katok and Dzogchen monasteries in Sichuan. Now there are Nyingma monasteries in Bhutan, Nepal, India, Belgium, Greece, France, and the United States.

## 二、道教
## Daoism

### 1. 道教与道家的区别
### The Difference Between Daoism and Daoist School

简单地说，道教是宗教；道家是哲学，是学术派别。道家创始人是春秋战国时期人老子，道教创始人是东汉时期人张道陵。

Simply put, Daoism is a religion, while the Daoist School is a philosophy or academic school of thought. The founder of the Daoist School was Laozi in the Spring-Autumn/Warring States period. The founder of Daoism is Zhang Daoling (34 – 156) of the Eastern Han.

道家，主要指先秦诸子百家中以老子、庄子为代表的学派，它把"道"作为最高哲学范畴，主张效法自然，清净无为，治国修身。

The Daoist School primarily refers to the school of thought in the pre-Qin Hundred Schools of Thought represented by Laozi and Zhuangzi. It takes *dao* as the highest philosophical category and stands for imitating nature, pure non-action, rule of the country and cultivation of the self.

道教是通过信奉"道"，修炼精神形体而"得道成仙"。

道家的黄老思想被道教吸收，并以此为基础创立了道教，道家与道教有渊源关系，但是不能完全等同。

Daoism, or the Daoist Religion, via faith in the "*dao*" cultivates spiritual form and upon "attaining the *dao* and becoming immortal".

Daoism absorbed the Daoist School's *Huanglao* thought and with this as its foundation created the religion. So, Daoism and the Daoist School have an originary relationship, but they are not entirely the same.

## 2. 道教的创立、教义
### Daoism's Founding and Creed

与佛教传入大体同时，中国本土宗教——道教创建。

东汉时期，道教成为一个有教义、教主、经典、组织的宗教，创始人是张道陵，《太平经》为道教主要经典。

At about the same time as the importation of Buddhism, China's native religion, Daoism, was founded.

In the Eastern Han, Daoism became a religion with a doctrine, founder, scriptures, and organization. The founder was Zhang Daoling, and its primary scriptural text was the *Taipingjing*.

道教的思想来源有三：一是古代民间的鬼神崇拜活动，二是战国以来的神仙方术，三是秦汉时期的道家思想。这是道教宗教神学、修炼方术和宗教仪式的三个主要来源。

There are three sources for Daoism's ideas: 1) ancient folk activities worshipping gods and spirits, 2) the supernatural entities and arts of the Warring States period and later, and 3) the ideas of the Daoist School of the Qin-Han period. These are the three primary sources of Daoism's religious theology, cultivation of supernatural arts, and religious ceremony.

道教尊奉三清尊神——道教根据《道德经》的"道生一，一生二，二生三，三生万物"的思想，把道家的"道"演变为"洪元""混元""太初"三个不同的世纪，再人格化为神，即三清尊神。元始天尊，手拿圆珠，象征"洪元"；灵宝天尊怀抱坎离匡廓图，象征"混元"；道德天尊手持扇子，象征"太初"。道教的三清尊神也是受到佛教的过去、现在、未来三世佛的影响而形成。

道教修行的终极目标是长生不老"得道成仙",使人成为灵魂常在、肉体永生的神仙。

Daoism reveres the "Three Clears Deity" based on the idea from the *Dao De Jing* that "The *dao* generates the one, the one generates the two, the two generates the three, and the three generates all things." The Daoist School's *dao* evolved into the three ages of the "Primary Flood", "Primary Chaos", and "Great Beginning". These are then anthropomorphized into spirits, i.e., the Three Clears Deity. The Primary Deity holds a round ball in his hand, symbolizing "Primary Flood"; the Lingbao Deity clutches to his chest the *Kanli Sketch*, symbolizing "Primary Chaos"; and, Virtue Deity holds a fan in his hand, symbolizing the "Great Beginning". The Three Clears Deity was formed under the influence of Buddhism's Buddha of the three ages: past, present, and future.

The ultimate goal of Daoism's practice is to "attain the *dao* and become an immortal", making the person become an immortal with a soul that exists forever, and with a physical body that lives forever.

## 3. 道教对中国文化的影响
### The Influence of Daoism on Chinese Culture

道教对中国文化有多方面影响:古代不少学科和道教关系密切。道士们为了长生不老而炼造金丹的实验,推动了古代化学制药技术的发展。为了延年益寿寻找能够帮助道士们成仙的药,积累了很多药方,是中医药物学的宝贵资料。为了长生不老而训练的方法演化为太极拳、武术、气功等体育项目。民俗中对土地神、灶神、门神等各路神仙的崇拜,都来自道教。传统的中国画中出现了佛、道画的新品种;山水花鸟画追求"无为"境界,形成了淡泊、超脱的艺术风格。传统文学作品中产生出一批以佛、道为题材的作品,描述神仙、鬼怪的故事,带来了新的意境、文体,对中国通俗文学的形成产生了影响。

The influence of Daoism on Chinese culture is multifaceted, including an intimate relationship between it and many ancient branches of learning. Daoist priests, in order to attain immortality, did experiments on smelting gold and cinnabar amassing vast chemical knowledge. In order to promise longevity, they looked for medicines that would enable Daoist priests to become immortal, amassing a great number of medical prescriptions which are valuable data underlying Chinese medical pharmacology. In order to attain immortality, the methods they practiced evolved into tai-chi, martial arts, *qigong* and other physical exercises. The popular worship of all sorts of gods, including gods of the earth, hearth, door, etc., all originates in Daoism. New breeds of Buddhist and Daoist painting appeared among traditional Chinese painting. Mountain and river paintings or flower and bird paintings pursue a "non-action" realm, forming an artistic style around living a simple life and transcending worldliness. A batch of works taking Buddhism or Daoism as a theme appeared among traditional Chinese literary works, such as stories describing immortals or phantoms, which brought new literary forms and creative concepts, and influenced the formation of Chinese popular literature.

今天人们喜欢吃的豆腐,也是淮南王刘安(前179—前122)在炼丹药过程中发明的。

鲁迅(1881—1936)说"中国的根柢全在道教",认为最深刻地表现中国人的生活传统、最本质地反映古代中国人性的就是道教。

The bean curd many people like to eat today was discovered by Liu An (179 – 122 B. C.), the King of Huainan, while in the process of concocting medicines for immortality.

Lu Xun (1881 – 1936) said, "The root of China is entirely in Daoism," believing it was Daoism that most deeply expressed Chinese people's living tradition, and most fundamentally reflected ancient Chinese people's natures.

## 三、中西宗教比较
## Comparison of Chinese and Western Religions

### 1. 中西不同的宗教态度
### Different Religious Attitudes Between China and the West

在对待宗教的态度上,中国文化从一开始就倾向于入世和人伦的价值取向,不是很关注超越现实人生的来世的彼岸世界,具有人本的价值尺度。中国文化从诸子百家开始,基本上不系统讨论彼岸世界的问题,不系统论证一个人格化的神的存在问题,不大讨论神学问题,而讨论人与人关系的伦理学特别发达。这一点从孔子说"敬鬼神而远之"的时候就开始了,儒家把关注点放到了人身上,关注人伦道德,关注的是现实世界的人生际遇,强调的是"入世"。作为现代新儒学代表的梁漱溟在1949年11月出版的《中国文化要义》一书中,认为中国文化有十四大特征,其中第六条就是"几乎没有宗教的人生"。

In the attitudes treating religions, Chinese culture from the beginning has tended toward the value orientations of secular and human relationships, rather than overly concerned with the future world on the other shore that transcends human life. Chinese culture possesses a human-based value scale. Starting from the time of the Hundred Schools, Chinese culture did not systematically discuss the problem of the world on the other shore, nor systematically expound on the question of the existence of an anthropomorphized god, and rarely discusses theological questions. On the other hand, discussions on the ethics of interpersonal relationships are particularly well developed. This point started with Confucius saying, "While respecting ghosts and spirits, be distant from them." Ru-ists placed their point of interest on the personal, paying attention to the morality of human order, the ups and downs of one's life in the real world, emphasizing the secular. Liang Shuming (1893 – 1988), as a representative of the modern Neo-Confucianist, in his *Essentials of Chinese Culture* (November, 1949), believed Chinese culture has fourteen major characteristics, and number six among them is, "there is practically no religious life."

西方文化对待宗教的态度,表现出了对一个超越的彼岸世界的向往,在价值上是以神为本的,上帝是人的尺度。在基督教看来,尘世的超脱需要靠上帝,人的存在是有限的和罪性的,因而人类的自救和自我解脱是不可能的,人只能把得救的希望寄托于彼岸的上帝。人是灵魂和肉体的结合物,其中灵魂是属于上帝的,属于自己的只有肉体。对人来说,真正的幸福是彼岸天国的永生。

Western culture's treatment of the religious attitude is expressed in a yearning for a transcendant world on the other shore, and in terms of values, it regards God as the root of all things. God is the measure of humans. In the Christian view, one must rely on God to transcend the mortal world; human existence is limited and of a sinful nature, so humanity's self-salvation and self-extirpation is impossible. Humans can only entrust their hopes for salvation in God of the other shore. Humans are spirit and flesh integrations, among which the spirit belongs to God, and only the flesh belongs to oneself. As far as the individual is concerned, true happiness is eternal life in Heaven on the other shore.

## 2. 中西不同的宗教信念
### Different Religious Beliefs Between China and the West

中国文化关注现世多于来世,呈现出信仰的多元化、泛神化特征。信仰的核心不是宗教经典的约束,更多的是为自己求得现世生活中的福报。

Chinese culture pays attention to this life more than the next life, demonstrated through the pluralistic and animistic traits. The core of belief is not the constraints of religious scripture, but rather the karmic reward one tries to obtain for oneself in life in this world.

中国人对待宗教信仰缺乏真正意义上的超越精神与终极关怀,因此对待各种不同宗教的态度也较为宽容。既崇拜来自儒家的三皇、五帝、尧、舜、禹,以及天、地、祖先,也崇拜道教的三清尊神、玉皇大帝、王母娘娘,以及来自佛教的佛、菩萨等。总之,在中国民间的信仰习俗中,以上各路神仙的界限已经模糊了,民众对他们可以同时膜拜。所谓"见庙就烧香,见神就磕头"。无论是佛、菩萨还是神仙、圣人,无论是土地爷、财神爷还是关公,只要能保佑平安、赐福,都可以去拜,许多节庆活动和祭祀礼仪交融在一起，体现出多元化和泛神的宗教精神。

Chinese people's treatment of religious beliefs lacks a real, meaningful transcendent spirit and final concern, and so the attitude to the various different religions is comparatively tolerant. They worship the Three Sovereigns, Five Emperors, Yao, Shun, and Yu, and Heaven and Earth and ancestors, according to Ru-ist beliefs; they also worship the Daoist Three Clears Deity, Jade Emperor, and Queen Mother of the West from Daoism. Still, they worship the Buddha and Bodhisattvas from Buddhism. In the belief traditions among Chinese populace, the boundaries between the aforementioned supernatural entities are fuzzy, and the masses can worship them at the same time. As the saying suggests, "if you see a shrine, burn incense, if you see a god, prostrate". As long as it can protect one with peace and blessings, whether it is Buddha, Bodhisattva, an immortal or sage, or the Earth God, God of Fortune, or Lord Guan, they can all be paid respects. Many festival activities and sacrificial rites are blended together, reflecting the pluralistic and animistic religious spirit.

唐代以后，中国文化一个明显的走向是儒、佛、道"三教合流"。合流以后的中国文化以儒家传统的人伦价值观念和人生理想为核心，糅合了佛教注重心性修炼的思维和实践方式，加入了道教追求长生不老的诱惑，在宗教信仰方面就形成了一套多元化和泛神化的天人体系。

One clear direction in Chinese culture following the Tang Dynasty is the "Convergence of the Three Doctrines (Ru-ism, Buddhism, Daoism)". After the convergence, Chinese culture regarded traditional Ru-ist human ethical values and life ideals as the core, mixed together Buddhism's thought and practices emphasizing mental cultivation, and added the Daoist pursuit of immortality. This formed a set of pluralistic and animistic human-heaven systems with regards to religious belief.

在西方，宗教观念是一元神的上帝崇拜。无论是基督教（新教）、天主教、东正教，在基本的宗教观念上是一致的，认为统治宇宙万物的是绝对的、唯一的和至上的上帝，代表着永恒、完美、至善和绝对，掌握着人类的命运和世间的一切。宣称这个世界是上帝创造的产物，人世间的一切都是上帝预先安排和决定的。上帝观念是西方大多数人价值观和人生观的根基和支柱。

In the West, religious thought is about worship of a monotheistic God. Regardless of whether it is Protestantism, Catholicism, or Eastern Orthodox Christianity, they are uniform in the basic religious notion, believing the ruler of all things in the universe is an absolute, singular, and most high God. God represents the eternal, the perfect, the ultimate good and the absolute, and controls human fate and all things in the world. The world is a product of God's creation, and all things between humans and the world are preordained and decided by

God. The notion of God is the foundation and support for the vast majority of Western people's values and outlook on life.

## 3. 中西不同的宗教际遇
### The Different Ups and Downs of Religions in China and the West

因为儒家思想在中国传统文化中居于主导地位，宗教文化在社会政治生活中一直被边缘化，始终臣服于世俗的政治权力。在中国古代，王权在社会生活中处于一种绝对至上的地位，宗教一直处于附属的地位。如果要立足扩展，必须采取会通和改革的态度，这是佛教道德化和世俗化的开始。

Because Ru-ist ideas occupy the dominant position in traditional Chinese culture, religious culture has always been marginalized in socio-political life, all along serving secular political power. In ancient China, royal power was in an absolute supreme position in social life, and religion was always in a subsidiary position. If it wanted to gain a footing and expand, it had to adopt an attitude of getting involved and reforming. This was the beginning of the moralization and secularization of Buddhism.

北宋的时候，有一次，宋太祖（赵匡胤，927—976）到相国寺，走到佛像前烧香的时候，他不知道是否需要拜佛。因为，面对佛像如果不跪拜，则显不出敬佛的真心；可是一旦跪拜了佛像，则又失去了天子的威仪。宋太祖便问旁边陪同的赞宁（919—1001）和尚："你看，朕是拜佛呢，还是不拜佛？"赞宁和尚回答了一句："现在佛不拜过去佛。"巧妙的回答，突出了皇上的地位，还尊皇上为现世佛，把人间帝王的地位和天上佛的地位对等。于是，宋太祖将这个规矩定为正式的礼仪，故宋朝的历代皇帝在见到佛像时都不必跪拜。

在中国，世俗王权拥有独尊地位，绝不容许宗教越权。

而在西方，按照灵肉二分的原则，世俗政权管理人的肉身，灵魂则应该交给上帝。多数西方人也是按照这一点来处理生存与信仰的问题，通过宗教为自己的灵魂找到依托。

In the Northern Song, Emperor Taizu (Zhao Kuangyin, 927 – 976) went to the Xiangguo Temple one time, and when he approached the image of the Buddha to light incense, he did not know whether to kneel or not. If one does not kneel to worship the image of the Buddha, then one is not showing a sincere respect for the Buddha. But, if he knelt, he would then lose the majestic presence of the Son of Heaven. Taizu then asked Zanning (919 – 1001), the monk who was accompanying him, "What do you think? Should I kneel before the Buddha?" Zanning responded, "The Buddha of the present does not kneel before the Buddha of the past." This clever response gave prominence to the imperial position and honored him as the Buddha of the present, equating the position of the monarch among people with that of the

Buddha in Heaven. Hence, Taizu fixed this practice as the official ceremony, and successive Song emperors had no need to kneel when seeing an image of the Buddha.

In China, the existing secular royal power holds the dominant position, and absolutely does not allow religious arrogation.

In the west, based on the principle of the distinction between spirit and body, the secular political power manages the person's corporeal body, while the spirit should be delivered to God. The majority of Westerners also deal with the problem of existence and faith according to this principle. They seek support for their soul through religion.

**思考题**

1. 道教与道家的区别在哪里？
2. 汉传佛教与藏传佛教的区别是什么？
3. 比较中西不同的宗教态度。

***Questions***

1. What is the difference between Daoism and the Daoist School?
2. What is the difference between Chinese (Han) Buddhism and Tibetan Buddhism?
3. Compare the different religious attitudes between China and the West.

# 第六章　中国古代教育
# Ancient Chinese Education

## 一、古代教育制度
## Ancient Educational System

### 1. 学校教育机构
### School Education Organizations

中国古代教育制度主要是学校教育制度，在夏商周时期初步建立，到清末新式学堂建立，开始向近代教育逐步过渡。

The ancient Chinese educational system was primarily a school-based educational system preliminarily established in the Xia-Shang-Zhou period; the establishment of new-style schools at the end of the Qing was the beginning of the gradual transition toward modern education.

中国教育的目的，从汉代开始一直就是为了培养中央集权统治所需要的社会治理人才。学生学习的目的就是"学而优则仕"。中国人把是否做官作为衡量学习成败的标准，官越大越成功。因此，中国人尊师重教。

The goal of Chinese education ever since the Han Dynasty was for the development of talent for managing society as needed by the central ruling regime. The students' goal for studying was "if one is successful in studying one can be an official". Chinese people measured the standard of whether one succeeded in studies by whether one became an official, and the higher the official the more successful the study. So, Chinese people respect teachers and value education.

夏时已有正式的学校出现，以校、序、庠为学校的名称。西周时期，学校分"国学"和"乡学"两类。"国学"是大贵族子弟的学校，"乡学"是一般贵族子弟的学校。春秋时期私学出现后，学校自此分为官学、私学两大类别。到汉代，官学、私学并举，官学在中央设太学，是全国最高学府，以后历代沿用。地方上府、州、县、卫设立各级儒学，私学主要是由老师自己在家聚集学生授课。

Formal schools had already appeared in the Xia period, schools names being *xiao*, *xu*, or *xiang*. In the Western Zhou, schools were divided into "national schools" and "countryside schools". "National schools" were schools for the sons of high-level aristocrats; "countryside schools" were for the sons of ordinary aristocrats. After the appearance of private schools in the Spring-Autumn period, schools were divided into official schools and private schools. In the Han Dynasty, official and private schools developed simultaneously. The official schools set up an Imperial College of Supreme Learning at the capital as the highest educational establishment in the country, a practice that was followed in later dynasties. Ru-ist schools were established at all levels of province, prefecture, county, and township. Private schools mainly involved teachers themselves gathering students at their own house for lessons.

隋朝开始设置的国子寺，是中央专门负责管理教育的行政机构，下辖国子学、太学、四门学、书学、律学，唐代增加算学，共六学。唐代地方官学主要有府学、州学、县学三级学校。唐朝时，国子监是最高教育行政机关，宋元明清基本承袭。

The Sui Dynasty began establishing the "Office of the State's Sons", the central administrative organ that was specifically responsible for managing education. It administered State's sons education, the Imperial College, the Four Gates School, School of Letters, Law School, and the Tang added the Math School, for a total of six. In the Tang, the local schools were mainly at the province, prefecture and county level, and the highest educational administrative organ was the Imperial College. This was basically followed in the Song, Yuan, Ming and Qing.

唐宋时期是教育制度发展成熟的时期，随着科举制度的兴起，教育开始以服务于科举制度为学校的中心任务。

In the Tang-Song period the educational system developed to maturity. Following the rise of the imperial examination system, school-based education started to change so that their core task was in service to that examination system.

明清时期，学校教育制度基本沦为科举考试的附庸。中央官学不再分国子学和太学，也没有唐宋时期那么多的专科学校，地方官学有府、州、县学。到清朝末年（1905年）废除国子监，设立学部，并逐渐引进新式学制。

In the Ming-Qing era, the school-based educational system basically sank to being an appendage of the imperial examination system. Central official schools no longer distinguished the State's Sons' School from the Imperial College of Supreme Learning, and there were not as many specialized schools as in the Tang-Song period. Local official schools were at the province, prefecture and county level. In 1905 toward the end of the Qing, the Imperial College was eliminated and the Ministry of Education was established, gradually leading toward a new-style education system.

## 2. 学校教材
### Educational Materials in the Schools

学校的基本教材是儒家的经典著作四书五经。四书是《大学》《中庸》《论语》《孟子》，五经是《诗》《书》《礼》《易》《春秋》。后来发展为十三部，即"十三经"。到清朝末年学习西方，开始设置新式学校，教育从此逐渐和西方教育体系相连接。

The basic educational materials in schools were the Four Books and Five Classics, the classic works of the Ru-ists. The Four Books were *The Great Learning*, *The Golden Mean*, *The Analects*, and *The Mengzi*; the Five Classics were *The Book of Poetry*, *The Book of Documents*, *The Book of Rites*, *The Book of Changes*, and *The Spring and Autumn Annals*. This later grew to be thirteen volumes, or "The Thirteen Classics". Toward the end of the Qing, they began to learn from the West and set up new-style schools, and the curriculum gradually resembled the Western educational system.

学校教育方法上，继承孔子的教育思想，主张因材施教，言传身教，循序渐进，教学相长。学校注重道德教育，把对学生的道德培养放在第一位。

In terms of pedagogical methods, having inherited Confucius' educational theory, they advocated teaching in line with the student's ability, teaching by words and example, making steady progress incrementally, and they held the idea that when you teach someone, both the teacher and student will benefit. Schools paid attention to moral education, placing development of the students' moral character in the primary position.

## 3. 书院
### Academies

到了唐代，兴起了一种新的私学形式——书院。

书院是把教育、学术、藏书合为一体的文化教育机构。早期书院大多属于自由办学的私学，元代以后大多由政府控制，变成官学。最早的书院出现在唐代，最兴盛的时期是宋代，出现了著名的四大书院。

In the Tang Dynasty there arose a new form of private school—the academy.

Academies were cultural educational institutions that combined teaching, scholarship, and library collection into one entity. The early academies largely belonged to independent private schools, but after the Yuan they were largely controlled by the government and became official schools. The earliest academies appeared in the Tang, and academies most flourished in the Song when there appeared the famous Four Academies.

宋代四大书院是指江西庐山的白鹿洞书院、河南商丘的应天府书院、湖南长沙的岳麓书院和河南登封太室山上的嵩阳书院。

The Four Great Academies of the Song refer to the White Deer Cave Academy of Lushan, Jiangxi; the Yingtianfu Academy of Shangqiu, Henan; the Yuelu Academy of Changsha, Hunan; and the Songyang Academy in Taishi Mountain of Dengfeng, Henan.

书院地址大多选在山林风景区，主持人称"洞主"或"山长"。书院尊崇孔子，院内须立孔子像。书院不仅是学习的地方，士人们也是社会良知的代表，担当着社会道义。书院的这一特点，集中体现在明代顾宪成（1550—1612）为东林书院题写的一副对联上：

风声、雨声、读书声，声声入耳；
家事、国事、天下事，事事关心。

The academy locations were mostly chosen to be in scenic places among mountains and forests. The hosts were called "cave masters" or "mountain elders". The academies revered Confucius, and there was inevitably a statue honoring Confucius inside the academy. These were not only places to learn, the scholars also represented the social conscience, bearing the role of social morality. This characteristic of the academies is embodied in this couplet written for the Donglin Academy by Gu Xiancheng (1550 – 1612) of the Ming Dynasty:

"The sound of wind, of rain, or reading books; every sound enters the ear;
Family affairs, national affairs, the world's affairs; every affair is of concern."

1905年科举制度废除，书院被新式学堂代替。

In 1905 the imperial examination system was abolished, and the academies were replaced by new-style schools.

## 二、选官制度的演变
## The Evolution of the Official Selection System

中国古代的选官制度有一个演变过程。科举考试出现以前，选拔官员的办法主要有以下三种。

There was a developmental course of events in the system for selecting officials in ancient China. Prior to the appearance of the imperial examination system, there were basically the following three methods.

## 1. 世卿世禄制
### System of Hereditary Appointment

夏商周三代的官吏选拔主要是世卿世禄制，即当权者权力的位子由自己的后代世袭地继承，他们世世代代拥有权力和地位，享受各种经济特权。

Selection of officials in the Xia-Shang-Zhou period was primarily through the system of hereditary appointment. That is, the position of a person in power was inherited by his own descendants, so they had position and power generation after generation, enjoying all kinds of economic privileges.

## 2. 察举征辟制
### The Observe, Raise, Recruit, and Enlist System

两汉时期，主要推行察举、征辟制度。"察举"，又叫荐举，是三公九卿、地方郡国守相等高级官员根据考察，将有德有才的平民或下级官吏推荐给朝廷，授予他们官职或提高其官位。"征辟"，就是高级官吏把有声望、有才干的人推荐给朝廷，由朝廷聘任为官的称为"征"，由地方官聘用的称为"辟"。

The two Han dynasties primarily carried out this system. "Observe and raise" was also called "recommendation". The three dukes and nine ministers, local officials, national defense ministers and other high-ranking officials based on their own observations recommended common people or lower officials of talent and good moral standing to the imperial court who awarded them with official positions or raised their official position. "Recruit" refers to high-level officials recommending prestigious and talented people to the court, and the court appointing them as officials; those employed by local officials were "enlisted".

## 3. 九品中正制
### The Fair and Honest System of Nine Ranks

魏晋南北朝时期，由政府派中央官员到地方选拔人才，郡叫"中正"，州叫"大中正"，负责把当地人士按照品德才识分别评定为上上、上中、上下、中上、中中、中下、下上、下中、下下九等，中央再根据等级录用，也叫"九品官人法"。品评人只看门第出生高低，并不看重实际才能。选官的权力由世家大族控制，形成了"上品无寒门，下品无势族"的局面，到南北朝以后逐渐打破。

In the Wei-Jin Northern-Southern Dynasties period, officials were dispatched from the government to go to localities to select people of talent. Those that went to the counties were called "*zhongzheng*" (fair and honest) and those that went to prefectures were "da zhongzheng" (greatly fair and honest). They were tasked with evaluating the people in the localities according to their moral character and erudition based on a nine-rank system: upper-high, upper-middle, upper-low; mid-high, mid-middle, mid-low; low-high, low-middle, and low-low. The central government would then make hires based on these rankings. It was also called the "Nine-rank Official Method". In practice, the evaluators only looked at the family status and whether they were born high or low. They didn't care about real ability. The authority to select officials was controlled by powerful clans, forming a situation in which, "the upper ranks have no poor families, and the lower ranks lack powerful clans". The system was gradually smashed after the Northern-Southern States period.

## 三、科举考试制度
## The Imperial Examination System

隋朝建立初期，就开始了用科举考试选拔官员的制度。606年进士科的创设，标志着科举制度的开始，唐代进一步完善了该制度。这一新的选官制度同以前选官制度的根本区别在于允许读书人自愿报名参加官府的考试，这为广大中小地主及普通士人做官参政提供了可能。

In the early years of the Sui Dynasty they began to use the system of examinations to select officials. The establishment of the palace graduate division in 606 marks the beginning of the imperial examination system. The Tang further perfected it. The fundamental difference between the new system to select officials and the previous one is: allowing scholars to voluntarily sign up to participate in the official government examination, which provides the possibilities for the majority of landlords and ordinary scholars to participate in politics.

### 1. 科举制度产生的社会条件
### The Social Conditions that Produced the Imperial Examination System

科举考试制度之所以在隋唐时期形成，是因为具备了发生变化的社会条件。隋朝建立后，一方面，士族门阀势力衰落，中小地主势力得到加强，有了更多对政治权力的要求，注重门第选官的九品中正制已无法继续下去。同时官僚机构的完备，提供了补充大量官吏的可能。另一方面，隋唐时期物质生产水平的提高，也为科举制度的实行提供了必要的物质条件。唐代手工造纸已经较为普遍，书籍大量印行，笔墨制造水平得以提高，使读书人便于阅读、书写和参加考试。这一切都为科举制度的实行提供了物质基础。这些条件，促成了科举制度在隋唐时期形成。

The reason the examination system formed in the Sui-Tang period was because the period satisfied the social conditions for change to take place. After the establishment of the Sui Dynasty, the power of the land-owning class and rich-and-powerful families declined, and the power of small and mid-sized landlords increased, and they demanded more political power. The nine-rank system of picking officials that relied on family status could no longer continue. At the same time, the completion of the bureaucratic system supplied the possibility of filling a large number of official positions. Another aspect was the rise in levels of material production in the Sui-Tang period which supplied the necessary material conditions for implementing the examination system. The hand-made-paper industry was fairly widespread, books were printed in large numbers, and the manufacture of ink was raised to a new level, all of which made it easier for scholars to engage in reading, writing, and participating in exams. These conditions facilitated the formation of the examination system in the Sui-Tang period.

## 2. 科举制度的沿革
### The Course of the Examination System's Development

科举制度在其存在的 1300 年里，从内容到形式在不同时期都有着不同的发展与演变。

In its 1300 year existence the examination system had different growth and evolution in different time periods in terms of both content and form.

隋唐时期，科举制得到初创及完善。隋朝创建科举考试，为地方荐举与中央考试相结合。隋文帝仅设二科，由京官五品以上和地方总管、刺史荐举考生。

隋炀帝时扩大为十科。606 年开设进士科，以诗赋、试策进行考试，被认为是科举制正式确立的重要标志。

The Sui-Tang period was the startup and improvement period. The Sui Dynasty established the examination system as an integration of the recommendation by localities and central exam. The Wen Emperor of Sui (541–604) only set up two exams, and all the examinees were recommended by capital officials of the fifth rank and higher and by local managers and governors.

The Yang Emperor of the Sui (569–618) expanded this to ten exams. In 606 he opened the palace exam, carrying out the test with poetry composition and policy proposals. This is recognized as an important symbol of the formal establishment of the examination system.

唐代是科举考试制度化并逐步完善的时期。考试分常科、制科两种。常科考试每年举行，分秀才科、进士科、明书科、明算科等多种。考试人数最多的是进士科、明经科。进士科往往是百人中取一二名，明经科则是十取一二。进士科虽最难考，可是一旦考上，升官也很快，所以，许多宰相是进士科出身。

The Tang was a period of systemization and gradual improvement of the imperial examination system. Exams were divided into two kinds, regular exams and specialized exams. The regular exam was held every year, divided into such types as the county exam, palace exam, elucidator of texts exam, and elucidator of calculations exam. The exam with the most people was the palace exam and the elucidator of texts. Only one or two out of a hundred candidates passed the palace exam, while one or two out of ten passed the elucidator of texts exam. Although the palace exam was the most difficult, if one passed it, one rapidly ascended the ranks of the bureaucracy. Many of the prime ministers were palace exam graduates.

进士科很重要的一个考试内容，就是写诗作赋，这也是历史上唐代诗歌发达的原因之一。例如王勃、王维、白居易、韩愈、柳宗元、杜牧、李商隐等著名诗人，都是科举出身，且绝大多数都是进士。

One important part of the palace exam was composing poetry, one of the reasons Tang poetry was so highly developed. For example, Wang Bo, Wang Wei, Bai Juyi, Han Yu, Liu Zongyuan, Du Mu, Li Shangyin, and other famous poets, were all successful examinees, and the vast majority of them were palace exam graduates.

制科，就是皇帝临时设立考试科目来选拔需要的人才。

Special exams were ad hoc exams the emperor held to select people of talent he needed.

武则天（624—705）时又设立武举科，由兵部主持，选拔军事人才。

武则天时发明了考卷"糊名"（密封考卷上姓名）制，以能公平地选拔人才，为后世沿袭。今天考卷的匿名制就是来源于这个时候。

In Wu Zetian's (624 - 705) time the military exam was started, held by the Board of War to select military talent.

In Wu Zetian's time they invented the system of "sealed names" (sealing up the name of the candidate on the exam paper), so as to fairly select people of talent, which was followed in later dynasties. The modern anonymous exam-paper system was started in this period.

宋元科举制度基本沿袭隋唐。科目以进士科为重，增加殿试，由皇帝亲策。考试规则在"糊名"基础上实行匿名"誊录"，即另派抄书手将试卷用正楷誊录，使考官无法辨认考生笔迹，以保证公正阅卷。考试时"锁院"，严禁出入，以防作弊。

The Song-Yuan exams basically followed the pattern of the Sui-Tang. The palace exam was considered important, but they added a court exam, personally administered by the emperor. On top of the "sealed names" rule they carried out the anonymous "copied out" rule, which was to assign a copyist to copy out the exam papers, making it impossible for the test officials to identify candidates by their writing in order to ensure equitable exam grading. At the time of the exam, the test location was locked so no one was allowed to enter or exit as a way to guard against cheating.

元朝蒙古贵族有做官的特权,无须通过考试,所以开国之初不重科举。中期以后开科取士。不同的是考试结果分两榜发布:蒙古人、色目人为右榜,汉人、南人为左榜,元朝录取人数低于前代。

The Mongol nobility of the Yuan Dynasty had the right to be officials without passing exams, so at the beginning of the dynasty they did not put much emphasis on exams. After the middle period though, they started using exams to pick officials. What was different was that the results were reported on two lists: Mongols and "people with colored eyes" on the list on the right, and Han and southerners on the left. The number of accepted applicants under the Yuan was lower than in previous dynasties.

明代科举仅进士一科,考试分乡试(见图6-1)、会试、殿试(见图6-2、图6-3)三级。

连中三元:乡试第一名称解元,会试第一名称会元,殿试一甲第一名称状元,合称三元。连中三元,是科举场中的佳话,明代连中三元者仅二人而已。

Under the Ming there was only the palace exam, divided into three levels: provincial exam (see Figure 6-1), metropolitan exam, and court exam (see Figure 6-2, Figure 6-3).

"Getting all three *yuán*": The person with the highest score on the provincial exam was the *jièyuán*; the person with the highest score on the metropolitan exam was the *huìyuán*; the person with the highest score on the court exam was the *zhuàngyuán*; together they were the three *yuán*. Getting all three yuán was a story that circulated around testing places that captured people's imagination. In fact, there were only two people who accomplished the feat in the Ming Dynasty.

明代考试命题取四书五经中的文句,试卷用八股文体写作。

Ming exam essay topics were taken from lines in the Four Books and Five Classics, and answers were written in the form of the eight-legged essay.

1904年,清朝最后一次举行科举考试。

1905年,清政府宣布废除科举考试,科举取士与学校教育实现了彻底分离。从606年(隋大业二年)起实行1300年之久的科举制度正式结束。

In 1904, the Qing held the last imperial exam.

In 1905, the Qing government announced the imperial exam was abolished. Using exams to select officials was thoroughly separated from school-based education. The imperial examination system that began in 606 and lasted 1300 years was formally ended.

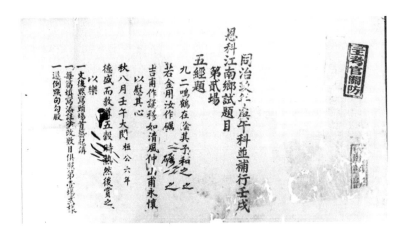

图 6-1 江南乡试题目，恩科，清代同治九年（1870 年）

Figure 6-1　Exam question from a Jiangnan Provincial beneficence exam in 1870

图 6-2　明代绘画中的殿试场景

Figure 6-2　Palace exam scene from a Ming Painting

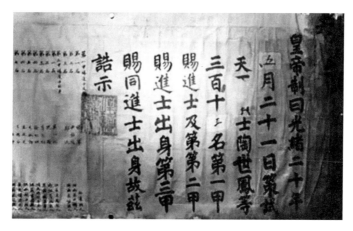

图6-3 殿试发榜，清代光绪二十年（1894年）5月21日
Figure 6-3 Exam List from May 21 1894

## 四、科举制度的影响
## Impact of the Examination System

### 1. 科举制度的积极意义
### Positive Aspects of the Examination System

首先，把选用官吏权力从世家大族收归朝廷，加强了中央集权制。

其次，以考试成绩而非出身选用官吏。科举考试的实行，改变了以往只有贵族才有资格参加的选官，让一般百姓走上仕途成为可能。让中小地主认识到只要自己努力读书，通过考试，做官就成为可以实现的目标。

First, it took the power to select officials away from powerful families and returned it to the court, increasing the power of the central regime.

Second, selecting officials was based on their exam scores rather than the circumstances of their birth. The implementation of the system changed the previous pattern in which only nobles were selected to be officials, so it allowed the possibility that commoners could become officials. Small and medium landlords recognized that if they worked hard at studying and passed the exam, then becoming an official became an attainable goal.

最后，推动了文化教育的普及。还有，和以前的选官制相比，科举制相对来说不容易作弊，客观公正。

Third, it made cultural education more widespread. Also, in comparison with previous methods of selecting officials, the exam system was more difficult to cheat and so it was objectively fairer.

英国在19世纪中期开始学习中国的科举取士,实行文官考试录用的办法,后来传播到欧美国家。

In the middle of the 19th Century, England learned from China and began using exams to select officials. They implemented the civil service exams, which later spread through Europe and the Americas.

## 2. 科举制度的消极影响
### Negative Effects of the Examination System

科举制的弊端,首先在于科举制把受教育和升官、发财直接联系起来。从此,天下读书人只知道读书、考试、做官,怀着"朝为田舍郎,暮登天子堂"的梦想,整日埋头读书,不务实学,只知道服从朝廷的安排,逐渐失去知识分子应该有的个性。

其次,科举考试偏重经书文章,忽略才干德行,束缚了士人思想的自由发挥。鸦片战争后,传统教育空疏无用的弱点日益暴露,清政府遂废科举,兴学校。

The corrupting influence was firstly in that the exams directly linked getting an education with becoming an official and getting rich. Because of this, every student simply thought about studying, exams and being an official, harboring the fantasy they would "in the morning be a farmhouse youth, and by night ascend to the emperor's court." Burying their heads in books, they didn't study practical things. All they knew to do was obey the court's arrangements, and so they gradually lost the individuality an intellectual should have.

Second, the exam system overly favored the classics and writing essays, neglecting ability and moral character; this restricted the free exhibition of scholars' thinking.

After the Opium Wars, the shallow, impractical weaknesses of traditional education were revealed day by day. The Qing government thereupon abandoned the exam system, and encouraged schools.

# 五、中西教育比较
# Comparison of Chinese and Western Education

中国古代教育自孔子开始就重视道德修养以及如何治理国家,不太重视自然科学知识。

欧洲教育的源头在古希腊、罗马,从一开始,欧洲教育比较突出的表现就是对知识的追求和探索。

Since the time of Confucius, ancient Chinese education has emphasized moral cultivation and the question of how to order society, but it did not emphasize knowledge of nature.

The origin of Western education lies in ancient Greece and Rome. From the beginning, the relatively prominent characteristic of European education was the pursuit and investigation of knowledge.

中国教育注重知识的积累,注重培养学生对知识和权威的尊重,注重对知识的掌握和继承。

西方教育则更重视学生运用知识的实际能力,注重培养学生对知识和权威的质疑、批判精神,注重对知识的拓展和创造。这反映出不同的教育观念。

Chinese education put emphasis on the accumulation of knowledge, cultivating student's respect for knowledge and authority, grasping it and carrying it forward.

Western education valued even more the practical ability to use knowledge, emphasizing the cultivation of the student's questioning and critical spirit with regard to knowledge and authority, paying attention to the expansion and creation of knowledge. This reflects different ideas of education.

中国教育重点是培养学生严谨、认真的精神,西方教育注意培养学生的自信、自主的精神。中国学生善于自我约束,固守规范,考虑周全,但是这也会成为创造性思维的障碍。

The focus of Chinese education was cultivating the student's spirit of rigor and conscientiousness; Western education emphasized cultivating the student's spirit of self-confidence and autonomy. Chinese students excel at self-constraint, clinging to standards, thorough consideration, but it also can become a barrier to creative thinking.

## 思考题

1. 为什么科举考试促进了唐代诗歌的兴盛?
2. 科举制度对中国社会产生了哪些影响?
3. 比较中西教育的培养目标有什么不同。

## *Questions*

1. Why did the examination system promote the flourishing of Tang poetry?
2. What influences did the examination system have on Chinese society?
3. What differences are there in the goals of Chinese and Western education?

# 第七章 中国古代文学
## Chinese Ancient Literature

在中国古代的文化书籍中，文学类作品远远多于其他类书籍。文学在中国古代文化中占据了非常重要的地位，魏晋以后的士大夫几乎人人都会写文学作品。在文学发达的唐宋时期，作家成为人数最多、身份最复杂的一个庞大群体，为世界文化史上所罕见。

Among ancient Chinese cultural works, literary works far outnumber those of other kinds. Literature occupies an extraordinarily important position in ancient Chinese culture. Virtually all scholars after the Wei-Jin period could write literary works. Writers in the Tang-Song period when literature flourished became an enormous community with the most people and most complicated identities, a situation rarely seen in the cultural history of the world.

## 一、中国古代文学发展进程简述
## Summary of the Growth of Ancient Chinese Literature

中国文学的历史，从有文字算起，已有了三千多年的历史。在文学的历史上，每一个朝代都有其代表性的文学形式，涌现出诸多杰出的文学作品、文学家。文学随着历史的进程，连续不断、持续稳定地向前发展，各类题材的文学作品、文学家灿若繁星。

The history of Chinese literature, starting from the invention of writing, is a history of over 3000 years. In that history, each dynasty had its representative literary form and put forth a good deal of outstanding literary works and writers. Following the course of history, literature grew onward in a steady, continuous march, and writers and literature on all subject matters were as splendid as the stars in the sky.

中国文学发展的初期，诗、文是主要样式。早期的诗来自民间，多数为民间创作。《诗经》305 首，即是经过采集删订而成的民间诗。以屈原（约公元前340—公元前278）为代表的楚辞，是在楚地风俗与楚地歌谣的文化土壤上产生的。屈原的作品，是最早士人的个人之作。文是文章，也是最早的文学样式。先秦诸子散文，以《孟子》《庄子》《荀子》《韩非子》为代表。

In the early period of Chinese literary development, verse and essays were the primary form. The early period verse came from among the common people, the majority of these pieces were folk creations. The *Book of Poetry*, a collection of 305 poems, mostly folk poems, was created through a process of collection and refinement. The *Songs of Chu* represented by Qu Yuan (340 – 278 B. C.) was born on the soil of Chu customs and Chu ballads. The works of Qu Yuan himself are those of the earliest individual poet. Essays, primarily literary essays, were also an early literary form. Among the essays of the various sages of the pre-Qin period, *Mencius*, *Zhuangzi Xunzi and Hanfeizi* are representative examples.

汉代文学的最主要成就是赋。赋这种文体,是在诗、骚的基础上发展起来的。以铺陈排比为主要手法的"大赋",是汉赋的主流,主要代表人物有司马相如(前179—前118)和扬雄(前53—公元18)等。

The main literary achievement of the Han Dynasty is the rhapsody (*fù*). The rhapsody developed on the basis of verse and *sāo* (a kind of metered writing most closely associated with Qu Yuan). The "Great Rhapsody" which uses lengthy description and parallelism as its primary technique, is the mainstream of Han rhapsody, and the works of Sima Xiangru (179 – 118 B. C.) and Yang Xiong (53 B. C. – 18 A. D.) are the primary representative writers.

魏晋南北朝时期,出现了著名山水诗人"大小谢"(谢灵运和谢朓)和田园诗人陶渊明(365—427)。

The famous "fields and gardens" poet Tao Yuanming (365 – 427) and landscape poets known as the "greater Xie and lesser Xie" (Xie Lingyun and Xie Tiao) appeared in the Wei-Jin Northern and Southern Dynasties period.

诗是唐代文学的代表,唐诗是我国诗歌发展的顶峰,诗坛群星灿烂,以李白(701—762)、王维(701—761)、王昌龄(698—756)、高适(704—765)、岑参(715—770)、杜甫(712—770)、白居易(772—846)、李商隐(813—858)、杜牧(803—852)等为代表。唐代散文以韩愈(768—824)、柳宗元(773—819)为代表。唐传奇是我国小说走向成熟的标志。

Verse poetry (*shī*) is the representative of Tang Dynasty literature. Tang poetry is the apex in the development of China's poetry, and the poetry community was as splendid as groups of stars, represented by Li Bai (701 – 762), Wang Wei (701 – 761), Wang Changling (698 – 756), Gao Shi (c. 704 – c. 765), Cen Shen (715 – 770), Du Fu (712 – 770), Bai Juyi (772 – 846), Li Shangyin (c. 813 – c. 858), and Du Mu (803 – 852). Tang literary essays are represented by Han Yu (768 – 824) and Liu Zongyuan (773 – 819). Tang *chuánqí* (short stories) are a major milestone on Chinese fiction's trend toward maturity.

词是宋代文学的代表,流派纷呈,风格各异,以柳永(约987—约1035)、苏轼(1037—1101)、秦观(1049—1110)、周邦彦(1057—1121)、李清照(1084—1155)、辛弃疾(1140—1207)、姜夔(1155—1221)等为代表。

Lyric poetry (*ci*) is the representative form of the Song Dynasty. Genres were brilliant and varied, and the styles were all different. The lyric poets are represented by Liu Yong (c. 987 – c. 1053), Su Shi (1037 – 1101), Qin Guan (1049 – 1100), Zhou Bangyan (1057 – 1121), Li Qingzhao (1084 – c. 1155), Xin Qiji (1140 – 1207), and Jiang Kui (1155 – 1221).

元曲,包括戏剧与散曲。戏剧最能代表元代文学成就,包括杂剧和南戏,以关汉卿(约1235—约1300)、王实甫(1260—1336)、马致远(1250—1321)、白朴(1226—1306)等人为代表。

Yuan opera included drama (*zaju*) and independent lyric (*sanqu*), and representative authors are Guan Hanqing (c. 1235 – c. 1300), Wang Shifu (1260 – 1336), Ma Zhiyuan (c. 1250 – 1321), and Bai Pu (1226 – 1306).

小说是明清文学的代表,出现了明代"四大奇书":《三国演义》《水浒传》《西游记》《金瓶梅》。清代的《儒林外史》《红楼梦》《聊斋志异》等作品成为不朽之作。戏曲中如明代汤显祖(1550—1616)的《牡丹亭》,清代洪昇(1645—1704)的《长生殿》、孔尚任(1648—1718)的《桃花扇》,都是经典之作。

Fiction is the representative form of Ming-Qing literature. In the Ming there appeared the "Four Marvelous Novels", i. e., *Romance of the Three Kingdoms*, *Water Margin*, *Journey to the West*, and *Plum in the Golden Vase*. The Qing works, *Scholars*, *Dream of the Red Chambers*, and *Strange Stories from a Chinese Studio*, became timeless classics. Among operas, the Ming's *Peony Pavilion* by Tang Xianzu (1550 – 1616) and the Qing's *Palace of Eternal Youth* by Hong Sheng (1645 – 1704) and *Peach Blossom Fan* by Kong Shangren (1648 – 1718), are classic works.

## 二、中国古代文学成就
## Literary Accomplishments of Ancient China

### 1.《诗经》与《楚辞》
### Book of Poetry and Songs of Chu

《诗经》是中国最早的一部诗歌总集,共收入自西周初年至春秋中叶(前11世纪

—前6世纪）的诗歌共305篇。按音乐类型分为风、雅、颂三个部分。风即《国风》，为地方小调，共160篇。雅即《大雅》《小雅》，是宫廷宴饮的乐歌，共105篇。颂即《周颂》《鲁颂》《商颂》，是宗庙祭祀的乐歌。

The *Book of Poetry* is China's earliest poetry anthology, collecting 305 poems from the Western Zhou to the Spring Autumn period (11<sup>th</sup> Century B.C. to 6<sup>th</sup> Century B.C.). Based on music type, they are divided into the following three major types：Airs, Elegentia, and Odes. Airs refers to the "Airs of the States", 160 pieces of folk poems from different places. Elegentia refers to the "Greater Elegentia" and "Lesser Elegentia", 105 pieces of poetry for music at court banquets. Odes refers to "Zhou Odes", "Lu Odes", and "Shang Odes", which are poetry for music at ancestral shrines sacrificial ceremonies.

先秦《诗经·国风·周南·关雎》是一首爱情诗：

关关雎（jū）鸠（jiū），在河之洲。窈（yǎo）窕（tiǎo）淑女，君子好（hǎo）逑。

参差荇（xìng）菜，左右流之。窈窕淑女，寤（wù）寐（mèi）求之。求之不得，寤寐思服。悠哉悠哉（aāi），辗（zhǎn）转反侧。

参差荇菜，左右采之。窈窕淑女，琴瑟友之。参差荇菜，左右芼（mào）之。窈窕淑女，钟鼓乐（yào）之。

The pre-Qin poem "Guan Ju", from the *Book of Poetry* (*Airs. Zhou Nan*) is a folk love poem：

"Guan, guan" cry the ospreys, on the islet in the river
The beautiful and good young lady, is a fine mate for the lord

Varied in length are the water plants, left and right we catch them
The beautiful and good young lady, waking and sleeping he wished for her

He wished for her without getting her, waking and sleeping he thought of her
Longingly, longingly, he tossed and turned from side to side

Varied in length are the water plants, left and right we gather them
The beautiful and good young lady, zithers and lutes greet her as friend

Varied in length are the water plants, left and right we cull them as vegetables

The beautiful and good young lady, bells and drums delight her

先秦《诗经·国风·周南·桃夭》是一首贺婚诗：

桃之夭夭，灼灼其华。之子于归，宜其室家。
桃之夭夭，有蕡其实。之子于归，宜其家室。
桃之夭夭，其叶蓁蓁。之子于归，宜其家人。

The poem "Tao Yao", from *Book of Poetry* (*Airs. Zhou Nan*) is an epithalamium (poem celebrating a marriage):

The peach tree is young and elegant;
Brilliant are its flowers.
This young lady is going to her future home,
And will order well her chamber and house.

The peach tree is young and elegant;
Abundant will be its fruits.
This young lady is going to her future home,
And will order well her house and chamber.

The peach tree is young and elegant;
Luxuriant are its leaves.
This young lady is going to her future home,
And will order well her family.

楚辞是战国时期在楚国兴起的一种新诗体，有浓郁的地方色彩及浪漫主义特点，代表作者是屈原、宋玉，《楚辞》是诗歌总集。

*Chu Ci* (the song of Chu) is a new poetic style that emerged in Chu during the Warring State period. It has strong local and romantic characteristics, the representative authors are Qu Yuan and Song Yu. *Chu Ci* is a collection of poetry.

屈原（约前340—前278）（见图7-1），战国时楚国人，曾经官居要职，后来被放逐。屈原的《离骚》内容丰富，是我国文学史上第一篇具有强烈政治倾向的抒情长诗，全诗大约有370多句，2400多字。诗歌表达了屈原对国家命运的关心，充满浪漫主义色彩，想象丰富，对我国诗歌的发展有深远的影响。

《离骚》的主题思想是忠君爱国,《离骚》运用了"香草美人"的比兴手法。

Qu Yuan (c. 340 – 278 B.C.) (see Figure 7 – 1), a person of Chu during the Warring States period, had once been an official in a key position, but was later exiled. The content of his *Li Sao* is rich; it is China's first long lyric poem that has strong political orientation. The poem is around 370 lines long, written with more than 2400 characters. It expresses Qu Yuan's concern for the fate of his country, and is permeated with a romantic tone and rich imagination. It had a profound influence on the growth of poetry in China.

The main idea of the *Li Sao* is loyalty to one's lord and love of one's country, and it uses the "Loyal, dependable person and the beauty" as its central metaphor.

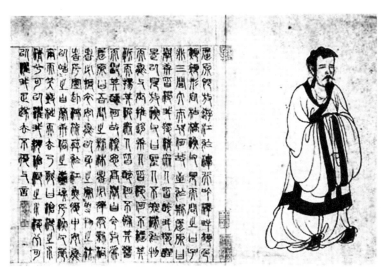

图 7 – 1  屈原(约公元前 340—公元前 278)
Figure 7 – 1  Qu Yuan

屈原的名句:

路漫漫其修远兮,吾将上下而求索。
举世皆浊我独清,众人皆醉我独醒。

Celebrated phrases from Qu Yuan:

The road is long, it's built into the distance; I will go up and down exploring.
All in the world is turbid, only I am clean; all the people are drunk, and only I am sober.

## 2. 先秦散文
**Pre-Qin Essays**

先秦散文主要分为历史散文和诸子散文两大类。

Pre-Qin essays are divided into two categories: historical essays and essays of the various philosophers.

历史散文：史官记录的史书，就是历史散文。主要有《左传》《国语》《战国策》等。《左传》是其中文学价值最高的一种，记载了春秋时代250多年间各国的政治、外交和军事行动，其中的人物都是真实的历史人物，丰富了传记文学的内容。

Historical essays are texts recorded by court scribes. These are primarily found in the *Zuo Zhuan*, *Guo Yu*, and *Strategies of the Warring States*. Among these, the literary value of the *Zuo Zhuan* is the highest. It records more than 250 years of political, diplomatic and military activities in the Spring and Autumn period using characters that are real historical people, enriching the biographical literature.

诸子散文：春秋战国时期，"士"阶层兴起，他们针对社会现实，提出各自的主张，展开论辩，形成了思想史上百家争鸣的局面，产生了以论说为主的诸子散文。
主要代表作有《论语》《孟子》《庄子》《荀子》《韩非子》等。

Philosophers' essays: The Warring States period saw the rise of the class of the *shi* (gentleman). They faced the social realities of their day, put forth their own positions about them and opened debate and discussion, forming the "Hundred Schools of Thought Contend" period in Chinese intellectual history. They produced philosophical essays that mainly rely on discussion and persuasion.

The main representative works are *Analects*, *Mencius*, *Zhuangzi*, *Xunzi*, and *Han Feizi*.

《论语》是语录体论集，记录的是孔子及其弟子的言行。

The *Analects* is a collection of sayings, recording the words and actions of Confucius and his disciples.

《孟子》是对话体的论集。主张儒家的"仁政"。论辩时多用比喻和寓言，例如"五十步笑百步""揠苗助长"等寓言故事。

The *Mencius* is a collection in the form of dialogues, advocating for Ru-ist "Humanistic Governement". It uses many metaphors and parables in the course of its arguments, such as "the person who retreats 50 paces laughs at the one who retreats 100" and "pull up the sprouts to aid the growth".

《庄子》是寓言体论集,主张顺应自然、清静无为,名篇是《逍遥游》。《庄子》的散文成就在先秦诸子散文中独树一帜,对后世文学的影响很深。

The *Zhuangzi* is a collection of essays characterized with fables. It advocates Daoists' following the nature, peaceful non-action, etc. One famous chapter is "Wandering Free and Unfettered". The *Zhuangzi*'s prose achievements stand out among the philosophical essays of the pre-Qin period, deeply influencing the literature of later generations.

荀子(前 310—前 237)是先秦最后一位儒家大师。荀子隆礼重法,所以他的弟子韩非(前 280—前 233)成为法家的代表。《荀子》善于使用比喻。《劝学》一篇最为突出,名句有:"青,取之于蓝,而青于蓝;冰,水为之,而寒于水。"《韩非子》收集了大量的寓言故事,著名的有《老马识途》《远水不救近火》《守株待兔》等等。

Xunzi (310 – 237 B.C.) was the last of the great pre-Qin Ru-ist teachers. Xunzi considered the rites as grand and the law as important, and so his disciple Han Fei (280 – 233 B.C.) became representative of the Legalist School. *Xunzi* is good at employing metaphors; the section "Quan Xue" is most notable. The *Han Feizi* collects a large number of narrative fables, famous among which are "The Old Horse Knows the Route" (an old hand knows the ropes), "Distant Water Does Not Extinguish Nearby Fires" (a slow remedy does not address the current emergency), and "Guard the Tree-stump Waiting for Rabbits" (wait idly for opportunities).

## 3. 汉乐府
### Han Music Bureau Poetry

"乐府"原是汉初采诗制乐的官署,这些采集来的歌谣和其他经乐府配曲入乐的诗歌即被后人称为乐府诗。汉乐府是继《诗经》之后古代民歌的又一次大汇集,是中国诗史五言诗体发展的一个重要阶段。

Originally, "the Music Bureau" was a state office in the beginning of the Han Dynasty charged with gathering folk songs and regulating music. The ballads the office collected and other poems that passed through the Music Bureau's office were matched with tunes and enrolled among the court's music, and later generations lumped them all together and called them Music Bureau Poetry. Following in line with the *Book of Poetry*, Music Bureau poetry is another collection of ancient folk poetry. It is also an important stage in the history of Chinese poetry in the development of the five-word-line poetic form.

《陌上桑》和《孔雀东南飞》都是汉乐府民歌,后者是我国古代最长的叙事诗,《孔雀东南飞》与《木兰辞》合称"乐府双璧"。

*Mulberry on the Foot Path* and *Southeast the Peacock Flies* are Music Bureau ballads, the latter being the longest narrative poem in ancient Chinese literature. *Southeat the Peacock Flies* and *The Ballad of Hua Mulan* are together referred to as the "Twin Jades of the Music Bureau".

## 陌上桑

Mòshàng sāng *Mulberry on the Foot Path*

(Translation by Joseph Roe Allen III, "From Saint to Singing Girl: The Rewriting of the Lo-fu Narrative in Chinese Literati Poetry", *Harvard Journal of Asiatic Studies* 48.2 (1988) p. 321 – 361)

日出东南隅，照我秦氏楼。秦氏有好女，自名为罗敷。罗敷喜蚕桑，采桑城南隅。青丝为笼系，桂枝为笼钩。头上倭堕髻，耳中明月珠。缃绮为下裙，紫绮为上襦。行者见罗敷，下担捋髭须。少年见罗敷，脱帽著帩头。耕者忘其犁，锄者忘其锄。来归相怨怒，但坐观罗敷。

使君从南来，五马立踟蹰。使君遣吏往，问是谁家姝？"秦氏有好女，自名为罗敷。""罗敷年几何？""二十尚不足，十五颇有余。"使君谢罗敷："宁可共载不？"罗敷前致辞："使君一何愚！使君自有妇，罗敷自有夫！"

"东方千余骑，夫婿居上头。何用识夫婿？白马从骊驹，青丝系马尾，黄金络马头；腰中鹿卢剑，可值千万余。十五府小吏，二十朝大夫，三十侍中郎，四十专城居。为人洁白皙，鬑鬑颇有须。盈盈公府步，冉冉府中趋。坐中数千人，皆言夫婿殊。"

The sun rises from the southeast quarter
To shine on the chambers of our Ch'in house.
The Ch'in family has a fine daughter,
She calls herself Lo-fu.
Lo-fu is skilled in silkworms and mulberry,
She picks their leaves south of the city wall.
Blue silk are her basket ties,
Cassia branches are her basket handles.
On the side of her head a hanging chignon,
In her ears bright moon-like pearls.
Yellow silk is her skirt,
Purple silk is her jacket.
When passers-by see Lo-fu,
They put down their loads and stroke their whiskers.
When young men see Lo-fu,

They doff their hats and adjust their hair-bands.
Those cultivating forget their hoes,
Those plowing forget their plows.
When they return home they complain,
All because they have seen this Lo-fu.

A Governor comes up from the south,
His five-horse team stops and lingers.
The Governor sends a runner,
Asking to whose house this beauty belongs.
The Ch'in family has a fine daughter,
She calls herself Lo-fu.
What is the age of Lo-fu?
Not yet a full twenty,
But somewhat more than fifteen.
The Governor asks Lo-fu
If she would like to ride with him.
Lo-fu answers straight to his face,
"How can the Governor be so foolish?
You already have your own wife,
And Lo-fu has her own husband.
In the east, in charge a thousand horsemen,
My husband is their leader.
And how would one recognize my husband?
On a white horse followed by a black yerling,
Blue silk binds his horse's tail,
Yellow gold halters his horse's head.
At shirt waist a sword with an ornate hilt,
It is worth more than a million.
At fifteen he was a Grandee,
At thirty he was a Palace Gentleman,
At forty he is Prefect Mayor.
He is one with fair clear skin,
And a fine light beard.
Stately he walks the halls of his office,
Slowly he moves about his residence.

Seated among a thousand others,
All say my husband is quite special."

## 4. 魏晋南北朝文学
### The Literature of Wei-Jin Northern and Southern Dynasties

政治上混乱的魏晋南北朝,却是文化上多元走向的时代。文学思潮与文学流派此起彼伏,从建安文学、正始文学、太康文学、玄言文学、田园山水文学、永明文学、宫体文学、北朝文学到南北朝乐府民歌,它们异象纷呈,各具风姿,远较两汉更有特色。就文学的主体而言,魏晋南北朝文学把目光更深刻地投向现实人生和个人的精神世界,从而使人成为文学的真正主题。

The politically chaotic Wei-Jin Northern and Southern dynasties, however, are the era of cultural diversity. The revolution of literature and literacy schools have emerged one after another, including Jian-An Literature, Zhengshi Literature, Taikang Literature, Xuanyan Literature, Idyllic Literature, Yongming Literature, Palace Style Literature, Northern Dynasty Literature, and Yuefu Folk Songs in the Southern and Northern Dynasties. They have distinctive differences, and far more distinctive than those in the Han Dynasties. As far as the main body of the literature is concerned, the literature of Wei-Jin Northern and Southern Dynasties have more focused on real life and the spiritual world of individuals, thus has made "human" become the real theme of literature.

建安"三曹七子":三曹指汉魏间曹操(155—220)与其子曹丕(187—226)、曹植(192—232),后人合称之为"三曹";七子,指建安年间(196—220)七位文学家,孔融(153—208)、陈琳(？—217)、王粲(117—217)、徐干(170—217)、阮瑀(约165—212)、应玚(？—217)、刘桢(？—217)。他们的诗与曹氏父子有许多共同之处。

The "Three Caos" and "Seven Masters" of Jian'an period: "Three Caos" refers to Cao Cao (155 – 220) of the Han-Wei transition and his sons Cao Pi (187 – 226) and Cao Zhi (192 – 232). The "Seven Masters" were seven literary talents of the Jian'an period (196 – 220): Kong Rong (153 – 208), Chen Lin (d. 217), Wang Can (117 – 217), Xu Gan (170 – 217), Ruan Yu (c. 165 – 212) Ying Yang (d. 217) and Liu Zhen (d. 217). The poetry of these seven talents had similarities to those of Cao Cao and his sons.

### 短歌行
### 东汉·曹操

*Short Song Style*

Cao Cao (Eastern Han)

对酒当歌,人生几何?譬如朝露,去日苦多。慨当以慷,忧思难忘。何以解忧?唯有杜康。青青子衿,悠悠我心。但为君故,沉吟至今。呦呦鹿鸣,食野之苹。我有嘉宾,鼓瑟吹笙。明明如月,何时可掇?忧从中来,不可断绝。越陌度阡,枉用相存。契阔谈䜩,心念旧恩。月明星稀,乌鹊南飞,绕树三匝,何枝可依?山不厌高,海不厌深。周公吐哺,天下归心。

I lift my drink and sing a song, for who knows if one's life is short or long
Man's life is like the morning dew, past days many future days few
The melancholy my heart begets, comes from cares I cannot forget
Who can unravel these sorrows of mine, I know of only one man, the God of Wine
Disciples dressed in blue, my heart worries for you
You are the cause of this song without pause
Across the banks a deer bleats, in the wilds where it eats
Honored guests I salute, strike the drums, and play the flute
Bright is the moon's sparkle; Will there be a time it can be grasped?
Thoughts of you from deep inside, never settling never ceasing
Friends drop by via a country road, the respect they pay really shows.
A long due reunion we feast, sharing past stories we possessed
The moon outshines the sparse stars; the crows fly to the south
Circling the tree three times; on what branch they find rest?
Mountains do not despise height; Seas do not despise depth
The sage pauses when guests call, so at his feet the empire does fall!

东晋陶渊明(365—427)是中国第一位田园诗人,被称为"古今隐逸诗人之宗"。

Tao Yuanming of the Eastern Jin (317 – 420) is China's first "field and garden" poet and has been called "the model for ancient and modern recluse poets".

## 饮酒·其五
东晋·陶渊明
*Drinking Wine—Number 5*
Tao Yuanming (Eastern Jin)

结庐在人境,而无车马喧。
问君何能尔,心远地自偏。
采菊东篱下,悠然见南山。
山气日夕佳,飞鸟相与还。
此中有真意,欲辨已忘言。

My home is built where other people live,
Yet there is no clamor from horses and carts.
One may ask, *Sir, how can this be*?
When the mind is distant, the place itself is remote.
While picking chrysanthemum beneath the eastern fence,
The South Mountain appears languidly into view.
The mountain atmosphere is fine as the sun sets;
Birds in flight return to roost with their companions.
Within all this is true meaning;
Though I wish to distinguish it, the words have already been forgotten.

## 5. 唐诗
**Tang Poetry**

唐代是中国古典诗歌的黄金时代,产生了许多著名的诗人和诗作。从数量来看,清代编订的《全唐诗》一共收录作者2200多人,诗歌48900多首,还有许多失散的作品没有收录。可谓名家辈出,也是人类文化史上的一大奇观。

The Tang Dynasty is the golden age of ancient Chinese poetry, producing numerous famous poets and poems. In terms of numbers, the *Quan Tang Shi* (*Complete Collection of Tang Poetry*) compiled in the Qing Dynasty includes 2200 poets and over 48900 poems, and there are many missing that were not included. So, one can call it an age when renowned masters came forth in large numbers. Truly, this is a great marvel in human cultural history.

唐诗之所以繁荣,主要有以下四点原因。
There are the following four primary reasons that poetry flourished in the Tang.

第一，唐朝国力富强，人民生活安定，这是唐诗繁荣的物质原因。
First, the Tang Dynasty was rich and strong, and the people's lives were peaceful; this is the material reason for the flourishing of Tang poetry.

第二，自东晋、十六国以来，边疆的少数民族不断进入中原地区，与汉族不断融合，使华夏民族有了新的气质和形态。
Second, since the Eastern Jin and the Sixteen Dynasties period, minority peoples on the border continuously migrated into the Central Plains and fused with the Han, causing the Hua-Xia people to have a new tempermant and form.

第三，唐代对外交通发达，和其他国家不同文化之间的文化交流，为中国文学输入了新鲜血液。
Third, the Tang had well developed diplomatic relations, together with cultural interactions among people of culturally different countries, which imported fresh blood for Chinese literature.

第四，科举考试的一项重要考试科目就是写作诗赋，写诗成为文人学士必须掌握的一项技能。
Fourth, one of the important parts of the imperial examination system was poetic composition, so writing poetry became a skill literati had to master.

唐诗的发展过程大致分为四个阶段，即初唐、盛唐、中唐和晚唐。
The development of Tang poetry is generally divided into four stages: Early Tang, High Tang, Mid-Tang and Late Tang.

## (1) 初唐时期 (618—712)
### The Early Tang Period (618 - 712)

代表诗人有王勃、杨炯、卢照邻、骆宾王，被称为"初唐四杰"。
Representative poets of the Early Tang are Wang Bo, Yang Jiong, Lu Zhaolin, and Luo Bingwang, who collectively are known as "The Four Great Poets of the Early Tang".

王勃（650—676），山西人，著名诗作有《送杜少府之任蜀州》，名句有"海内存知己，天涯若比邻"。其《滕王阁序》有名句"落霞与孤鹜齐飞，秋水共长天一色"。
Wang Bo (650 - 676) was a native of Shanxi, whose works include the famous "On Seeing Off Vice Prefect Du on His Appointment in Shu Prefecture" with the lines, "As long as there exists a close friend within the border, even if at the ends of the earth it is like they are

right next door". His "Prelude to the Pavilion of Prince Teng" is well-known for the lines, "Descending clouds at sunset fly off together with the lone duck; the river in autumn mirrors the color of the extended sky."

杨炯(650—693),陕西人,主要写边塞征战诗,如《从军行》《出塞》《战城南》等,名句有"宁为百夫长,胜作一书生"。

Yang Jiong (650 – 693) was a native of Shaanxi, who primarily wrote poems about frontier campaigns, such as *Traveling in the Army*, *Beyond the Frontier*, and *Fighting South of the City Wall*; famous lines include, "I would rather be the leader of a hundred soldiers, than act as a single intellectual."

卢照邻(637—689),河北人,代表作是《长安古意》,名句有"得成比目何辞死,愿作鸳鸯不羡仙"。

Lu Zhaolin (637 – 689) was a native of Hebei, whose representative work is *Thoughts on Old Chang'an*, with the famous lines, "As long as I am able to hold together with one that I love dearly, I would rather be an ordinary person and not envy the immortals."

骆宾王(619—684),浙江人,七岁就能写诗,写了《咏鹅》。曾经跟随徐敬业起兵反对武则天。

Luo Bingwang (619 – 684) was a native of Zhejiang, who was able to compose verse at the age of seven and wrote the *Song for the Goose*. At one point, he took up arms in rebellion following Xu Jingye (d. 684) against Wu Zetian (624 – 705).

咏鹅

骆宾王

*Song for the Goose*

Luo Bingwang

鹅,鹅,鹅,
曲项向天歌。
白毛浮绿水,
红掌拨清波。

Goose, goose, goose,
With craned neck sing to the skies,
white feathers float on green waters,
red feet paddle clear waves.

## (2) 盛唐时期（713—761）
### High Tang (713 -761)

国力强盛的盛唐时期也是唐诗最为繁盛的时期。盛唐诗歌以浑厚、雄壮为其风格特征。

The High Tang, when the country was rich and powerful, is also Tang poetry's most thriving period. Poetry in the High Tang has a vigorous and majestic style.

盛唐时期，作家辈出，作品丰富，流派众多，诗人中最负盛名者是李白和杜甫，韩愈评价杜甫和李白："李杜文章在，光焰万丈长。"

此外还有以写田园生活著称的王维、孟浩然等人，称为田园诗派；以写边塞生活著称的高适、岑参、王昌龄等人，称为边塞诗派。

Poets emerged in large numbers and grouped in numerous schools and styles. Among the most famous were Li Bai and Du Fu. Han Yu said, "With the literary works of Li and Du in existence, the light and flames reached lofty heights."

Also, there were such people as Wang Wei and Meng Haoran, widely known for writing about the bucolic life, and known as the school of "fields and gardens" poets. There were poets such as Gao Shi, Cen Shen, and Wang Changling who were widely known for writing about life on the frontier, and thus known as the school of frontier poets.

田园诗派以描写田园生活著称的王维、孟浩然为代表。

Wamg Wei and Meng Haoran here represent the "fields and gardens" poets.

### 送元二使安西
### 王维

### *Seeing off Yuan Er on His Mission to Anxi*
### Wang Wei

渭城朝雨浥轻尘，
客舍青青柳色新。
劝君更尽一杯酒，
西出阳关无故人。

Morning rain at the city on the Wei moistens the light dust,
the green of the willow appears so fresh on the guest house.
I urge you to finish one more cup of wine,
for west through South Pass there are no old friends.

## 春晓
### 孟浩然
*Spring Sleep*
Meng Haoran

春眠不觉晓，
处处闻啼鸟。
夜来风雨声，
花落知多少。

From my spring sleep I do not feel like waking,
yet everywhere I hear birds chirping.
Last night was the sound of wind and rain,
in which how many blossoms fell?

边塞诗派以写边塞生活著称的高适、岑参、王昌龄等人为代表。
Here, Gao Shi, Cen Shen, and Wang Changling represents the "frontier" poets, writing about life in the border areas.

## 从军行
### 王昌龄
*Traveling with the Army*
Wang Changling

青海长云暗雪山，
孤城遥望玉门关。
黄沙百战穿金甲，
不破楼兰终不还。

Extended clouds over Kokonor darken the snowy peaks,
The city wall gazes far into the distance at Jade Gate pass;
On yellow sands through 100 battles I have worn metal armor,
If we do not destroy Loulan, we will not return in the end.

"诗仙"李白（701—762），字太白，号青莲居士，祖籍甘肃。诗富于浪漫气息和理想色彩。代表作有《望庐山瀑布》《行路难》《蜀道难》《将进酒》《早发白帝城》等。

Li Bai (701－762), styled Taibai, with the assumed name Qinglian jushi, known as

"The Immortal Poet", was originally from Gansu Province. His poetry is full of a romantic flavor and idealistic character. Representative works include *Gazing on the Waterfall at Mt Lu*, *Traveling Is Hard*, *The Road to Shu Is Difficult*, *Invitation to Drink*, and *Setting out Early from Baidi City*.

**静夜思**

李白

*Quiet Night Thoughts*

Li Bai

床前明月光，
疑是地上霜。
举头望明月，
低头思故乡。

Bright moonlight in front of my bed
I suspect it is frost on the ground.
I raise my head to gaze at the bright moon
Then lower my head to think of my home town.

**望庐山瀑布**

李白

*Gazing on the Waterfall at Mt Lu*

Li Bai

日照香炉生紫烟，
遥看瀑布挂前川。
飞流直下三千尺，
疑是银河落九天。

Sun shines on Xianglu Peak giving rise to purple mist.
Looking at it from afar the waterful seems to hang like a river.
3000 feet of water vigorously dashing downward,
I suspect it is the Milky Way descending from the highest heaven.

"诗圣"杜甫（712—770年），字子美。"安史之乱"以后，杜甫经历动荡的生活，所以他的诗歌较多地反映了社会现实，他的诗就是一幅生动的历史画卷。代表作有《春望》《北征》《三吏》《三别》等。

Du Fu (712 –770), styled Zimei, known as "The Sage Poet", lived a life of upheaval following the "An-Shi Rebellion". His poems more generally reflect real social conditions, creating a kind of vivid historical picture scroll. Representative works include *Spring Gaze*, *Northern Expedition*, *Three Officials*, and *Three Farewells*.

春望

杜甫

*Spring Gaze*

Du Fu

国破山河在,
城春草木深。
感时花溅泪,
恨别鸟惊心。
烽火连三月,
家书抵万金。
白头搔更短,
浑欲不胜簪。

The capital is destroyed, but the rivers and mountains live on
The city in spring is overrun with grass and trees.
In times of sorrow, flowers are splashed with tears
Regretfully departing a bird startles my heart.
Warning fires have continued for three months
A letter from home is worth 10000 in gold.
The white on my head is even shorter from scratching
Though I want to, I simply cannot pin it up.

(3) 中唐时期(*762—835*)

***Mid Tang (762 -835)***

代表诗人有白居易、元稹、韩愈、柳宗元、贾岛(779—843)、李贺(790—816)、刘长卿(709—约786)、韦应物(737—792)、卢纶(739—799)等人。

白居易的诗歌题材广泛,语言通俗生动。代表诗作有《长恨歌》《卖炭翁》《琵琶行》《赋得古原草送别》等。

Representative poets include Bai Juyi, Yuan Zhen, Han Yu, Liu Zongyuan, Jia Dao (779 –843), Li He (790 –816), Liu Changqing (709 – c. 786), Wei Yingwu (737 –792), and Lu Lun (739 –799).

The subject matter of Bai Juyi's poetry is far ranging, and his language is common and lively. Representive works include *The Song of Everlasting Regret*, *The Old Charcoal Seller*, *Song of the Pipa Player*, and *Grass*.

**赋得古原草送别**

白居易

*Grass*

Bai Juyi

离离原上草,
一岁一枯荣。
野火烧不尽,
春风吹又生。

Green grass thriving on the plain,
Year after year withered then lush.
Wild fires can't burn you all away
The spring wind blows and you live again.

**早春呈水部张十八员外**

韩愈

*Early Spring – In Honor of Zhang Ji*

Han Yu

天街小雨润如酥,
草色遥看近却无。
最是一年春好处,
绝胜烟柳满皇都。

The streets of the capital in the light rain are shiny as butter;
Grass color looked at from afar up close turns out to be nothing.
This is the best time of the year, early spring
Far better than when the willow seeds fill the imperial capital.

## 江雪
### 柳宗元
### *River and Snow*
### Liu Zongyuan

千山鸟飞绝,
万径人踪灭。
孤舟蓑笠翁,
独钓寒江雪。

Thousands of birds fly away,
People have all disappeared on the road,
There is a man who wearing a palm-bark rain cape on the lonely boat,
Alone, he is fishing on the river in a cold snowy day.

### (4) 晚唐时期 (*836—907*)
### *Late Tang (836 -907)*

"小李杜"指李商隐(约813—约858)、杜牧(803—852)。杜牧的诗歌以七言绝句著称,代表诗作有《过华清宫绝句》《清明》《赤壁》《泊秦淮》《山行》等人。

The "Lesser Li Du" are Li Shangyin (c. 813 – c. 858) and Du Mu (803 – 852). Du Mu's fame is largely because of his seven-syllable quatrains; representative pieces include *Quatrain on Passing Huaqing Palace*, *Qingming*, *Red Cliffs*, *Anchored at Qinhuai*, and *Mountain Travel*.

### 山行
### 杜牧
### *Moutain Travel*
### Du Mu

远上寒山石径斜,
白云深处有人家。
停车坐爱枫林晚,
霜叶红于二月花。

The stone path on far off the cold mountain is steep;
In a spot deep within the clouds there is person's home.
I stop the carriage because I love the maple forest in the evening;
Frost on the leaves makes them more red than flowers in the spring.

夜雨寄北

李商隐

*A Poem Sent North in the Evening Rain*

Li Shangyin

君问归期未有期,
巴山夜雨涨秋池。
何当共剪西窗烛,
却话巴山夜雨时。

You ask my return date though it's not been decided.
Evening rain on Mt Ba swells the autumn pools.
When will we together clip the candle wick by the western window?
We will then speak of the evening rain on Mt Ba.

## 6. 宋词

## Song Lyrics

词是诗歌的一种。最初的词都是配乐来歌唱的,句子有长有短,便于歌唱。词兴于唐,盛于两宋。宋词数量巨大,《全宋词》里收录的有两万多首。

宋朝词人的创作风格大体上分为婉约派、豪放派两大类。

Lyrics are a kind of poetry. The earliest were set to music for singing, so line lengths are long and short to make singing convenient. Lyrics first became popular in the Tang Dynasty, but reached their flourishing stage in the Northern and Southern Song Dynasties. The number of them that survive from the Song is huge. The *Complete Song Lyrics* includes more than 20000 pieces.

Lyricists from the Song are generally divided into two categories: graceful and subdued, and bold and unconstrained.

### (1) 婉约派

### *The Graceful and Subdued School*

婉约,即婉转含蓄,主要内容侧重于儿女风情。主要代表人物有李煜(937—978)、柳永(984—1053)、周邦彦、李清照、姜夔等人。

The school has language that is indirect with implicit meanings, and such lyrics primarily are about amourous relationships between men and women. Representative poets of this school are Li Yu (937 - 978), Liu Yong (984 - 1053), Zhou Bangyan, Li Qingzhao, and Jiang Kui.

## 虞美人
### 五代·李煜
*To the Tune of "The Beauty Yu"*
Li Yu (Five Dynasties)

春花秋月何时了?
往事知多少。
小楼昨夜又东风,
故国不堪回首月明中。
雕栏玉砌应犹在,
只是朱颜改。
问君能有几多愁?
恰似一江春水向东流。

When do spring flowers and autumn moons meet their end?
How many past matters there are!
Again last night an east wind blew on the small tower,
Under this bright moon I can't bear to reminisce over the old country!
The carved balustrades and jade steps must still be there,
Only the folks I remembered will all have aged.
If you ask how sorrowful I can be,
It is like a river of vernal water flowing east.

## 如梦令
### 北宋·李清照
*To the Tune of "Like a Dream Writ"*
Li Qingzhao (Northern Song)

昨夜雨疏风骤,浓睡不消残酒。
试问卷帘人,却道海棠依旧。
知否?知否?应是绿肥红瘦。

Rain last night was sparse, but the wind sharp,
Deep sleep does not extinguish the cruelties of liquor.
I ask the one rolling up the curtain, who says the crabapple blossom is as it ever was.
Do you know? Do you know? It should be in full green with sparse red flowers.

## 钗头凤
*南宋·陆游*
*To the Tune of "Phoenix Hairpin"*
Lu You（Southern Song）

红酥手，黄縢酒，
满城春色宫墙柳。
东风恶，欢情薄，
一怀愁绪，几年离索。
错，错，错！

春如旧，人空瘦，
泪痕红浥鲛绡透。
桃花落，闲池阁。
山盟虽在，锦书难托。
莫，莫，莫！

Soft red hands, fine wine.

Willows growing at the palace walls fill the city with spring color.

The east wind is vicious and joy is meager,

When my mind thinks of melancholy, several years resurface from memory—

Wrong, wrong, wrong!

Spring is as it ever was, the person is thinner.

Her tears leave traces in rouge, thoroughly dampening the fine silk.

Peach blossoms fall leisurely into the courtyard pool,

Though our promise exists before the mountains and seas, it's difficult to trust in a letter from home—

No, no, no!

### (2) 豪放派
**The Bold and Unconstrained School**

豪放派词是士大夫所作的抒情诗，风格雄壮、豪放，主要代表人物有苏轼、辛弃疾。

This school refers to poetry composed by scholar-officials, stylistically majestic and powerful. Primary representative poets are Su Shi and Xin Qiji.

## 水调歌头
### 北宋·苏轼
*Prelude to Water Melody*
Su Shi (Northern Song)

明月几时有,
把酒问青天。
不知天上宫阙,
今夕是何年。
我欲乘风归去,
又恐琼楼玉宇,
高处不胜寒,
起舞弄清影,
何似在人间。

转朱阁,
低绮户,
照无眠。
不应有恨,
何事长向别时圆。
人有悲欢离合,
月有阴晴圆缺,
此事古难全。
但愿人长久,
千里共婵娟。

When will there be a bright moon?

I raise a glass to ask the clear sky.

In the Heavenly Palace

I do not know what year this night is.

I want to ride the wind to return,

Yet also fear the bejeweled Jade Palace,

Highly placed and unbearably cold,

So starting to dance I make fun with clear shadows.

How can it compare to the mortal world?

Turning around the vermillion room, descending into the carved window, and shining on the sleepless...

It ought not to have a grievance. Yet why is it round when people have departed?
People have sorrows, joys, separations, and reunions,
Just as the moon is dark, clear, full, and crescent.
This business has always been difficult.
I only wish people endured,
And though miles apart can join in appreciating the moon.

## 江城子
### 北宋·苏轼
*To the Tune "Son of the River City"*
Su Shi (Northern Song)

十年生死两茫茫。
不思量，自难忘。
千里孤坟，无处话凄凉。
纵使相逢应不识，
尘满面，鬓如霜。

夜来幽梦忽还乡。
小轩窗，正梳妆。
相顾无言，惟有泪千行。
料得年年断肠处，
明月夜，短松冈。

Ten years full of life and death—
Don't think on it; it will be hard to forget.
Her solitary tomb is miles away, I have no place to talk of my melancholic mourning.
If by chance to meet, I presume we won't recognize each other, as dust of the world covers my face and my temples are all white.

In a deep dream last night I hurried back to my hometown.
In a small pavilion window you were grooming.
Looking at each other without speaking, only tears streamed down thousands of trails.
Thinking on it year after year, that heartbreaking place,
The bright moon at night shines on the mound with the lone pine.

## 丑奴儿·书博山道中壁
南宋·辛弃疾
*To the Tune "Clown boy" —Written on the Wall on the Road to Mt. Bo*
Xin Qiji (Southern Song)

少年不识愁滋味，
爱上层楼。
爱上层楼，
为赋新词强说愁。

而今识尽愁滋味，
欲说还休。
欲说还休，
却道天凉好个秋。

In my youth I knew not the flavor of melancholy
I adored ascending towers
I adored ascending towers
To express new lyrics in which I force out speech on melancholy.

Yet now I know the flavor of melancholy in full,
I wish I could say I still did not
I wish I could say I still did not
And speak of the cold weather this fine autumn.

## 7. 元曲
## Yuan Opera

元曲包括杂剧和散曲两部分。

杂剧在元代极为盛行。它把歌唱、舞蹈、念白、杂技等多种艺术形式融为一体表演，剧本主要由唱词、对白、动作三个部分组成，一般分为四场表现一个完整的故事。

Yuan Opera includes *zaju*, a kind of musical drama, and *sanqu*, verse or songs from theatrical performances.

*Zaju* was exceedingly popular in the Yuan. It combined many kinds of artistic performances, such as singing, dancing, dialogue, and acrobatics, into a single show. The screenplays are made up of three elements: verse to songs, dialogues, and actions; and, a complete performance was usually divided into four acts.

散曲，是歌曲的词，用来清唱和阅读。

*Sanqu* is the lyrics to songs, which can be sung in an opera or read aloud.

元代著名的剧作家200多人，剧目700多种。主要代表作家及其代表作有关汉卿（约1235—约1300）《窦娥冤》、马致远（约1250—约1321）《汉宫秋》、王实甫（1260—1336）《西厢记》、白朴（1226—1306）《墙头马上》、纪君祥《赵氏孤儿》等。《赵氏孤儿》在18世纪传入欧洲，被改编成《中国孤儿》上演。

There were over 200 famous playwrights in the Yuan Dynasty with over 700 plays. The primary representatives and their representative works are: Guan Hanqing (c. 1235 – c. 1300) *The Injustice to Dou E*; Ma Zhiyuan (c. 1250 – c. 1321) *Autumn in the Han Palace*; Wang Shifu (1260 – 1336) *Romance of the West Chamber*; Bai Pu (1226 – 1306) *Pei Shaojun and Li Qianjin*; Ji Junxiang (Late 13th Century) *The Orphan of Zhao*. In the 18th Century, *The Orphan of Zhao* was imported into Europe, where it was performed with the title *L'Orphelin de la Chine* (*The Chinese Orphan*).

王实甫《西厢记》写的是相府的小姐崔莺莺和穷书生张珙的爱情故事。两人一见钟情，但是遭到崔莺莺母亲的反对，后来在崔莺莺的侍女红娘的帮助下，最终结合。所以，后来人们把恋爱、婚姻的中间介绍人也叫作"红娘"。《西厢记》的故事也表达了"愿天下有情人终成眷属"的美好愿望。

The *Romance of the West Chamber* by Wang Shifu is a love story between Ms Cui Yingying, from a minister's family, and a poor student named Zhang Gong. It was love at first sight for the two of them, but they ran into opposition from Yingying's mother. Later, with the help of Yingying's servant, "Red Girl", they were able to get together in the end. Thus, up to modern times, a person who acts as a go-between for an affair or a marriage is called a "red girl". The story of *Romance of the West Chamber* expresses the beautiful wish that "love will find a way" for everyone in the world.

元杂剧体现出的一个特征是以浪漫的理想化方式处理现实主义的题材。例如《窦娥冤》中的弱女子窦娥，被恶霸贪官迫害，含冤致死，但是死后申冤。《赵氏孤儿》写春秋时期忠臣赵盾被奸臣诬陷后，赵家300余人被斩尽杀绝，奸臣还要追杀赵家孤儿以斩草除根。一批仁人志士想方设法制止追杀，最后赵氏孤儿得到保护，正义得到伸张。元杂剧最后的结局大多都是圆满的结局，是"大团圆"，并成为写作套路。

马致远是元朝散曲成就最高的作家。

One characteristic embodied in Yuan *zaju* is the use of romanticized, idealized ways to deal with realistic material. For example, the weak woman Dou E in *The Injustice of Dou E* is exploited by the evil, corrupt official, such that she is hounded to a wrongful death. But, after her death her injustices are redressed. *The Orphan of Zhao* writes of Zhao Dun, the loyal minister in the Spring and Autumn period, who is entrapped by a treacherous official. His family, all 300 members, are to be decapitated to exterminate the clan. To completely eliminate the clan, the orphan of the Zhao family is pursued by the traitor. A group of people with lofty ideals devise plans to stop the chase, and in the end the orphan is protected and righteousness is upheld. The final scene of a *zaju* is generally a perfect conclusion, the "great reunion" that also became routine in written works.

Ma Zhiyuan is a writer with the highest achievements in Yuan *sanqu*.

秋思<br>
元朝·马致远<br>
Autumn Thoughts<br>
Ma Zhiyuan (Yuan Dynasty)

枯藤老树昏鸦,
小桥流水人家,
古道西风瘦马。
夕阳西下,
断肠人在天涯。

Dried vines, an old tree, a crow in the evening light.
A small bridge, flowing water, a farmhouse.
An ancient highway, the western wind, a thinning horse.
The late day sun sets in the west;
The person who breaks my heart is far away.

## 8. 明清小说
## Ming-Qing Fiction

明清时期是中国小说的繁荣时期,出现了中国文学史上最伟大、最有影响力的四部古典小说:14世纪的《三国演义》《水浒传》,16世纪的《西游记》和18世纪后期的《红楼梦》,被誉为中国文学四大古典名著。

The Ming-Qing period was Chinese fiction's most prosperous period. The four classical novels, the greatest, most influential novels in Chinese literary history, appeared: *Romance of the Three Kingdoms* and *Water Margin* in the 14th Century, *Journey to the West* in the 16th Century, and *Dream of the Red Chambers* in the 18th Century. These have been acclaimed as the four great classical works of Chinese literature.

《三国演义》的作者是罗贯中（约1330—1400年）。这是一部章回体长篇历史演义小说。小说描写了东汉末年大小军阀发展势力，扩展地盘，为争夺全国统治权而展开斗争的故事。其中曹操（155—220）、刘备（161—223）、孙权（182—252）各据一方，争夺的结果是三家谁也消灭不了对方，最后建立三国：曹操儿子在北方建立魏国，刘备在四川地区建立汉国（世称蜀汉），孙权在长江中下游地区建立吴国，历史进入三国鼎立时期。

*Romance of the Three Kingdoms* was written by Luo Guanzhong (c.1330 – 1400). It is a type of traditional Chinese history novels with captions for each chapter. The novel described the growing power of greater and lesser warlords in the end of the Eastern Han as they expanded their territory and carried out wars to contest ruling authority over the whole country. Cao Cao (155 – 220), Liu Bei (161 – 223), and Sun Quan (182 – 252) each occupied one area, and the results of their struggle is that none was able to eradicate the others and three kingdoms were established. Cao Cao's son Cao Pi set up the Wei Kingdom in the north, Liu Bei set up the Shu Kingdom in Sichuan, and Sun Quan set up the Wu Kingdom in the middle and lower Yangtze valley. With that, the country entered the Three Kingdoms period.

小说反映了动荡时代里群雄逐鹿的历史画面，描绘了壮观的战争场面，刻画了许多栩栩如生的人物，每个人物都有其独特的个性。典型人物有智慧、奸诈的曹操，足智多谋的诸葛亮，英勇、忠义的关羽，勇猛粗犷的张飞，知人善任的刘备，等等，他们都已经成为家喻户晓的人物。见图7–2。

The novel reflects the historical tableau of great heroes pursuing prizes in a time of turmoil. It describes magnificent battle scenes and portrays many vivid characters; each character is drawn with a unique personality. The prototypical characters are the knowledgeable and devious Cao Cao, the wise and strategic Zhuge Liang, the brave and loyal Guan Yu, the bold, crude and violent Zhang Fei, and Liu Bei, who is expert at appointing the right people. These characters have all become household names (see Figure 7 – 2).

《水浒传》的作者是施耐庵（1296—1371）。这是一部描写农民起义的长篇小说，反映的是北宋末年宋江等人起义反抗官府的故事，写出了"官逼民反"的社会现实。一共描写了12世纪初期的108位英雄好汉，塑造了宋江、武松、林冲、鲁智深、李逵等性格各异的典型人物，他们是一群志同道合、充满正义的绿林好汉。其中"武松打虎"等故事家喻户晓。见图7–3至图7–6。

*The Water Margin* written by Shi Nai'an (1296 – 1371) is a novel that describes a peasant rebellion. What it reflects is the story of the final years of the Northern Song when Song

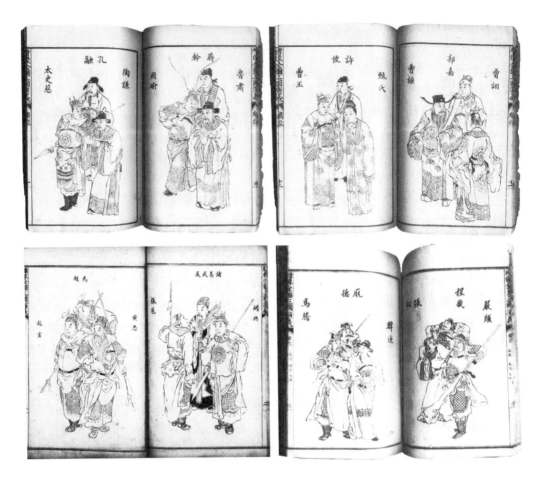

图 7-2 《三国演义》人物图（清光绪善本·点石斋）

Figure 7-2　Portraits of the characters from the *Romance of the Three Kingdoms* (from the Qing Guangxu edition by Dianshi Studio)

Jiang and others rose up in opposition to official authorities, describing the social reality of "government officials driving the people to revolt". All together it describes 108 heroes from the early 12$^{th}$ Century, modeling Song Jiang, Wu Song, Lin Chong, Lu Zhishen, Li Kui and others as prototypical characters. They are a group of Robin Hood style heroes with kindred spirits and righteousness. Among the episodes related in the novel, the story of "Wu Song fights a tiger" is known to everyone (see Figure 7-3—Figure 7-6).

第七章 中国古代文学

图 7-3 《水浒传》人物——行者武松
Figure 7-3 *Water Margin* character—Wu Song the Pilgrim

图 7-4 《水浒传》人物——双枪将董平
Figure 7-4 *Water Margin* character—Dong Ping the Two-speared General

图 7-5 《水浒传》人物——神算子蒋敬
Figure 7-5 *Water Margin* character—Jiang Jing the Counting Expert

图 7-6 《水浒传》人物——一丈青扈三娘
Figure 7-6 *Water Margin* character—Hu Sanniang Ten Feet of Blue

《西游记》的作者是吴承恩（约1506—1583年）。《西游记》是一部充满神奇色彩的长篇神话小说，描写了唐代僧人玄奘（602—664）在徒弟孙悟空、猪八戒、沙僧的保护之下，远赴天竺（印度）取经的故事。他们一路上降伏妖魔，与魔鬼怪兽作战，历经八十一难，最终到达印度，取回真经。故事充满了奇特的想象，中心人物是石猴孙悟空。他机智勇敢、行侠仗义、正直无私。还有贪吃的猪八戒、踏实的沙和尚，以及唐僧骑的白马，都很受人们喜爱。孙悟空大闹天宫时高喊"皇帝轮流做，明年到我家"，反映了现实社会人们的幻想。"孙悟空三打白骨精"、"猪八戒背媳妇"等故事广为流传（见图7-7、图7-8）。

*Journey to the West* written by Wu Cheng'en (1506 – 1583) is a long, legendary novel full of magical flavor. The novel portrays the Tang Dynasty monk Xuanzang (602 – 664) who, with the help of his disciples Sun Wukong (Monkey), Zhu Bajie (Pigsy), and Sha Seng (Sandy), travels west to India to get Buddhist scriptures. All along the route they vanquish demons, do battle with devils and monsters, experiencing 81 trials in total. In the end they arrive in India and retrieve the true scriptures. The story is full of unusual fantasy. The central character is the stone monkey Sun Wukong, who is resourceful, brave, chivalrous, upstanding and unselfish. There is also the gluttonous Zhu Bajie, solid Sha Seng, as well as White Horse who is ridden by Xuanzang, all of whom are much loved by the people. In the episode in which Sun Wukong "wreaks havoc in heaven", he yells out, "The emperor serves in turns, next year come to my house," reflecting the fantasy of real people. Also, the stories of Sun Wukong Fighting the White Bone Spirit and Zhu Bajie Carrying a Wife on His Back, and many others, are widely retold and well known (see Figure 7-7, Figure 7-8).

图7-7 《西游记》电视剧照，1986年版

Figure 7-7 Photo from the Television Show *Journey to the West* from 1986

图 7-8　《西游记》壁画（明朝）
Figure 7-8　Mural of the *Journey to the West* (Ming Dynasty)

图中的人物从右至左为唐僧、沙和尚、猪八戒、孙悟空。出自陕西渭南韩城大禹庙。

The characters from right to left are Xuanzang, Sha Seng, Zhu Bajie and Sun Wukong. From the Temple to Yu the Great in Hancheng, Weinan, Shaanxi Province.

《红楼梦》的作者是曹雪芹（1715—1763）。《红楼梦》是一部杰出的古典长篇小说，以贾宝玉、林黛玉、薛宝钗三人的悲惨爱情故事为主要线索，描写了贾、史、王、薛四大家族由盛而衰的过程，塑造了薛宝钗、王熙凤、袭人等四百多个人物的形象。

*Dream of the Red Chambers* was written by Cao Xueqin (1715 – 1763). This is a remarkable classical novel. It takes the tragic romance of Jia Baoyu, Lin Daiyu, and Xue Baochai as the main narrative thread and describes the process of going from flourishing to decline among four large clans, the Jia, Shi, Wang, and Xue, and portrays more than 400 characters including Xue Baochai, Wang Xifeng, and Xi Ren.

小说主要内容是讲一个生活在有很多女孩子和女佣人的富裕之家的公子贾宝玉，爱上了他的表妹林黛玉，但是贾家不赞成，结婚的时候，贾宝玉被欺骗娶了表姐薛宝钗。小说较为全面而真实地反映了清朝中期中国南方的社会现实。

《红楼梦》是中国古代文学中最优秀的现实主义巨著。

The main contents of the novel discuss Jia Baoyu, a son of nobility living in a wealthy family among many young women and female servants. He falls in love with a cousin, Lin Daiyu, but the Jia family does not approve, and when it is time to marry, he is tricked into marrying another cousin, Xue Baochai. The novel comprehensively and realistically reflects the social reality of mid-Qing China.

*Dream of the Red Chambers* is the most outstanding monumental work of realism in ancient Chinese literature.

## 三、中西文学比较
## Comparison of Chinese and Western Literature

中西方文学内涵不同,风格各异。大体上来说,传统中国文学以抒情为主,重视作者个人的主观情意的表达。西方古典的文学传统则更加关注反映客观现实,以此来认识人们的生存状态与生活中的真善美。

There are differences in content among Chinese and Western literature, and each of their own style. Generally, traditional Chinese literature relies mainly on expression of emotion, emphasizing the subjective, friendly expression of the individual writer. The western literary tradition, on the other hand, pays more attention to reflecting objective reality and by means of this becoming familiar with the conditions of the people's existence and life's truth, goodness, and beauty.

### 1. 神话比较
### Comparison of Myths

神话文学主要描写人类诞生、宇宙起源、氏族英雄以及洪水、猛兽等内容,但是具体表现却有很大不同。

Mythological literature primarily describes such contents as the birth of humankind, the origin of the universe, clan heroes, as well as floods and ferocious beasts. However, the concrete manifestation of these things is very different.

#### (1) 自然神和社会神
#### *Natural Gods Versus Social Gods*

中国神话中的神灵以自然神为主,有天神、地神、山神、河神、日神、月神、动物神、植物神等。汉代以前就写成的《山海经》中,仅山神就有四五百之多。

Supernatural entities in Chinese mythology are mainly natural gods, so there are such gods as the God of Heaven, God of Earth, Mountain Gods, River Gods, Sun God, Moon God, Animal Gods, and Plant Gods. In the *Classic of Mountain and Sea* written before the Han Dynasty, there are four to five hundred different mountain gods alone.

与此相对,西方神话中的神灵以社会神为主,例如命运女神阿忒洛波斯、报复女神涅墨西斯等,都是人类观念的化身。自然神也兼社会神,如太阳神阿波罗,兼管战争、农业、医药等；月神阿尔忒弥斯，监管分娩等。神话作品大多折射出的是社会现象和人际关系，如希腊生活中的仇杀、爱情故事，含有较多的社会因素。

In contrast, supernatural entities in Western mythology are primarily based on social gods. For example, the goddess of fate Atropos, the goddess of revenge Nemesis, etc., are all incarnations of human concepts. Gods of nature also serve as social gods. For example, Apollo, god of the Sun, also manages warfare, agriculture, medicine, etc.; God of Luna Artemis also oversees parturition, etc. Mythological works generally reflect social phenomena and interpersonal relationships. For example, stories of revenge killings and romance in Greek life contain relatively numerous social elements.

(2) 对神灵的不同道德要求
***Different Moral Requirements for Supernatural Entities***

中国神话中的神灵大多是道德楷模，例如黄帝、大禹等。黄帝是善良和正义的化身，是后世帝王的师表。中国神话表现出强烈的伦理意识，侧重于现世道德教化，神灵往往被改造为道德偶像的"圣"。

Supernatural entities in Chinese myths are generally moral models, as in the Yellow Emperor and Yu the Great. The Yellow Emperor is the incarnation of goodness and justice, the exemplary character for monarchs of later generations. Chinese myths express a strong ethical consciousness, particularly emphasizing real moral education. The supernatural entities always become refashioned into "sages" that are moral idols.

西方神话中的神灵，并不比人更有道德，只是比人更有力量、更美，是一种美的理想。神灵们有优美的形体、卓越的智慧，是人类的生活理想。如俊美的太阳神阿波罗，威严的宙斯，睿智的女神雅典娜，美丽的神后赫拉，等等。这些神灵大多具有双重品质，例如宙斯既威严又荒淫，赫拉既端庄又有嫉妒心，道德上都不完满，但是个性丰满，令人亲近。

Supernatural entities in Western myths are not necessarily more moral than humans; they are simply stronger or more beautiful than humans, a kind of aesthetic ideal. Gods have exquisite forms, outstanding knowledge, and reflect the ideal life of humankind; as in the handsome Sun God Apollo, the awe-inspiring Zeus, the Goddess of Wisdom Athena, and the beautiful Hera, wife of Zeus. These gods generally all have a dual character, like Zeus who is both awe-inspiring, but also licentious, or Hera who is both beautiful, but also jealous. None of them are morally perfect, but they are full personalities, causing one to feel close to them.

## 2. 诗歌比较
### Comparison of Poetry

中国古代文学"抒情言志"的宗旨在诗歌中表现得最充分,而西方文学中诗歌形成了以叙事为主的史诗传统。

The ancient Chinese literary goal of "expressing emotion and speaking of ambition" is most fully expressed in poetry. Poetry in the Western tradition formed the epic tradition that mainly relies on narration.

抒情是中国诗歌的本质特征。诗歌追求的艺术境界不是真实而是空灵,不是形似而是神似。中国文学的源头是《诗经》《楚辞》,内容都是以抒情为主。例如《诗经》中的名句"蒹葭苍苍,白露为霜,所谓伊人,在水一方……"等等。

Expression of emotion is the basic characteristic of Chinese poetry. The artistic world pursued in poetry is not a real one, but one of exquisiteness; not similar in shape and appearance, but similar in expression and spirit. The fountainheads of Chinese literature are the *Book of Poetry* and *Chu Ci*, and the contents of both are primarily about expressing emotions, as in the famous line from the *Book of Poetry*, "Thick grow the rush leaves; their white dew turns to frost. He whom I love, must be somewhere along this stream...", etc.

西方最早的诗是叙事诗,最完美的诗的形式就是史诗。西方文学的源头是《荷马史诗》与《圣经》。《荷马史诗》以重大的历史事件为题材,以英雄人物为中心,规模宏大的叙事方法,让我们可以看到希腊民族的形成和发展。

The earliest poetry in the West was narrative, and the most beautiful poetic form was the epic. The fountainheads of Western literature are the Homer's Epic and *The Bible*. *Homer's Epic* uses important historical events as their subject matter, is centered on heroic characters, and employs a large-scale narrative technique, allowing us to see the formation and growth of the Greek people.

## 3. 塑造的人物形象比较
### Comparing Portrayal of Characters

群雄同在、集体为重的人物特征是中国古典小说描写人物时的主要方法。中国文化在宗法制度影响下,以群体为本位,重视群体关系,轻视个体自我。体现在文学作品里,大多数以写一群人物为主。例如《水浒传》里的一群梁山好汉;《三国演义》里曹操、刘备、诸葛亮、关羽、张飞等一群英雄;《红楼梦》里贾宝玉、林黛玉、王熙凤、薛宝钗等一群人物;虽有核心角色,但和出场的群体一起构成了作品的主体。

In describing characters in ancient Chinese fiction the primary method is characterized as the importance of the collective and the heroic group existing together. Under the influence of the patriarchal system, Chinese culture regards the groups as the basic unit, emphasizing group relationships, somewhat scornful of the individual and ego. As manifested in literary works, the great majority of them write about groups of characters; e. g. , the group of heroes on Mt Liang in the *Water Margin*, or the group of heroes, Cao Cao, Liu Bei, Zhuge Liang, Guan Yu, and Zhang Fei in *Romance of the Three Kingdoms*; or the group of characters in *Dream of the Red Chambers* Jia Baoyu, Lin Daiyu, Wang Xifeng, Xue Baochai, etc. Although there are central roles, the group that enters the stage together forms the main subject of the piece.

与之相对,个性张扬、英雄为主的人物描写方法是西方文学作品的主要目标。西方文化基本上是以个人为中心,追求个性解放,探索自我存在的价值。体现在文学形象上,主要描写具有独特个性的人物,即以"英雄"为主线的叙事模式。例如《红与黑》里的于连,《王子复仇记》里的哈姆雷特,《堂·吉诃德》中的堂·吉诃德,等等。

On the contrary, western literary works' character portrayal mainly relies on heroes and individual display. Western culture basically takes the individual as the center, pursues individual liberation and the value of self-existence. As manifested in literary figures, it lies in primarily describing uniquely individual characters; that is, the narrative model that takes the hero as the main thread; e. g. , Julien in *Le Rouge et le Noir*, or Hamlet in *Hamlet*, or Don Quixote in *Don Quixote*.

**思考题**

1. 朗诵一首你喜欢的唐诗或宋词。
2. 观看电视剧《红楼梦》(1986年版)。
3. 比较西方和中国传统文学作品有哪些不同特点?

***Questions***

1. Recite your favorite Tang poem or Song lyric.
2. Watch the 1986 TV adaptation of *Dream of the Red Chambers*.
3. Compare different characteristics of traditional Chinese and Western literatures.

# 第八章 中国古代书法、绘画
## Ancient Chinese Calligraphy and Painting

中国艺术里的书法、绘画、音乐、戏曲等，从艺术作品的美学风格上来看，都有着追求意境的特点。中国艺术在儒家"温、良、恭、俭、让"的中庸思想影响下，注重情感表现的委婉与节制，追求怨而不怒、哀而不伤、乐而不淫的温柔敦厚的含蓄表达。西方艺术则崇尚刚性之美，提倡英雄主义与悲剧精神，在艺术作品中充满了率性、浪漫、博大的气势。本章及后文关于书法、绘画、音乐、戏曲等内容能让我们感受到中国艺术追求"中和"的审美理想。

Chinese arts, such as calligraphy, painting, music, and opera, from the perspective of the works' aesthetic style, all possess the characteristic of seeking a creative concept. Under the influence of Ru-ist ideas of the Golden Mean, including "tender, good, respectful, frugal, and yielding", Chinese art emphasizes tactful and moderated emotional expression, in pursuit of the tender, honest implicit expression of "blame but not anger", "deep feeling but not mawkishness", "joyful but not licentious". Western art, on the other hand, reveres rigid beauty, advocating heroicism and the tragic spirit, and the art is filled with a willful, romantic, broad grandeur. From the content of the following sections on calligraphy, painting, music and opera, we can get a sense of the "central harmony" aesthetic ideal pursued in Chinese art.

## 一、书法
## Calligraphy

世界文化领域，汉字、藏文、阿拉伯文等，都把书法作为了一门艺术。

把书写汉字作为一种艺术，就叫"书法"，书法历来与绘画并列，合称"书画"。书法作为一门艺术出现在汉末魏晋时期。受中国书法的影响，用过或仍使用部分汉字的日本和朝鲜半岛等地区也讲书法，日本称之为"书道"。

Among writing cultures in the world, Chinese character, Tibetan writing, and Arabic writing, etc. all regard calligraphy as an art form.

Calligraphy is the writing of Chinese characters in an artistic way. Historically, it has been on par with painting, and they are often discussed together. As an art form, calligraphy appeared in the late Han and Wei-Jin period. Under the influence of China, areas such as Japan and the Korean peninsula that use, or have used, Chinese characters also are particular about calligraphy. In Japan it is called *shodō* "the way of writing".

## 1. 书法的工具
### The Tools of Calligraphy

书法的书写工具是文房四宝：笔、墨、纸、砚。在后来的使用过程中，文房四宝越来越富于赏玩性、装饰性。宋代开始，文房四宝不仅是书画工具，而且是颇富文人情趣的工艺品。不论写文章还是绘画，每一个中国古代文人都离不开这四样东西。

The implements used for calligraphy are the "four treasures of the study": brush, ink, paper, and inkstone. Later the four treasures have become more and more enjoyable and decorative. From Song Dynasty, the four treasures are not only the tool of calligraphy and painting, but also crafts to show scholars' interests. Whether writing an essay or painting, every ancient Chinese literatus could not be apart from these four things.

### (1) 毛笔
#### Brush

传统上用来写字的工具是毛笔，一般用狼、羊等动物毛制成（见图 8 - 1）。按笔头大小，毛笔可分为大、中、小三种，俗称大楷笔、中楷笔、小楷笔，春秋战国时期已经开始普遍使用毛笔。

Traditionally the tool used for writing was the brush, generally made from the hair of a wolf or sheep (see Figure 8 – 1). Based on the size of the tip, brushes are divided into three kinds: large, medium and small; commonly referred to as the large-model brush, medium-model brush, and the small-model brush, respectively. The widespread use of brushes had already begun in the Spring and Autumn, and Warring States periods.

图 8 - 1　清朝乾隆时期玉管珐琅斗毛笔

Figure 8 – 1　Jade Shaft with Enamel Cup Brush from the Qianlong Period

(2) 墨汁
## *Ink*

制作墨的原料一般取自松烟,墨色乌黑而有光泽,捏成方、圆各种形状的墨块,使用的时候将墨块用水研磨成墨汁使用。汉魏以后,制墨技术愈益精良,到宋朝,徽州府(今安徽省黄山地区)成了全国的制墨中心,以徽州产的"徽墨"最好(见图8-2)。

The raw material for making ink is generally taken from pine soot. The color is jet-black yet has luster. It is kneaded into ink blocks that are square or round. The block is ground into ink using water when it's time to write. After the Han and Wei periods, ink manufacture became increasingly refined, and by the Song Dynasty, Huizhou Prefecture (the present Yellow Mountain Prefecture) in Anhui Province became the center of ink manufacture in the country, so the best ink was considered to be "Anhui Ink" made in Huizhou (see Figure 8-2).

图 8-2　徽墨
Figure 8-2　Anhui Ink

(3) 宣纸
## *Xuan Paper*

毛笔书写的传统用纸是宣纸(见图8-3)。宣纸是唐、宋年间留传下来的一种手工纸,唐代开始使用,最好的纸产自宣州府(今安徽省泾县),故因地得名宣纸。宣纸的特点是轻、薄、柔韧性强、纯净、不易被虫蛀、不褪色。宣纸是自古以来可以保存时间最长的纸,所以有"纸寿千年"之说。

The paper traditionally used for brush calligraphy is called *xuānzhǐ* (Xuan paper) (see Figure 8-3). It is a kind of hand-made paper which has been used since Tang and Song times. The best kind of this paper is made in Xuanzhou Prefecture (modern Jing County, Anhui Province), which is why it is called "*Xuan* paper". This paper is light, thin and with a strong pliability; it is not easy to be damaged by moths or worms and it is colorfast. Since ancient times it is the paper that can be preserved the longest, so it is said to be "the paper with a thousand year lifetime".

图 8-3 宣纸
Figure 8-3 *Xuan* paper

品质良好的宣纸看上去颜色洁白，抓在手里像一团绵；听声音，用手把宣纸提起来，轻轻摇一摇，好宣纸发出的声音柔和、绵软；有良好的吸水性，能较快地吸收墨汁，又能适当扩散墨液。墨汁干后，画面尚能保持润湿的感觉，墨色乌黑鲜艳，不发灰色，纸面平整不褶皱。尤其在拓片制作方面，宣纸的柔韧性表现突出，专门制作拓片的宣纸，贴在凹凸不平的表面上，反复敲打，依然能够保持伸缩自如、裂而不断的完美状态。

The quality *Xuan* paper is pure white in color and feels like cotton to the touch. If you pick it up and gently shake it, good *Xuan* paper sounds gentle and silky soft. It has a good ability to absorb water, and takes up ink readily. It also has the ability to diffuse ink appropriately. After the ink dries, the surface still keeps a sense of being wet; the ink is jet-black, not fading to gray; and the surface stays smooth, not crinkling. The pliability of *Xuan* paper comes to the fore especially when used for making rubbings from a tablet. The paper that is especially manufactured for rubbings is stuck to the uneven surface and then repeatedly beaten on, and it is still able to preserve its flexible, smooth, bending-but-not-breaking appearance.

宣纸具有胶性，将字体写入宣纸内，待墨迹晾干后，把晾干字迹后的生宣纸泡在清水里，即使泡上半天，着墨的生宣纸也不会发生跑墨现象，即墨汁不会因为水的浸泡而化开。

The paper also has a kind of stickiness. After writing characters on the paper and letting the ink dry, if you soak the paper with dried characters on it in clear water, even if you soak it for a good long time, the ink will not run. There is not problem with the ink dissolving in the water.

### (4) 砚台
### Ink Slabs

墨必须加水研磨、调和之后才能使用，用来研磨墨块的器皿就叫砚台，一般用石块等耐磨材料制成，最常见的是石砚（见图 8-4）。砚台除了实用之外，因为可以雕刻花纹图案，所以还有收藏、观赏的价值。三大名砚是：端砚，产于广东端溪；歙砚，产于安徽歙县；洮砚，产于甘肃临洮。

Ink must be mixed with water and milled before it can be used, and the thing on which ink is ground is an ink slab (yan). Since ink slabs are generally made from wear resistant materials, such as stone, the most commonly seen slabs are ink stones (see Figure 8-4). In addition to being useful, because they can be carved with beautiful designs, they also have value as collectibles to be appreciated. The three most famous inkstones are: Duanyan, made in Duanxi, Guangdong Province; Sheyan, made in She County, Anhui Province; and, Taoyan, made in Lintao, Gansu Province.

图 8-4　雕席地龙纹钟禄松花方砚·清朝

Figure 8-4　Square Inkstone of Green Marble, Bell-shaped with Deer, Dragon Design on Mat Pattern (Qianlong era, Qing Dynasty)

## 2. 书法的类型
## Categories of Chinese Calligraphy

书法从字体类型上可分为篆书、隶书、楷书、行书、草书五类。

Based on the form of the characters, there are differentiated five categories: seal script, official/clerical script, regular script, running/semi-cursive script, grass/cursive script.

(1) 篆书

***Seal Script***

篆书分为大篆、小篆。篆书保存有象形文字的特点，笔法直线较多，字形修长，笔画均呈粗细划一。

Seal Script has great seal and small seal. Preserving the characteristics of pictographic writing, there are comparatively more straight lines, the characters are long and slender, and the strokes present a unified thickness.

《石鼓文》（见图 8-5），字体属于大篆，秦朝时期刻在石头上的文字，因为石头外形像鼓而得名，出土于陕西省宝鸡，现收藏于北京故宫博物院石鼓馆。

*Stone Drum Text* (see Figure 8-5), the characters are in the Great Seal style, a text carved on stone in the Qin Dynasty. Because the stone's outer appearance was that of a drum, thus it is named "Stone Drum Text". Unearthed in Baoji, Shaanxi Province, it is currently stored in the Stone Drum Hall of the Palace Museum in the Forbidden City in Beijing.

图 8-5 《石鼓文》·秦朝

Figure 8-5　Great Seal *Stone Drum Text*

释文：吾车既工，吾马既同，吾车既好。

The characters in the picture read, "My chariot has been built, my horse has been equipped. My chariot is already fine…"

《宋枢密副使赠礼部尚书孝肃包公墓铭》（见图 8-6），包拯墓碑铭文。包拯即包青天、包公（999—1062 年），北宋宋仁宗（1010—1063）时任监察御史，官至枢密副使（最高军事机构的副长官），去世后被赠（追封）为礼部尚书，赠"肃孝"谥号。包公墓在他的故乡安徽省合肥市。

Lord Bao Tomb Inscription (see Figure 8-6), the inscription on the tomb of Bao Zheng (999-1062), also known as Bao Qingtian. He served as censor in the time of Emperor Renzong (1010-1063) of the Northern Song, rising to the rank of assistant to the Privy Council (assistant commanding officer of the highest military institution). After his death, he was posthumously made the Director of the Board of Rites and given the name Xiaosu. Lord Bao's tomb is in his hometown of Hefei City, Anhui Province.

图 8-6 《宋枢密副使赠礼部尚书孝肃包公墓铭》·北宋

Figure 8-6 Seal Script, "Inscription on the Tomb of Lord Bao, Song Assistant to the Privy Council, posthumously named Xiaosu Director of the Board of Rites"

(2) 隶书

### Clerical or Official Script

隶书在东汉时期定型并流行，因而称为汉隶，隶书结构扁平、工整。

The Clerical script's design was finalized and became widely used in the Eastern Han Dynasty, and so it is also known as "Han clerical". Clerical script is planar in structure, careful and neatly composed.

汉隶《曹全碑》（见图 8-7）全称为《汉郃阳令曹全碑》，东汉汉灵帝 185 年立，记述曹全（字景完）功绩。出土于陕西郃阳县，现收藏于陕西西安碑林博物馆。

Han clerical *Cao Quan Stele* (see Figure 8-7), its complete title is *Stele of Cao Quan, Magistrate of Han's Heyang County*. It was erected in 185 AD under Emperor Ling (156-189) of the Eastern Han commemorating the achievements of Cao Quan (styled Jingwan). It was excavated in Heyang County, Shaanxi Province, and is currently stored in the Beilin Museum, Xi'an, Shaanxi.

图 8-7 《曹全碑》·东汉

Figure 8-7 Han Clerical *Cao Quan Stele*

释文：君讳全，字景完，敦煌效谷人也，其先盖周之胄。

The text in the picture reads: The gentleman's given name, Quan, is to be avoided; he was styled Jingwan, a native of Xiaogu, Dunhuang; his ancestors were descendants of the Zhou.

(3) 楷书

**Regular Script**

楷书形体方正，笔画平直，可作楷模，故称楷书。楷书字体端正，现在通行的汉字手写正体字就是楷书。

Regular Script：square in form, the strokes are level, and can be used as a model. Regular script's calligraphic style is upright and regular. The modern characters in circulation are in regular script when handwritten in traditional style.

楷书的代表作是唐代颜真卿的《颜勤礼碑》（见图 8-8），笔力深沉，端庄雄伟，大气磅礴。《颜勤礼碑》是颜真卿在 71 岁时为自己的曾祖父颜勤礼写的墓碑，是现在中国书法界楷书入门的经典范本。颜真卿的颜勤礼碑，被认为有"雄强的美"，现收藏于陕西碑林博物馆。

Representative of the "regular script" is the *Stele for Yan Qinli* by Yan Zhenqing (709 – 784) of the Tang Dynasty (see Figure 8 – 8). The brush work is profound, dignified, and impressively majestic. The "Stele for Yan Qinli" is the gravestone written for his paternal great-grandfather, Yan Qinli, when Yan Zhenqing himself was 71 years old. It is the classic model for the contemporary Chinese calligrapher's introduction to regular script. Yan Zhenqing's "Stele for Yan Qinli" (regular script), known to have "the beauty of the bold and powerful", currently preserved in the Beilin Museum, Xi'an, Shaanxi.

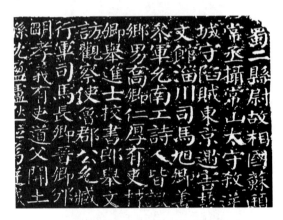

图 8 – 8　颜勤礼碑（楷书）（唐代颜真卿）
Figure 8 – 8　Yan Zhenqing's "Stele for Yan Qinli" (Regular Script)
图中文字前两句是：蜀二县尉，故相国苏颋……常丞摄常山太守杀逆……城守陷贼东京遇害……

楷书《胆巴碑》全名为《大元敕赐龙兴寺大觉普慈广照无上帝师之碑》，碑文记述元朝帝师哲布尊丹巴的功德事迹（见图 8 – 9）。"大觉普慈广照无上帝师"就是哲布尊丹巴，被皇帝尊为帝师，故又称《帝师胆巴碑》，字体严谨秀美。此碑是元仁宗延祐三年（1316 年）奉敕书写，时赵孟頫年 63 岁，写有感怀诗："齿豁头童六十三，一生事事总堪惭，惟余笔砚情犹在，留与人间作笑谈。"现收藏于北京故宫博物院。

Regular Script, *Dampa Stele*, known in full as *Stele for the Imperial Preceptor, the Greatly Enlightened Whose Universal Kindness Broadly Shines and Is Unsurpassed, Ordered by the Great Yuan to Be Bestowed on Longxing Temple*. The inscription describes the merits of the Yuan imperial's teacher Dampa (see Figure 8 – 9). The Imperial Preceptor, The Great Enlightened One Whose Universal Kindness Broadly Shines and Is Unsurpassed is Jetsun Dampa, who was honored as the imperial preceptor (teacher), and thus it is also called the "Imperial Presceptor Dampa Stele". The calligraphic style is rigorous and elegant. The stele was written and submitted to the emperor in the third year of the Yanyou Reign (1316) of Emperor Renzong (Buyantu Khan) of the Yuan Dynasty. When Zhao Mengfu wrote it, he was 63 years old, and he attached a sentimental poem that reads: "With cracked teeth and head like a child I am 63 years old; everything I've done my whole life has always been pitiful; only when I am with brush and inkstone is there still some passion; so I leave this among the living to serve as an object of ridicule." It is currently preserved in the Palace Museum in the Forbidden City.

图 8-9 《胆巴碑》（楷书）（元朝赵孟頫）
Figure 8-9 *Dampa Stele*, Regular Script, by Zhao Mengfu, Yuan Dynasty.

### （4）行书
***Running Script***

行书：介于楷书、草书之间，近于草书的称行草，写得比较端正平稳，近于楷书的称行楷。

Running Script: Running script is intermediate between regular and grass/cursive. The running type closer to cursive is known as "running grass", while the style that is more upright and steady is closer to regular script, and is known as "running regular".

行书的代表作是东晋王羲之（303—361）的《兰亭集序》（行楷）（见图 8-10），被奉为"登峰造极，风神盖代"，是"天下第一行书"，有"超逸的美"。《兰亭集序》从头到尾信手写来，浑然天成，其中有 20 个"之"字，8 个"以"字，7 个"不"字，反复出现，各有其妙，却不雷同。王羲之有"书圣"之称。

The representative of "running script" is the *Preface to the Orchid Pavilion Collection* (running regular) (see Figure 8 – 10) by Wang Xizhi (303 – 361) of the Eastern Jin, esteemed as "the greatest stylistic heights, the god of style, a canopy over the age". It is the "the best running script in the world", with "a beauty beyond outstanding". The "Preface to the Orchid Pavilion Collection", written from beginning to end by hand is of the highest quality. There are 20 之 *zhī* characters, eight 以 *yǐ* characters, and seven 不 *bù* characters, each with their own cleverness, yet not repetitive of each other. Wang Xizhi is thus known as the "Sage of Calligraphy".

王羲之的《兰亭集序》被誉为"天下第一行书",摹本众多,世人最看重唐代冯承素的"神龙本兰亭"摹本,现收藏于北京故宫博物院。

Wang Xizhi's *Preface to the Orchid Pavilion Collection* (running script) is "the best running script in the world"; there are numerous copies, but everyone regards most highly the Tang Dynasty's Feng Chengsu copy entitled "Shenlong Edition of the Orchid Pavilion", currently preserved in Beijing's Palace Museum in the Forbidden City.

图 8 – 10　王羲之《兰亭集序》(行楷)

Figure 8 – 10　Wang Xizhi's *Preface to the Orchid Pavilion Collection* (Running regular script)

兰亭集序

　　永和九年,岁在癸丑,暮春之初,会于会稽山阴之兰亭,修禊事也。群贤毕至,少长咸集。此地有崇山峻岭,茂林修竹,又有清流激湍,映带左右,引以为流觞曲水,列坐其次。虽无丝竹管弦之盛,一觞一咏,亦足以畅叙幽情。是日也,天朗气清,惠风和畅。仰观宇宙之大,俯察品类之盛,所以游目骋怀,足以极视听之娱,信可乐也。夫人之相与,俯仰一世。或取诸怀抱,悟言一室之内;或因寄所托,放浪形骸之外。虽趣舍万殊,静躁不同,当其欣于所遇,暂得于己,快然自足,不知老之将至;及其所之既倦,情随事迁,感慨系之矣。向之所欣,俯仰之间,已为陈迹,犹不能不以之兴怀,况修短随化,终期于尽!古人云:"死生亦大矣。"岂不痛哉！每览昔人兴感之由，若合一契，未尝不临文嗟悼，不能喻之于怀。固知一死生为虚诞，齐彭殇为妄作。后之视今，亦犹今之视昔，悲夫！故列叙时人，录其所述，虽世殊事异，所以兴怀，其致一也。后之览者，亦将有感于斯文。

*Preface to the Orchid Pavilion Collection*

On this late spring day, the ninth year of Yonghe (353 AD), we gathered at the Orchid Pavilion in Shaoxing to observe the Spring Purification Festival. All of the prominent people were there, from old to young. High mountains and luxuriant bamboo groves lie in the back; a limpid, swift stream gurgles around, which reflected the sunlight as it flowed past either side of the pavilion. We sat by the water, sharing wine from a floating goblet while chanting poems, which gave us delight in spite of the absence of musical accompaniment. This is a sunny day with a gentle valley breeze. Spreading before the eye is the beauty of nature, and hanging high is the immeasurable universe. This is perfect for an aspired mind. What a joy.

Though born with different personalities—some give vent to their sentiment in a quiet chat while others repose their aspiration in Bohemianism—people find pleasure in what they pursue and never feel tired of it. Sometimes they pause to recall the days lapsed away. Realizing that what fascinated yesterday is a mere memory today, not to mention that everyone will return to nothingness, an unsuppressible sorrow would well up. Isn't it sad to think of it?

I am often moved by ancients' sentimental lines which lamented the swiftness and uncertainty of life. When future generations look back to my time, it will probably be similar to how I now think of the past. What a shame! Therefore, when I list out the people that were here, and record their musings, even though times and circumstances will change, as for the things that we regret, they are the same. For the people who read this in future generations, perhaps you will likewise be moved by my words

行书的代表作之一是赵构的《洛神赋》（行草）（见图8-11）。赵构即宋高宗（1107-1187），建立南宋后，在位36年（1127—1162）。《洛神赋》曹植撰，赵构于55岁时书《洛神赋》，笔力沉着、浑厚、流畅。赵构做皇帝无能，艺术上却有天赋，他的书法被誉为"六朝风骨，自成一家"。

One of the masterpieces for running script is the *Rhapsody on the Goddess Luo* (Running cursive) by Zhao Gou (see Figure 8 – 11). Zhao Gou (1107 – 1187), i. e., the Gaozong Emperor of the Song Dynasty, after establishing the Southern Song sat on the throne for 36 years (1127—1162). The *Rhapsody on the Goddess Luo* was authored by Cao Zhi (192 – 232), and Zhao Gou at the age of 55 wrote *Rhapsody on the Goddess Luo* in running cursive script; the vigor of the strokes is steady, unsophisticated, and fluent. As an emperor, Zhao Gou was powerless, but he was a gifted artist, his calligraphy in particular having been praised as "the vigorous style of the Six Dynasties, unique unto itself".

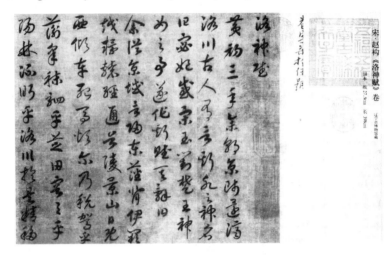

图 8-11　赵构《洛神赋》

Figure 8-11　Zhao Gou's *Rhapsody for the Goddess Luo*

赵构《洛神赋》，绢本，笔法稍瘦，气势苍逸。赵构在55岁（1162年）让位于子（赵昚）时书写，现收藏于辽宁省博物馆。

Zhao Gou's *Rhapsody for the goddess luo* in Grass Script (running grass) on silk. The calligraphy is somewhat thin, with an imposing and leisurely manner. It was written when Zhao Gou, at the age of 55 (1162), ceded his throne to his son (Zhao shen). It is currently preserved in the Liaoning Provincial Museum.

洛神赋

曹植（东汉）

　　黄初三年，余朝京师，还济洛川。古人有言，斯水之神，名曰宓妃。感宋玉对楚王神女之事，遂作斯赋，其词曰：余从京域，言归东藩，背伊阙，越轘辕，经通谷，陵景山。日既西倾，车殆马烦。……

*Rhapsody for the Goddess Luo*

Cao Zhi (Eastern Han Dynasty)

In the third year of Huangchu, I attended court, and returned home crossing the Luo River. The ancients once said that the goddess of this river is called Mifei by name. Moved by Song Yu's (c. 319-298 B.C.) service to the Chu King's goddess, I thereupon composed this rhapsody. Its words are as follows: From the capital territory I said I would return to my eastern vassal state. With Mt Yi to my back, I crossed Huanyuan, passed through Tong Valley, and crossed Mt Jing; the sun already leaning in the west, my carriage in danger, and my horse troubled.

(5) 草书

***Grass/Cursive Script***

草书结构简省，笔画上下勾连。草书艺术性高，但是实用性不强。草书贵在传神。唐代的张旭（约685—约759）、怀素（737—799）是古代草书名家，两人合称"颠张狂素"，他们常常在喝醉酒后书写，被称为"狂草"。

Grass/cursive script is structurally simple and economized, and the strokes interconnect top and bottom. The artistic nature of the script is foregrounded, but its practicality suffers. The script values its vivacity. Zhang Xu (c.685 – c.759) and Huai Su (737 – 799) of the Tang Dynasty are the most famous writers of this script in ancient times, and they are referred together as "inverted Zhang and crazy Su". They often wrote after getting drunk, and the calligraphy they produced has been called "crazy grass/cursive".

狂草的代表作是张旭的《古诗四帖》（见图 8 – 12），用笔肥厚，表现了一种"奔放的美"，现收藏于辽宁省博物馆。

One of the masterpieces for crazy cursive is the *Four Rubbings of Ancient Poetry* by Zhang Xu (see Figure 8 – 12). The brush lines are heavy and thick, expressing a "beauty of the bold and unrestrained". This piece is currently stored in the Liaoning Provincial Museum.

图 8 – 12  狂草《古诗四帖》唐朝·张旭

Figure 8 – 12  Crazy Grass *Four Rubbings of Ancient Poetry*, Tang Dynasty Zhang Xu

怀素的《自叙帖》(见图 8 – 13)是狂草的另一个代表作,先后写过几本,北宋时能看到三本,今天看到的是《苏本自叙帖》纸本,共 126 行,698 字,卷首有清乾隆皇帝为此帖题写的赞诗,卷中还有诸多历代皇帝、显贵的题记,笔力瘦而有劲。原帖现收藏于台湾故宫博物院。

Huai Su's crazy cursive *Rubbing of the Self-narrative* (see Figure 8 – 13) is another masterpiece. Several editions, earlier and later, were written, and in the Northern Song there were three editions extant. The one seen today is the "Su Edition Rubbing of the Self-narrative", on paper, with 698 characters in 126 lines. The opening of the folio includes a poem praising the work attached to it from the Qianlong Emperor of the Qing Dynasty. Throughout the folio there are numerous epigraphs from historical emperors and dignitaries. The vigor of the strokes is thin yet powerful. The original rubbing is preserved in the Palace Museum in Taiwan.

图 8 – 13  《自叙帖》(唐朝·怀素)

Figure 8 – 13  Tang Dynasty Huai Su grass script *Rubbing of the Self-narrative*

## 3. 如何欣赏中国书法?
### How Does One Appreciate Chinese Calligraphy?

中国书法要看笔画、整体、布局,一幅书法作品就像一幅写意的绘画。

中国书法追求动感,靠点线的变化表现美。线条千变万化,书法作品的神采也千差万别。纸是白色,字是黑色,一阴一阳,虚实相生,书法以线条的流动而成字。从书法的线条、绘画的线条中可以感受到中国艺术中线条美的特点。

One should look to the strokes, the entire body, and the composition; a work of calligraphy is like a freehand style painting.

Chinese calligraphy pursues dynamism relying on changes in lines and dots to express beauty. Any particular line may have countless permutations, and the spirit of a calligraphic work is diverse in innumerable ways. The paper is white, the ink is black; one *yang* and one *yin*, empty and full engender one another; calligraphy creates characters by the circulation of lines. From within calligraphic lines and the lines of a painting, one can sense the characteristic linear beauty of Chinese art.

笔力：书法审美，首先看笔力，就是看如何操纵毛笔。笔力是从字的点画形态中体现出来的"力"的感受。笔力弱的书法，不是好的作品；只有笔力强健的，才能显示出书法的造诣。所谓"力透纸背""入木三分"，都是称赞书法笔力的雄健。

Vigor of strokes: In appreciating the beauty of Chinese calligraphy, one first considers the vigor of the strokes, or how the brush is controlled. Vigor is the perception of the "power" experienced from the form of the strokes themselves. Calligraphy with weak strokes is not good work; only when strokes are sturdy is the calligraphic achievement able to be expressed. The sayings, "the power permeates the back of the paper", and "able to penetrate into wood three inches deep" are praising the vigorousness of the calligraphic strokes.

墨法：是在黑白中体现书法艺术形式美的重要因素。墨法是在白纸上使用黑色的墨表现出枯、湿、浓、淡，可以造出雄奇、秀媚的书法意境。不同的书法家对墨色的浓淡有不同的爱好。

Methods with ink: It is an important element of the beauty of the calligraphic art form experienced within the black-and-white. It is the use of black ink on white paper to express "dried up", "wet", "thick", and "light"; it can create a calligraphic concept that is grandly strange and elegantly charming. Different calligraphers have different preferences for the thickness or lightness of the color black.

气韵：气是无形的，气韵说的是书法的意境之美，是从整体中得到的。气是一种运动，韵是一种节奏，表达的是书法抽象生动的意境。

*Qìyùn* "rhyme of energy", i.e., spirit, flavor, or distinct style: *qì* or "vital energy" is formless; what *qìyùn* refers to is the beauty of the calligraphic artistic conception. It is attained from the entirety of the piece. *Qì* is a kind of movement, and *yùn* is a kind of rhythm; what they express is the abstract, vivid artistic conception of calligraphy.

## 4. 书法与货币
### Calligraphy and Currency

生活中，书法处处可见。与我们每个人息息相关、为大家熟悉的是人民币上的书法——"中国人民银行"六个大字，被评价为笔力浑厚、字体俊秀、刚柔并济，重笔势、讲韵度，既有隶书的庄秀，又有魏碑的刚劲。"中国人民银行"于1950年由时任中国人民银行金融研究所的研究员马文蔚题写。

Calligraphy can be seen everywhere in daily life, but the calligraphy intimately related to each of us and most familiar to everybody is the calligraphy on the Renminbi. The six characters in "People's Bank of China" have been evaluated as having simple and honest strokes, elegant characters, and coupling strength and gentleness; it has strong force of the brush, and emphasizes charm; it has both the solemn elegance of clerical script and boldness of the Wei stele. It was written in 1950 by Ma Wenwei, a researcher in the financial institute at the People's Bank of China.

马文蔚（1904—1988），山西人，毕业于南京国立中央大学。"中国人民银行"和人民币上的其他汉字，从第二套人民币开始使用，到现行的第五套人民币，迄今已经使用了60多年，也是家喻户晓的书法（见图8-14、图8-15）。

Ma Wenwei (1904 - 1988), a native of Shanxi, graduated from Central University in Nanjing. "People's Bank of China" and the other characters on the currency started being used in the second set of Renminbi, and have been in use for more than 60 years up to the presently circulating fifth set. Thus, it is the calligraphy familiar to everyone. See Figure 8 - 14, Figure 8 - 15.

图8-14　第四套人民币面值伍元纸币，面币汉字由马文蔚题写

Figure 8 -14　The fourth set of Renminbi Paper Currency, the face value 5 yuan note (the characters on which were created by Ma Wenwei)

第八章 中国古代书法、绘画

图 8 – 15　第二套人民币面值叁元纸币，面币汉字由马文蔚题写

Figure 8 – 15　The second set of Renminbi paper currency, the face value 3 yuan note,
( The characters on which were created by Ma Wenwei)

1955 年发行第二套人民币，其中包括叁元面值在内的共十一种新版人民币，流通 9 年，至 1964 年停用。以后发行的人民币依旧采用马文蔚题字，至今未变。

The second set of Renminbi was issued in 1955, all together eleven new versions, including the 3 Yuan note. It circulated for 9 years until it was suspended in 1964. The Renminbi issued afterward still used the Ma Wenwei characters, and that has not changed even up to today.

交通银行始建于清光绪二十四年（1908），"交通银行"四字为郑孝胥（1860—1938）所书（见图 8 – 16）。郑孝胥是福建省闽侯县人，清末官员，伪满洲国总理。"交通银行"属北魏碑体，字体苍劲朴实，既肃穆典雅，又险峻纵逸，既不出规范，又奇姿流美。

The Bank of Communications was founded in the 24th year of Guangxu (1908) in Qing Dynasty. The word "Bank of Communications" was written by Zheng Xiaoxu (1860 – 1938) (see Figure 8 – 16). Zheng Xiaoxu was born in Minhou County, Fujian Province, and he was an official of the late Qing, and a puppet Prime Minister of Manchuria. "Bank of Communications" is written in Northen Wei Stele script. The script is vigorous and simple, it is solemn and elegant. It is both normative and creative.

图 8 – 16　交通银行（郑孝胥题写）

Figure 8 – 16　Bank of Communications ( by Zheng Xiaoxu)

中国银行成立于1912年,"中国银行"原为孙中山题写,现中国银行上海分行营业部(原中国银行总部)大楼上的石刻银行名仍为原题。现行字体为郭沫若(1892—1978)题写(见图8-17),1980年开始使用,字体粗笔不臃肿,细笔不柔弱,字字精到。

Bank of China was established in 1912. The "Bank of China" was originally inscribed by Sun Yat-sen. Now, the original title is on the stone inscription on the building of the business department of the Bank of China Shanghai Branch (formerly the headquarters of Bank of China). The current font is inscribed by Guo Moruo (1892 – 1978) (see Figure 8 – 17), which was started to use since 1980. The thick strokes are not bloated, and the thin strokes are not weak, so the font is done to a turn.

图 8 – 17 中国银行(郭沫若题写)
Figure 8 – 17 Bank of China (by Guo Moruo)

## 二、绘画
## Chinese Painting

中国画是用毛笔、墨和颜料,在特制的宣纸或绢上作画。

中国画简称国画,按内容分,主要有人物画、山水画、花鸟画三大类。此外,还有民间画、民俗画。

Chinese painting uses brushes, to apply ink and pigments onto especially made *xuan* paper or silk.

Chinese painting is also called "national painting", and is classified by the contents of the painting into basically three large categories: "characters" (portraits), "mountain and river" (landscapes), and "flower and bird" paintings (still lifes). Besides, there are folk paintings such as illustrations and paintings of door gods.

## 1. 人物画
**Portrait Painting**

人物画在唐朝时达到了顶峰。著名的人物画画家有东晋的顾恺之（约 346—407）、中唐的吴道子（680—740）等。

Portrait painting reached to a peak in the Tang Dynasty. Famous portrait painters include Gu Kaizhi (346 – 407) of the Eastern Jin, Wu Daozi (680 – 740) of the mid Tang and others.

顾恺之是六朝时期艺术成就最高、对后世影响最大的画家，以《女史箴图》《洛神赋图》传世。

Gu Kaizhi is a painter of Eastern Jin with the highest achievements and the greatest influence on later generations. His work includes *Admonitions of the Instructress to Court Ladies* and *Luoshen Appraisal Painting*.

《女史箴图》（见图 8 – 18）传世的是两幅摹本，隋唐摹本现收藏于英国大不列颠博物馆，宋代摹本现收藏于北京故宫博物院。

There are two copies of "Admonitions" (see Figure 8 – 18) still in existence from ancient times. The Sui-Tang copy is stored in the British Museum, and the Song copy is stored in the Palace Museum in the Forbidden City in Beijing.

图 8 – 18 《女史箴图》（东晋·顾恺之）

Figure 8 – 18 *Admonitions of the Instructress to Court Ladies* (by Gu Kaizhi from Eastern Jin)

《洛神赋图》（见图 8 – 19）以曹植的文学作品《洛神赋》为题材，描绘曹植渡洛水时与洛水女神相遇而恋爱，最终因为人神难以共存于同一世界而无奈分离的故事。两幅画被历代视为珍宝。

The "Luoshen" painting (see Figure 8-19) takes Cao Zhi's *Rhapsody on the Goddess Luo* as subject matter and portrays the story of Cao Zhi crossing the Luo River, meeting and falling in love with the Luo River goddess, and in the end, because humans and gods cannot inhabit the same realm, they grudgingly separate. The two paintings have been regarded as treasures for generations.

《洛神赋图》原件现已遗失,现在传世的是宋代的四件摹本,分别收藏于北京故宫博物院(二件)、辽宁省博物馆和美国弗利尔美术馆。

The original has been lost; there are four Song dynasty copies extant, two of which are in the Palace Museum in the Forbidden City, one is in the Liaoning Provincial Museum, and one in the Freer Gallery of Art in the United States.

图 8-19 《洛神赋图》(东晋·顾恺之)

Figure 8-19 *Luoshen Appraisal Painting* (By Gu Kaizhi from Eastern Jin)

《簪花仕女图》(见图 8-20),纵 46 厘米,横 180 厘米。现藏于辽宁省博物馆。

*Court Ladies Adorning Their Hair With Flowers*, (see Figure 8-20) 46 cm high, 180 cm long, is stored in the Liaoning Provincial Museum.

图 8-20 《簪花仕女图》(唐朝·周昉)

Figure 8-20 *Court Ladies Adorning Their Hair With Flowers* (By Zhou Fang from Tang Dynasty)

还有一类是描绘历代帝王、文臣武将,以宣扬其文治武功。如唐代阎立本(600—673)的《历代帝王图》(见图 8-21)。

Another type portrays historical monarchs, ministers, and generals, proclaiming their civilian and military achievements; for example, the *Portraits of Monarchs of Past Dynasties* by Yan Liben (600 – 673) of the Tang Dynasty (see Figure 8 – 21).

图 8 – 21　《历代帝王图》（局部）（唐朝·阎立本）

Figure 8 – 21　*Portraits of Monarchs of Past Dynasties* (By Yan Liben from Tang Dynasty)

阎立本的《历代帝王图》，又称《古帝王图》，绢本，全卷画有自汉代至隋代的 700 多年中十三位帝王的画像（如图 8 – 22 即为其中刘备画像），现收藏美国波士顿美术馆。

Yan Liben's *Portraits of Monarchs of Past Dynasties*, also known as *Paintings of Ancient Emperors*, on silk, includes portraits of thirteen emperors from the 700 years of Han to Sui history (see Figure 8 – 22, the portrait of Liu Bei). It is currently stored in the Boston Museum of Fine Arts.

图 8 – 22　《历代帝王图·刘备画像》（局部）（唐朝·阎立本）

Figure 8 – 22　Portrait of Liu Bei from Yan Liben's *Portraits of Monarchs of Past Dynasties*

刘备（161—223），谥号昭烈皇帝，字玄德，东汉末年幽州涿郡涿县（今河北省涿州市）人，221 年在成都称帝，国号汉，史称蜀或蜀汉，魏、蜀、吴三国鼎立局面形成。刘备在位两年过世，终年 63 岁。

Liu Bei (161 - 223), posthumously the Zhaolie Emperor, styled Xuande, a native of Zhuo County, Zhuo Prefecture (modern Zhuozhou city, Hebei Province) in the later years of the Eastern Han. He proclaimed himself emperor in 221 in Chengdu, and took the name Han, but in history is known as the Shu Kingdom, or the Shu-Han, which together with the Wei and Wu, formed the Three Kingdoms. Liu Bei reigned for two years before passing away at the age of 63.

从画像来看，虽仍有程式化的倾向，但在人物个性刻画上表现出很大的进步，不落俗套，而显得个性分明；画中按等级森严的封建伦理观念处理人物的大小。《历代帝王图》用重色设色和晕染衣纹的方法，有佛教艺术的影响。

The portraits, though they still tend toward formalization, show a great advance in the portrayal of individual characters. The portraits are unconventional, appearing individually distinct; within the paintings, the size of the representation conforms to the idea of strict ranks in feudalistic ethics. The *Portraits of Monarchs of Past Dynasties* uses the techniques of bright coloring and dyeing of clothes and designs, influenced by Buddhist arts.

阎立本的《步辇图》（见图 8 - 23），绢本，现存画被认为是宋代摹本，画的中央上方有"步辇图"三字，是宋高宗赵构的手笔，并盖有印记。画以唐太宗李世民（599—649）将文成公主（628—680）嫁给吐蕃王松赞干布为背景，描绘了吐蕃使者禄东赞（590—667）来唐迎亲并和唐太宗会面的场景。唐太宗李世民坐在由六名宫女抬着的步辇上，他的前方三人，站立在中间的是禄东赞，画中包括唐太宗在内共有 13 个人物，时间是贞观十五年（公元 641 年）。现收藏于北京故宫博物院。

Yan Liben's *Emperor Taizong Receiving the Tibetan Envoy* (see Figure 8 - 23), on silk, the current painting is believed to be a Song copy. In the middle of the top of the painting are the three characters *Bu Nian Tu*, meaning "Painting of Sedan", which are in the hand of Zhao Gou, Gaozong Emperor of the Song, and it has his seal on it. The painting takes as its background Li Shimin (599 - 649), the Taizong Emperor of the Tang, giving Princess Wencheng (628 - 680) in marriage to the Songtsen Gampo, founder of the Tubo (Tibetan) Empire. It portrays the Tubo emissary Gar Tongtsen Yulsung (590 - 667) coming to the Tang to escort the bride and his meeting with Taizong. Taizong sits on a sedan carried by six palace women, and there are three people in front of him, standing in the middle is Gar Tongtsen Yulsung. There are thirteen people in the painting including Taizong. The date of the meeting was 641. The painting is in the Palace Museum in the Forbidden City.

图 8-23 《步辇图》唐朝·阎立本

Figure 8-23  Yan Liben's *Emperor Taizong Receiving the Tibetan Envoy*, *Tang Dynasty*

## 2. 山水画
## Landscape Painting

山水画以表现山川自然景色为主题，讲究山水位置的安排、表达意境。现存最早的山水卷轴画《游春图》（见图8-24），是北齐至隋之间大画家展子虔（约550—约604）的作品，这幅画在处理空间远近关系方面有特色。

Landscape painting takes as its theme the display of mountains, rivers and natural scenery, paying particular attention to arranging the position of the mountains and rivers to express its creative conception. The earliest preserved landscape painting is the scroll painting *Spring Outing* (see Figure 8-24), a work by Zhan Ziqian (c. 550 - c. 604), a great painter of the period between the Northern Qi and Sui. This painting is distinguished by its handling of the relationship of near and distant space.

图 8-24 《游春图》（隋朝·展子虔）

Figure 8-24  Zhan Ziqian's *Spring Outing*, Sui Dynasty

展子虔的《游春图》，绢本，画中右上"展子虔游春图"六个字为宋徽宗题写。现收藏于北京故宫博物院绘画馆。

Zhan Ziqian's *Spring Outing*, on silk, in the upper write are the words "Zhan Ziqian Spring Outing" written by Emperor Huizong of the Song Dynasty. It is stored in the painting hall of the Palace Museum in the Forbidden City.

### 3. 花鸟画
### Paintings of Flowers and Birds

花鸟画以自然界中的花草、石竹、鸟兽、鱼虫为描绘对象。宋徽宗赵佶（1082—1135），是一个天才的书画家，他对山水、人物、花鸟画样样精通。他的《芙蓉锦鸡图》（见图8-25），画一只羽毛绚丽的锦鸡，圆目注视着飞舞的蝴蝶，巧妙地表现出锦鸡在一瞬间跃跃欲试的神情。此外，宋代还兴起了以梅、兰、竹、菊为内容的"四君子图"，代表画家有苏轼、赵孟坚（1199—1264）等。之后著名的花鸟画家有明末擅长画花鸟的朱耷（1626—1705）、清乾隆时期擅长画竹子的郑板桥（1693—1765）（见图8-26）、现代擅长画鱼虾的齐白石（1864—1957）等。

图8-25 《芙蓉锦鸡图》（北宋·赵佶）

Figure 8-25 Zhao Ji's *Hibiscus and Golden Pheasant*, Northern Song Dynasty

These paintings take elements of the natural environment, such as grass, stone, bamboo, birds, animals, fish, and insects, as their subjects. Zhao Ji (1082-1135), Emperor Huizong of the Song Dynasty, was a talented calligrapher and painter, proficient in landscapes, portraits, and flower and bird paintings. His *Hibiscus and Golden Pheasant* portrays (see Figure 8-25) a golden pheasant in glorious plumage, whose round-eyed gaze is fixed on a pair of flitting butterflies, cleverly expressing the pheasant's instantaneous feeling of wanting to give it a try. The Song Dynasty also saw the rise of the so-called "Four Gentlemen Paintings" which include plum blossoms, orchids, bamboo, and chrysanthemums, representative painters of which are Su Shi and Zhao Mengjian (1199-1264). Later famous flower and bird painters include the Ming-Qing master Zhu Da (1626-1705) (see Figure 8-26), the Qing master of bamboo painting Zheng Banqiao (1693-1765), and the modern master of fish and shrimp paintings Qi Baishi (1864-1957).

图 8-26 《竹石图》(清·郑板桥)
Figure 8-26 Zheng Banqiao's *Bamboo and Stone*, Qing Dynasty

宋徽宗赵佶的《芙蓉锦鸡图》,绢本,纵 81.5 厘米,横 53.6 厘米,双勾重彩工笔花鸟画。现收藏于北京故宫博物院。

Zhao Ji's *Hibiscus and Golden Pheasant*, made of silk, 81.5 cm in length, 53.6 cm in width, double-hook and heavy color painting of flowers and birds. It is now collected in the Palace Museum in Beijing.

郎世宁(1688—1766),意大利米兰人。27 岁时来到中国,康熙末年入宫当宫廷画师,从此开始了长达五十多年的宫廷画家生涯,为宫廷创作了大量的作品(如图 8-27),深受康熙、雍正、乾隆三代皇帝的器重,特别是乾隆的宠爱。70 岁时,乾隆皇帝为其举行庆寿仪式,去世后赏其三品顶戴。他的作品融合中西技法,细腻逼真,创造出了新的画风。他还在宫内培养了一批学生,为促进中西文化艺术交流作出了特殊贡献。

Giuseppe Castiglione was a native of Milan, Italy. At the age of 27, he came to China and in the latter years of the Kangxi reign he entered the court to serve as a painting teacher. Thus began a career as court painter that lasted more than 50 years. He created a large number of pieces for the court (see Figure 8-27), having been highly regarded by the Kangxi, Yongzheng, and Qianlong emperors. Qianlong especially doted on him. Qianlong held a ceremony in celebration of his 70th birthday, and after he died bestowed a cap badge of the third rank (relatively high rank in the bureaucracy). His work fused Chinese and Western techniques, meticulous and true to life; he created a new painting style. He also trained a group of students in the court, and thereby made a particular contribution to furthering Chinese and

Western artistic interaction.

图 8 -27 《百骏图》(意大利籍清代宫廷画家郎世宁)
Figure 8 -27 Giuseppe Castiglione' *Hundred Steeds*, Qing Dynasty

《百骏图》,此图共绘有100匹骏马,姿势各异,或立、或奔、或跪、或卧,可谓画尽骏马之态。该图稿本为纸质本,纵102厘米、横813厘米,收藏于美国纽约大都会博物馆,绢本收藏于中国台北故宫博物院。

The painting *Hundred Steeds* indeed depicts 100 spirited horses in all kinds of postures, some standing, some running, some kneeling, some laying down. One might say he exhausted the form of spirited horses. The sketch draft is on paper, 102 cm by 813 cm, and is currently in the Metropolitan Museum of Art in New York. A version on silk is in the Palace Museum in Taiwan.

(4) 民间绘画
***Folk Painting***

民间绘画有两类,一类是小说、戏曲读本中的插图,如图 8 -28。

There are two categories of folk painting. The first is illustrations within novels and opera books, as Figure 8 -28.

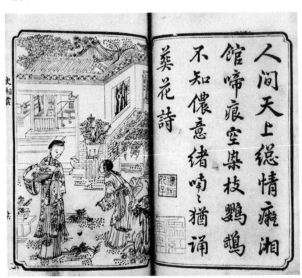

图 8 -28 《红楼梦》清朝·程甲本插图
Figure 8 -28 *Dream of the Red Chambers*, Illustration for the Chengjia Edition, Qing Dynasty

图中文字：人间天上总情痴，湘馆啼痕空染枝。鹦鹉不知侬意绪，喃喃犹诵葬花诗。图中印章一：潇湘妃子；印章二：聚红轩。

The characters in the illustration read: "Among people in the world and in the heavens there are always the lovesick ones; traces of a hoot in Xiang Hall and emptiness infects the branch. The parrot doesn't know of my mind and mood, yet still murmurs a recitation of a poem for funeral flowers." One of the seals in the illustration reads: Imperial Concubine of the Xiaoxiang (Lin Daiyu's nickname). The second of the seals in the illustration reads: Gathering Red Pavilion.

还有一类是民间年画、风俗画，与民间习俗有关，表达民众的愿望，以财神、门神、送子图、福寿图之类为主，如图 8-29 所示。

Another category are the New Year's paintings and social customs paintings; i.e., those that are related to folk customs. They express the wishes of the people, relying mostly on paintings of such things as the God of Wealth, the Door God, Delivering a Baby, Happiness and Long-life, etc., as Figure 8-29.

图 8-29 门神

Figure 8-29 Door God

门神：是民间信仰中守卫门户的神灵，将其神像贴于大门，用以驱邪避鬼、保平安。图中门神为秦叔宝（秦琼）、尉迟恭（尉迟敬德），他们是唐代的两位武将。

Door God: the spirit that protects the household in folk beliefs. The image is pasted on main gates to expel evil, avoid demons and keep the household safe and sound. The Door Gods depicted here are Qin Shubao (d. 638, Qin Qiong) and Yuchi Gong (585-658, Yuchi Jingde), two Tang Dynasty generals.

唐朝以后，人们开始把唐代的秦叔宝和尉迟恭两位武将当作门神的原因：

据民间相传，某一日，唐太宗生病，听见门外鬼魅呼号，彻夜不得安宁。于是他让这两位将军手持武器立于门旁镇守，第二天夜里就再也没有鬼魅骚扰，唐太宗得以安睡。以后，唐太宗让人把这两位将军的形象画下来贴在门上，从此，这一习俗开始在中国民间广为流传。

In the years after the Tang Dynasty, the reason the two Tang generals Qin Shubao and Yuchi Gong came to serve as Door Gods is：

According to popular legend, on a certain day, Emperor Taizong of the Tang became ill and heard a monster wailing outside his doorway. He was unable to calm down for the whole night. So, he made these two generals stand guard beside the door with weapons in their hands. The next night, there was no more harassment from monsters, and the emperor was able to sleep well. Afterward, the emperor allowed people to paint images of these generals and attach them to their doorways, and from this incident, this wide-spread folk custom started in China.

## 三、如何欣赏中国画
## How to Appreciate Chinese Painting

中国画以整体为主，平面构图着眼，以线条造型为基本原则。

中国画的艺术特色有三点。

Chinese painting relies mainly on synthesis, so the eye focuses on the planar composition and takes the linear appearance as the main principle.

There are three points to consider with regards the artistic characteristics of Chinese painting.

第一，中国画讲究整体性，画面首先要突出主要人物或主峰。人物画中主要人物形象总是画得大于其他人。例如前面《历代帝王图》中，帝王高大，次要人物则矮小。雕塑也是如此，云冈石窟中的主佛高大，旁边的其他人物则矮小。山水画中山一定有主峰，其他山围绕着主峰。

First, Chinese painting pays particular attention to the synthetic whole, while the tableau first will give prominence to the main character portrait or the main mountain peak. In portraits, the image of the main character is always painted larger than other people. For example, in *Portraits of Monarchs of Past Dynasties*, the monarchs are large, and the secondary characters are smaller. The same principle holds in sculpture, as in, for example, the main Buddha in the Yungang Caves is large, while the other characters beside him are small. In landscape painting, there will certainly be a main mountain peak, and the other mountains revolve around that peak.

第二，气韵生动是中国画的生命力所在。由于绘画的整体性要求，中国画内在的生动气韵被看作第一重要的表现手法。对实物的描绘，不求相似，但见气韵。

Second, the liveliness of the *qìyùn* (spirit, style, lasting appeal) is the location of the vitality of Chinese painting. Owing to the requirements of the synthetic whole of the painting, the intrinsic, vivid *qìyùn* has been regarded as the most important method of expression. In the portrayal of objects, one does not pursue resemblance, only the appearance of *qìyùn*.

第三，要求构造独特的意境。国画的画面不是把一切都画出来，而是要留有让欣赏者想象的空间。绘画的时候注重留白处理，讲究虚实相生，无画处有妙境，偏重传神达意。国画始终以线为主，以面为辅，要求画家善于用线条表达思想、感情，构出意境。

Third, it requires an artistic conception that is compositionally distinct. The tableau of a Chinese painting does not depict everything, but rather leaves empty space to allow the viewer to imagine. When painting, one pays attention to dealing with leaving empty spaces, paying attention to the notion that the full and the empty engender each other; and there are marvelous scenes in places with no painting, biased toward expressing one's idea by vivid representation. From beginning to end, Chinese painting relies mainly on the lines, with the surfaces as complementary, requiring painters to excel at using lines to express their thoughts, feelings and construct their artistic conception.

线条在中西绘画中都使用，但是有所不同。

西方绘画中使用线条主要是为了精确描绘物体的真实感。

中国画非常讲究笔墨技巧，主要用线条造型，勾画线条和大块的墨色有丰富的用笔技巧，这一点和中国书法有相通之处。墨的用法通过浓淡干湿的变化运用，形成画面效果。

中国有诗、书、画一体的艺术传统，一幅作品上，书法、绘画、诗文、题跋、印章等往往都可以看到。

Lines are used in both Chinese and Western painting, but there are differences.

In Western painting, lines are used primarily for the precise portrayal of the real sense of the thing.

Chinese painting very much pays attention to brush and ink skills, mainly using lines to shape something; there is rich brush technique in sketching out lines and large portions of ink and color. This point is similar to Chinese calligraphy.

The ink is manipulated through changes of richness or thinness, dryness or wetness, which forms the result on the tableau.

There is the artistic tradition of integrating poetry, calligraphy, and painting in China. One can see on a particular piece calligraphy, painting, poetry, short comments, and seal inscriptions.

## 四、中国画与西方画的比较
## Comparison of Chinese Painting and Western Painting

西方绘画强调真实，追求写实。充分运用光学、几何学，讲究比例的真实，讲究光线的明暗，对光、色的掌握是西方绘画的主要造型技法。讲究设色，尤其是油画，颜料丰富多彩，覆盖面大，有一定的厚重感，容易创造出立体效果和不同于中国画的写实性和艺术感染力。

从形式上来说，中国画以散点透视为主，画面布局具有平面性特点；西方画以焦点透视为主，画面布局具有立体性特点。

中国画体现出强烈的写意性、程式化、整体感，追求内容与形式的和谐。西方画体现出强烈的写实性、科学性、真实感，在追求内容与形式的和谐的同时，更偏重形式。

中国画追求写意，是根据作者个人的主观感受，不是实际的物体形象，不求形似，以写意为主。作者要借物抒怀，追求情与景的统一。

Western painting emphasizes the real and pursues realism. Making full use of optics and geometry, it pays attention to the reality of the scale, and the lightness or darkness of the illumination. Mastering light and color is the main modeling technique of Western painting. Paying attention to the application of paint, especially oil paints, the paints are richly colorful, the coverage is large, and there is a definite sense of thickness, making it easier to create a three-dimensional effect and an idea of realism and artistic inspiration that is very different from Chinese painting.

In terms of form, Chinese painting relies on scattered point perspective, so the tableau's arrangement has the characteristic of flatness; Western painting relies on single point perspective, so the tableau's arrangement has the characteristic of three-dimensionality.

Chinese painting displays a strong suggestiveness, patternization, and sense of the synthesis, pursuing harmony between content and form. Western painting displays a strong sense of realism, science, and sense of the genuine; while pursuing harmony between content and form, it is more biased toward form.

Chinese painting's pursuit of suggestiveness is based on the subjective perception of the individual creator. It is not the actual material image, not in pursuit of the form itself, but the suggestion of it. The creator expresses emotion by borrowing something material and pursues the unity of emotion and scene.

梁楷（？—1210）的《泼墨仙人图》（见图8-30）开创了人物画的泼墨法，塑造了中国乃至世界史上的稀有形象，是中国画写意传神、追求神似的典型作品。现收藏于台北故宫博物院。

*Portrait of an Immortal in Splashed Ink* by Liang Kai (d. 1210) (see Figure 8-30) initiated the splash-ink technique in portrait painting, creating a rare image in Chinese, or indeed world, history. It is the archetype of Chinese paintings suggestive vividness and pursuit of semblance of spirit. It is stored in the Palace Museum in Taiwan.

图8-30 《泼墨仙人图》（南宋·梁楷）

Figure 8-30 Liang Kai's *Portrait of an Immortal in Splashed Ink*, Southern Song

中国画的散点透视体现在画面布置上。透视点是上下移动的，由高到低，视线由远至近，后面的山不受前面山的遮挡，画家可以根据写意的需要自由表现。作品要视野宽广，一张纸上要看到万里之势。没有散点透视，对事物的多方观照便无法统一于一幅画中，例如，像《清明上河图》（见图8-31）那样的作品，采用焦点透视的西方绘画就较难表现。

Chinese painting's scattered perspective is displayed on the tableau's arrangement. The point of perspective moves up and down, from high to low, and the line of sight moves from near to far, so that mountains in the back are not obscured by mountains in the front. Based on the needs of suggestiveness, the painter can freely show off. The work must have a broad field of view so that on a single sheet of paper one must see the condition of thousands of miles. Without scattered perspective, there is no way to integrate into a single painting the diverse treatment of the subject. For example, a work like *Along the River During the Qingming Festival* (see Figure 8 – 31) could not be depicted using the single-point perspective in Western painting.

图 8 – 31　《清明上河图》（北宋·张择端）

Figure 8 – 31　Zhang Zeduan's *Along the River During the Qingming Festival*, Northern Song

《清明上河图》，宽 25.2 厘米，长 528.7 厘米，绢本，作品记录了北宋都城东京（古名汴梁，又称汴京，今河南开封）的城市面貌和当时社会各阶层人民的生活状况。现收藏于北京故宫博物院。

*Along the River During the Qingming Festival*, 25.2 cm high, 528.7 cm long, on silk; the piece records the city features of the Northern Song Eastern Capital (also called Bianliang, modern Kaifeng, Henan Province) and situations of the life of all classes of people at the time. It is stored in the Palace Museum in the Forbidden City.

西方绘画的焦点透视是在平面的画布上通过透视精确的明暗光影、色彩渲染凸显出有深度、有层次、细节逼真的立体空间的真实感。所以，重视有助于表现真实的各种技术，例如几何透视法，以解剖学为基础的人体结构，等等。此外，也重视数学和逻辑思维在艺术创作中的应用。

Single-point perspective in Western painting, through the precise shading of light and dark and color rendering on the surface of the painting, expresses a sense of the real in three-dimensional space that is deep, layered, detailed, and true to life. So, it attaches importance to the various techniques that are an aid to showing realism, such as geometric perspective, human composition based on anatomy, etc. It also values the use of mathematical and logical reasoning in the creation of art.

## 五、中西对待雕塑的不同态度
## Different Attitudes Toward Sculpture in China and the West

### 1. 中国人对待雕塑的态度
### The Chinese Attitude Toward Sculpture

雕塑只是民间工匠的体力活。在中国人的传统观念中，绘画是一种艺术形式，而雕塑没有获得这种美学高度的认识，雕塑被看作是民间工匠从事的体力活。所以，绘画有士人的参与，是士人必须具备的修养，但中国文人几乎不参与雕塑创作，没有哪位名家留下任何雕塑作品。

In China, sculpture is the product of the physical labor of folk craftsmen. In the traditional conception of Chinese people, painting is an art form, but sculpture did not receive this aesthetic recognition. Sculpture was seen as physical labor carried out by folk craftsmen. So, scholar officials participated in painting, indeed, it was a kind of training that all of them must possess. But Chinese literati basically never participated in creating sculpture, and there were never any famous people who left behind works of sculpture.

中国的雕塑整体以实用功利为主要目的。今天我们看到的古代雕塑作品绝大多数是陵墓、宗教雕塑。例如，陵墓前的"石像生"、秦始皇兵马俑、石窟的塑像、唐三彩乐舞俑等数量最多。

Chinese sculpture regarded practical utility as the main purpose. The majority of ancient sculptures that we can see today are in tombs or are religious sculptures. For example, the most numerous are the "Stone Statues of the Living" in front of mausoleums, Qin Shihuang's terra-cotta warriors, the sculptures in stone grottoes, and Tang era tri-color singing-and-dancing figures.

中国雕塑在美学上没有理论与规范，这是其发展的障碍，但是也就可以自由灵活地使用雕塑技法，这样雕塑的结果，让中国古代雕塑形成了自己独特的风格，具有很强的艺术表现力,有着灵活、传神、写意的特点。

Chinese sculpture was never theorized or categorized in aesthetic terms, which was an impediment to its development. However, one could freely and flexibly apply sculptural techniques, the result of which was to allow ancient Chinese sculpture to form its own unique style possessed of strong artistic expressive power with agile, vivid and suggestive characteristics.

## 2. 中国古代雕塑作品选
## Selection of Ancient Chinese Sculptures

### (1) 兵马俑
### *Terracotta Army*

兵马俑是中国历史上第一个皇帝——秦始皇(公元前259年—前210年)陵墓的陪葬坑,被称为世界第八大奇迹。

The Terracotta Army was found in a pit for accompanying the burial of China's first emperor, Qin Shihuang (259 – 210 B.C.). It has been called the eighth wonder of the world.

先秦时期的丧葬实行人殉,即用活人陪葬;战国时期发生变化,出现以俑殉葬。"俑"的本意就是人殉,即用陶俑、木俑等来代替人殉。当人殉消失后,"俑"便成了墓葬中陶塑、石雕、人像的专有名词。秦始皇陵陪葬坑里的兵马俑,是想让这些兵马俑帮助死后的秦始皇统治另一个帝国。

Burials in the pre-Qin era included the practice of including human sacrifices to accompany the person being buried. This started to change in the Warring States Period, when figurines appeared as sacrificial grave goods. That is, they began to use clay and wooden figurines as replacements for sacrificing live human beings. The Terracotta Army that accompanied the burial of Qin Shihuang was meant to allow this army to help the emperor to govern another empire after he died.

兵马俑(见图8-32)位于陕西省西安市临潼区东部,南部是骊山,北部是渭水。据史书记载,当时约有70万人次参与建设。兵马俑坑是地下坑道式的土木结构建筑,是从地面挖下去的一个深约5米的大坑,俑坑的底部铺的是青砖。最早发现的是一号俑坑,呈长方形,东西向230米,南北向62米,深5米,坑里有6000多个兵俑和马俑排列成古战阵形状,10扇墙把地下士兵分成不同的列。从东到西五个有坡度的入口可到达底部。一号俑坑左右两侧是二号坑和三号坑。坑内出土了大量的士兵俑、马俑和1万多件青铜武器,集中展示了秦朝的军事文化,这里也是世界最大的地下军事博物馆。

The Terracotta Army (see Figure 8 – 32) is located in the eastern part of Lintong, in Xi'an; to the south is Lishan, to the north is the Wei River. According to historical records, at the time there were around 700000 workers engaged in constructing it. The pit where the

Terracotta Army was found is an underground wood-and-earth structure. It is a large pit, about five meters deep, that was dug out from the surface. Along the bottom of the pit are green tiles. The earliest pit discovered is known as Pit #1; a rectangle 230 meters from east to west, 62 meters from north to south, and five meters deep. In the pit were found 6000 soldiers and horse figurines arranged in a battle formation, with ten walls separating the underground soldiers into different ranks. From east to west there are five sloping entrances into the floor of the pit. On the left and right of Pit #1 are Pit #2 and Pit #3. A large number of soldiers and horse figurines, and more than 10000 pieces of bronze weaponry unearthed from the pits reveals the Qin military culture. This is also the world's largest underground military museum.

图 8 - 32　秦陵兵马俑（位于陕西省临潼）

Figure 8 - 32　Terracotta Army at Qinling, Located in Lintong, Shaanxi Province

## （2）云冈石窟
### *Yungang Caves*

云冈石窟（见图 8 - 33）位于山西省大同市西郊 17 公里处的武周山，石窟依山开凿，东西长约 1 公里，存有主要洞窟 45 个，大小佛像 10 万余尊，最高的 17 米，最小的仅有几厘米，最早建于北魏文成帝兴安二年（453 年），其他大多建于北魏孝文帝时期。为中国规模最大的古代石窟群之一，与敦煌莫高窟、洛阳龙门石窟和天水麦积山石窟并称为中国四大石窟。

The Yungang Caves (see Figure 8 - 33) are located in Wuzhou Mountain, in a western suburb 17 kilometers from Datong, Shanxi Province. The caves are carved into the mountain, running east to west for about a kilometer. There are primarily 45 cave openings, with more than 100000 Buddhist statues of different sizes, the tallest at 17 meters, and smallest a few centimeters. It was first constructed in 453 A. D. under Emperor Wencheng (440 - 465) of the Northern Wei, and mostly completed under Emperor Xiaowen (467 – 499). Yungang is one of China's largest cave complexes. Together with Mogaoku in Dunhuang, Longmen in Luoyang, and Maijishan in Tianshui, they constitute the four great cave complexes in China.

由于这里的石头质量较好,所以石窟全部用石头雕刻而成。石窟吸收了很多外来文化,例如印度的塔柱,希腊的卷涡柱头,中亚的兽形柱头以及卷草等装饰纹样。

Because the quality of the stone in this cave is quite good, they are entirely constructed of stone. The caves reflect the assimilation of a great deal of foreign culture. For example, there are such decorative shapes as the Indian pagoda pillars, the Greek curled column caps, the Central Asian animal shaped column caps, as well as curled grass decorations.

图 8 – 33 云冈石窟(北魏,位于山西省大同)

Figure 8 – 33 Yungang Caves built in Northern Wei, located in Datong, Shanxi Province

### (3) 击鼓说唱俑
### The Drum-Playing Speaking-Singing Figurine

东汉击鼓说唱俑(见图 8 – 34)的造型处理不讲求真实形体,只求形似,胸腹部大块平面,下肢比例压缩,但是,整体上却有一种洒脱灵动的气势,把说唱艺人的表演形态塑造得很传神。

击鼓说唱俑现收藏于中国国家博物馆。

The handling of the appearance of the drum-playing speaking-singing figurine from the Eastern Han (see Figure 8 – 34) does not strive for realistic form; rather, it only seeks a semblance of the form. The chest and belly are a large flat surface, while the lower limbs are on a compressed scale. However, on the whole, it has a kind of unconstrained, quick-witted vigor, vividly modeling the form of the speaking-singing artist's performance.

The drum-playing speaking-singing figurine is currently stored in the National Museum of China.

图 8-34 击鼓说唱俑（东汉，四川省郫县出土）

Figure 8-34　The Drum-Playing Speaking-Singing Figurine ( Excavated in Pi County, Sichuan Province)

## 3. 西方人对待雕塑的态度
### The Western Attitude Toward Sculpture

西方雕塑通过人体的健美来表达崇高的写实精神。古代西方人信奉"神人同形同性"，认为只有健全的身体才能产生健全的精神，因此，他们在生活中追求体格健壮，并使身体保持完美状态，在艺术上崇尚裸体的美，把人体作为雕塑的主要题材。例如米隆（约前480—前440）的《掷铁饼者》、米开朗基罗（1475—1564）的《大卫》（见图 8-35）、罗丹（1840—1917）的《思想者》等等，表现的是人体真实的比例，通过美的体态、肌肉和筋骨展现时代精神。

Western sculptures convey a sublime realistic spirit through the healthy and beautiful human body. Ancient Westerners believed "gods were the same as man in form and in characteristics", and they thought only through a sound body could one produce a sound spirit. Therefore, they pursued physical training in their lives and keeping a perfectly healthy condition. In art, they esteemed the beauty of the nude, and made the human body the primary subject matter of sculpture, as for example, Myron's (c. 480 – 440 B. C.) *Discobolus*, Michelangelo's (1475 – 1564) *David* (see Figure 8 – 35), Rodin's (1840 – 1917) *The Thinker*, etc. These display actual proportions of the human body, and through beautiful poses, flesh, muscle and sinew display the spirit of their age.

中国画里,除了工笔画以外,写实并不是第一要务。这可以从《大卫》与东汉《击鼓说唱俑》和《泼墨仙人图》表现出的形体直观地比较出来。

Realism was not the most important thing in Chinese painting, with the exception of "tidy brush" paintings. One can directly perceive this through the comparison of Michelangelo's *David* with the Eastern Han's *Drum-Playing Speaking-Singing Figurine* and *Portrait of an Immortal in Splashed Ink*.

图 8 –35 米开朗基罗的《大卫》
Figure 8 –35 Michelangelo's *David*

米开朗基罗·博那罗蒂(Michelangelo Buonarroti, 1475—1564)的《大卫》,创作

于 16 世纪初,像高 3.96 米,连基座高 5.5 米,用整块大理石雕刻而成,重量达 5.46 吨。人体结构符合严格的几何比例,体格健美,神情坚定,气势凛然,每一块肌肉都表现出内心的激烈情绪,整个人像洋溢着健康的生命气息,表现出严格的写实,是文艺复兴时期乃至整个人类社会的男性美的化身。现收藏于意大利佛罗伦萨美术学院。

Italian Michelangelo Buonarroti (1475 – 1564) created *David* in the early 16$^{th}$ Century. The figure is 3.96 meters tall, but with its stand is 5.5 meters high. It was carved from a single piece of marble, and it weighs 5.46 tons. The human composition rigorously adheres to geometric proportion; his physique is healthy and beautiful, his expression is resolute; its imposing manner is awe-inspiring. Every muscle manifests his internal, intense mood, so the entire sculpture is brimming with the breath of healthy living, displaying a strict realism. The piece is the beautiful incarnation of the male figure in Renaissance, even all of human, society. It is stored in the Accademia di Belle Arti di Firenze.

**思考题**

1. 中西绘画有什么不同的特点?

2. 欣赏一幅中国绘画,感受其所表达的意境。例如,郑板桥画的《竹石图》,是要通过竹子的空心、挺直来表达士人的虚心和傲骨等精神气节。

**Questions**

1. How is Chinese painting different from western painting?

2. Appreciate a Chinese painting and feel the artistic conception it is expressing. For example, Zheng Banqiao's paintings of *Bamboo and Stones* express the spiritual integrity, open-mindedness and uprightness of scholars/officials through the empty middle and straightness of the bamboo.

# 第九章 中国古代音乐、戏曲
# Ancient Chinese Music and Opera

古代的"乐"不只是音乐,而是音乐、舞蹈以及诗歌的组合,音乐与舞蹈相伴随。青海大通县上孙家寨墓地出土的舞蹈纹盆(见图9-1),内壁绘着三组舞蹈人的形象,每组5人,手拉着手跳舞,动作整齐协调,似乎在边舞边唱,反映出新石器时代人们文化生活的片段,表明从人类之初,音乐、舞蹈就相伴相生。

Ancient "yuè" is not just music, but a combination of music, dance and poetry. Music and dance accompany one another. The inner walls of the Basin with Dancing Design unearthed in the Upper Sunjiazhai cemetery in Datong County, Qinghai Province, depict three groups of dancers with five dancers in each group (see Figure 9-1). They hold each others' hands as they dance, and the action is orderly and harmonious, as if they are singing and dancing at the same time. This is a reflection of a fragment of popular cultural life in the neolithic era, making clear that from the beginning of humanity music and dance accompany and engender one another.

图9-1 马家窑文化中的舞蹈纹盆(青海大通县上孙家寨出土)
Figure 9-1 Basin with Dancing Design, Majiayao Culture
(Unearthed in the Upper Sunjiazhai, Datong County, Qinghai Province)

青海大通县上孙家寨墓地出土的舞蹈纹盆,是青海马家窑文化的代表性作品,绘有三组舞蹈人形,每组5人,各垂一发辫,摆向一致,服装下缘处还各有一尾饰。现收藏于中国国家博物馆。

Basin with Dancing Design, excavated in the Upper Sunjiazhai cemetery, Datong County, Qinghai Province, is a represtative piece from Qinghai's Majiayao Culture. The design has three groups of dancers with five people in each group, and each person with a braid swinging in unison. At the lower edge of the clothing of each, there is a tail decoration. The basin is stored in the National Museum of China.

# 一、中国古代代表性乐器
# Representative Instruments of Ancient Chinese Music

中国最早的乐器出现在新石器时代,以骨哨(浙江余姚河姆渡出土,距今7000年新石器时代)、陶埙(陕西西安半坡出土,距今6700年)为主要代表。到隋唐时期,乐器品种已经达到300多种,主要乐器全部出现。

The earliest Chinese musical instruments appeared in the Neolithic Era, primarily represented by the bone whistle (7000 years ago, in Neolithic Era, excavated in Hemudu, Yuyao, Zhejiang Province) and the clay *xūn* (6700 years ago, unearthed in Banpo, Xi'an, Shaanxi). By the Sui-Tang period, there were more than 300 different types of musical instruments, and all the primary types of instruments were in use.

## 1. 鼓
## Drum

### (1) 概述
### *General Remarks*

远古时期,鼓主要用作祭祀的器具。在狩猎征战活动中,鼓也被广泛地使用。鼓作为乐器从周代开始。

In ancient times drum was primarily used as an implement in sacrifices to anscetors, but was also widely used in hunts and warfare. As a musical instrument, the drum was first used in the Zhou Dynasty.

虎座鸟架鼓(见图9-2):战国时期楚国乐器,距今有2200多年。底座是双虎,背鼓的是双凤,中间是扁鼓,楠木制作。战国时期人们认为凤凰与音乐有关系,所以用凤凰做鼓架。湖北省江陵望山1号墓出土,现收藏于湖北省荆州博物馆。

Drum on Tiger Stand with Phoenix Frame (see Figure 9-2): a musical instrument from the Chu state of the Warring States period, more than 2200 years old. The base is two tigers, with a pair of phoenixes carrying the drum on their back, and the drum itself is a flat drum, made of Chinese cedar. People in the Warring States period believed there was a relationship between music and the phoenix, so the phoenix here forms the frame for the drum. It was excavated in the #1 tomb in Wangshan, Jiangling, Hubei Province, and is currently stored in the Jingzhou Museum, Hubei Province.

图 9-2 虎座鸟架鼓（战国）

Figure 9-2 Drum on Tiger Stand with Phoenix Frame (from the Warring States period)

(2) 关于鼓的诗词
**Poems about Drums**

鼓钟
《诗经·小雅》（西周）
Drum and Bell
"Book of Poetry, Lesser Elegentia" (Western Zhou)

鼓钟将将，
　　淮水汤汤，

忧心且伤。
淑人君子,
怀允不忘。

His bells ring out qiang-qiang
While the waters of the Huai go sweeping on;
Sad is my heart and wounded.
The virtuous sovereigns [ of old ]
In my heart, indeed, I cannot forget them.

## 菩萨蛮·画船捶鼓催君去
### 舒亶（北宋）
### To the Tune Pusaman: The Hanging Drum on the Painted Boat Presses You to Go
### Shu Dan (Northern Song)

画船捶鼓催君去,
高楼把酒留君住。
去住若为情,
西江潮欲平。

江潮容易得,
只是人南北。
今日此樽空,
知君何日同!

The hanging drum on the painted boat presses you to go,
Holding wine in a high tower pulls you to stay.
To go or stay is a matter of the heart,
The tide on West River desires calm.

Rivers and tides are easy to attain,
Only that people are separated in the north and south.
On this day, the wine goblet is empty,
I know not what day I will be together with you.

## 2. 埙

*Xun*

### (1) 概述

***General Remarks***

埙是中国最古老的吹奏乐器之一,早在新石器时代的红山文化时期,埙就已经出现。古代用陶土烧制,也叫"陶埙"(见图9-3),圆形或椭圆形,有六孔(现在有八孔、九孔、十孔、双八度等),上端为吹孔。

相传埙起源于一种叫作"石流星"的狩猎工具。古时候,人们常常用绳子系上一个石球或者泥球,投出去击打鸟兽。有的球体中间是空的,抡起来一兜风能发出声音。后来人们觉得挺好玩,就拿来吹,于是这种石流星就慢慢地演变成了吹奏乐器——埙。

据考古学家考证,全国多地都曾出土过形状各异的陶埙。

Xūn, one of China's oldest wind instruments, first appears in the Hongshan culture period of the Neolithic Era. It was made of clay fired in kiln, so it is also called the "clay *xūn*" (see Figure 9-3). It is round or oval, with six holes (there are also eight-hole, nine-hole, ten-hole, and double-octave versions), and the upper end is the blow hole.

Tradition has it that the *xūn* was originally a kind of hunting tool, known as a "stone meteor". People in ancient times would attach a string to a clay ball or stone ball and throw it as a means of hunting animals. Some of the balls had hollow centers and when they were swung around, they would catch the wind and produce a sound. Later, people decided this was a lot of fun, so they started to blow on it, and gradually this "stone meteor" evolved into a wind instrument.

According to archeological research, clay *xūn* of various shapes have been excavated in many places around the country.

图9-3 陶埙(春秋战国时期)

Figure 9-3 Clay *Xūn* (the Spring and Autumn, and Warring States Period)

## (2) 关于埙的诗词
***Poems about Xūn***

### 何人斯
《诗经·小雅》（西周）
What Person Is This?
"Book of Poetry, Lesser Elegentia" (Western Zhou)

伯氏吹埙，
仲氏吹篪。
及尔如贯，
谅不我知。
出此三物，
以诅尔斯。

The elder of us blew the porcelain whistle,
And the younger blew the bamboo flute;
I was as if strung on the same string with you.
If indeed you do not understand me.
Here are the three creatures [for sacrifice],
And I will take an oath to you.

### 贺田都弦再帅夔
阳枋（南宋）
Congratulating Tian Duxian on Again Proceeding to Kui
Yang Fang (Southern Song Dynasty)

桃李三生黄口儿，
春回桑梓放埙吹。

The peach and plum have bloomed thrice for the little child.
When Spring returns to his hometown, he can freely blow his whistle.

## 3. 琴
### Qin

**(1) 概述**
**General Remarks**

在古代，人们的文化修养是用琴、棋、书、画四方面的才能高低来表现的，弹琴为四大才能之首（见图9-4、图9-5、图9-6）。

Cultural accompliment among people in ancient times was expressed through levels of talent in the four aspects of *qín*, chess, calligraphy, and painting. So, playing *qín* was the first among the four important talents of the cultivated class. See Figure 9-4 to Figure 9-6.

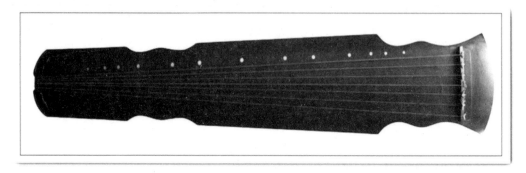

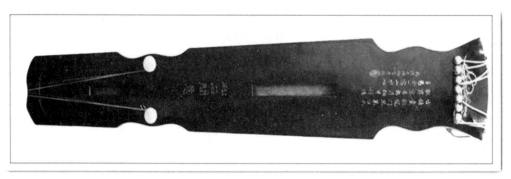

图9-4 古琴［北宋宣和二年（1120）宋徽宗御制］
Figure 9-4 Guqin

图9-5 弹琴图（徐州铜山苗山汉墓出土，现藏于江苏省徐州市汉画像石艺术馆）
Figure 9-5　Playing *Qin* (Excavated at the Han tomb on Miaoshan, Tongshan, Xuzhou, currently stored in the Xuzhou Art Museum of Han Stone Engravings, Jiangsu Province)

图9-6 听琴图（北宋·宋徽宗赵佶）
Figure 9-6　Listening to *Qin* (By Zhao Ji from Northern Song)

## (2) 关于琴的诗词
### Poem about Qin

**竹里馆**

王维（唐朝）

Room in the Bamboo

Wang Wei (Tang Dynasty)

独坐幽篁里,
弹琴复长啸。
深林人不知,
明月来相照。

I sit alone deep within a bamboo grove,
Playing my *qín* zither I again let out a long whistle.
Deep in the forest no one knows of it,
The bright moon comes out and we shine upon each other.

## 4. 笛子和箫
### Flutes and Xiao

### (1) 概述
#### General Remarks

笛子和箫两者均为古老的吹奏乐器。笛子吹孔在侧面，横吹；箫吹孔在上端，竖吹。笛子和箫的简单区别是：横吹为笛，竖吹为箫；笛子音量较大，箫的音量较小；笛子有一个孔上贴膜，箫一般不贴膜；笛子音质清脆，箫相对浑厚。笛子一般都是用竹子制作，故称竹笛。笛子因为制作容易，携带方便，是一种在民间较为普及的乐器，所以也留下了很多和笛子相关的诗歌。

Among ancient wind instruments, the flute's blow hole is on the lateral side, and it is played horizontally; the *xiao* blow hole is on the end, and it is played vertically. So, the simplest distinction between the two is the flute is played horizontally, and the *xiao* is played vertically. The volume of the flute is greater, and the flute has a membrane over the hole, whereas the *xiao* does not. The sound quality of the flute is sharp and crisp, while the *xiao* is relatively deep and resounding. Flutes are generally made of bamboo, so it is referred to as the "bamboo flute". Because they are relatively easy to make and very portable, it is a musical instrument that is relatively popular among folk musicians, and so there are numerous poems about the flute.

骨笛（见图9-7），出土于河南省舞阳县贾湖村新石器时代遗址，发掘出了随葬的21支骨头制成的笛子，全部用鹤类尺骨制成，长约20厘米，大多钻有七个孔，这是迄今发现的世界上最早的笛子，比古埃及出现的笛子要早2000年左右；开有五孔、六孔的两支骨笛，能奏出四声音阶和完备的五声音阶，是世界上出土年代最早、保存最为完整、出土个数最多且现在还能用以演奏的乐器。现收藏于河南省博物馆。

Bone flutes (see Figure 9-7) were excavated in a Neolithic site in Jiahu Village, Wuyang County, Henan Province. The site produced 21 bone flutes that accompanied the burial, all made from the ulnar bones of cranes, around 20cm long. Most had seven holes drilled in them. These are the world's earliest flutes, around 2000 years earlier than flutes found in ancient Egypt. Two bone flutes with five and six holes can play a four-note scale and a complete five note scale. These are the world's earliest musical instruments, preserved most intact, and the largest cache of them. Moreover, when they were unearthed they could still be played. They are currently stored in Henan Provincial Museum.

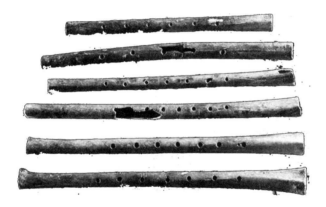

图9-7 骨笛（河南省舞阳县贾湖村出土的新石器时代文物）

Figure 9-7 Neolithic Bone Flutes (excavated in Jiahu Village, Wuyang County, Henan Province)

## (2) 关于笛子的诗词
## *Poems about Flutes*

### 春夜洛城闻笛
李白（唐朝）

### Hearing the Flute in Luoyang on a Spring Night
Li Bai (Tang Dynasty)

谁家玉笛暗飞声，
散入春风满洛城。
此夜曲中闻折柳，
何人不起故园情。

From whose home does the jade flute darkly let fly that sound?
Floating into the spring breeze it fills Luoyang.
On this night in this tune I hear "Breaking Willows"
Who could not reminisce over their hometown?

### 凉州词二首·其一
王之涣（唐朝）

### Two Lyrics in Liangzhou—Number One
Wang Zhihuan (Tang Dynasty)

黄河远上白云间，
一片孤城万仞山。
羌笛何须怨杨柳，
春风不度玉门关。

The source of the Yellow River, distant and lofty, between the white clouds,
A solitary city-wall among mountains thousands of feet high.
How could the barbarian's flute complain of poplars and willows,
When the spring wind does not cross the Jade Gate?

## 塞上听吹笛
### 高适（唐朝）
### Hearing a Flute on the Frontier
### Gao Shi (Tang Dynasty)

雪净胡天牧马还，
月明羌笛戍楼间。
借问梅花何处落，
风吹一夜满关山。

The snow melts under a barbarian sky, the horse-herder returns;
The moon is bright, the barbarian's flute resounds among the garrison.
May I ask where the "Plum Blossoms Fall"?
The tune blows all night filling mountains and passes.

(3) 关于箫的诗词
***Poems about Xiao***

### 松风阁
### 薛嵎（南宋）
### Pine Wind Pavilion
### Xue Yu (Southern Song Dynasty)

何处笙箫起半空，
满山斜日动蛟龙。
老僧无语凭栏久，
过尽白云千万重。

Wherein do the reeds and pipes arise in midair?
They fill the mountain under a tilting sun and move the rain-dragon.
The old monk leans on the parapet silently for a long time,
Crossing white clouds to the end ten million times.

## 湖上
### 徐元杰（南宋）
### On the Lake
### Xu Yuanjie (Southern Song Dynasty)

花开红树乱莺啼，
草长平湖白鹭飞。
风日晴和人意好，
夕阳箫鼓几船归。

Flowers in bloom on a red mangrove, the riotous orioles sing;
Grass is long, the lake is calm, the white egret takes flight.
The sun and wind are clear and harmonious, the people's minds are well;
Under the setting sun, among flutes and drums, several boats return.

## 5. 编钟
**Serial Bells**

编钟是大型打击乐器，兴起于西周，盛于春秋战国直至秦汉。编钟用青铜铸成，由大小不同的扁圆钟按照音调高低的次序排列悬挂在钟架上，用木槌和棒敲打发出不同的音调。编钟的钟体小，音调就高，音量也小；钟体大，音调就低，音量也大。

Serial Bells: a large-scale percussion instrument that arose in the Western Zhou and flourished in Spring-Autumn/Warring States period all the way up to the Qin-Han. Serial bells use bells cast of bronze; the oblate bells of different sizes are arranged on a hanging bell frame according to the height of their pitch, and they produce notes upon being struck by a wooden hammer or club. If the bell is smaller, the pitch it produces is higher, and the volume is lower; if the bell is bigger, the pitch is lower, and the volume is greater.

曾侯乙编钟（见图9-8）：战国早期文物，湖北随州曾侯乙墓出土。由大小不同的扁圆钟按照音调高低的次序排列起来，悬挂在一个巨大的钟架上，用丁字形的木槌和长形的棒分别敲打铜钟，能发出不同的乐音。由于每个钟的音调不同，按照音谱敲打，可以演奏出美妙的乐曲。总重量达5000多斤，由65件青铜编钟组成，音域跨五个半八度，12个半音齐备。钟架为铜木结构，呈曲尺形（如 ┌），全长10米以上，上下3层，高273厘米，由6个佩剑的青铜武士和几根圆柱承托。整套编钟和梁架气势宏大、壮观无比。演奏时乐队由几个人组成，用6只丁字形木槌敲高、中音，用两根长形棒撞低音。经声学专家研究，编钟中的每只钟都可以发出两个不同的乐音，只要准确地敲击钟上标音的位置，它就能发出合乎一定频率的乐音，整套编钟能奏出现代钢琴上的所有黑白键的音响。这套编钟的定音频率为256.4赫，与如今钢琴上的中央"C"频率几乎完全相等。它比欧洲十二平均律的键盘乐器的出现要早将近 2000 年。现收藏于湖北省博物馆。

The serial bells of Zeng Hou Yi (see Figure 9-8) are a cultural relic of the early part of the Warring States period, unearthed in Zeng Hou Yi's tomb, Suizhou, Hubei Province. Oblate shaped bells of different sizes are arranged in the order of the height of the pitch and hung on a massive bell frame; separately struck with a T-shaped hammer or a long club, the bells are able to produce different musical notes. Because the tone of each bell is different, when struck according to a musical score, one can perform marvelous musical compositions. The overall weight is more than 2500 kg, and it is made of 65 bronze bells. The register covers five and a half octaves, and twelve semitones are complete. The frame is made of copper and wood in the shape of a set square, more than ten meters long; there are three levels from top to bottom, 273 cm high. It is held up by six sword-bearing bronze warriors and several round columns. The bells and frame as a set are imposing and grand in appearance, an incomparable spectacle. It was played by a group of several musicians using six T-shaped wooden mallets for striking high and medium notes, and two long clubs for the lower notes. Accoustic research shows that each bell is able to produce two different notes, so the complete set of bells is able to play sounds of all the black and white keys on a modern piano. The tune frequency for this set of bells is 256.4 Hz, just about the same as Middle C on a modern piano. It appeared nearly 2000 years earlier than European twelve tone equal treatment keyboard instruments. It is currently stored in the Hubei Provincial Museum.

图 9-8 曾侯乙编钟（战国）

Figure 9-8 The Serial Bells of Zeng Hou Yi (Warring States Period)

## 6. 二胡
**Erhu**

二胡（见图9-9）早期也叫胡琴，因为用两根弦拉奏，所以叫二胡，原是北方少数民族乐器，后经不断改良。二胡名曲有《二泉映月》《赛马》等。

Erhu (two-string fiddle) (see Figure 9-9) was earlier called the *húqín*, but because it is played by drawing a bow across two strings, it is called *èrhú* (two-*hú*). It is a musical instrument originally of northern ethnic minorities that later continued to be improved. Famous tunes on the erhu include *Two Springs Reflect the Moon* and *Horse Racing*.

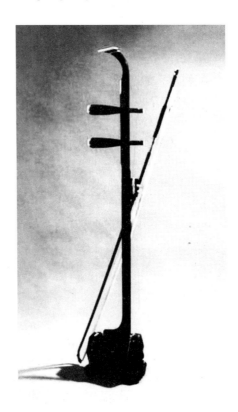

图9-9 二胡
Figure 9-9 Erhu

## 7. 琵琶
## Pipa

### (1) 概述
### *General Remarks*

琵琶是拨弦类弦鸣乐器。木制,音箱呈半梨形,上装四弦,演奏时竖抱,左手按弦,右手五指弹奏,是独奏、伴奏、重奏、合奏的重要乐器。

唐代的五弦琵琶,是古代北方少数民族弹拨乐器,简称五弦,造型可见于敦煌壁画。五弦琵琶自西域传入中原,公元五六世纪盛行于北朝,隋唐时期尤为盛行。

琵琶名曲有《十面埋伏》《春江花月夜》等。

*Pipa* is a plucked-string musical instrument. Made of wood, the resonating chamber is shaped like half of a pear. Equipped with four strings, it is held vertically as it is played, with the left hand pressing on the strings and the five fingers of the right hand pluck or strum the strings. It is an important instrument for solos, accompaniment, and ensemble performances.

The five-string *pipa* of the Tang Dynasty was a musical instrument of ancient northern ethnic minorities, referred to simply as the "five-string". It appears in Dunhuang murals. The five-string *pipa* spread from the western regions to the Central Plains, and was prevalent in the Northern Dynasties in the 5$^{th}$ and 6$^{th}$ Centuries, but became especially popular during the Sui-Tang period.

Famous *pipa* tunes include *Ambush on Ten Sides* and *River on a Spring Night*.

唐朝的五弦琵琶(见图9-10),目前世界上仅存的五弦琵琶,是唐朝宫廷送给日本圣武天皇的礼物,由紫檀木制成,全长108.5厘米,腹宽31厘米。日本圣武天皇非常喜爱这张五弦琵琶,公元756年,圣武天皇去世后,献给了东大寺,现收藏于日本奈良东大寺的正仓院。

Currently, the only extant five-string *pipa* from Tang Dynasty (see Figure 9-10) is a present the Tang court gave to the Japanese Emperor Shōmo. Made of red sandalwood, it is 108.5cm long and 31cm wide in the belly. Emperor Shōmo very much enjoyed this instrument, and after his death in 756, he gave it to the Tōdai-ji, a temple in Nara, where it is currently stored in the Shōsō-in, their repository of imperial treasures.

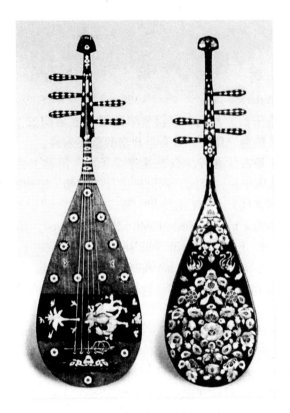

图 9-10　唐朝五弦琵琶

Figure 9-10　Tang Dynasty Five-string *Pipa*

### (2) 有关胡琴（二胡）的诗词
**Poems about the Erhu**

白雪歌送武判官归京<br>
岑参（唐朝）<br>
A Song of White Snow on Seeing Off the Military Magistrate on His Return to the Capital<br>
Cen Shen (Tang Dynasty)

北风卷地白草折，胡天八月即飞雪。
忽如一夜春风来，千树万树梨花开。
散入珠帘湿罗幕，狐裘不暖锦衾薄。
将军角弓不得控，都护铁衣冷犹著。
瀚海阑干百丈冰，愁云惨淡万里凝。

中军置酒饮归客，胡琴琵琶与羌笛。
纷纷暮雪下辕门，风掣红旗冻不翻。
轮台东门送君去，去时雪满天山路。
山回路转不见君，雪上空留马行处。

A north wind curls on the ground and the white grass bends,
Under the barbarian sky, snow already flies in the eighth month.
As if suddenly a night of spring wind blows,
And thousands and ten thousands of pear blossoms bloom.
Scattering into the bejeweled screen and dampening the gauze canopy,
The fox-fur coat is not warm, and the embroidered quilt is thin.
The general's horned bow cannot be controlled,
The governor's armor still must be worn.
The frozen desert is criss-crossed with acres of ice,
Worrisome clouds dark and gloomy congeal over thousands of miles.
The colonel lays out drinks to toast to the guest who will go back.
There is a *húqín*, *pipa*, and the barbarian flute.
Continuously the evening snow comes in under the barracks' gate,
Wind flashes past the red flag, but frozen it doesn't turn over.
Out the east gate of Luntai I see you off as you go,
When you go the the snow covers the road over Tianshan.
Around the mountain the road bends, and I do not see you,
On the snow are the empty tracks where the horse traveled.

## 池边即事
### 白居易（唐朝）
### A Prompt Affair Beside the Pond
### Bai Juyi (Tang Dynasty)

毡帐胡琴出塞曲，
兰塘越棹弄潮声。
何言此处同风月，
蓟北江南万里情。

In a felt tent the *húqín* produces a frontier tune
Thoroughwort on the pond climbs over the paddle and plays a damp sound.
How can one say this place is the same as the romance of wind and moon?
The Central Plains and Lower Yangtze feel a thousand miles away.

## (4) 有关琵琶的诗词
### *Poems about the Pipa*

#### 琵琶行
#### 白居易（唐朝）
#### Song of the *Pipa* Player
#### Bai Juyi (Tang Dynasty)

忽闻水上琵琶声，
主人忘归客不发。
寻声暗问弹者谁？
琵琶声停欲语迟。
移船相近邀相见，
添酒回灯重开宴。
千呼万唤始出来，
犹抱琵琶半遮面。
............

Suddenly from across the river came the sound of the *pipa*
The host forgot to leave and the guest did not depart.
We searched for the sound and asked in the dark who the player was
The *pipa* playing stopped, but the desired words were slow to come.
We moved the boat to draw nearer and requested a chance to meet
Refilling the wine cups and relighting the lamps the party started anew.
After beseeching time and again did she first come out
Still holding the *pipa* that shadowed half her face.
...

#### 五弦行
#### 韦应物（唐朝）
#### Song on the Five-String
#### Wei Yingwu (Tang Dynasty)

美人为我弹五弦，
尘埃忽静心悄然。
A beauty plays the five-string for me,
And the dust of life suddenly calms from my heart and I am quiet.

## 二、十大古典名曲
## Ten Famous Classical Songs

### 1.《高山流水》
### *Towering Mountains Flowing Water*

传说先秦时琴师俞伯牙一次在荒山野地弹琴，樵夫钟子期竟能领会曲中高山流水之意，伯牙感到惊讶，子期心中所想竟然和我一样。子期死后，伯牙因为失去知音而感到痛苦，于是摔断了琴和弦，一生都没有再碰它。

Legend has it that in pre-Qin times the *qín* master Yu Boya was playing the *qín* (zither) on a barren hill in the wilderness. The woodcutter, Zhong Ziqi was surprisingly able to understand the reference to lofty mountains and flowing water in the piece Boya was playing. Boya was amazed that what he had been thinking and what Ziqi was thinking were identical. After Ziqi's death, Boya was pained at losing a "knower of the sounds" (i.e., intimate friend), and so he gave up playing the *qín* and never touched the instrument again.

### 2.《梅花三弄》
### *Thrice Worked Plum-blossoms*

此曲是借物咏怀，即通过梅花的洁白、芬芳和耐寒等特征，来赞颂具有高尚情操的人，因为曲子中泛奇曲调在不同的徽位上重复了三次，所以称为"三弄"。

This tune uses an object to sing about one's feelings, i.e., through characteristics of plum blossoms like pure whiteness, fragrance, and resistance to cold, one praises a person possessed of noble character. Because the odd melody in the song is repeated three times at different positions, it is called "thrice worked".

### 3.《春江花月夜》
### *River on a Spring Night*

该曲原来是一首琵琶独奏曲，演奏中运用了各种琵琶技法，后被改编成民族管弦乐曲，又名《夕阳箫鼓》。乐曲通过委婉质朴的旋律，流畅多变的节奏，形象地描绘了月夜春江的迷人景色，赞颂的是江南水乡的风姿异态。

This was originally for a *pipa* solo performance which made use of various kinds of *pipa* techniques. Later it was adapted as a folk orchestral piece. It is also called *Flutes and Drums under a Setting Sun*. By means of a tactful, simple melody and flowing, multivariate rhythm, it figuratively depicts a charming scene of a moon-lit night in spring on a river, praising the charmingly unusual state of patchwork waterways in the lower Yangtze region.

### 4.《汉宫秋月》
*Autumn Moon in the Han Palace*

此曲意在表现古代深宫中的宫女们的幽怨悲泣情绪,从而唤起人们对她们不幸遭遇的同情。

This piece's meaning lies in expressing the bitter, grief-filled mood of palace maids in ancient times, and thereby awakening people's sympathy for their unfortunate experiences.

### 5.《阳春白雪》
*White Snow in a Sunny Spring*

此为琵琶独奏古曲,以清新流畅的旋律、活泼轻快的节奏,生动地表现了冬去春来大地复苏、万物向荣、生机勃勃的初春景象。

This is an ancient tune for *pipa* solo performance; by means of a clean flowing melody and lively, quick rhythm it vividly displays an early spring scene as winter retreats, mother earth resuscitates, living things begin to thrive, and vitality returns.

### 6.《渔樵问答》
*Questions and Answers Between the Fisherman and Woodcutter*

此曲在历代传谱中有30多种版本,有的还附歌词。乐曲旋律飘逸,采用渔夫和樵夫之间对话的方式,以上升的曲调表示问句,下降的曲调表示答句,表现渔樵在青山绿水间自得其乐的情趣。

There are over thirty versions of this tune among transmitted scores over the centuries, some of which include lyrics. The composition's melody is graceful, employing the form of a dialogue between a fisherman and a woodcutter. It uses rising tunes to express questions, and falling ones to express answers, showing the delight of the two as they each find amusement in their own way among the green hills and clear waters.

### 7.《胡笳十八拍》
*Eighteen Beats with a Barbarian's Whistle*

"胡笳"原来是我国北方少数民族的吹奏乐器,它音量宏大,用作军乐以壮声威,十八拍即十八首之意。《胡笳十八拍》反映的主题是著名的"文姬归汉"的故事:汉末,著名文学家蔡邕的女儿蔡文姬被匈奴所获,成为匈奴王的妃子,生了两个孩子,在匈奴生活了十二年。后来曹操派人把她接回,她喜悦于回乡,却痛苦于和孩子别离。于是她写诗叙述她的身世和思乡别子的感情。情绪悲凉激动,感人颇深。

The "barbarian's whistle" was originally a wind instrument used among northern ethnic minorities, which had great volume, and when used for military music it had robust resonance. The "eighteen beats" means eighteen pieces. The main theme it renders is the famous story of "Wenji's return to the Han". In the latter years of the Han Dynasty, Cai Wenji, the daughter of the famous literatus Cai Yong, was captured by the Xiongnu and became an imperial concubine of the Xiongnu king. As such, she gave birth to two sons and lived among the Xiongnu for twelve years. Later, Cao Cao sent someone to get her back, and she was happy to return home, but pained about being separated from her sons. So, she wrote a poem narrating her life history and feelings about separating from her sons. The mood is sorrowful, exciting and deeply moving.

## 8.《广陵散》
### *Guangling Verse*

"广陵"是指琴曲的流传地在广陵（今天的江苏扬州），"散"是操、引、曲的意思。《广陵散》题材源于古代的《聂政刺韩王曲》。该作品讲的是一个造剑工匠被韩王无辜杀害，他的儿子聂政为了报仇，以泥瓦匠身份混入韩宫；刺杀失败后，他逃入深山刻苦学琴，十年时间练成绝技以后，再次混入宫中，利用弹琴的机会刺死了韩王，自己也为此而牺牲。

"Guangling" (modern Yangzhou) refers the the area where this tune on the *qin* was in circulation. The tune's subject matter is the story of "Nie Zheng Assassinates the King of Han". This story relates how a sword-maker was killed for no reason by the King of Han. The sword-maker's son, Nie Zheng, in order to get revenge, sneaks into the Han palace in the guise of a bricklayer. After his attempt at assassinating the king fails, he escapes to the mountains where he undertakes rigorous training in the *qin*. After ten years during which time he perfected his supreme feat, he again sneaks into the Han palace. He takes advantage of the opportunity of a *qin* performance to assassinate the king and then sacrifices himself for doing so.

## 9.《平沙落雁》
### *Wild Geese Descending on the Sand Bank*

此曲曲调悠扬流畅，通过时隐时现的雁鸣，描写雁群在天空盘旋的情景。表现手法新颖、别致，容易为听众理解。

The melody is mellifluous and fluent; through intermittently audible wild goose calls, it depicts a scene in which a flock of wild geese circle in the sky. The technique on display is new and unusual, and it is easily understood by the audience.

## 10. 《十面埋伏》
### *Ambush on Ten Sides*

这是一首历史题材的大型琵琶曲,描写公元前202年楚汉战争时,刘邦、项羽决战的情景。汉军用十面埋伏的阵法击败楚军,项羽自刎于乌江,刘邦取得胜利。

This is a large-scale *pipa* piece based on historical subject matter. It describes the situation in 202 B. C. during the Chu-Han Civil War when Liu Bang and Xiang Yu fought their decisive battle. The Han army used the "ambush on ten sides" battle formation to attack the Chu army. Xiang Yu committed suicide at the Wu River, and Liu Bang emerged victorious.

# 三、中国古典音乐的特点
# Characteristics of Chinese Classical Music

第一,以旋律为主。西方音乐注重合声和配气,给人一种浑厚之美。中国音乐以旋律为主,带给人们的是一种气韵生动的线条之美。

First, rely mainly on the melody. Western music emphasizes joined sound and matched energy, giving listeners a kind of deep and resounding aesthetic. Chinese music relies mainly on the melody, giving listeners a kind of linear aesthetic that is distinctly lively.

第二,理性精神。古人认为音乐是表达内心情志的一种方式或途径,情志属于人,用嘴吟唱比非人体乐器更接近情的本性。

Second, rationalist spirit. The ancients believed music was a method or path for expressing inner emotions; emotions belong to people; using one's mouth to chant was closer to the emotion itself than a non-human musical instrument.

第三,节奏宣泄。主要表现在民间音乐中,如陕北腰鼓、山西锣鼓等,在喧闹的节奏中凸显出一种粗犷的阳刚之气。

Third, rhythmically unburden oneself. This is primarily manifest in folk music, such as the waist drums of northern Shaanxi and the gongs and drums of Shanxi; within the noisy rhythm, a crude, wild, masculine energy is magnified.

## 四、中国戏曲的种类
## Types of Chinese Opera

中国戏剧发端于远古时期祭祀鬼神的仪式。按照当时的习俗，祭祀鬼神时要用人装扮成"尸"，作为鬼神所依附的实体。同时，巫师穿着巫服，手拿道具，在音乐的伴奏下载歌载舞，以此来娱乐神灵，这种仪式便是后世戏剧的萌芽。

Chinese theater originated in ceremonies for making sacrifices to gods and spirits in ancient times. According to the customs of the time, when making sacrifices, they needed a person to dress up as the "corpse" to serve as the entity the spirits adhered to. At the same time, wizards wearing shaman's costume and holding props danced and sang with the musical accompaniment and in so doing would entertain the spirits. These sorts of ceremonies were the seed for later theatrical performances.

中国各民族地区的戏曲剧种约有 360 多种，传统剧目数以万计。比较著名的戏曲种类有昆曲、粤剧、淮剧、川剧、秦腔、晋剧、汉剧、河北梆子、河南坠子、湘剧、黄梅戏、湖南花鼓戏等。

中国戏曲主要的五大剧种是京剧、越剧、黄梅戏、评剧、豫剧。

Dramatic and operatic types among the various ethnic regions of China total some 360 types with traditional repertoires in the tens of thousands. Relatively well-known operatic genres include: Kunqu, Cantonese opera, Huai (Jiangsu) opera, Sichuan opera, Qinqiang (Shaanxi), Jin opera (Shanxi), Han opera (Hubei), Hebei opera, Henan opera, Xiang opera (Hunan), Huangmei opera (Anhui), and Huagu opera in Hunan.

The five main types of opera in China are Peking opera, Shaoxing opera, Huangmei opera, Ping opera (north and northeast China), and Henan opera.

### 1. 京 剧
### Peking Opera

京剧形成于清朝，民国年间得到空前的繁荣。用胡琴和锣鼓等伴奏，被视为中国国粹。由于京剧在形成之初就进入了宫廷，这使得它的发育成长不同于其他地方剧种，要求也就更高。

Peking opera took shape in the Qing Dynasty and attained unprecedented prosperity in the Republican period. Accompanied by the *húqín* and percussion instruments, it has been considered the national essence of China. Because during its formative years it entered the imperial court, its development and maturation was different from other types of regional operas, and the demands were even higher.

京剧表演的四种艺术手法——唱、念（人物的内心独白和对话）、做、打，也是京剧表演四项基本功。角色性格化的脸谱，分为生、旦、净、丑四大基本类型。各种角色的性格品行、唱腔念白、动作造型、穿着打扮等都有着严格的规定。

The four types of artistic skills in Peking opera performance are singing, reciting (soliloquies and dialogues), acting, and fighting. These are also the four fundamental skills of the performance. The types of facial makeup which characterize the roles are differentiated as "male lead", "female roles", "painted face male role", and "clown", and these are the four basic types of roles. There are strict provisions for each role's temperament and moral conduct, singing and speaking voices, style of action and style of dress.

生：男性角色的统称，分老生、小生等。著名老生演员有余叔岩（1890—1943）、马连良（1901—1966），都形成了自己的派别。

Male lead: A general term for male roles, which can be differentiated as venerable male and young male. Famous venerable male actors include Yu Shuyan (1890 – 1943) and Ma Lianliang (1901 – 1966), both of whom have already formed their own school of acting.

马连良（见图 9 – 11 和图 9 – 12），回族，经名尤素福，原籍陕西扶风，生于北京，中国著名京剧艺术家。

Ma Lianliang (see Figure 9 – 11, Figure – 12), whose family was from Fufeng, Shaanxi, was a famous Chinese Peking opera artist born in Beijing.

图 9 –11　马连良扮演的京剧老生
Figure 9 –11　Peking Opera Venerable Male Played by Ma Lianliang

图 9 –12　马连良
Figure 9 –12　Ma Lianliang

旦：女性角色的统称，分青衣（正旦）、花旦等。由于受传统礼教的影响，舞台上不允许男女同台演出，直到民国初年还是如此。男女若同台，是"有失风化"的大事，不仅会受到老百姓的唾弃，也会受到当局的干涉。所以，在戏台上扮演女性形象的"旦角"都是男演员。民国时期著名的旦角演员有梅兰芳（1894—1961）、程砚秋（1904—1958）、荀慧生（1900—1968）、尚小云（1900—1976）等，称为"四大名旦"，都形成了自己的派别。梅兰芳于1919年赴日本公演，1930年赴美国公演，第一次将京剧传播到了海外，受到观众喜爱。

Female roles: The general term for female parts in the performance, and is differentiated as "black shirt" (starring role) and "colored shirt" (vivacious young female role). Owing to the influence of Ru-ist ethics, men and women were not permitted to appear on stage together, a rule which lasted to the early years of the Republican era. If a man and woman appeared together, it was considered a "loss of public morality", a situation spurned by the common people, and subject to interference from the authorities. So, the female roles on stage were played by male actors. Famous female role actors of the Republican period include Mei Lanfang (1894 – 1961), Cheng Yanqiu (1904 – 1958), Xun Huisheng (1900 – 1968), Shang Xiaoyun (1900 – 1976), the so-called "four great female roles" actors. They each have formed their own school of acting. Mei Lanfang performed in Japan in 1919, and in 1930 traveled to the United States to perform. He was the first to spread Peking opera abroad and was greatly appreciated by audiences.

梅兰芳（见图9-13和图9-14）的祖籍是江苏泰州，中国京剧表演艺术大师。抗日战争爆发后，1941年，梅兰芳蓄起胡须，息影舞台，表明支持抗日。1945年抗战胜利，10月重新登台。1949年获美国波摩那学院和南加州大学的荣誉文学博士学位。

Mei Lanfang's family was from Taizhou, Jiangsu Province. He was a great master of Peking opera performing arts (see Figure 9 – 13, Figure 9 – 14). After China's War of Resistance against Japan broke out, starting from 1941, he grew a beard and stopped performing on stage as an expression of his support for the resistance. In October 1945, after the War of Resistance was won, he again appeared on stage. In 1949 he received an honorary doctorate from Pomona College and the University of Southern California.

图9-13 京剧旦角（梅兰芳演出剧照《贵妃醉酒》）
Figure 9-13 Female role in Peking Opera (Photo of Mei Lanfang Performing *The Drunken Beauty*)

图9-14 梅兰芳
Figure 9-14 Mei Lanfang

净：俗称花脸（见图9-15），用来扮演性格、品质或相貌上有些特异的男性人物，分为文净、武净两大类。

Painted face male role (see Figure 9-15): Commonly called the colorful face role, it is used to perform male characters with special features in their temperament, intrinsic quality, or outward appearance. They are generally differentiated as civilian painted faces and military painted faces.

架子花脸（张飞）　　白净（曹操）　　红净（关羽）

图9-15 京剧花脸（净脸）
Figure 9-15 Peking Opera Painted Faces (Jing Face)

丑：扮演喜剧角色，因在鼻梁上抹一小块白粉，俗称小花脸（见图9-16）。分文丑、武丑等。

Clown：A clown performs comic roles. Because there is a smear of white powder on the bridge of the nose, it is commonly called the lesser colored face (see Figure 9-16). They are differentiated as civilian clowns and military clowns.

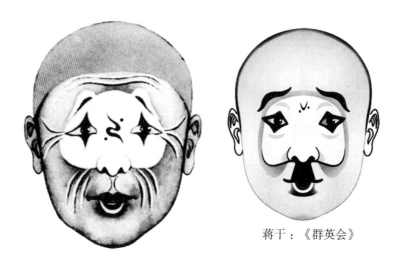

蒋干：《群英会》

图9-16 京剧丑角脸谱
Figure 9-16 Peking Opera Clown Facial makeup

京剧的脸谱（见图9-17），主要表示人物的性格、特征或其他特点，变形大胆而夸张，但是有一定的规律和方法，不同颜色有不同的含义：红色表示忠烈正义，例如关羽；黑色表示耿直、豪爽，例如张飞；紫色表示刚正稳健；蓝脸、绿脸表示草莽英雄；黄脸、白脸表示阴险狡诈，例如曹操；金脸、银脸是神秘，代表神妖，例如孙悟空。

Peking opera's facial makeup (see Figure 9-17) mainly expresses the character's temperament, trait, or other special features. The changes are brazen and exaggerated, but there is a definite pattern and method to it. Different colors have different connotations: red expresses sacrificing for one's country and righteousness, as in Guan Yu; black expresses frankness and forthrightness, as in Zhang Fei; purple expresses honest and stable; blue faces and green faces express heroism in the wilderness; yellow and white faces express sinister and cunning, as in Cao Cao; gold and silver faces are mysterious, representing spirits or goblins, such as Sun Wukong.

图 9-17 京剧脸谱
Figure 9-17 Peking Opera Facial Makeup

京剧常见剧目有《霸王别姬》《贵妃醉酒》《四郎探母》《铡美案》等。京剧行当全面、表演成熟、气势宏美,是近代中国戏曲的代表。

The commonly performed repertoire for Peking opera includes *Farewell My Concubine*, *The Drunken Beauty*, *The Fourth Son Visited His Mother*, and *The Case of Chen Shimei*. Peking opera, comprehensive in its professionalism, mature in its performances and grandly beautiful in its vigor, is the representative of modern Chinese opera.

## 2. 越剧
### Shaoxing Opera

越剧以抒情见长,唱腔委婉细腻,具有江南地方色彩,被称为中国第二大剧种。多以"才子佳人"题材为主,艺术流派众多,主要流行于南方地区。越剧常见剧目有《梁山伯与祝英台》《红楼梦》《五女拜寿》《西厢记》等。

Shaoxing opera takes emotional expression as its forte, with arias that are tactful and exquisite, possessed of the character of the lower Yangtze valley area. It has been called the second greatest operatic type in China. It mostly relies on "gifted scholars and beautiful ladies" for its subject matter, and there are many schools of the art. It is most popular in the south. The repertoire includes *The Butterfly Lovers*, *Dream of the Red Chambers*, *Five Daughters Offering Felicitation*, and *Romance of the West Chamber*.

## 3. 黄梅戏
### Huangmei Opera

黄梅戏起源于湖北黄梅县,发展壮大于安徽安庆地区,所以戏曲语言用安庆方言。黄梅戏唱腔流畅,以抒情见长。黄梅戏常见剧目有《天仙配》《女驸马》《牛郎织女》等。

Huangmei opera, originating in Huangmei County, Hubei Province, grew and expanded into Anhui's Anqing prefecture, so the language the opera uses is Anqing dialect. The arias are smooth and flowing, taking the expression of emotion as its forte. The repertoire includes *Goddess's Marriage*, *The Female Prince Consort*, and *The Cowherd and the Weaving Girl*.

## 4. 评剧
### Ping Opera

评剧的艺术特点是表演生活气息浓厚,故事性强,善于表现民间生活。评剧在华北、东北等地流行较广,于清末时形成于河北唐山,所以又名"唐山落子"。1923年,创建该剧种的警世戏社在天津演出时,因其上演剧目多有惩恶扬善、评古论今之新意,随后就改称"评剧"。评剧常见剧目有《杜十娘》《杨三姐告状》《小二黑结婚》等。

Ping opera's artistic characteristics are its strong narrativity, with the strong interest in the breath of life. It also excels at displaying folk life. It is broadly popular in north and northeast China. Having formed in the Qing Dynasty in Tangshan, Hebei Province, it is also called "Tangshan opera". In 1923, the Startle the World Opera Society which was founded around this type of opera performed in Tianjin. Because the repertoire they performed included many new ideas about "condemning evil and praising the good", as well as "criticizing the old and discussing the modern", so its name was changed to Ping (criticize) opera. The common repertoire includes *Du Shiniang*, *Yang Sanjie Lodges a Complaint*, and *Xiao Erhei's Marriage*.

### 5. 豫剧
### Henan Opera

豫剧主要流行于河南等地，因河南省简称"豫"，所以定名为豫剧。豫剧唱腔有口语化特点，地方特色浓郁，通俗自然，紧贴老百姓的生活。豫剧常见剧目有《花木兰》《穆桂英挂帅》《七品芝麻官》《朝阳沟》等。

Henan opera is mainly popular in Henan. Because the literary name for Henan is "Yu", this form is called Yu (Henan) opera. Its arias have the characteristic of being very colloquial, with strong local features, making it natural and common, sticking close to the lives of the common people. The common repertoire includes *Hua Mulan*, *Mu Guiying Takes Command*, *The Presumptuous Mr. Nobody*, and *Chaoyang Village*.

中国戏剧虽然剧种繁多，流派复杂，但总体特点大致相似。

Though there a many kinds of Chinese opera and the styles are complicated, in general they are mostly very similar.

## 五、中国戏曲的特点
## Characteristics of Chinese Opera

第一，综合性。唱念做打样样齐全，融合了文学、音乐、舞蹈、绘画、雕塑等艺术。

First, synthesis. With singing, dialogue, acting and fighting, it includes everything, welding together the arts of literature, music, dance, painting and sculpture.

第二，动作的虚拟化。戏剧在音乐、服装、舞台设计与表演动作等方面，都是借助意境表现实际，例如用扬鞭表示骑马，用划桨表示行船，用抬轿的动作表示有轿，用开关门的动作表示有门，等等。可以三五步行遍天下，六七人百万雄兵（见图 9 – 18 和图 9 – 19）。还有眼睛的各种看法，脚的各种走法，都是把实际生活的特点高度集中，用艺术夸张来表现。

Second, fictitiousness of the action. In regards to music, costumes, stage design, and the performance of action, opera draws on the artistic conception to represent reality. For example, raising a whip expresses riding a horse (see Figure 9 – 18), or paddling an oar means traveling by boat, or using the motion of raising a sedan chair to express that there is such a chair in the scene, or using the motion of opening and closing a door to show that there is a door in the scene. An actor can stride across the world in several steps, or six or seven people can stand for an army of myriad warriors (see Figure 9-19). There are also various techniques with moving the eyes and several ways of taking steps with the feet, all of which highly concentrate the features of real life and use artistic exaggeration to express them.

图 9-18 京剧中的策马扬鞭

Figure 9-18 Urging a Horse On by Raising a Whip in Peking Opera

图 9-19 京剧中的战争场面

Figure 9-19 A Fight Scene in Peking Opera

第三，表演的程式化。程式是戏曲反映生活的表现形式。它是指对生活动作的规范化、舞蹈化表演并被重复使用。程式直接或间接来源于生活，但它又是按照一定的规范对生活经过提炼、概括、美化而形成的。戏曲以唱、念、做、打的综合表演为主，戏曲表演中的程式指的是关门、推窗、上马、登舟、上楼等，皆有固定的格式。此外，戏曲从剧本形式、角色当行、音乐唱腔、化妆服装等各个方面，都有固定的程式。

Third, formulization of the performance. Formulas are the expressive form by which opera renders life. It refers to the standardized, dancified performance of life's actions and their repeated use. The formula directly or indirectly originates in life, but it also is formed according to certain standards to purify, generalize and beautify life experience. Opera relies on the composite performance of singing, reciting, acting and fighting; the formulas in operatic performance refers to the closing of doors, pushing of windows, mounting horses, boarding boats, ascending towers, and all such fixed patterns. In every aspect, such as the form of the script, roles of the characters, music and singing, and makeup and costumes, all have fixed formulas.

第四，抒情性。也是表情性。中国传统戏曲经典剧目大多是抒情戏。

Fourth, emotional expressiveness: the Chinese traditional repertoire of operatic classics are mostly operas about expressing emotions.

**思考题**

1. 欣赏十大名曲中的一曲，并了解乐曲背后的历史故事。
2. 简要总结中国戏曲的特点。
3. 列出中国戏曲的五大剧种。

***Questions***

1. Listen to one of the ten famous songs and find out about the historical story behind the song.
2. Simply summarize the characteristics of Chinese opera.
3. List the five great types of Chinese opera.

# 第十章 中国建筑
## Chinese Architecture

## 一、中国建筑类型
## Types of Chinese Architecture

中国古代建筑大体上分为宫殿、陵墓、寺庙、园林和民居。

Ancient Chinese architecture can largely be divided into the following types: palaces, tombs and mausoleums, temples and monasteries, parks and gardens, and homes.

### 1. 宫殿
### Palaces

宫殿建筑代表了建筑技术与艺术的最高水平,以皇宫为代表性建筑。皇宫作为皇帝办公和居住的场所,目的是显示帝王的威严,因此有房屋高、空间大、布局深、庄重肃穆四大特点。

宫殿建筑采取严格的中轴线对称排列的布局方式,建筑排列深长,占有空间众多,传统格局为两部分,即"前朝后寝"。"前朝"是帝王日常朝会、举行庆典之处,"后寝"是皇帝与后妃们居住生活的地方。

Palace architecture represents the highest level of architectural art and technique, and imperial palaces serve as the representative construction. The imperial palace was the location the emperor worked and lived, so the goal was to display the emperor's majesty. Thus it had the four characteristics of having high roofs, covering a large area, a depth of composition, and being dignified and solemn.

Palace construction adopted the compositional pattern of strict adherence to central axis symmetry. The building arrangement was deep and long, and the space it occupied was large. The traditional arrangement was in two parts, i.e., the so-called "front (south) for ruling, back (north) for sleeping". "Front for ruling" is the place for daily court meetings and holding ceremonies. "Back for sleeping" is the place where the emperor and his consorts resided.

现在比较完整地保存下来的帝王宫殿只有两处，一是北京的明、清故宫；二是沈阳的清故宫，是清朝入关前创建的宫殿，原称盛京宫阙，建成于后金时期（1636年），清朝称作奉天行宫，有房屋三百余间，建筑具有东北地方风格。

There are two places where imperial palaces are preserved relatively completely: Beijing's Forbidden City of the Ming and Qing, and Shenyang's Forbidden City of the Qing, which is the palace the Qing Dynasty built before they entered the pass and took over the rest of the country. The Shenyang palace was originally called the Shengjing (an old name for Shenyang) Palace, and was built in 1636. After taking over the country in 1644, the Qing called it Fengtian (Bestowed Heaven, an old name for Shenyang) Imperial Residence. It has over 300 buildings, and the construction possesses a regional northeastern style.

北京位于华北平原的北端，处于通向东北平原的要冲地带。战国时，这里已经形成城市，辽代在此建陪都，金时建为都城，称为中都。元朝灭金以后，建成大都城。明朝灭元后，大都改称北平。明成祖朱棣为了把都城从南京迁到自己以前的驻地北平，从永乐五年（1407）起开始营建北平宫殿，修建了13年以后，迁都北平，之后南京就成为明朝的陪都。清朝灭明后，继续沿用明代旧宫。

1949年之后，对北京城进行了大规模的拆除工作。北京的外城城墙、城门和角楼于1951年至1958年拆除。内城城门和城墙先后于1965年至1969年拆除。只有紫禁城（故宫）较为完整地保存下来。

Beijing is located in the northern end of the North China Plain, positioned in a major crossroad leading to the Northeast Plain. In the Warring States period, this place had already had a city, and a secondary capital was built here in the Liao Dynasty. In the Jin Dynasty a capital city was built here, called Zhongdu. After the Yuan Dynasty wiped out the Jin, they built Dadu City here. After the Ming wiped out the Yuan, Dadu's name was changed to Beiping (northern peace). Zhu Di, the Chengzu Emperor of the Ming, began to construct the Beiping Palace in fifth year of his reign (1407) in order to move the capital from Nanjing to his former encampment. After 13 years of construction, the capital moved to Beiping, and Nanjing became a secondary capital for the Ming. After the Qing wiped out the Ming, they continued to use the Ming palaces.

After 1949, large-scale demolition work was carried out in Beijing. The outer city walls, city gates and corner towers were demolished between 1951 and 1958. The inner city walls and gates were demolished between 1965 and 1969. Only the Forbidden City was relatively completely preserved.

北京故宫，旧称紫禁城，明朝从永乐四年（1406）开始准备修建，1402年竣工。北京故宫南北长961米，东西宽753米，共有房屋9999间半。

Beijing's Forbidden City, whose construction started in 1406, was completed in 1420. West to east, it is 760 meters wide, north to south is is 960 meters long, and it includes 9999 and a half buildings.

北京紫禁城（故宫）是庭院式平面建筑群布局的典型例子（见图 10 – 1）：三大殿——太和殿、中和殿、保和殿以及三个后宫——乾清宫、交泰殿、坤宁宫位于中轴线上，其他次要的建筑位于两边，在到达主殿太和殿之前，需经过 1600 余米长的中轴线以及五门五院（自南向北是大清门、天安门、端门、午门、太和门），其他建筑相对降低、减小，形成逐步展开的建筑序列来衬托三大殿的庄严、崇高、宏伟，以强调皇帝的权威和至高无上的地位，反映出中国建筑文化中的等级观念。

Beijing's Forbidden City, the archetypical example of planar-building-complex layout in the courtyard style (see Figure 10 – 1); three large main halls (Hall of Supreme Harmony, Hall of Central Harmony, and the Hall of Preserving Harmony) together with three back palaces for imperial concubines (Palace of Heavenly Purity, Hall of Union, and Palace of Earthly Tranquility), all positioned on the central axis. Other secondary buildings are located on either side of the axis. Before arriving at the main hall, the Hall of Supreme Harmony, one must travel along the 1600-meter central axis, as well as pass through five gates and courtyards (from south to north they are Gate of China, Gate of Heavenly Peace, Gate of Uprightness, Meridian Gate, and the Gate of Supreme Harmony). Other buildings are relatively low and small, forming a building sequence that progressively unfolds, setting off the solemn, imposing, magnificence of the three main halls, thereby emphasizing the authority of the emperor and his supreme position, reflecting the concept of rank in the Chinese architectural culture.

北京故宫建筑为木结构，黄琉璃瓦顶、青白石底座，饰以金碧辉煌的彩画，与一般的青灰瓦顶住房形成强烈对比，是世界皇宫之最。故宫周围有两道坚固的防线，外围是一条宽 52 米，深 6 米的护城河环绕；护城河外是周长 3 公里的城墙，墙高近 10 米，底宽 8.62 米。城墙四面开有 4 门：南面正门叫午门，北面神武门，东面东华门，西面西华门。城墙四角，耸立着 4 座角楼，角楼有 3 层屋檐，72 个屋脊，造型华美。北京故宫是现存最大、最完整、最精美的木结构宫殿建筑群，最能全面体现中国古建筑特色。

Beijing's Forbidden City construction is wood structured, with golden yellow glazed roof tiles on white marble foundations, and it is decorated with dazzling color paint. It forms a strong contrast with the generally gray tile roofs on the residences around it. It is the largest imperial palace in the world. The palace is ringed by two firm defensive perimeters. The outer one is the 52-meter wide, six-meter deep moat, outside the moat is the three kilometer long city wall, nearly 10 meters high and 8.62 meters wide at the base. There are four gates in the city wall: the main gate in the south is the Meridian Gate; in the north is the Gate of Divine

Might; to the east is Donghua Gate, and Xihua Gate is to the west. Standing at the four corners of the city wall are four corner towers, each three levels of eaves totaling 72 roof ridges, each of which is stylistically ornate. Beijing's Forbidden City is the largest, best preserved wood-constructed palace complex in existence, and it is best able to comprehensively reflect ancient China's architectural characteristics.

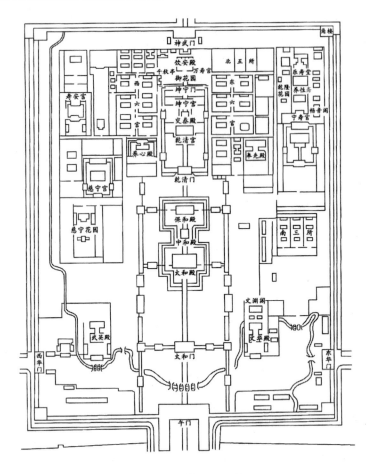

图 10 – 1　北京紫禁城（故宫）
Figure 10 – 1　Beijing's Forbidden City

紫禁城内部分为外朝、内廷两大部分。外朝是皇帝处理朝政的地方，内廷是生活场所。

外朝包括太和殿、中和殿、保和殿三大殿以及文华殿、武英殿。主殿太和殿是天子登基、颁布重要政令、元旦和冬至的大朝会、皇帝庆祝生日等活动的地方，中和殿是大朝会前的预备室以及休息处，保和殿是殿试进士、宴会等使用。

内廷，乾清门以北就是内廷，包括以乾清宫为中心的中路和左右侧嫔妃们居住的寝宫。其中乾清宫是皇帝寝宫，坤宁宫是皇后居所。

The inside of the Forbidden City is divided into two main parts, the outer and inner courts. The outer court is for imperial government affairs, while the inner court is the living quarters.

The outer court includes the Hall of Supreme Harmony, Hall of Central Harmony, and the Hall of Preserving Harmony, along with Wenhuadian and Wuyingdian. The Hall of Supreme Harmony, the main building, is where the emperor ascends the throne, issues important government decrees, holds important court meetings on New Year's Day and the Winter Solstice, and where the emperor celebrates his birthday. The Hall of Central Harmony is the preparatory room and resting room for large court meetings. The Hall of Preserving Harmony is used for the top grade imperial examination, banquets, etc.

The Gate of Heavenly Purity and north is the inner court, which includes the central road that has the Palace of Heavenly Purity at its center, and the sleeping palaces where imperial concubines reside on the left and right of it. Among them, the Palace of Heavenly Purity is where the emperor sleeps, and the Palace of Earthly Tranquility is where the empress resides.

## 2. 陵墓
### Tombs and Mausoleums

古人视土地为生命之本，讲求入土为安，故标准的埋葬习俗是土葬。一般人的通称"墓"，君主的墓通称"陵"。

陵墓，一般利用自然地形，靠山而建。陵墓建筑除了封土坟头之外，地面建筑一般分作三部分：祭堂、墓道、墓穴。

The ancients regarded the earth as the basis of life and were particular about finding peace by entering the earth. So, the standard burial custom was to be interred in the ground. The common ones were called "graves" or "tombs", while rulers' graves were generally called "mausoleums".

Tombs generally take advantage of the natural topography and were built into mountains. Besides mounds for the burial itself, tomb buildings generally were divided into three parts: sacrificial hall, tomb passage, and grave.

祭堂就是祭祀大殿，规模庞大。例如，乾陵的地面建筑就有房378间之多。墓道即神道，两旁立有成对的"石像生"，即石头雕刻的石人、石兽以及石柱和门阙等。墓穴即地宫，是埋葬死者的地方，是帝王陵的主要部分。因为实行厚葬制度，许多帝王陵和大墓都是极好的文物仓库和地下博物馆。

The sacrificial hall is the main hall for making sacrificial offerings. They were enormous in scale. For example, the surface buildings at Qianling (See Figure 10–2) number more than

378. The tomb passage is also known as the spirit path, along which stand in paired stone statues of people, animals, stele, and gates. The grave itself is the underground palace, the place where the deceased is interred, the main part of an imperial tomb. Because of carrying out the system of lavish burials, many imperial tombs and large mausoleums are excellent storehouses of cultural relics and underground museums.

陕西西安附近是我国皇帝陵墓较为集中的地方,除了骊山秦始皇陵墓外,还有西汉11个皇帝的陵墓,唐代18个皇帝的陵墓。

The place in China with a relatively large concentration of imperial tombs is around Xi'an, Shaanxi. In addition to Mt. Li where the tomb of Qin Shihuang is, there are eleven Western Han imperial tombs and 18 Tang imperial tombs.

乾陵(见图10-2)是唐高宗李治与皇后武则天的合葬墓,位于陕西省咸阳市乾县县城北部6公里的梁山上,采用"因山为陵"的建造方式,墓室藏于梁山中。乾陵选址极佳。除主墓外,乾陵还有17座陪葬墓,葬有其他皇室成员与功臣。

Qianling (see Figure 10-2) is the joint tomb for Tang Gaozong and Empress Wu Zetian. Located in Mount Liang, six kilometers north of the county seat of Qian County, Xianyang City, Shaanxi Province, it adopts the construction method of "following the mountain to make a tomb". The tomb chambers are hidden within Mount Liang, an extremely good site. In addition to the main tomb, Qianling has seventeen subsidiary tombs where other members of the imperial family and important ministers were buried.

图 10-2 乾陵
Figure 10-2 Qianling

皇帝陵墓中保存最为完整的是明清两代的皇陵。明朝皇帝的陵墓主要是位于北京的明十三陵。其中规模最大最宏伟的是明成祖朱棣的长陵和明神宗朱翊钧的定陵。明神宗朱翊钧 10 岁做皇帝，22 岁就开始为自己修建坟墓。

The best preserved tombs are the imperial tombs of the Ming and Qing dynasties.

The Ming Dynasty tombs are primarily located in Beijing's mausoleum park of the Ming emperors. The largest, most imposing of them are Changling, the tomb of Zhu Di, the Chengzu Emperor, and Dingling, the tomb of Zhu Yijun (1563 – 1620), the Shenzong (Wanli) Emperor. Zhu Yijun took the throne at the age of 10, and began construction on his tomb when he was 22.

清东陵是我国现存陵墓建筑中规模最宏大、建筑体系最完整的皇家陵园。这里埋葬着顺治（孝陵）、康熙（景陵）、乾隆（裕陵）、咸丰（定陵）、同治（惠陵）5个皇帝，15位皇后，136位嫔妃，3位阿哥，2位公主共161人，共15座陵园，占地约2500平方公里。

Dongling of the Qing Dynasty is the imperial tomb site on the largest scale and with the most complete architectural setup. Buried here are five emperors (Shunzhi, Kangxi, Qianlong, Xianfeng, Tongzhi), fifteen empresses, and 136 concubines, with 3 princes, 2 princesses, a total of 161 people and 15 cemeteries. It occupies an area of 2500 square kilometers.

## 3. 寺庙
### Temples and Monasteries

佛教传入中国后，兴建的第一座官办寺院是河南省洛阳的白马寺（见图 10 – 3），修建于东汉时期。"寺"，是古代高级官府的名称，以寺称呼，表示尊重，所有的佛教寺院便通称为寺。佛寺建筑依据当时大臣的办公场所修建，所以与印度寺庙建筑不同。寺庙建筑整体对称，基本布局以平面方形为主，沿南北这条中轴线，前后建筑按照顺序排列为山门殿——天王殿——大雄宝殿——本寺主供菩萨殿——法堂——藏经楼。

After Buddhism spread to China, the first officially run monastery to be built was the White Horse Temple in Luoyang, Henan Province (see Figure 10 – 3). It was built in the Eastern Han period. The term for temple/monastery *sì* (寺) in ancient times referred to a high level government office. Using the term for the religious structures was an expression of respect, and all Buddhist temples and monasteries were then generally designated with that term. Buddhist temple architecture was built according to the places where important officials of the time would conduct official business, so they are different from Indian temple buildings. On the whole, temple buildings are symmetrical, basically relying on flat plane shape for their lay out and following the north-south central axis. From front to back the order of arrangement is as follows: Main Monastery and Hall, Maitreya Hall, Hall of Great Strength (hall where the hosts of the temple make offerings to Bodhisattvas), Dharma Hall, Sutra Hall.

图 10 -3　白马寺（洛阳）
Figure 10 -3　White Horse Temple (Luoyang)

白马寺位于河南省洛阳市老城以东 12 公里，创建于东汉永平十一年（公元 68 年），是中国第一座佛教寺院，距今已有 1900 多年的历史。现存古迹为元、明、清时所留。寺内保存了大量元代夹纻干漆造像如三世佛、二天将、十八罗汉等，弥足珍贵。

The White Horse Temple is located twelve kilometers east of the old city of Luoyang, Henan Province. It was built in 68 A. D., in the Eastern Han period. It is the first Buddhist temple in China, with a history of over 1900 years. Extant relics date from Yuan, Ming and Qing periods. There are a large number of painted statues from Yuan period housed in the temple, including highly valuable ones of the Buddha of the Three Ages, Two Heavenly Generals, and the Eighteen Arhats.

## 4. 园林

**Parks and Gardens**

园林建筑是供人们娱乐、游赏的庭院式建筑，亭台楼阁、山石花木随自然之势修建。园林布局、造景有较高的境界，在世界建筑领域独树一帜。

园林的建造，一是讲究亭台轩榭的布局，二是讲究假山池水的配合，三是讲究曲折变化和远景、近景的层次。建筑巧妙运用花墙和游廊，使园林显得层次多，景物逐次展露，宛如一幅幅连绵不断的天然图画，引导观看的人从小空间进到大空间，会感受到一种移步换景的乐趣。中国园林追求意境和实境的交融转换，让人的感情和自然交流。

中国四大名园：江苏苏州留园、拙政园、北京颐和园、河北承德避暑山庄。

Garden buildings are courtyard-style buildings that provide people with amusement and a place to enjoy sights. Kiosks, pavilions, rocks, and plants are built and cultivated in accordance with the natural conditions. Garden arrangement and manufacture of scenery are carried out to a relatively high level, unique in the field of the world's architecture.

Garden construction first tastefully chooses the arrangement of pavilions, kiosks, and rooms. Second, particular attention is paid to the rapport between rockery and water features.

Third, the alternation of views around bends and turns is highly regarded, as is the layering between long-range views and close-up scenery. The ingenious use of flower walls and verandas makes the garden appear to have numerous layers, so the scenery gradually unfolds before the visitor. Like a continuous landscape painting, it leads the viewer from small spaces into larger spaces, so the viewer/traveler senses the joy of enjoying a new scene with every footstep. Chinese gardens pursue a blended interchange between artistic conception and actual boundaries, allowing the interaction between the individual's emotions and nature.

China's four great gardens are: the Lingering Garden and Humble Administrator's Garden in Suzhou, Jiangsu province, Beijing's Summer Palace, and Chengde's Qing Imperial Summer Residence in Hebei province.

苏州留园（见图 10 – 4）位于苏州阊门外留园路，明朝嘉靖年间修建，光绪年间改名为"留园"，面积约 50 亩，以园内建筑布置精巧、奇石众多而知名。

Lingering Garden (see Figure 10 – 4) in Suzhou is located at Lingering Garden Road, Changmenwai, Suzhou. It was built during the Jiajing era of the Ming Dynasty. Its name changed to "Lingering Garden" in the Guangxu era of Qing. It covers an area of around 3.3 hectares and is famous for the arrangement of buildings in the garden and numerous fantastic rocks.

图 10 – 4  苏州留园

Figure 10 – 4  Lingering Garden in Suzhou

## 5. 民居
### Homes

在中国的民居中，最有特点的是北京四合院，西北黄土高原的窑洞，福建、广东等地的客家土楼等。

Among Chinese homes, the most characteristic are Beijing's courtyard homes, the cave homes on the northwest Loess Plateau, and the earth towers of the Hakkas (the Kejia people) in Fujian and Guangdong.

四合院是中国传统的合院式建筑，其格局为一个院子四面建有房屋，合在一起，形成一个口字形，这就是四合院的基本特征（见图10-5）。院落封闭独立，最常见的是一进院或二进院。

Courtyard Homes are the traditional Chinese courtyard style buildings. Their layout consists of a courtyard with buildings on all four sides, joined together they form a hollow square shape; this is the basic characteristic of the courtyard home. The courtyard is closed off and independent. The most common types have a single or double courtyard.

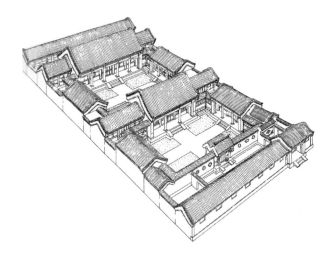

图10-5 北京典型三进院四合院图（马炳坚《北京四合院建筑》图1-9）

Figure 10-5 Diagram of Beijing's Typical Three-courtyard Courtyard Home [Ma Bingjian: *Beijing Siheyuan Jianzhu* (Architecture of Beijing's Courtyard Homes), diagram 1-9]

四合院院子被房屋和高高的围墙封闭，窗子不开向院外，通向院外的大门只有一个，门外有石狮子把守，大门上贴门神守护，层层封闭的居住结构展现出隐秘、内向的文化心态。院子一般分正房、偏房、前房、后房等，中轴线上的正房是位置最好、最重要的屋子，由长辈居住，子女住在两侧的厢房，女子闺房不允许外人随便进入。一个大家庭的成员居住在一个院落，共居、共财、共食，不能随便分家，"父母在，不远游"的伦理也体现在日常的居住生活中。

The yard in a courtyard home is enclosed by rooms and high walls. Windows do not open to the outside of the yard, and there is only one gate leading out from the yard. There is a pair of stone lions guarding the gate, which is also protected by a pair of door gods pasted to the gate. The layered-confinement residential structure reveals a secretive, reserved cultural psychology. The courtyard typically distinguishes the main room, side rooms, front rooms and back rooms. The main room on the central axis is in the best position and is the most important room, where family elders reside. Children live in rooms on the two sides. Outsiders are generally not allowed to enter the women's boudoir. The members of a large family live together in one courtyard, sharing residence, wealth, and food, and the household cannot be casually split up. The ethic of "when father and mother are alive, one does not wander far" is manifest in daily residential life.

窑洞是中国西北黄土高原上居民的古老居住形式，常见的土窑，是在黄土崖壁上挖出的拱洞，在洞口安设门窗。

Cave homes are an ancient form of residence in China's northwestern Loess Plateau. The typical loess caves are arched caves dug out of the loess cliffs. Doors and windows are installed at the mouth of the cave.

陕北窑洞（见图 10 - 6）是以前陕西的一种传统民居。挖窑洞时，先修"窑面"，即在山坡上挖一竖截面，然后向纵深挖掘。一般窑高 3 米左右、宽 3 米左右、深 6 至 8 米，门窗用木框，窗户上糊纸或镶玻璃，窑洞冬暖夏凉。

Cave dwelling in northern Shaanxi, a kind of traditional residence in Shaanxi's past (see Figure 10 - 6). When digging a cave dwelling, one first builds a "cave face", that is, digging a vertical cross-section on the hillside. Then, one excavates the depth from front to rear. Typically the caves are around three meters high, three meters wide and six to eight meters deep. Doors and windows are wood-framed, and the windows are covered with paper or inlaid with glass. Caves are cool in summer and warm in winter.

图 10 - 6　陕西北部的窑洞
Figure 10 - 6　Cave Dwelling in Northern Shaanxi

客家土楼（见图10-7）的整体布局是一个大圆形，是具有防御性的城堡式住宅，规模大，聚族而居，大的土楼可以容纳上百户，近千人居住。主要分布在中国东南部的福建、江西、广东三省的客家地区。土楼、排屋、围屋是客家民居的三大主要形式。

Earth Tower of the Hakkas (see Figure 10-7), the overall layout of which is a large circle, is a defensive, castle-style residence. Large in scale, they are occupied communally. Larger ones will accommodate up to 100 households, or nearly 1000 people. They are mainly distributed in the Kejia (Hakka) areas in the provinces of Fujian, Jiangxi, and Guangdong in Chinese southeast. The main form of Kejia homes are three major categories: earth towers, row houses and circular houses.

图 10-7 客家土楼（福建永定）
Figure 10-7 Earth Tower of the Hakkas (in Yongding, Fujian)

客家的先民是黄河流域的汉人，东晋时为了躲避中原的战乱开始向南方迁移。南宋以后主要居住在岭南山区。客家人因为是移民，为了安全，迁到陌生地方后就修建土楼集中居住，厚实的墙用土夯成，故称土楼。土楼墙厚达1米，高可达5层，圆形平面直径最大可达70余米，有300余间房，一个土楼内可以居住上百户人家，结实安全。保存较好的明代土楼，至今仍然在使用、居住。

The ancestors of the Kejia were Han people from the Yellow River valley. In the Eastern *Jin* period, in order to avoid the chaos of war, they started to migrate to the south. After the Southern Song, they mostly lived in the mountainous areas of the Lingnan region. The Kejia, being immigrants, built these earth towers and lived communally for protection after moving to a strange land. The thick walls are made of tamped earth, nearly one meter thick, and can be five storeys tall. The diameter of the circle is as long as 70 meters. With more than 300 rooms, one earth tower home can house over 100 households safely and securely. This Ming Dynasty example is preserved relatively well, and is still used as a residence today.

中国人有恋家、守家的传统。离开家园是迫不得已才去做的事情，所以，历代文人把对家的思恋作为写作的一大主题，在诗歌里可以处处看到。例如，马致远在秋日里思念家乡，想起的是"小桥流水人家"；杜甫梦想的是"青春作伴好还乡"；离开家乡的人都是"断肠人在天涯"。无论如何，人老了都要"叶落归根"回到家乡。家园就是中国人的根。

Chinese people have a tradition of loving their homes and protecting their homes. Leaving the home is something one would only do if there were no alternative. So, people of letters over the generations have taken love for one's home as a major point of subject matter for compositions, and one sees it everywhere in poems and songs. For example, Ma Zhiyuan on an autumn day when longing for his home thinks of "a small bridge, a running stream, a home"; what Du Fu dreamt was of "a youth accompanying me, I am fond of returning home"; a person who has left their home is always "a heartbroken person at the ends of the earth". No matter what, an old person "like a fallen leaf returning to its roots" wants to return home. The home is really the foundation of Chinese people.

## 二、中国古代建筑的主要特点
## Main Traits of Ancient Chinese Architecture

### 1. 梁柱式的框架结构
### Pillar and Beam Frame Construction

西方古建筑大多以砖石结构为主，中国古建筑在结构上最重要的一个特征是梁柱式的框架结构，即采用木柱、木梁构成房屋的框架，屋顶与房檐的重量通过梁架传递到立柱上，以梁柱承重，墙壁只起隔断的作用，而不承担房屋重量（见图 10-8）。它突出的优点是抗震性能强，可以把巨大的震动能量分散在弹性很强的接点上。例如，天津蓟州区辽代独乐寺观音阁，高 23 米，曾经经历了附近 8 级以上大地震，1976 年又经历唐山大地震而没倒塌。所以，民间有"墙倒屋不塌"之说，正反映了梁柱式结构的特点。

The majority of Ancient Western buildings relied on brick structures; whereas, most important trait in the structure of ancient Chinese architecture is pillar-and-beam frame construction. That is, using wooden pillars and wooden beams to form the frame of the building. The weight of the roof and eaves is transmitted to the pillars through the beams, the load-bearing elements of the structure. Walls only serve as partitions; they are not load-bearing (see Figure

10 – 8). Its prominent advantage is its anti-seismic performance is powerful. It can dissipate huge vibration energy on nodes which are flexible and strong. For example, the Liao Dynasty Guanyin Pavilion in Dule Temple in Ji County, Tianjin, is 23 meters high and has experienced an nearby earthquake of 8 degrees on the Richter scale as well as the great Tangshan earthquake of 1976 without toppling. Therefore, there is a popular saying that, "the walls may fall, but the roof stays up", which precisely reflects the advantages of pillar-and-beam construction.

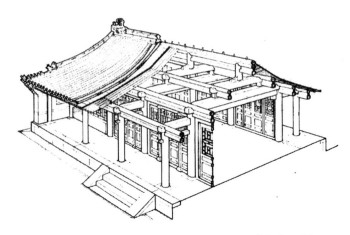

图 10 – 8　大木作制度示意（厅堂）（北宋《营造法式》）

Figure 10 – 8　Song Schematic for Wooden Building System (Hall) (in *Building Methods* of Song Dynasty)

## 2. "斗拱"结构
### "Bucket-and-arch" Bracket Structure

"斗拱"结构是中国古建筑结构的一种重要特征，这是框架式木结构所有的一种独特构件。"斗拱"由形状像量谷物用的斗和升一样的木块和好像弯弓一样的拱形构件所组成，所以称之为斗拱（见图 10 – 9）。斗拱位于柱子与梁和其他构件的交接处，纵横交错，逐层向外挑出，形成上大下小的托座。既有支承梁架的作用，又有装饰作用（见图 10 – 10）。

"Bucket-and-arch" bracket structure is an important trait of ancient Chinese architecture. This is a unique component in the wooden framing structure. It is made up of a wooden piece shaped like the bucket or scoop used to measure grains and a bending arch component, hence the name "bucket-and-arch" (see Figure 10 – 9). It is positioned at the node where the pillar joins with the beam and other components. Criss-crossing and jutting out in gradual layers, it forms a support base that is big on the top and small on the bottom. It serves both to bear the weight of the roof beams and as a decorative feature. (see Figure 10-10)

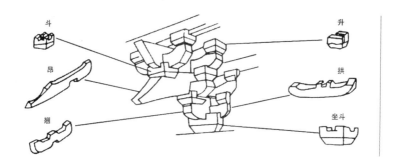

图 10-9 斗拱组成
Figure 10-9 Bucket-and-arch Form

图 10-10 天津蓟州区独乐寺观音阁上的斗拱
Figure 10-10 Bucket-and-arch, on the Guanyin Pavilion in Dule Temple in Ji County, Tianjin

## 3. 布局的中轴对称
**Layout and Central Axis Symmetry**

中国建筑的空间组合遵循平衡和对称原则,平面布局最大的特征是中轴对称。

整个建筑或建筑群是沿中轴线按左右对称的格局分布的。中轴线上布置重要的建筑物,在中轴线的两旁布置次要的建筑物,这种布局主次分明、左右对称、封闭性强。住宅、官方建筑、寺庙和宫殿都遵循这些基本原则。这样的安排适合中国古代社会的宗法和礼教制度,"礼"强调尊卑有序,"中"突出了权威居中。这种布局也与中华民族心理相关，中国人追求审美心理上的平稳、沉静，在建筑中也就强调了中轴对称的均衡。

例如，北京故宫的平面布局，自南至北以正阳门、大明门、天安门、端门、午门、太和门、太和殿、中和殿、保和殿、乾清门直到鼓楼，形成一个突出的中轴序列，这个中轴序列位于全城的中轴线上，左为祖庙，右为社稷。太和殿中的皇帝宝座也精密地设在全城的中轴线上。

Space in Chinese architecture is assembled to follow the principles of balance and symmetry. The surface layout's largest characteristic is central axis symmetry.

The entire building or building complex is distributed according to left-right symmetry following the central axis. Important buildings are arranged on the central axis, and secondary buildings are placed on the two sides of the axis. In this kind of layout, primary and secondary are clearly distinct, left and right are symmetrical, and there is strong encapsulation. Residences, government buildings, temples and palaces all follow these basic principles. This arrangement accords with ancient Chinese society's patriarchal and Ru-ist ethical system. "etiquette" emphasizes respect for orderliness; "center" gives prominence to authoritativeness of living in the middle. This layout is also related to the Chinese people's psychology. Chinese people pursue steadiness and quietude in their aesthetic psychology, and in their buildings, they emphasize the balance of central axis symmetry.

For example, the planar layout of the Forbidden City in Beijing forms a prominent central axis sequence, from south to north with Zhengyang Gate, Gate of China, Gate of Heavenly Peace, Duan Gate, Gate of the Meridian, Gate of Supreme Harmony, Hall of Supreme Harmony, Hall of Central Harmony, Hall of Preserving Harmony, Gate of Heavenly Purity, all the way to the Drum Tower. This central axis sequence is positioned on the central axis of the entire city. On the left is the ancestral temple, and on the right is the temple for the gods of earth and grain. The imperial throne in the Hall of Supreme Harmony is also exquisitely set up on the central axis of the entire city.

### 4. 人文性
**Humanness**

中国建筑明显地存在着中国文化价值观念的表达。

讲究秩序、注重等级的观念表达最突出。在同一个建筑物组合中，建筑物之间的排列有着明确的正偏、内外之别，这种区别象征着使用者的地位尊卑。

建筑物上色彩的使用也能体现出地位的尊卑。明清时期，琉璃瓦的使用，一般是黄色为最高贵，只用在皇宫、社稷、坛庙等主要建筑上。王府、寺观一般不能使用全黄琉璃瓦顶。清朝雍正时，皇帝特准孔庙可以全部使用黄琉璃瓦，以表示对儒学的独尊。

The expression of Chinese culture's value conception clearly exists in Chinese architecture.

Paying particular attention to order and emphasizing the concept of rank are expressed most prominently. Within the same building assembly, there are clear distinctions among buildings between straight and oblique, inside and outside. These distinctions symbolize the senior or junior status of the users.

The use of colors on a building can also manifest the status rank. In Ming-Qing times, yellow glazed roof tiles were the noblest and only used on imperial palaces, temple for the gods of earth and grain, altars, and other important structures. Prince's quarters, Buddhist and Daoist temples and monasteries were generally not allowed to use yellow glazed roof tiles. In the Yongzheng reign of the Qing Dynasty, the emperor especially permitted the Confucian Temple to use yellow glazed roof tiles as a statement that Ru-ism was the sole orthodoxy.

## 三、长城及其他代表性建筑
## The Great Wall and Other Representative Buildings

### 1. 长城
### The Great Wall

长城,是古代中原王朝抵御北方游牧民族入侵的防御工事,也是世界上修建时间最长、工程量最大的一项古代防御工程(见图 10 – 11)。长城上一个很重要的建筑是方形的烽火台,7 米见方,为传递军事信息时使用。当出现敌情时,白天点燃狼烟报警,因为狼粪的烟可以上升得高而直,晚上点燃火把。所以,古代把战争的场面形容为"狼烟四起"。烽火台与敌台、关城卫所一起,构成了一套较为完整的军事防御体系。从战国到明朝,各朝各代在各地都有修建长城,前后 2000 多年。

The Great Wall is a defensive structure the ancient kingdoms of the Central Plains used to defend against invasions of northern nomadic peoples (see Figure 10 – 11). It is also an ancient defensive project and the world's largest scale engineering project built over the longest amount of time. An important structure on the Great Wall is the Fire Beacon Towers, which are square (7 meters by 7 meters) structures used to transmit military information. When enemy activity occurred during the day, they alarm people by sending up smoke from burning wolf feces because such smoke ascended high and straight. If it was at night, they lit torches. In ancient times, a battle and war scene was often described as, "wolf smoke all around". Fire beacon towers, lookout towers, defensive forts all taken together constitute a relatively complete military defensive system. From the Warring States to the Ming Dynasty, a period of over 2000 years, each dynasty in each age in various places contributed to the construction.

长城保存较为完整的是明代长城,一般墙体有 3 米多高,走道有 5—8 米宽。各地长城中,北京八达岭长城特别坚固,保存也较为完整。此外还有慕田峪长城、司马台长城、天津黄崖关长城、河北山海关长城,最西边的甘肃嘉峪关长城等等。

The Ming Great Wall is preserved relatively well today. It is generally around three meters high with a corridor of five to eight meters wide. Among the various portions of the Great Wall, Beijing's Badaling is rather stable and preserved largely intact. Also, there is Mutianyu, Simatai, Tianjin's Huangyaguan, Hebei's Shanhaiguan, and on the western end there is Jiayuguan in Gansu.

图 10-11 万里长城(东起山海关,西至甘肃省嘉峪关)

Figure 10-11 The Great Wall (Rising in the east from Shanhai Pass and extending in the west to Jiayuguan, Gansu Province)

**(1) 烽火戏诸侯**

***Fire Beacons Trick the Various Lords***

西周的周幽王(795—771 B.C.)有个宠爱的妃子,叫褒姒,长得很美丽,但是从来没有笑过。周幽王出告示说,谁要能让娘娘一笑,就给一千两金子。于是有人出主意:"在烽火台上点火,诸侯们以为要打仗了,就会跑来,这样褒姒也许会笑。"周幽王听从了这个计划,晚上在骊山烽火台上点燃火堆,熊熊火焰照亮天空,诸侯们看到信号,果然很快赶来。褒姒看到诸侯们被愚弄,就笑了。后来,周幽王又多次燃放烽火,以致诸侯们都不相信了。公元前771年,当时北方的一支少数民族——犬戎进攻西周,国王紧急下令烽火台放狼烟发信号,让诸侯们来打仗。但是,因为诸侯们不再相信,都没有赶来。周幽王战败被杀。后来周幽王的儿子周平王继位,开始了东周时期。

King You (795-771 B.C.) of the Western Zhou had a concubine on whom he doted excessively, named Baosi. She was very beautiful, but she never smiled. King You made an announcement that anyone who could make her smile would be granted one thousand ounces of gold. Someone came up with an idea: "Light the fires on the fire beacons; the various lords will think there is a war brewing and come running out. This will surely make Baosi smile." King You followed this plan and that night had the becons on Lishan lit. A great blaze illuminated the night sky. The various lords saw the signal, and sure enough, quickly came running out. When Baosi saw that the lords had been duped, she smiled. King You again on many occasions had the beacon fires lit to amuse her, and the lords were again fooled, until in the end, they no longer trusted the signal. In 771 B.C. the Quanrong, a minority group in the north, attacked the Western Zhou. The king urgently ordered the beacon fires lit to send the signal to the lords to prepare for war, but because they didn't trust the signal anymore, none of them came. The war was lost, and King You was killed. King You's son inherited the throne as King Ping and started the Eastern Zhou Dynasty.

(2) 关于长城的诗词
**Poems About the Great Wall**

古筑城曲<br>陆游（南宋）<br>Ancient Wall Tune<br>Lu You (Southern Song Dynasty)

长城高际天，三十万人守。
一日诏书来，扶苏先授首。
The Great Wall is as high as the sky,
and three hundred thousand men stand guard.
One day an imperial order arrives,
And Fusu (eldest son of Qin Shihuang) is the first to lose his head.

清平乐·六盘山<br>毛泽东<br>To the Tune Qingpingle on Liupan Mountain<br>Mao Zedong

天高云淡，望断南飞雁。
不到长城非好汉，屈指行程二万。

六盘山上高峰，红旗漫卷西风。
今日长缨在手，何时缚住苍龙？

Heaven is high and the clouds wispy,
I gaze at south flying geese.
If one hasn't ascended the Great Wall, one isn't a real hero.
By rough count its journey is 10000 miles.

On Liupan Mountain I ascend the highest peak,
The red flag gently flutters in the west wind.
Today, the long ribbon is in hand,
When will it bind the Blue Dragon?

## 2. 故宫
### The Forbidden City

北京故宫（见图 10-12），也叫紫禁城，前身是元朝在 1264 年营建的大都城。大都城规划严整，设施完善。明代第三位皇帝明成祖朱棣取得帝位后，决定把首都从南京迁到北京，于是依照历代建设都城的成规和明太祖朱元璋（1328—1398）在南京的宫殿样式，对元代的大都城实施大规模改建，改建后成为明清两个朝代的都城。

图 10-12　北京故宫
Figure 10-12　The Forbidden City in Beijing

明清两个朝代统治中国 540 多年，两朝共有 28 位皇帝，有 24 位皇帝在这里居住，最后一个居住在这里的皇帝是清朝宣统皇帝溥仪。1924 年，溥仪被逐出紫禁城，这里作为皇帝宫殿的历史就此结束。

The Forbidden City in Beijing (see Figure 10-12), or the Imperial Palace, was in 1264 the site of the Yuan Dynasty capital Dadu. Dadu was neatly planned, its facilities complete. After the third emperor of the Ming, Chengzu (named Zhu Di, the Yongle Emperor, 1360-1424) ascended the throne, he decided to move the capital from Nanjing to Beijing. Thus, according to the established rules of building a capital with the style of palaces built by Ming Taizu (Zhu Yuanzhang, 1328-1398) in Nanjing, he undertook a grand rebuilding of the Yuan Dadu.

The Ming-Qing period extended for more than 540 years, with a total of 28 emperors across both dynasties, 24 of whom lived in this palace. The last emperor to live here, Puyi (1906-1967), was driven out in 1924 and the history of this site as an imperial palace came to an end.

### 3. 布达拉宫
**Potala Palace**

西藏布达拉宫（见图 10-13）建造在拉萨市西北的玛布日山上，依山建造，高 200 余米，外观 13 层，内为 9 层，主体建筑分为白宫和红宫两部分，整体为石木结构。始建于公元 7 世纪吐蕃王朝藏王松赞干布时期，距今已有 1300 年的历史。

Tibet's Potala Palace (see Figure 10-13) is built on Moburi Mountain northwest of Lhasa. Built into the side of the mountain, it rises over 200 meters high, with 13 exterior storeys and 9 interior storeys. The bulk of the structure is divided into a white palace and a red palace, and the whole is stone and wood structure. Construction first started in the $7^{th}$ Century under Songtsen Gampo (604-650) of the ancient Tubo Dynasty, so it has more than 1300 years of history.

1645 年（清顺治二年）布达拉宫重建之后，成为历代达赖喇嘛冬宫居所，以及重大宗教和政治仪式举办地，旧时与驻藏大臣衙门共为统治中心，也是供奉历世达赖喇嘛灵塔之地，五世和十三世达赖喇嘛的金制灵塔，是布达拉宫里的艺术珍品的代表作。内有 2500 余平方米的壁画、近千座佛塔、上万座塑像、上万幅唐卡，还有贝叶经、甘珠尔经等珍贵经文典籍，明清两代皇帝封赐西藏地方政府和达赖喇嘛的金册、金印、玉印以及大量的金银品、瓷器、珐琅器、玉器、锦缎品及工艺品。

After it was rebuilt in 1645, the Potala Palace became the winter palace of the Dalai Lama, as well as the major site of religious and government ceremony. In old times it served as the center of control together with the cabinet minister offices stationed in Tibet. It is also the site of memorial pagodas for historical Dalai Lama. The 5$^{th}$ and 13$^{th}$ Dalai Lama's golden pagodas are representative of the artistic treasures found in the palace. The interior has over 2500 square meters of wall paintings, nearly a thousand pagodas, more than 10000 statues, and more than 10000 thangkas. It also has such literary treasures as the sutra written on leaves of pattra palm and the Kangyur. There are also the golden books, seals, and jade stamps the Ming-Qing emperors bestowed on the government of Tibet and the Dalai Lama, as well as a large number of gold and silver pieces, pottery, enamel ware, jade artifacts, brocades and other craftwork.

布达拉宫是世界上海拔最高（3700 m），集宫殿、城堡和寺院于一体的宏伟建筑，也是藏区最庞大、最完整的古代宫堡建筑群，是第五套人民币50元纸币背面的风景图案。

The Potala Palace is the world's highest palace (3700m), a magnificent architectural work that combines a palace, fortress, and monastery into a single structure. It is also Tibet's largest, most complete ancient palace/fortress architectural complex. It is also the scenic picture on the back of the 50 RMB bill.

图 10 -13　西藏布达拉宫
Figure 10 -13　Potala Palace of Tibet

## 4. 承德避暑山庄
### Qing Imperial Summer Residence at Chengde

承德避暑山庄（见图 10 – 14）又叫热河行宫，位于河北省承德市，距离北京 230 公里。由皇帝宫室、皇家园林和寺庙群组成，是清代皇帝夏天避暑和处理政务的场所。始建于 1703 年，历经清朝康熙、雍正、乾隆三代皇帝，耗时 89 年。清朝的康熙、乾隆皇帝每年约有半年时间要在承德度过，因此，承德避暑山庄也就成了北京以外的第二个政治中心。乾隆在这里接见并宴赏过厄鲁特蒙古杜尔伯特台吉三车凌、土尔扈特台吉渥巴锡，以及西藏政教首领六世班禅等重要人物，还在此接见过以特使马戛尔尼为首的第一个英国访华使团。清朝皇帝嘉庆、咸丰皆病逝于此。

The Qing Imperial Summer Residence at Chengde (see Figure 10 – 14) is also called the Temporary Imperial Residence at Rehe, located in Chengde, Hebei Province, about 230 kilometers from Beijing. Composed of palace rooms, gardens and temples, it is the site where Qing emperors escaped the summer heat and carried out the government's business. First built in 1703, construction lasted through the reigns of Kangxi, Yongzheng, and Qianlong, lasting a total of 89 years. The Kangxi and Qianlong emperors every year spent nearly half a year at this residence, so this summer residence became a second governmental center outside of Beijing. Qianlong met and feasted such important dignitaries here as the the Three Tserens of the Oirat Mongol Dörbod nobility, Ubashi of the Torghut nobility, as well as the Sixth Panchen Lama, the Tibetan theocratic leader. It was also here that Qianlong met the first British diplomatic mission to China, the Macartney Mission in 1793. Both the Jiaqing and Xianfeng emperors died in this palace.

图 10 – 14　河北承德避暑山庄
Figure 10 – 14　Imperial Summer Residence in Chengde, Hebei Province

## 5. 苏州园林
### Gardens in Suzhou

苏州园林（见图 10 – 15）也称为苏州古典园林，是指苏州城内的园林建筑，以私家园林为主。起始于春秋时期，全盛时 200 多处园林遍布古城内外，至今保存完好的尚存数十处，代表了中国江南园林风格。

苏州园林占地面积不大，但以意境见长，以独具匠心的艺术手法在有限的空间内点缀安排，移步换景，变化无穷。

Gardens in Suzhou (see Figure 10 – 15) are also called the Classical Suzhou Gardens, referring to the garden buildings within the city of Suzhou. Mainly this refers to the private gardens which first appeared in the Spring-and-Autumn Period. During the heyday, there were more than 200 garden sites spread inside and outside the old city, and now there are still dozens of well preserved locations that represent the Chinese Jiangnan garden style.

Suzhou gardens do not occupy a lot of space, but using a strong creative concept and original artistic technique, decorously arranged in a limited space, it seems the scenery changes with every step and there are innumerable variations in the view.

图 10 – 15　苏州园林
Figure 10 – 15　Gardens in Suzhou

苏州园林是文化意蕴深厚的"文人写意山水园"。古代的造园者都有很高的文化修养，能诗善画，造园时多以画为本，以诗为题，通过凿池堆山、栽花种树，创造出具有诗情画意的景观，被称为是"无声的诗，立体的画"。在园林中游赏，犹如在品诗，又如在赏画。为了表达园主的情趣、理想、追求，园林建筑与景观又有匾额、楹联之类的诗文题刻，有以清幽的荷香自喻人品（拙政园"远香堂"），有以清雅的香草自喻性情高洁（拙政园"香洲"），有追慕古人似小船自由漂荡怡然自得的（怡园"画舫斋"），还有表现园主恬淡生活的（留园"小桃源"），等等，不一而足。

Suzhou gardens are "literati's suggestive landscape gardens" with deep cultural connotations. Garden designers in ancient times had a high level of cultural training, able to paint and write poetry. When they built gardens they took painting as the root inspiration, and poetry as the theme. Through chiseling out ponds and piling up mountains, planting trees and flowers, they created landscapes with idyllic appeal, known as "voiceless poems and three-dimensional paintings". Traveling through a garden is like appraising a poem, or like appreciating a painting. To express the interests, ideals, and pursuits of the owner, the scenery and buildings have poetry in the form of couplets and inscribed boards. So, there is the self-reference to one's moral character by means of the fragrant lotus [as in the Zhuozheng Garden's (Humble Administrator's Garden) "Distant Fragrant" Hall]; or there is the reference to one's lofty and clean-living temperament by means of a refined aromatic herb (as in Zhuozheng Garden's "Fragrant Island"); or the pursuit of imitating the ancients, like contentedly adrift freely on a small boat (as in Yi Garden's "Painted Boat Study"); or the expression of the owners simple and contented life (as in Liu Garden's "Lesser Peach Spring"). Examples such as these are too numerous to list exhaustively.

**思考题**

1. 中国传统建筑有什么特点？
2. 中国古代建筑风格中蕴含的伦理观念是什么？

***Questions***

1. What are the main traits of ancient Chinese architecture?
2. What is the ethical conception contained in ancient Chinese architectural style?

# 第十一章　中国古代科技——四大发明

## Ancient Chinese Science and Technology—Four Great Inventions

中国古代产生世界影响力的科技，是四大发明——造纸术、印刷术、指南针和火药，其文化价值为世界所公认。

In ancient times China produced science and technology that influenced the world, i. e., the four great inventions of paper-making technology, movable-type printing technology, the compass, and gunpowder. Their cultural value is recognized around the world.

马克思在《机器、自然力和科学的应用》中对于火药、罗盘、印刷术的世界意义曾做总体性的阐述：

> 火药、罗盘、印刷术——这是预兆资产阶级社会到来的三项伟大发明。火药把骑士阶层炸得粉碎，罗盘打开了世界市场并建立了殖民地，而印刷术却变成新教的工具，并且一般地说变成科学复兴的手段，变成创造精神发展的必要前提和最强大的推动力。

In Karl Marx's *Machinery*, *Utilisation of the Forces of Nature and of Science* as regards the world significance of gunpowder, the compass, and movable-type printing, he made the following overall elaboration:

> Gunpowder, the compass, and the printing press were the three great inventions which ushered in bourgeois society. Gunpowder blew up the knightly class, the compass discovered the world market and founded the colonies, and the printing press was the instrument of Protestantism and the regeneration of science in general; the most powerful lever for creating the intellectual prerequisites.

英国学者培根在《新工具》中说道：

> 这三种发明已经在世界范围内把事物的全部面貌和情况都改变了：第一种是在

学术方面,第二种是在战事方面,第三种是在航行方面。并由此又引起难以数计的变化来,竟至任何帝国、任何教派、任何星辰对人类事务的力量和影响都仿佛无过于这些机械性的发现了。

British scholar Francis Bacon in his *Novum Organum* said:

For these three have changed the appearance and state of the whole world: first in literature, then in warfare, and lastly in navigation; and innumerable changes have been thence derived, so that no empire, sect, or star, appears to have exercised a greater power and influence on human affairs than these mechanical discoveries.

# 一、造纸术
# Papermaking Technology

造纸术发明以前,古代埃及人使用纸草茎部的薄皮(莎草纸),欧洲人用羊皮,中国人用甲骨、竹片、丝帛等作为书写材料。但是,这些材料要么太贵、要么太重不宜广泛使用,纸的发明使书写材料发生了革命,为印刷技术的产生做好了准备。中国最早的纸出现在西汉时,发现于新疆、陕西、甘肃等地。东汉时期的蔡伦(d. 121)改进了造纸术,让造纸术很快推广开来,蔡伦也就被后世认为是纸的发明人。

Prior to the invention of papermaking, ancient Egyptians used the thin skin of the stalks of papyrus, Europeans used sheepskins, and Chinese people used bones, bamboo, and silk as the medium for writing. These materials are all either too expensive, or too heavy, and therefor inconvenient for wide-scale use. The invention of paper revolutionized writing materials, preparing the way for printing technology. The earliest paper appeared in the Western Han period, showing up in Xinjiang, Shaanxi, and Gansu. Cai Lun (d. 121) of the Eastern Han period improved papermaking technology, allowing it to quickly spread, and thus later generations recognize Cai Lun as the inventor of paper.

6世纪起,造纸术传到日本、朝鲜、越南等东南亚国家,751年传到中亚的撒马尔罕、西亚的大马士革。阿拉伯纸大批生产后,源源不断地输往欧洲的希腊、意大利等地。1150年西班牙开始造纸,建立了欧洲第一家造纸工厂。此时离蔡伦的发明已有一千多年。后来法国(1189)、意大利(1276)在13世纪开始造纸,德国(1391)、英国(1495或1498)、荷兰(1586)、美国(1690)都先后设厂造纸。16世纪,纸开始流行于欧洲。

Starting from the 6th Century, papermaking technology was transmitted to Japan, Korea, Vietnam and other Southeast Asian countries. By 751, it had spread to Samarkand in Central Asia and Damascus in Southwest Asia. After the large-scale production of Arabic paper, a steady flow of it was transported into Greece, Italy and other European countries. In 1150, Spain began making paper, establishing the first European papermaking factory, at a time that was more than 1000 years after Cai Lun's invention. Later, France (1189) and Italy (1276) began making paper in the 13$^{th}$ Century, then Germany (1391), England (1495 or 1498), Holland (1568), and the United States (1690) one after the other set up factories for making paper. In the 16$^{th}$ Century, paper started being fashionable in Europe.

"纸对后来西方文明整个进程的影响无论怎样估计都不过分。"① 中世纪的欧洲，主要使用羊皮为书写材料，据估计，生产一本羊皮纸的《圣经》，至少需要300多只羊的皮，文化传播受到材料的限制。

"The influence of paper on the whole course of later Western civilization can hardly be overestimated" (Derk Bodde *China's Gifts to the West*, 1942, p.19). Medieval Europe primarily used sheepskin as their writing material. According to some estimates, producing a single sheepskin *Bible* required at least the skins of three hundred sheep. Clearly, cultural propagation suffered material limits.

## 二、印刷术
## Printing Technology

中国古代印刷术的发展，可分为两个阶段，一是雕版印刷术，二是活字印刷术。

The development of printing technology in China can be divided into two stages: carved block printing and movable type printing.

### 1. 雕版印刷术
### Carved Block Printing

最早的印刷术是雕版印刷术，方法是把图画或文字反刻在一块平整的木板上，然后着墨印刷（见图11-1）。

The earliest printing technology was carved block printing. The method is to reverse carve the picture or text onto a level piece of wood, and then smear it with ink and print with it (see Figure 11-1).

---

① [美]德克·卜德：《中国物品西传考》，《中外关系译丛》第一辑，上海译文出版社1984年版。

## 第十一章　中国古代科技——四大发明

图 11-1　雕版印刷术

Figure 11-1　Carved Block Printing

现存最早的雕版印刷品《金刚经》（见图 11-2）是唐代（868 年）印的《金刚经》，长约 496.1 厘米，由 7 个印张粘贴连接而成。卷首是释迦牟尼的说法图，卷尾题写"咸通九年四月十五日王玠为二亲敬造善施"。此卷雕刻精美，印刷清晰，是世界上现存最早的印刷物，1900 年发现于敦煌千佛洞。欧洲现存最早的、有确切日期的雕版印刷品，是德国南部 1423 年的《圣克里斯托菲尔》画像。

The earliest extant carved block print product is the Tang Dynasty (868) printing of the *Diamond Sutra* (see Figure 11-2). It is about 496.1 cm long, made by sticking together and joining seven printed pieces. At the head of the scroll is an image of Sakyamuni Buddha expounding on Buddhist teachings, and at the end is written, "On the 15th day of the 4th Month in the 9th year of Xiantong (May 11, 868) Wang Jie on behalf of his parents respectfully made and universally distributed." The carving for this text is delicate, and the printing is distinct, and it is the world's earliest extant printed document. It was discovered in 1900 in the Buddhist grottoes at Dunhuang. The earliest European block print product that can be dated with precision is the portrait of *Saint Christopher* from southern Germany in 1423.

图 11-2　《金刚经》

Figure 11-2　*Diamond Sutra*

## 2. 活字印刷术
### Movable-type Printing Technology

活字印刷术是由北宋时期毕昇（990—1051）发明的。他用胶泥刻字，每字一印，用火烧硬。另准备一块铁板，铁板上面放上松香、蜡、纸灰等合制而成的粘胶物。印刷时把铁框放在铁板上，在铁框内排列活字，一铁框为一版，再用火在铁板底下烤，使松香和蜡等熔化，再用另一块平板把字压平，冷却后就可以上墨印书。用完以后，再用火烤铁板，就可以将字型拆下。活字印刷术工艺简单，使用和保存方便，效率高。

Movable-type printing technology was invented by Bi Sheng (990 – 1051) in the Southern Song. He carved the characters in clay, then fired them until they were hard. Then he prepared an iron panel, and placed on the panel a glue-like substance made of pine rosin, wax, and paper ashes. He put a metal frame in the iron panel and arranged the movable type inside the frame, each frame making a single page. Then he heated the bottom of the iron panel causing the rosin and wax to melt, and using a different flat plate he pressed the characters until they were even. After it cooled, he could smear on ink and print a book. After he finished printing, he would again heat the iron panel and dismantle the characters. The technology is simple, convenient to use and preserve, and it is highly efficient.

中国的雕版印刷大约在公元8世纪传到日本，12世纪或略早传入埃及。波斯也很早便熟悉了中国的印刷术，并曾经用来印造纸币。著名历史学家拉希德·丁（Rashid al-Din Hamadani，1247—1318）在其1310年完成的著作《世界史》中，还专门介绍了中国雕版术。活字印刷术则于14世纪传到朝鲜。欧洲接触中国印刷术是在13世纪（元代），此时，中西交通活跃，不少欧洲旅行家远涉中国，亲眼看到中国人用雕版和活字印刷图书、纸币和纸牌，从中受到启发。于是，14—15世纪，雕版与活字印刷开始流行于欧洲。1455年，德国谷腾堡（Johannes Gutenberg，1397—1468）出版《圣经》，这是欧洲人用活字印刷的第一部重要作品。1460年，意大利建立了欧洲第一家印刷厂。印刷术在欧洲的出现，从根本上改变了欧洲的社会文化环境，也改变了只有僧侣才能读书写字的状况。从此，欧洲的学术中心由修道院转移到了各地的大学。

China's block printing spread to Japan around the 8th Century, and around the 12th Century or a bit earlier spread to Egypt. Persia early became familiar with Chinese printing technology and used it to print paper money. The famous historian Rashid al-Din Hamadani (1247 – 1318) in his *Jāmi'al-tawārīkh* (*Compendium of Chronicles*) completed in 1310 especially introduced Chinese block printing. Movable type printing spread to Korea in the 14th Century. Europe first came into contact with Chinese print technology in the 13th Century (Yuan Dynasty). Chinese and Western communication at that time was lively, and quite a few European travelers crossed into China, seeing with their own eyes Chinese people using block prints and movable-type printing to print books, paper money and playing cards. Inspired by this, by the 14th to 15th Centuries block printing and movable type printing became fashionable in Europe. In 1455 Johannes Gutenberg (1397 – 1468) printed the *Bible* in Germany, the first movable type printed work in Europe. In 1460, Italy established Europe's first printing house. The appearance of printing in Europe fundamentally changed its socio-cultural environment. It changed the situation in which only monks were able to read and write. After this, the academic centers of Europe moved from monasteries to universities.

## 三、指南针
## Compass

司南是中国最早的指向南北方向的设备,出现在春秋战国时期(见图 11 – 3)。"司"有"主管、执掌"的意思,"南"是南方。古人把"磁石",即一种有磁性的石头磨光,凿成长柄勺子的形状,放在刻有图案表明方向的光滑青铜板镜上转动,长柄勺停止时,勺柄指向正北方,另一端则指向正南方。宋代对此有了进一步改进。

The ancient compass (*sīnán* "observe the south") was China's earliest device for pointing in the direction of north-south (see Figure 11 – 3). It appeared in the Spring-Autumn/Warring States period. "*Si*" means "supervisor, in charge". "*Nan*" means "South". The ancients polished magnetic rocks, rocks with magnetic properties, then chiseled them into the shape of a long handled spoon, then placed it on a smooth brass plate/mirror that had a pattern carved into it for showing the directions, and on which the spoon rotated. Where the spoon stopped, the handle pointed toward north and the other end pointed to the south. There were improvements made to it in the Song Dynasty.

图 11 – 3 汉代司南方盘复原
Figure 11 – 3 Reconstruction of Han Dynasty Compass

指南针在航海上使用的时间，大约在 12 世纪初北宋末年的时候。指南针为远洋航行创造了条件，由此开辟了海上丝绸之路。大约在 1180 年左右，经阿拉伯人之手，指南针传入欧洲。

指南针给世界航海业带来了划时代的影响。15—16 世纪，葡萄牙人达·伽马（约 1469—1524）环绕非洲到达印度，哥伦布发现美洲新大陆，麦哲伦（1451—1506）环球航行，这些地理上的大发现都是借助了指南针。海上丝绸之路促进了中国和世界各国的交往。

The time when the compass was used for sea navigation is around the later years of the Northern Song, or the end of the 12$^{th}$ Century. The compass created the conditions for long distance ocean voyages, and therefore opened the Maritime Silk Road. Around 1180, the compass was spread to Europe through the hands of the Arabs.

The compass had an epoch-making effect on the world's navigation industry. In the 15$^{th}$ – 16$^{th}$ Century, the Portuguese Vasco Da Gama (c.1469 – 1524) sailed around Africa to India, Columbus (1451 – 1506) discovered the New World, Magellan (1480 – 1521) circumnavigated the globe. These geographic discoveries were all aided by the compass. The Maritime Silk Road boosted the contact between China and other countries of the world.

## 四、火药
## Gunpowder

火药起源于古代炼丹术。炼丹家在炼丹的实践中，经常使用硫黄、硝石等材料，他们从意外的爆炸中得到了启示，经过反复实践，发现了火药的配方。至迟在唐代已经发明了火药，并开始用于军事。宋代出现管状火器，元代改进为"火铳"，这是世界上最早的原始步枪，普遍用于战争中。10 世纪左右，蒙古人、阿拉伯人先后学会了使用火药、火器。13 世纪以后传入欧洲。

管状火器的出现，标志着火器制造史上一个划时代的进步，它使整个作战方式发生了重大的变革，标志着从冷兵器时代进入了热兵器时代。

Gunpowder has its origins in the ancient concocting of immortality pills through alchemy. The alchemists in the practice of concocting their immortality pills frequently used sulfur, saltpeter and other materials. They got inspiration from the accidental explosion, and through repeated practice discovered the formula for gunpowder. At the latest, it was already invented by the Tang Dynasty, and began to be used for military purposes. Tube-shaped firearms appeared in the Song Dynasty, which was improved in the Yuan Dynasty into a "blunderbuss", the first primitive rifle commonly used in warfare. In the 10$^{th}$ Century the Mongols and then the Arabs learned the use of gunpowder and firearms. After the 13$^{th}$ Century, it spread to Europe.

The appearance of tube-shaped firearms symbolizes an epoch-making advance in the history of manufacturing weapons, an important transformation in the whole way wars were fought. It symbolizes the era of cold weapons evolving into the era of hot weapons.

## 五、近代中国科技不发达的原因
## Reasons for the Lack of Growth in Chinese Science and Technology in Modern Times

中国古代以四大发明领先的科技能力,到了明代中期以后远远落后于世界,究其原因,主要有以下三点。

China's ancient science and technological capabilities, with the four great inventions at the lead, fell far behind the rest of the world after the middle of the Ming Dynasty. Upon investigating the reasons for this, there are primarily the following three points.

第一,皇权宗法专制社会里"重农抑商"的经济政策,限制手工业、商业的发展,是中国没有产生近代自然科学技术的根本原因。传统的小农经济政策阻碍了工商业的发展,社会对技术的需求很少,机器生产没有出现。科技人员地位低、待遇低、人数少,知识分子普遍以从事技术工作为耻,这在中国历史上是一个奇特的现象。例如写了《茶经》的陆羽(733—804),在御史大夫季卿召见他的时候,却不以士人之礼相待,让陆羽深以为耻。

First, the economic policy in the imperial, patriarchal society of "favor agriculture and constrain the mercantile" restricted the development of handicrafts and commerce; this is the basic reason China did not produce natural science and technology in the modern era. Traditional small-scale farming economic policy blocked the growth of business. Social needs for new technologies were small, and mechanical production did not arise. Personnel involved in science and technology were in a low social position, not paid well and small in number. Intellectuals generally regarded engaging in technological work as shameful, which was a peculiar phenomenon in Chinese history. For example, when Lu Yu (733 – 804) who wrote the *Classic of Tea*, was called to see the imperial censor, a high official, he was not received with the ceremony appropriate to a scholar. This was a disgrace for Lu Yu.

第二,自给自足、温饱则安的小农思维方式,限制了对科学技术的探求精神。传统的以小农经济为主的生活方式,以经验为主,追求实用性,束缚了开拓创新的思维,科学技术的发展失去了原动力。诸多农学著作大都是农业生产经验的总结,没有提升到系统的理论性探讨。

Second, the small-farm thought mode of being content if adequately provided for and relying on self-sufficiency restricted the investigative spirit in science and technology. The traditional lifestyle of the small-farm economy relied mainly on experience and the pursuit of practicality, which tied down innovative, ground-breaking thinking, and the development of science and technology lost its motive force. Many agricultural science writings are largely summaries of farming production experience, not rising to the level of systematic theoretical investigations.

第三，早期科技发展方向的先天不正。早期的科技工作人员中主要的一些人是巫师，政府对他们给予了大量的支持，但是真正对经济生活产生影响的科技发明，政府却没有给予足够的重视，科技被视为"雕虫小技"。正因为这样，四大发明传入欧洲以后，火药被用来开山、开矿、制造枪炮，近代西方用枪炮打开了中国的大门；指南针用来航海，导致地理大发现。但是在四大发明的发明地中国，火药用来制造爆竹，指南针成了风水先生的必备工具。在近代向西方学习的过程中，由于中国文化的封闭性传统，加之"唯我独尊"的文化心态，虽然被动地接受近代科技，引进西方工业，对西方的科学思想却是排斥的。

Third, the early direction of scientific and technological development was innately skewed. The main people among the early science and technological workers were magicians/wizards, and the government provided them with a great deal of support. But the government did not sufficiently value the real technological inventions that influenced economic life, which were regarded as "minor accomplishments". Precisely because of this, after the four great inventions spread to Europe, gunpowder was used to open mountains, blast out mines and manufacture rifles and cannon, which Western countries later used to open China's gates. The compass was used for ocean navigation, bringing about the great geographic discoveries. But in China where the inventions were originally made, gunpowder was used to make firecrackers, and the compass became an essential tool of the geomancer. In the process of learning from the West in modern times, though China passively accepted modern technology, Chinese culture's tradition of closing itself off and the cultural psychology of "respecting only oneself", made it reject Western scientific thinking.

**思考题**

1. 中国古代的四大发明对世界产生了什么样的影响？
2. 近代中国科技发展迟滞的原因是什么？

***Questions***

1. What influence did ancient China's four great inventions have on the world?
2. What are the reasons for the sluggish development of science and technology in modern China?

# 第十二章 中国医学
## Chinese Medicine

中国传统医学有5000多年的历史,具有独特的诊断和治疗系统。中医体系是以中国古代盛行的阴阳五行学说来说明人体的生理现象和病理变化,说明二者之间的关系,并将生理、病理、诊断、用药、治疗、预防等有机地结合在一起,形成了一个整体的观念和独特的理论,作为中医的基础。

Traditional Chinese medicine has a history of more than 5000 years, with a unique diagnostic and therapeutic system. The system of Chinese medicine uses the ancient Chinese theories of Yin-Yang and the Five Phases to explain physiological phenomena in the human body, pathological changes, and the relationship between them. Moreover, it organically integrates physiology, pathology, diagnosis, medication, therapy and prevention into one, forming a holistic conception and unique theory as its foundation.

## 一、中医的起源
## Origin of Chinese Medicine

中医学始于神农氏,他是传说中著名的草药大师,生活在大约5000年前,《史记》《淮南子》等书里有"神农氏尝百草"的记载。到春秋战国时期,医学专业化,有专职的医生队伍,扁鹊及其弟子都是著名的职业医生,秦国有专门的宫廷医疗机构,设有"太医令"一职。医学著作也已经出现。

Chinese medical science originates with Shennong, the Farmer God. He is the famous master of herbal medicine from legend who lived around 5000 years ago. *The Records of the Grand Historian* and other history texts have records of "Shennong trying all kinds of plants." By the Spring-Autumn/Warring States period, medicine had specialized, with a specialized medical corp, and writings on medicine had already appeared. Bian Que and his disciples are well-known professional doctors. The Qin owned special court medical institution, and had the position of "minister of imperial physicians". The medical literature have also appeared.

## 二、中医药理论
## Theory of Chinese Medicine

### 1. 阴阳理论
### *Yin-Yang* Theory

汉语中阴和阳的直接含义是物体的阴暗和明亮两面。古代哲学家用阴和阳来表示宇宙中普遍相反的属性：冷与热、慢与快、静与动、男与女、低与高等。总之，任何移动的、上升的、明亮的、进步的、活跃的特性，包括身体的功能性疾病，都属阳。任何静止的、下降的、黑暗的、退化的、不活跃的特性，包括器质性疾病，都属阴。

The meaning of *yīn* and *yáng* in Chinese is the "dark" and "bright" sides of things, respectively. Ancient philosophers used *yin* and *yang* to express the general contrary attributes in the universe: hot and cold, slow and fast, quiescent and active, male and female, low and high, etc. In brief, anything with the characteristics of moving, rising, brightness, advancing and liveliness, including disease functionality in the body, is categorized as *yang*. Anything with the characteristics of quiescent, declining, dark, retreating, and not lively, including organic diseases is categorized as *yin*.

阴和阳既对立又统一，既相互冲突又互相依赖。阴和阳的性质是相对的，二者都不能孤立存在。没有冷就没有热，没有动就没有静，没有黑暗就没有光亮。

阴阳理论贯穿于中医学的各个领域，用来说明人体的组织结构、生理功能、病理变化，并指导养生和临床的论断与治疗。

*Yin* and *yang* are both in opposition and united, both in mutual conflict and mutually dependent. The nature of *yin* and *yang* is oppositional, and the two cannot exist in isolation. If there is no cold, then there is no hot; if there is no activity, there is no quiescence; if there is no dark, there is no light.

*Yin-yang* theory runs through every field of Chinese medicine, and is used to explain the structural composition of the human body, physiological function, pathological changes, and moreover, it directs maintenance of good health and clinical judgement and treatment.

### 2. 五行理论
### Five-Phase Theory

五行是木、火、土、金、水五种物质的总称，和阴阳理论一样，古代哲学家用这五种物质来揭示宇宙的构成和现象。中医用五行理论来解释人体的生理、病理和自然环境之间的关系。根据五行理论，五行是不断运动和变化的，五行的相互依存和相互制约说明了物质对象之间相互联系以及人体与自然界之间的统一。

中医中的内脏器官以及其他器官和组织，具有与五行相似的属性，它们像五行一样在生理和病理上相互影响（见图12-1）。

The five phases are the general term for five kinds of materials: wood, fire, earth, metal and water. Like *yin-yang* theory, ancient philosophers used these five materials to make known cosmological structure and appearance. Chinese medicine uses five-phase theory to explain human physiology and pathology and their relationship with the natural environment. According to the theory, the five phases are constantly moving and changing. The mutual dependence and mutual constraint of the five phases explains mutual connections between matter and object, as well as the unity between the human body and the natural world.

In Chinese medicine, the internal organs and other organs and systems have properties similar to the five phases. Like the five phases, they influence each other in physiology and pathology (see Figure 12-1).

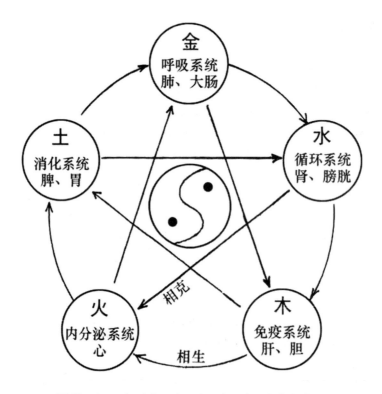

图12-1 五行（木、火、土、金、水）相生相克图

Figure 12-1 Map of the Mutual Engendering and Mutual Constraint of the Five Phases

五行相互促进相生、制约相克的关系如下。

五行相生：木生火，火生土，土生金，金生水，水生木。

五行相克：金克木，木克土，土克水，水克火，火克金。

The relationship of mutual promotion and engendering and mutual restriction and constraint among the five phases is as follows.

The five phases engender one another: wood births fire, fire births earth, earth births metal, metal births water.

The five phases constrain one another: metal constrains wood, wood constrains earth, earth constrains water, water constrains fire, fire constrains metal.

五行是在观察各群体的动态过程、功能及特征中形成的，五行大致涉及如下几个方面。

金：强度、硬度、杀害、切割、清理等。

木：萌发、扩展、柔软、和谐、灵活性等。

水：水分、寒冷、下降、流动等。

火：气流、热量、燃烧、优势、运动等。

土：增长、变化、滋养、生产等。

The five phases are formed in the observation of each community's active processes, function, and characteristics. The five phases generally touch upon the following aspects.

Metal: strength, hardness, murder, cutting, clearing up.

Wood: sprouting, expanding, softness, harmony, flexibility.

Water: moisture content, frigidity, declining, flowing.

Fire: breath, heat, combustion, superiority, activity.

Earth: growth, change, nourishment, production.

五行理论在春秋战国时开始用于中医学，用来说明脏腑的属性及其相互关系，分别把肝归属于木、肺归属于金、心归属于火、脾归属于土、肾归属于水。五行说在诊断和治疗上的运用，主要是根据五脏在五色、五味，以及脉象变化在五行分类归属上的联系，来推断病情或作诊断。

Five-phase theory began to be used in Chinese medicine in the Spring-Autumn/Warring States period to explain attributes of internal organs and their mutual relationships. The liver was classified as wood, lungs as metal, heart as fire, spleen as earth, and kidneys as water. The use of five-phase theory in diagnosis and treatment is primarily based on connections of the five organs in terms of the five colors and five tastes, as well as the connection to changes in pulse according to the five phase classification.

## 三、中医疗法
## Chinese Medical Therapy

### 1. 中草药
**Chinese Herbal Medicine**

中草药和针灸是中医的主要支柱。中药主要由植物药、动物药和矿物药组成。植物药以人参、灵芝、枸杞等最为著名。动物药以驴胶、熊胆、蛇毒等最为珍贵。矿物药以朱砂、赭石、芒硝等最为常用。中药以植物药为主,常见的草药有 600 多种。

中药有四性五味之分,四性是指药性的寒、热、温、凉。五味指药物的辛、酸、甘、苦、咸。中草药的气、味不同,其疗效也各异。

Chinese herbal medicine and acupuncture-and-moxibustion are the primary pillars of Chinese medication. Chinese medicines are mainly composed of plant-based medicines, animal medicines and mineral medicines. Among plant-based medicines, ginseng, reishi mushrooms (*ganoderma lucidum*) and wolfberries are the most famous. Among animal medicines donkey glue, bear gall, and snake venom are the most precious. Among mineral medicines cinnabar, ocher, and mirabilite are the most commonly used. Chinese medicine relies mainly on plant medicines, of which there are more than 600 different kinds of herbal medicine in common use.

Chinese medicines are classified based on four characteristics and five flavors. The four characteristics refer to the medicine's natural coldness, heat, warmth, and coolness. The five flavors refers to the medicine's pungency, sourness, sweetness, bitterness and saltiness.

The vital energy and flavor of Chinese herbal medicines are different, and so too are their healing efficacies.

### 2. 针灸
**Acupuncture and Moxibustion**

针灸包括针法和灸法,即在病人身体的穴位用针刺入或用火温热。针灸是用特制的毫针,从穴位刺入体内;艾灸是用燃烧着的艾绒温热穴位,利用热刺激身体表面的穴位;二者都是以运行经络、调解气血流通为目的来治疗疾病。针灸的理论基础是经络学说。经络学说认为经络遍布于人体各部位,气和血通过经络渠道系在体内循环,使身体内部器官与外部器官相连。

This is two types of treatment. Either needles are used to enter the acupuncture points of the patient's body, or fire is used to warm them. Acupuncture uses special needles to pierce into the body at the acupuncture points. Moxibustions is the use of burning moxa floss to warm the acupuncture point and taking advantage of heat to provoke the point on the body's surface. Both of these methods, by putting energy channels into operation, have the goal of mediating the flow of vital energy and blood to treat disease. The theoretical foundation of acupuncture-and-moxibustion is the theory of energy channels, which believes there are energy channels found throughout every part of the human body, and vital energy and blood circulate throughout the body through the system of energy channels, causing connections between internal and external organs.

穴位位于十多个主要经络两侧。有 12 对有规则的经络对称分布在身体两侧，另外两个主要经络分布在腹部和背部的中线。沿着这些经络，可以看到 300 多个穴位，每个穴位都有治疗效果。例如，太阳穴在外眼角外上方大概一寸左右，用手摸有一个很明显的凹陷。刺激太阳穴，可以缓解头痛、神经痛、眼睛疲劳等。太阳穴也是被武术拳谱列为要害部位的"死穴"之一。现代医学证明，打击太阳穴，可使人致死或造成脑震荡使人意识丧失。

Acupuncture points are positioned in more than ten primary energy channels along two sides. There are twelve pairs of regular energy channels symmetrically distributed on the two sides of the body, and two main energy channels are distributed on the central line of the abdomen and back. Following these energy channels, one can see more than 300 acupuncture points, each one with therapeutic efficacy. For example, the temple point is about an inch above the outer corner of the eyes. If you feel it with your hands, there is noticeable depression. Simulate the temple, and it can relax and undo headaches, neuralgia, and tired eyes. The temple point is listed by martial arts charts as one of the "lethal points" in a crucial position. Modern medical science has proved that a blow to the temple point can cause a fatality, or create a cerebral concussion causing one to lose consciousness.

针灸时，将针插入穴位，停留 15～30 分钟，银针从半寸到三寸长不等，一个治疗疗程一般为 10～15 次。

艾灸时，把干艾叶做的艾条点燃，放在离皮肤一英寸的特定穴位上方熏烤，以温热经络里的气和血，一次 10～15 分钟。艾灸通常用来驱寒气、除湿气、补气、补血的治疗。

When doing acupuncture, the needle is inserted into the acupuncture point and stays in place for fifteen to thirty minutes. Silver needles are varied in length from half an inch to three inches long. A course of treatment generally runs ten to fifteen times.

When doing moxibustion, moxa floss made from dried mugwort leaves are set on fire and placed at a specified acupuncture point an inch from the skin before smoldering, in order to warm the vital energy and blood in the energy channels for ten to fifteen minutes at a time. Moxibustion is usually used for treatments to expel cold energy, remove moist energy, supplement the vital energy, and supplement the blood.

### 3. 拔火罐
#### Suction Cups

拔火罐是以罐为工具,将点燃的酒精棉放在罐内烧一会儿再抽出,使罐子成为真空,然后把真空罐快速放在穴位上吸住,从而使吸附部分皮肤充血,以达到通经活络、行气活血、消肿止痛、祛风散寒等作用。

This technique uses a jar as a tool. Burning alcohol-soaked cotton is placed inside the jar and allowed to burn a moment and then extracted, causing the jar to become a vacuum. Then the vacuumized jar is quickly placed on an acupuncture point to draw on it. This causes the part of the skin being absorbed to fill with blood in order to attain such therapeutic effects as stimulating live channels, moving the energy to improve circulation, reducing swelling and relieving pain relief, dispelling pathogenic winds and dispersing cold.

### 4. 推拿
#### *Tuīná* (A Manual Therapy)

推拿是一种用手在人体上按照经络、穴位,用推、拿、提、捏、揉等手法进行治疗疾病的方法,以期达到治疗效果。

*Tuīná* is a method for conducting disease therapy by using the hands on the patient's body and pushing, holding, lifting, pinching, and rubbing along energy channels and acupuncture points in order to attain therapeutic results.

### 5. 刮痧
#### *Guāshā*

刮痧要先滑润皮肤,再用边缘光滑的石片、汤匙、铜钱等工具按压和刮,皮肤上会出现小红块瘀斑,叫"痧"。刮痧可促进正常循环和生理代谢,可快速减轻疼痛。

*Guāshā* first requires making the skin slippery and lubricated. Then, using a stone slab, soup spoon, or copper money and other such tools that have a smooth edge one presses and scrapes. Small red bruises will appear on the skin, known as *shā*. *Guāshā* can promote normal circulation and physiological metabolism; it can speed up the alleviation of pain.

### 6. 气功疗法
#### *Qìgōng* Therapies

中医学中的"气"被视为人体的基本物质,是生命之源,它的运行能说明各种生命过程。

气沿着经络和脉络循环，气的流通与精神状况密切相关，情绪不稳可能导致郁气，例如，愤怒可能会导致头晕、头疼、腹胀以及食欲降低。另一方面，心智锻炼可以帮助气的流通，这就是气功练习的目的。气功疗法主要是调解意念和呼吸的运动以控制或促进气的流动。

The *qì* (vital energy) of Chinese medicine has been regarded as the basic matter of the human body, the source of life. Its operation can explain various sorts of life processes.

Vital energy follows energy channels and the network of blood vessels. The flow of vital energy is closely related to the spiritual condition. If one's mood is unstable, it can lead to dense vital energy. Anger, for example, can lead to dizziness, headaches, swollen abdomen and decreased appetite. On the other hand, exercizing one's wisdom can aid the flow of vital energy, which is the goal of *qìgōng*. *Qìgōng* therapies primarily mediate thought and breathing activity to control or promote the circulation of vital energy.

### 7. 食疗
**Food Therapies**

把食物和草药结合起来用作药，以治疗疾病的做法称为食疗。例如，小米粥可养胃，菊花茶可清火明目，等等。

This is the combination of food and herbal medicines to treat illness. For example, millet porridge can nourish the stomach, and chrysanthemum tea can clear internal heat and brighten the eyes.

## 四、古代名医
**Famous Ancient Doctors**

扁鹊（约公元前407—前310）：神医，春秋战国时人，创造了望、闻、问、切的诊断方法，提倡整体治疗的中医方法，也被尊为医祖。

Bian Que (407 – 310 B. C.): in the Spring and Autumn and the Warring States period, he created the diagnostic method of "observing" "smelling" "inquiring" and "pulse-taking". He advocated a holistic treatment, and is honored as the Ancestor of Doctors.

华佗（约145—208）：外科手术鼻祖，生活在东汉末年，在外科手术中首次使用了麻醉药——麻沸散，麻沸散是世界上最早的麻醉剂。直至1805年，日本使用以曼陀罗花为主的麻醉剂，被认为是世界外科学麻醉史上的首创，实际上比中国要晚。华佗还模仿虎、鹿、熊、猿和鹤的动作编排了健身操——五禽戏。

Hua Tuo (145 – 208): originator of surgery who lived in the later years of the Eastern Han. He was the first to use anesthetic in surgery—*máfèisàn*, the world's first anesthetic. In 1805, Japan used the flower of the *datura stramonium* as an anesthetic, which was believed to be history's first surgical anesthesia. In fact, this is later than China's use. Hua Tuo also arranged a physical regimen imitating tigers, deer, bears, apes and cranes, called the Five Animal Play.

张仲景（约150—约216）：医圣，东汉时期人，他著有医学专著《伤寒杂病论》。
Zhang Zhongjing (a. 150 – a. 216): the Sage of Medicine, a person of the Eastern Han, who authored the medical text *Treatise on Febrile and Miscellaneous Disorders*.

葛洪（283—363）：生活在东晋，他注意研究急性传染病，著作《肘后备急方》，书名的意思是可以常常备在肘后（带在身边）的应急书，书中收集了大量救急用的药方。
Ge Hong (283 – 363): lived in the Eastern Jin. He paid attention to research on acute infectious disease. He wrote *The Handbook of Prescriptions for Emergencies* (literally, "emergency prescriptions prepared behind the elbow"); the meaning of the title is that it is a book for emergencies that one can keep prepared by one's elbow (carried with you). The book collects a large number of prescriptions for treating emergencies.

皇甫谧（215—282）：针灸鼻祖，魏晋时期人，著作《针灸甲乙经》，是我国第一部针灸学专著，总结了晋代以前的针灸学成就。此书也被传到国外，受到日本、朝鲜的重视，在日本法令《大宝律令》中，规定《针灸甲乙经》为必读的参考书之一。
Huangfu Mi (215 – 282): originator of acupuncture-and-moxibustion, a person of the Wei-Jin period. He wrote *The Systematic Classic of Acupuncture and Moxibustion*, China's first work on the topic. It summarized the achievements in acupuncture and moxibustion before the Jin Dynasty. The book was transmitted to foreign countries, and particularly highly regarded in Korea and Japan. The *Taihō Law* (701 A.D.) in Japan stipulated that the *The Systematic Classic of Acupuncture and Moxibustion* become one of the required reference texts of the land.

孙思邈（541—682）：药王，唐朝人。创立脏病、腑病分类系统，他认为"人命至重，有贵千金"，他的医学著作即《千金方》，是中国最早的临床医学百科全书。
Sun Simiao (541 – 682): King of Medicines, a person of the Tang Dynasty. He established the systematic distinction between diseases of the five *zang* (referring to heart, liver, spleen, lung and kidney) and those of the six *fu* (referring to stomach, gallbladder, *san-jiao*, bladder, large intestine, and small intestine). He believed, "The importance of a human life

is as valuable as 1000 pieces of gold." His medical text was *Prescriptions Worth a Thousand in Gold*, China's earliest encyclopedia of clinical therapeutics.

钱乙（1032—1117）：儿科鼻祖，北宋人，著有第一部儿科专著《小儿药证直诀》，比欧洲最早出版的儿科著作早300年。

Qian Yi (c. 1032 – 1117): originator of pediatrics. A person of the Northern Song, he wrote the first monograph on pediatrics *Direct Methods and Proven Medicines of Children*, which appeared three hundred years earlier than Europe's earliest work on pediatrics.

宋慈（1186—1249）：法医之鼻祖，南宋时期人。他在著作《洗冤集录》中提出滴血认亲的方法，开创了法医鉴定学。《洗冤集录》是中国第一部法医学专著，也是世界上最早的法医学专著。

Song Ci (1186 – 1249): originator of forensic investigation, a person of the Southern Song. In his master work, *Record of Washed Grievances*, he proposed the method of "dripping blood to identify relatives", initiating forensic science. *Record of Washed Grievances* is China's, indeed the world's, first monograph on forensics.

李时珍（1518—1593）：医药学家，明朝人，著作《本草纲目》是我国中医药学领域的不朽杰作，达尔文（1809—1882）称赞它是"中国古代的百科全书"。

Li Shizhen (1518 – 1593): pharmaceutical scholar of the Ming Dynasty. His *Compendium of Medicinal Herbs* is China's immortal masterpiece in the field of Chinese pharmacology. Charles Darwin (1809 – 1882) praised it as "the encyclopedia of ancient China".

## 五、中医主要典籍
## The Main Classics of Chinese Medicine

《内经》：约在公元前5—前3世纪，产生了我国最早的一部医学著作——《内经》。《内经》相传为黄帝所作，又称《黄帝内经》。春秋战国时期成书，较为全面地论述了人体的生理、病理、诊断、预防、针灸等方面的理论。

*Inner Classic* appeared around $5^{th}$ to $3^{rd}$ Century B. C. , and it is China's earliest medical text. By tradition, it was authored by the Yellow Emperor, so it is also known as *Yellow Emperor's Inner Classic*. It first appeared in the Spring and Autumn and the Warring States period. It comprehensively discusses various theoretical aspects such as the physiology of the human body, pathology, diagnosis, prevention and acupuncture-and-moxibustion.

《神农本草经》：出现于公元前 2 世纪，是我国第一部药物学著作。由于古代的药物主要来自自然界的植物，因而人们把药物学著作称作"本草"。这也是我国现存最早的药物学专著。全书分三卷，书中记载药物 365 种，对每一味药的产地、性质、采集和主治的病症都有详细的记载。

*Shennong's Compendium of Materia Medica*: appearing in the 2$^{nd}$ Century B.C., it is China's first pharmacological work. Because ancient medicines primarily came from plants in the natural world, so people referred to pharmacological works as *běncǎo* ("roots and plants", material medica). This is China's earliest extant pharmacological treatise. The book is in three chapters, and it records 365 herbal medicines. There are detailed records in the book of each medicine's place of origin, characteristics, collection, and illness it mainly treats.

《伤寒杂病论》：作者是东汉张仲景（150—216）。这本书比较系统地总结了汉代以前对伤寒和杂病在诊断和治疗方面的经验，确立了中医辨证论治的基本法则，是我国第一部临床治疗学方面的巨著。

*Treatise on Cold Damage Disorders*: The author was Zhang Zhongjing (150 – 216). This text relatively systematically summarizes experiences diagnosing and treating "cold damage" and various illnesses in the Han Dynasty. It established Chinese medicine's basic principle of a holistic diagnosis and treatment. It is China's first monumental work on clinical therapeutics.

《千金方》：作者是唐代孙思邈（c.541—682），有《千金要方》和《千金翼方》两部。《千金要方》共 30 卷，包括临床各科诊断、治疗、针灸、食疗以及预防、卫生等各个方面。《千金翼方》收载有 800 多种药物，内容以本草、伤寒、中风、杂病和疼痛等记述最为突出。

*Prescriptions Worth a Thousand in Gold*: The author was Sun Simiao (c. 581 – 682). It consists of two parts: *Important Prescriptions* and *Ancillary Prescriptions*. *Important Prescriptions* has thirty chapters on various aspects such as clinical subjects, diagnosis, therapy, acupuncture-and-moxibustion, food therapy, as well as prevention and hygiene. *Ancillary Prescriptions* collects around 800 herbal medicines. Notable contents include records of materia medica, "cold disorders", stroke, miscellaneous illnesses and pain.

《本草纲目》：作者是明朝李时珍（1518—1593）。全书共 52 卷，记载药物 1892 种，处方 11096 个，附有 1162 幅插图，总结了明清以前的药物知识。后来传到日本、欧洲，译成日、英、法、德、俄等多种文字。

*Compendium of Medical Herbs*: The author was Li Shizhen (1518 – 1593). The book has 52 chapters, recording 1892 types of herbal medicines, 11096 medical prescriptions with 1162 illustrations. It summarizes the knowledge of herbal medicine up to the Ming-Qing period. It later was transmitted to Japan and Europe and was translated into many languages, including Japanese, English, French, German and Russian.

### 思考题

1. 中医主要的治疗方法有哪些?
2. 中医是如何使用阴阳五行理论的?
3. 认识一个穴位,比如眼睛旁边的太阳穴,按摩并感受其作用。

### *Questions*

1. What are the main treatment methods of Chinese medicine?
2. How does Chinese medicine make use of *Yin-Yang* and Five-Phase theories?
3. Identify an acupuncture point, such as the temple point beside the eyes, massage it and feel its effects.

# 第十三章 中国古代服饰
## Ancient Chinese Apparel

中国人习惯把日常生活概括为衣、食、住、行，服饰排在了第一位。

中国民族众多，着装不同，各民族都有自己独特的服饰，多种多样的服饰体现着各民族不同的服饰文化，无法一概而论，但是穿着人数最多的是汉服。

Chinese people are in the habit of summarizing daily life as clothes, food, accommodations, and travel; apparel is in the first position.

There are many ethnicities in China that dress differently, each with their own unique apparel. These many varied pieces of clothing manifest each ethnicity's different culture of apparel, which is impossible to lump into a single discussion. Still, that which is worn by the most people is the traditional Han Chinese clothing.

今天说的汉服，是指古代传统的汉族服饰，即华夏衣冠，又称为华服。汉服是从夏商周时期到明朝末期，华夏民族（汉族）穿着的服饰。其源头从传说中的三皇五帝时期就已具备基本形式，历经周代的规范，到了汉代已全面完善并普及，汉人、汉族、汉服由此得名。

Han Chinese dress today refers to the ancient traditions of ethnic Han apparel, the attire of Hua-Xia, also known as Hua dress. It is the apparel the Hua-Xia (Han) wore from the Xia-Shang-Zhou era down to the end of the Ming era. Its source, according to legend, was already basically formed in the era of the Three Sovereigns and Five Kings. It went through standardization in the Zhou period, and was perfected and widespread by Han times. The Han people, the Han ethnicity and the Han dress get their names from this period.

## 一、传统汉服
## Traditional Han Chinese Apparel

传统的汉服样式有两种：一种是衣与裳，即上穿衣，下着裳，类似于今天的衣服、裤子，是上下分开的；一种是衣和裳连在一起，叫作"深衣"（见图13-1至图13-3）。

The traditional style of Han apparel is of two types: One is an upper garment (called "*yi*") and a lower garment (called "*chang*"), i.e., wearing a shirt on top and a skirt or petticoats below, similar to modern-day pants and a shirt with separations between the upper and lower garments. The other type is *shēnyī* ("robe", lit. deep shirt), and the upper and lower garments are connected together (see Figure 13-1—Figure 13-3).

图 13-1　汉服之深衣（1）

Figure 13-1　Traditional Han Chinese Apparel: "Robe" ( I )

图 13-2　汉服之深衣（2）

Figure 13-2　Traditional Han Chinese Apparel: "Robe" ( II )

图 13-3 汉服之深衣（3）
Figure 13-1 Traditional Han Chinese Apparel："Robe"（Ⅲ）

古代的衫、袍等都采用衣、裳连在一起的深衣样式。

汉服以周代的服装为标准，即束发为髻，上衣下裳，右衽交领，腰间束带。

The ancient jacket with open slits in place of sleeves and the lined gown all adopted this style of joined-together clothing.

Traditional Han apparel takes the clothing of the Zhou Dynasty as the standard. It was to bind one's hair into a topknot, shirt on the top and skirts/petticoats on the bottom, right lapel crosses the collar, and a belt binds the waist.

汉服衣领的主要特征：衣领有交领、圆领、对襟直领等（见图13-4）；袍衣用衣带、暗扣；袖子长短宽窄都有。

Main Characteristics of Han Apparel Collar: Collar varieties included crossed, round collars and buttoned straight collars (see Figure 13-4); gowns and shirts used belts and buttons; in sleeves there were long and short, as well as wide and narrow.

交领　　　　圆领　　　　对襟直领　　　　右衽

图 13-4 汉服衣领
Figure 13-4 Han Apparel Collar

三千年来，汉人服装的基本特征没有大的改变，后来的朝代虽然对汉服有不同程度的改变，但直到三百多年前的清初，受满族人服饰影响，汉服才发生彻底变化。

清末变革，康有为（1858—1927）等人提倡改革服饰，首先中国留学生开始行动，他们剪掉长辫子，改穿西服，服饰为之一变。1912年，国民政府发布《剪辫通令》，随后参考西方各国的服饰制度，又发布《服制条例》，不久又重新发布，主要规定男女礼服和公务人员制服。

Over three thousand years, there weren't any large variations in the basic characteristics of Han apparel. Later dynasties had different degrees of variation in Han apparel, but not until the beginning of the Qing Dynasty three hundred years ago when it was influenced by Manchu apparel, did Han apparel undergo a thorough change.

This situation changed at the end of the Qing Dynasty. Kang Youwei (1858 – 1927) and others advocated reforming apparel. First, Chinese students studying abroad began to mobilize. They cut off their long braids and changed to wearing Western clothes, apparel being one of their reforms. In 1912, the Republican government issued *The General Order on Cutting Off Braids*. Following that, upon consulting the systems of apparel among Western countries, it again issued *Regulations on the System of Clothing*, and reissued it after a short amount of time. It primarily stipulated formal attire for men and women and uniforms for public servants.

旗袍（见图13-5至图13-7）由满族服装演变而来，20世纪20年代开始流行，成为最普遍的女子服装。1929年，中华民国政府正式确定旗袍为国家礼服之一。中山装，从民国年间开始逐渐成为男子主要服装。

20世纪50年代以后，常见的男女装束是上衣下裤。80年代改革开放以后，传统服饰开始变得多样，牛仔裤、T恤、迷你裙等开始在中国流行。服饰的变化总是离不开文化变迁的大背景。

The *qípáo*, or cheongsam (see Figure 13 – 5—Figure 13 – 7), evolved out of Manchu clothing. It became popular in the 1920s, eventually becoming the most representative female dress. In 1929, the government of the Republic of China confirmed it as one of the national formal dresses. The Chinese tunic suit gradually became the primary male attire starting in the Republican years.

After the 1950s, the common attire for men and women was shirt and pants. After reform and opening in the 1980s, conventional attire began to diversify. Jeans, T-shirts, miniskirts, etc., began to become popular in China. Changes in apparel are always inserable from the larger cultural background.

图 13-5 旗袍
Figure 13-5 qípáo

图 13-6 旗袍
Figure 13-6 qípáo

图 13-7 旗袍
Figure 13-7 qípáo

## 二、五行与着装
## The Five-Phases Theory and Clothing

五行，即金、木、水、火、土，分别对应了不同的颜色：金——白色；木——青色；水——黑色；火——赤色；土——黄色。不同朝代崇尚的色彩与这个朝代的五行属性有关。

The five phases, i. e., metal, wood, water, fire, and earth, separately correspond to different colors. Metal corresponds to white; wood, blue and green; water, black; fire, red; earth, yellow. The colors revered by different dynasties are related to the category of the five phases the dynasty belonged to.

中国朝代五行属性和色彩的关系。

夏代木德，商代金德，周代火德，秦代水德，西汉土德，东汉火德，曹魏土德，西晋金德，东晋金德，隋代火德，唐代土德，宋代火德，元代金德，明代火德，清代水德，民国土德。

The relationship between colors and the five-phase category of Chinese dynasties:

Xia represents wood virtue; Shang, metal virtue; Zhou, fire virtue; Qin, water virtue; Western Han, earth virtue; Eastern Han, fire virtue; Cao's Wei Dynasty, earth virtue; Western and Eastern Jin, metal virtue; Sui, fire virtue; Tang, earth virtue; Song, fire virtue; Yuan, metal virtue; Ming, fire virtue; Qing, water virtue; Republican, earth virtue.

　　服饰的色彩：汉族把青、红、皂、白、黄五种颜色视为"正色"。不同朝代崇尚的色彩也不尽相同，一般是夏代尚青、商代尚白、周代尚赤、秦代尚黑、西汉尚黄、东汉尚赤、曹魏尚黄，唐服色尚黄，旗帜尚赤，到了明代，定赤色为正色。从唐代以后，黄色长期被视为尊贵的颜色，往往只有天子权贵才能穿用。

　　As for the colors of apparel, the Han ethnicity regards blue-green, red, black, white, and yellow as the "five colors". The colors revered by the different dynasties are not necessarily the same. Generally, it is Xia—black (blue-green); Shang—white; Zhou—red; Qin—black; Western Han—yellow; Eastern Han—red; Cao's Wei Dynasty—yellow. Tang clothes were yellow and banners red; by the Ming Dynasty, red was determined to be the fundamental color. But, after the Tang, yellow was regarded as the color of honor for a long time, and usually only the emperor and influential nobles could wear it.

## 三、服饰中的文化观念
## Cultural Notions in Apparel

　　一般而言，服饰以遮羞、保暖、舒适、实用为主。中国则是以人文精神为本，将尊严排于第一，舒适排于第二，这就从根本上决定了中国的服饰不是单纯的遮羞保暖，而是被赋予了更多的意义。古文献中谈到服饰时，说"非先王之法，服不敢服"（出自《孝经》），"变节易度，则为剽轻奇怪之服，故有服妖"（出自《汉书·五行志》），根据这些表述，可知古时对奇装异服是抱有敌视且恐惧的心理的。这也决定了中国服饰在漫长的五千年历史中并不会像西方服饰那样发生天翻地覆的变化。

　　Generally, apparel culture attaches significance to the practical aspects of covering the body, warmth, and comfort, but in China the humanistic spirit took primacy, placing honor above comfort. This basically determined that Chinese apparel was not simply about covering the body and keeping warm, but was rather invested with more significance. Ancient writings about apparel express such thing as, "If it is not the pattern of the first kings, one does not dare to wear it" (from the *Classic of Filial Piety*), "If their social customs are wild and slow, and they transgress rules and change norms, then they are marauders on horseback wearing strange clothes; thus, there is the Clothes Goblin" (from *Han Shu*, "Treatise on the Five Phases"). Based on these formulations, clearly in antiquity there was malicious and fearful psychology as regards wearing bizarre dress. This also determined that in the long, five thousand year history, Chinese apparel would not, like western apparel, undergo great changes.

首先，服饰与礼制相联系。正史"二十四史"里，每一部都有一章"舆服志"，详细地记载了天子、官员参加祭祀时的着装礼仪。古人的服饰中有祭服、吉服、丧服，出席的场合不同，穿着的服饰不同；服饰的颜色也是如此，不同的颜色有不同的含义。例如，红色是喜庆的色彩，黑色、白色是哀伤的色彩，如果在丧礼上穿着红色的衣服，会被认为无礼。

First, apparel is connected with systems of rites. In the official "Twenty-four histories", each one has a chapter on "Treatise on Chariots and Clothes", which meticulously records the clothing rituals of the emperor and nobility when they participated in sacrifices to the ancestors. The clothing of the ancients included apparel for sacrifices, auspicious clothing, and mourning garments; differences in what one attended meant differences in the apparel one wore. The color of the clothing was similar in that different colors had different meanings. For example, red was the color of celebration, black and white the colors of bereavement. If one wore red colored clothes at a funeral, it would be considered rude.

其次，服饰用来区分尊卑、等级。从黄袍、龙袍、乌纱帽，明清官服胸前补子上的图案，到百姓的布衣，从服饰可以直观区分等级。人们会严格遵守，不敢乱穿。

Second, apparel was used to distinguish seniority and rank. From the yellow robe, dragon robe, black hat, and designs worn on the chest of Ming and Qing Dynasty officials to the plain-cloth clothing of the common people, one could distinguish rank from the direct observation of clothing. People strictly abided by these rules and would not dare to mix them up.

再次，服饰是人的内在品格的外部表现。儒家追求"中和"的人格，认为做人要适度，要做到内在与外在的统一，因此服饰整体上追求温和内敛的审美，儒雅的服装要有相应的饰物佩戴，以表现谦谦君子的风度，玉为首选。在古代，君子大都要佩戴玉，因为玉用来比喻美德，人们普遍地认同这样的观念。在传统的着装观念中，正统的服饰标志着端庄、修养，裸露的服饰代表着轻浮、浅薄等等。这些观念只是在近几年才开始逐渐发生变化。

Third, apparel is the outer expression of one's inner character. Confucianism pursues the "neutral" personality, which believes that people should be modest, and need to achieve the internal and external unity. Thus, the overall aesthetical pursuit of clothing is gentle and reserved. The elegant clothing must be worn with corresponding ornaments to show the modesty of the gentleman; in this sense, the jade is a perfect choice. Most of the gentlemen in ancient times wore a piece of jade on their waist, because jade was used as a metaphor for virtue, and people generally identified with these ideas. In the traditional conception of clothing, orthodox apparel symbolized dignity and accomplishment; revealing clothing represented frivolousness and superficiality. Only in the last few years has this started to undergo change.

最后，服饰中蕴含着幸福吉祥的美好愿望。服饰上的各种装饰，特殊日子里的着装讲究，较为普遍地反映了中国人追求美满生活的心理。例如，牡丹花的图案表示富贵吉祥，喜鹊表示"喜上眉梢"，等等。

Finally, happiness and good luck accumulates in apparel. The various kinds of decorations on apparel and the attention paid to clothing for special days, generally reflect the Chinese people's pursuit of a happy life. For example, a peony flower design expresses wealth and good luck; the magpie expresses "happiness shown in one's countenance", etc.

**思考题**

中国古代服饰如何体现中国人的文化观念？

*Questions*

How does Chinese apparel manifest the cultural conception of Chinese people?

# 第十四章 中国饮食
## Chinese Food and Drink

"民以食为天",饮食对于中国人来说是头等大事。最幸福的时刻也就是合家团圆,一家人围坐在饭桌前一起吃团圆饭;最大的节日春节来临时,人们赶回家就是为了大年三十晚上的一顿团圆饭。

"The people regard food as God." Food is a big deal for Chinese people. In the happiest times, i.e., when the entire family gathers together, the whole family will sit around the dinner table and eat a meal together. On the last day of the lunar year as the most important holiday, the Spring Festival, draws near, people hurry home for the family meal.

《礼记》称:"饮食男女,人之大欲存焉。"把饮食之事和生儿育女之事看作是"大欲",是人类最大的欲望,认为应该慎重对待。因此,中国人特别讲究饮食。中国人的吃不仅仅是填饱肚子,也吃出了一种艺术,一种文化。中国、法国、土耳其一起被称为"世界主要三大烹饪王国"。

The *Classic of Rites* says, "Food, drink, men, and women; therein lies the great passions of the people." Sustenance and bearing children are the great desires of the people, and therefore these things should be treated prudently. Therefore, Chinese people pay special attention to food and drink. Eating for Chinese people is not simply about filling the stomach. It is also a kind of art, a kind of culture. China, France and Turkey have been called, "The three great culinary kingdoms of the world."

## 一、饮食原料和特点
## Materials and Characteristics of Food and Drink

一方水土养一方人。受地理环境的影响,中国菜大致可以分为南方做法和北方做法。

一般说来,北方盛产麦子,所以北方人以面食为主,面条、馒头、饺子、包子等是北方人日常的主食。南方盛产水稻,所以南方人以大米为主,米饭、糯米、米粉等是南方人日常的主食。

The place where people live is a contributor to our overall subjective well-being. Under the influence of geography, Chinese food can roughly be divided into northern and southern practices.

Generally, the north is rich in wheat, so northerners rely mainly on foods made from wheat flour, such as noodles, steamed breads, dumplings, etc., which are the staples of the northerner's diet. The south is rich in rice, so southerners rely mainly on rice-based foods, such as rice, sticky-rice and rice noodles. These are the staples of the southerner's diet.

北方地处内陆，多山地、草原，所以北方人以牛、羊、猪肉为主；南方多水，所以南方人以鱼虾以及猪肉为主。

口味上，北方人偏好咸味，南方人偏好甜味。中国饮食重视滋味，要达到滋味无穷，所以在滋味的基础上形成了各种菜系。

The north is located in the interior of the continent, with mountains and plains, so northerners rely mainly on beef, mutton and pork. The south has a lot of water, so southerners rely mainly on fish, shrimp and pork.

In terms of flavors, northerners tend to favor salty, and southerners tend to favor sweet. Chinese food values full flavoring. It must attain boundless full flavor, so on the basis of this full flavoring, various regional cuisines have evolved.

中国菜的烹饪讲究色、香、味俱全，认为食材的五味能满足人体五脏的营养需要，即甜、酸、苦、辣、咸五味能入心、肝、脾、肺和肾脏五个主要器官，强调五味能保持身体健康。认为"药食同源"，相信食物的药用价值，认为"药疗不如食疗"。

中国菜的烹调技巧，大体上有炒、干煸、油炸、烘焙、烤、蒸、煮、炖、熬、焖、煨、汆等。

Chinese cooking pays particular attention to the complete package of appearance, aroma and taste. Moreover, it is believed that the five flavors of food can fulfill the nutritional needs of the five *zang* (organs) in the human body; so, sweet, sour, bitter, spicy and salty can enter the heart, liver, spleen, lungs and kidneys, thus connecting the five flavors with maintaining physical health. It is thought that, "there is no distinction between food and medicine," a statement of the belief in the medicinal value of food, as is also found in the idea that, "medicinal treatments are not as good as treatment via food."

The techniques of Chinese cooking are stir-fry, sauté, deep-fry, bake, roast, steam, boil, braise, stew, decoct, simmer, and quick-boil.

## 二、素食
## Vegetarian Food

素食即以蔬菜、瓜果、蘑菇、豆制品为主要食材,用植物油做调料,不吃肉。素食源自佛教,佛教传入中国后,汉传佛教从南朝梁武帝时期开始,主张吃素,忌食荤腥。寺院的素食,除了不吃肉,不吃荤,也不吃腥物,例如葱、姜、蒜、韭菜都属腥臊物,吃了容易有味、燥热,不利修行,所以忌食。

Vegetarian food relies mainly on vegetables, melons and squashes, mushrooms, and beans for ingredients and uses vegetable oil as condiment. One does not eat meat. Vegetarian originated from Buddhism. After Buddhism spread to China, starting from the time of the Wu Emperor of the Southern Liang Dynasty, Han Buddhism advocated vegetarianism, making a taboo out of meat consumption. The vegetarian food of monasteries and temples, in addition to not including meat, does not include fish and strong-smelling vegetables. For example, green onions, garlic, ginger, and chives are all categorized as strong-smelling vegetables; if one were to eat them, they would be tasty and hot, not conducive to religious practice, so they are tabooed.

## 三、药膳
## Medicinal Cuisine

药膳即食疗,就是把药材与食材相配伍而做成食物,是把食物和传统医学结合起来,让疾病的预防和治疗变得简单而容易让人接受。人们在享受食物的同时,又可防病治病,保健强身,延年益寿。

药膳有很多种类,包括各种菜肴、汤、饮料、粥和糕点。药膳最基本的作用是增强身体的抵抗力,加强身体的免疫功能。最常见的药膳有八宝粥、莲子粥等。

Medicinal cuisine is treating illness via food, the joining of food with traditional medicine, making the prevention and treatment of disease simpler and easier for people to accept. While enjoying food, people can prevent and cure diseases, strengthen health and have a longer life.

There are many kinds of medicinal cuisines, including all kinds of dishes, soups, beverages, porridges, and cakes. The most basic effect of medicinal cuisine is to increase the body's resistance to disease, by increasing its immunity. The most common medicinal dishes are eight-treasure porridge and lotus seed porridge.

## 四、八大菜系
## Eight Great Regional Cuisines

形成不同菜系的原因包括历史因素、烹调特点、地理因素、气候、资源和生活方式等。早在春秋战国时期，中国的饮食文化就表现出了南北菜肴风味的差异。到唐宋时，南食、北食各自形成体系。到清代初期，鲁菜、川菜、粤菜、苏菜成为当时最有影响力的地方菜，被称作"四大菜系"。到清末，浙菜、闽菜、湘菜、徽菜四大新地方菜系分化形成，共同构成中国传统饮食的"八大菜系"。

The reasons for the formation of regional cuisines are historical factors, cooking techniques, geographic factors, climate, resources and lifestyle. As early as the Spring-Autumn/Warring States period, Chinese food culture already expressed differences between northern and southern dishes and flavors. By Tang times, the northern food and southern food had formed their own systems. By Qing times, Shandong, Sichuan, Cantonese and Jiangsu cuisines had become the most influential regional cuisines, and were known as "the four great cuisines". By the end of the Qing, Zhejiang, Fujian, Hunan and Anhui had separated out as four new regional cuisines. All together, these constitute the "eight great regional cuisines" of traditional China.

### 1. 鲁菜
### Shandong Cuisine

中国四大菜系之首为鲁菜。鲁菜即山东菜，鲁是山东省的简称。山东是中国古文化发祥地之一，地处黄河下游，气候温和，境内山川纵横，河湖交错，沃野千里，物产丰富。山东的粮食产量长期居中国前列，蔬菜种类多，品质优良，是中国重要的蔬菜产地。山东是孔子的故乡，鲁菜处处体现着孔子"食不厌精，脍不厌细"的饮食理念，讲究调味纯正，口味偏咸鲜。

Shandong Cuisine is the first of China's four great cuisines. Shandong is one of the cradles of ancient Chinese culture, situated on the lower reaches of the Yellow River. The climate is moderate, mountains and rivers, creeks and lakes criss-cross within its borders, fertile land stretches for hundreds of miles and its resources are abundant. Shandong's grain production is always in the forefront of the country. There are many kinds of vegetables with good quality. Shandong is an important vegetable producing area in China. Shandong is the homeland of Confucius, so Shandong cuisine everywhere manifests his dietary idea that one "eat but finely ground grain and finely chopped meat" (be fastidious about one's food). They pay attention to seasoning and purity, with flavors tending toward the bright and salty.

明清时期,鲁菜已是宫廷御膳主体。以清代国宴规格设置的"满汉全席",使用全套银餐具,196 道菜,全是山珍海味,奢华至极。作为北方第一菜系,喜庆寿诞的高档宴席和家常菜的许多基本菜式都是由鲁菜发展而来。鲁菜对北京、天津、东北等地菜肴也有着重要影响。山东人豪爽好客,特别讲究待客之道,唯恐客人吃不饱、吃不好,因此大盘大碗,菜量很大,在山东人家做客要有一吃到底的心理准备。典型的山东菜有糖醋鲤鱼等。鲁菜还善以葱香调味,什么菜都要用葱,山东人平日也极爱吃葱,家常饭就是大饼卷大葱。

In the Ming-Qing era, Shandong cuisine was already the main part of imperial meals in the palace. The "Manchu Han Imperial Feast" which had been installed as the national banquet norm under the Qing, used complete sets of silver tableware, 196 courses, all of which were treasures of the mountains and sea, luxurious to the extreme. As the No. 1 northern regional cuisine, fancy banquets for celebrating old age and birthdays and many basic recipes for home cooking developed out of Shandong cuisine. It has had an important influence on the regional cooking of Beijing, Tianjin and the northeast. Shandong people are outspoken and hospitable, especially particular about the ways of hosting guests. Their only fear is that the guest does not eat enough, so there is a great amount of food served in large platters and bowls. If you are going to be a guest in a Shandong person's house, one must be prepared to eat to the utmost. A typical Shandong dish is sweet-and-sour carp. Shandong cuisine excels at seasoning with green onions, so every dish includes them and they are eaten every day. A common home cooked dish is a large savory pancake wrapped around giant green onions.

## 2. 川菜
### Sichuan Cuisine

川菜即四川菜,特点是调料偏辣,调味离不开辣椒、胡椒、花椒这三椒,还有葱、姜、蒜三香,口味重酸辣麻香。

Sichuan cuisine is characterized as being spicy. Its flavorings are inseparable from hot pepper, black pepper, and Sichuan pepper (Chinese prickly ash), but they also use green onions, garlic, and ginger. The flavors are heavily sour, spicy and numbing.

### (1) 知名川菜
#### Famous Sichuan Dishes

宫保鸡丁:就是辣子鸡炒花生,主要以花椒调味。由清朝四川总督丁宝桢所创,"宫保"是丁宝桢的荣誉官衔,他发明的这道菜由此得名"宫保鸡丁"。

Palace Guard Chicken: chicken stir-fried with hot peppers and peanuts, flavored mostly with Sichuan pepper. It was invented by Ding Baozhen (1820 – 1886), a Qing Dynasty governor of Sichuan. His honorary title being "Gong Bao" (palace guard), and because he invented this dish, it is called Palace Guard Chicken.

麻婆豆腐：麻婆是指一位脸上有麻点的女子。据说在清朝末年的时候，一位脸上有麻子的女子，人们就叫她"麻婆"，她和丈夫一起在成都一座桥边开了一家饭店。麻婆做好这种辣炖豆腐卖给过往的小贩和船夫，后来她的这些客人把她做的豆腐叫作麻婆豆腐。

Ma Po Tofu："ma po" refers to a woman with a pock-marked face. According to legend, in the end of the Qing Dynasty, a woman with a pock-marked face was known to people as "ma po". She and her husband opened a restaurant beside a bridge in Chengdu. The woman made this dish of stewed hot peppers and tofu to sell to passing peddlers and boatmen. Later, these customers called her dish "Ma Po Tofu".

(2) 小吃
### *Snack Foods*
赖汤圆：百年前一位姓赖的小贩在成都街头贩卖汤圆，他卖的汤圆又好吃又好看，当地人就叫他的汤圆为赖汤圆。

Lai's rice dumplings：Around 100 years ago a peddler surnamed Lai sold tasty and attractive rice dumplings on the streets of Chengdu, so the local people called them "Lai's rice dumplings".

担担面：源于小贩们在街头挑着担担卖面，方便又便宜，因而得名。担担就是扁担。担担面是将面条煮熟，浇上用肉末、花生、芝麻、辣椒油及葱姜蒜炒制的卤汁而成。

Dandan noodles：This dish has its origin in pedlars who sold noodles on the streets shouldering a carrying pole. The dish was convenient and inexpensive, and it got the name "Dandan" meaning "carrying pole". The dish involves cooking the noodles thoroughly, then ladling on a gravy made of stir-fried minced pork, peanuts, sesames, hot pepper oil, green onions, ginger and garlic.

夫妻肺片：据说是名叫郭朝华的人和他的妻子发明了这道菜，人们就称这道菜为"夫妻肺片"。做法是把卤制好的牛肉及一些牛的内脏切片，以辣椒油、花椒面调拌而成。

Married couple lung slices：According to legend, a man by the name of Guo Chaohua and his wife invented this dish, so people called it "married couple lung slices". It's made by stewing beef and beef offal in spices, then cutting them into thin slices and tossing them with hot pepper oil and Sichuan pepper powder.

四川火锅：据说在清朝末年，四川长江边上的船工们跑船的时候，常住宿在码头，做饭只有一个瓦罐，罐中盛水，再加各种蔬菜，再添加辣椒、花椒等调料一起煮着吃，后来又有了一些加工，用牛内脏熬汤吃，后来逐渐成为人们喜爱的四川代表性菜肴。

Sichuan Hot Pot: According to legend, in the latter years of the Qing Dynasty, when boatmen along the Yangtze River in Sichuan were running boats, they often spent the night on the docks. They took a single pot, filled it with water, then added various vegetables and boiled them together with hot peppers, Sichuan peppers and other spices. Later, it was added to by using a broth made of decocted beef offal. Still later it gradually became the representative Sichuan dish that people so love today.

## 3. 粤菜
### Cantonese Cuisine

粤菜即广东菜，由于广东海外华侨数量占全国六成，因此，世界各国的中菜馆，多数是以粤菜为主。传统粤菜特点之一是食材广泛奇异，蛇、鼠、猫、虫等飞禽走兽及山珍海味均可食用。例如名菜龙虎凤大烩，选用蛇、豹狸和母鸡炖汤而成。粤菜烹调做法考究，风格别致。强调味道清而不淡、鲜而不俗、嫩而不生、油而不腻。受欢迎的菜点有蒸全鱼、鱼翅羹、烤乳猪等。

Cantonese Cuisine: i.e., the cuisine of Guangdong Province. Because around 60% of the overseas Chinese are from Guangdong, the Chinese restaurants found around the world are mostly based on Cantonese cuisine. One of the characteristics of traditional Cantonese cuisine is that the materials used are varied and strange, including snakes, rats, cats, and insects; flying animals and crawling beasts, treasures of mountains and seas, all can be eaten. For example, a famous dish known as "Great Braise of Dragon, Tiger and Phoenix" uses a fat, tender snake, an autumn leopard cat, and a hen stewed into a soup. Cooking methods in Cantonese cuisine are exquisite, and the style is unique. The favored flavors are clear, but not weak; fresh, but not common; tender, but not raw; oily, but not greasy. Popular dishes include steamed whole fish, shark-fin soup, and roasted suckling pig.

## 4. 苏菜
### Jiangsu Cuisine

苏菜即江苏菜，由四种地方风味组成，是宫廷第二大菜系，今天国宴仍以淮扬菜系为主。

江苏是南方的"鱼米之乡"，食材丰富。江苏菜的特点是选料讲究、时令鲜活，工艺注重刀工火候，调味突出本味清淡，造型强调色泽美观，烹制菜肴喜欢加糖。江苏菜新鲜、清淡、味醇。代表菜有蟹粉狮子头、三套鸭、常熟叫花鸡、盐焗鸭、扬州炒饭等。

Jiangsu Cuisine: Composed of the flavors of four areas, it was the second greatest cuisine of the palace. Today, national banquets mainly rely on Huai-Yang cuisine.

Jiangsu is the "land of rice and fish", so cooking materials are abundant. Jiangsu cuisine pays particular attention to the selection of foods, the seasoning is lively, knife-work is exquisite, and heat control is emphasized. Flavors make prominent the light basic flavors of the material, and in appearance it emphasizes a color and luster that is pleasing to the eye. In cooked dishes they are fond of adding sugar. The cuisine is fresh, light and pure of flavor. Representative dishes include: Crab-meat Lion's Head (pork meatball), Three-sets Duck, Changshu Beggar's Chicken, Salt Pot Duck, and Yangzhou Fried Rice.

## 5. 闽菜
### Fujian Cuisine

闽菜即福建菜，由福州、漳州、厦门、泉州菜组成，烹调技法以清汤、干炸、爆炒为主，调味偏重甜酸。闽菜三大特色，一喜欢用红糟调味，二善于制汤，三喜欢使用糖醋。

最著名的菜是佛跳墙，菜名的意思是佛闻到菜香都要跳过墙来尝一尝，它由海鲜、鸡、鸭、猪肉混合放进米酒缸里，用小火慢慢煨成。

Fujian Cuisine: Composed of the cuisines of Fuzhou, Zhangzhou, Xiamen and Quanzhou, cooking techniques rely mainly on clear broths, dry frying, and rapid stir-fry. Flavorings tend toward sweet and sour. Three characteristics of the cuisine are: the use of red-wine dregs, excellence in making soups, and the use of sugar and vinegar.

The most famous dish is "Buddha Jumping over the Wall". The story is that even a Buddhist who smelled the dish cooking would excitedly jump over a wall to taste it. It is made by placing seafood, chicken, duck and pork in a wine vat and then slowly simmering it over low heat.

## 6. 浙菜
### Zhejiang Cuisine

浙菜即浙江菜，由杭州、宁波、绍兴菜组成，讲究新鲜、嫩、软、滑，保持原味。

杭州曾经是南宋朝的都城，浙菜喜欢给菜配上秀美的名称，重视菜的造型，典型的浙江菜有龙井虾仁、西湖醋鱼、东坡肉、叫花鸡等。

东坡肉，即红烧肉，主料采用半肥半瘦的猪肉，成品菜码得整整齐齐的像麻将块儿，肉色红中透亮，色如玛瑙，形状软而不烂、味道肥而不腻。东坡肉相传为北宋词人苏轼（号东坡居士）创制。

Zhejiang Cuisine: Composed of the food of Hangzhou, Ningbo and Shaoxing, it pays particular attention to being fresh, tender, soft and slippery, preserving the original flavor of the ingredients.

Hangzhou was the capital of the Southern Song Dynasty. Zhejiang cuisine is fond of giving dishes elegant names, and it emphasizes appearance. Typical dishes include: Longjing Shrimp, West Lake Sour Fish, Dongpo Pork, and Beggar's Chicken.

Dongpo Pork is braised pork. The main ingredient is pork that is half fatty, half lean. The finished dish is stacked neatly like mahjong tiles, and the meat is reddish and shiny, cornelion-colored, soft but not mushy, fatty but not greasy. According to legend, the dish was invented by the Northern Song poet Su Shi (whose nickname was the Hermit of Dongpo).

## 7. 徽菜
### Anhui Cuisine

徽菜即安徽菜，起源于安徽省徽州地区。由于徽州多山多水，徽菜的大部分食材都来自山区。徽菜喜欢用火腿和糖作为调料，特点是"三重"：重油、重色、重火功，芡重，色深，味浓。代表菜肴有火腿炖甲鱼、黄山炖鸽、雪冬烧山鸡等。

Anhui Cuisine: Originating in the Huizhou area, home to many mountains and rivers, the cuisine's ingredients are mostly from the mountain areas. Anhui cuisine is fond of using ham and sugar as flavorings, and is characterized by the "three heavies": heavy oil, heavy color, and heavy fire. The dishes are heavy, the color is deep, and the flavors are strong. Representative dishes are: Turtle Stewed with Ham, Huangshan Stewed Dove, and Pheasant Cooked with Potherb Mustard and Winter Bamboo Shoots.

李鸿章大杂烩：李鸿章（1823—1901），安徽合肥肥东人，晚清名臣，淮军、北洋水师的创始人和统帅，洋务运动的领袖，官至直隶总督兼北洋通商大臣，授文华殿大学士等。他曾代表清政府访问美国，在使馆回请美国友人时，因中国菜可口而深受欢迎，宴会不久，李鸿章即命厨师加菜，但主菜已用完，厨师只得将做菜余料混合下锅，凑成一道菜。宾客尝后连声叫好，并问菜名，李鸿章答："好吃多吃！"后来此菜便被命名为"李鸿章杂烩"。

Li Hongzhang's Mixed Pot: Li Hongzhang (1823 - 1901) was a native of Feidong, Hefei, Anhui Province, and a famous minister in the late Qing; the founder and admiral of the Huai Army and North China Navy, and leader of the Self-Strengthening Movement. He rose to the rank of Governor-General of Zhili and Minister of Beiyang Trade, and was an imperial preceptor. He once represented the Qing government as a visitor to the United States. When hosting Americans at the embassy, because the Chinese food was tasty and so well received, not long into the banquet he ordered the chef to add a dish. The main ingredients had all been used up, so the chef mixed the remaining ingredients into a pot to put together a dish. After the guests tasted it, they repeatedly applauded it, and asked for its name. Li Hongzhang answered, "If you like it, eat more!" Later, the dish was named, "Li Hongzhang's Mixed Pot".

## 8. 湘菜
### Hunan Cuisine

湘菜即湖南菜。湖南菜口味也偏辣，有时很难分清四川菜和湖南菜。二者的区别是：四川菜的辣以"麻辣"为主，湖南菜的辣以"酸辣"为主。

湘菜采用熏腊原料较多，做法以熏蒸、干炒为主。

代表性菜肴有腊味合蒸、剁椒鱼头、红椒腊牛肉、浏阳蒸菜、吉首酸肉等。

Hunan Cuisine: The flavor of Hunan cuisine is spicy. Sometimes it is difficult to distinguish Hunan and Sichuan cuisines, but the difference is that Sichuan cuisine is spicy and numbing, while Hunan cuisine is spicy and sour.

Hunan cuisine uses a lot of smoked meats as flavorings, and the primary techniques are smoking, steaming and dry-frying. Representative dishes include: Mixed Steamed Pot with Dried Meat, Chopped Pepper Fish, Dried Beef in Red Peppers, Liuyang Steamed Vegetables, and Jishou Sour Meat.

中西方饮食观念的差异非常明显。西方人对待饮食更多的是理性，注重卫生，重视营养搭配。中国人则追求色香味俱全。正如林语堂在《吾国吾民》中所说，西方人对待吃，是把吃当成给机器加油，而中国人则视吃为人生至乐。

Differences between Chinese and Western food are obvious. Westerners treat food and drink with more rational considerations, emphasizing hygiene and paying attention to nutritional pairings. Chinese people on the other hand pursue smelling, looking and tasting great, the complete package. Just as Lin Yutang (1895 – 1976) said in *My Country and My People*, Westerners treat eating as if they are adding fuel to a machine, whereas Chinese people regard eating as the great pleasure of life.

# 五、茶
## Tea

### 1. 茶的历史
#### The History of Tea

茶，是把从茶叶树上采摘的嫩芽经过揉捻、焙火烤干而成，饮用时在煮沸的水中冲泡。采摘茶叶的最好时节是每年农历的二、三、四月份，茶农中流传着"谷雨前，嫌太早，后三天，刚刚好，再过三天变成草"的说法，所以，"吃好茶，雨前嫩尖采谷芽"。

　　Tea is made from the process of plucking the soft shoots of leaves from the tea plant, rubbing and twirling them in the fingers, and dry roasting them. As a drink, the leaves are steeped in boiled water. The best season for picking tea is the second, third and fourth months of the lunar year. Among tea growers there is a saying, "Before Grain Rain (the sixth of 24 solar terms, falling on 19 to 21 of April), suspect it's too early; three days later is just right; wait another three days and it turns to grass," so, "to taste good tea, pluck the sprouts before the rains when they are tender and pointed."

　　茶在秦汉之前被称为"荼"（*tú*），即苦涩的可食用的食物，到汉代时被正式称为"茶"。汉时对茶的种类、茶的烘焙技能、茶的冲泡、茶水的选择、茶具及其使用等，形成了一套饮茶礼节和习俗。

　　Prior to the Qin-Han period, it was known as *tú*, a bitter, astringent food that could be made into a drink. In Han times it was formally referred to as *chá* "tea", and a set of drinking rituals and customs formed around the types of tea, the techniques for roasting it, infusing it, selecting the water, and tea implements.

　　从历史看，茶的使用是从药用、食用再到饮用。春秋战国时期更多的是用于祭祀、治病，贵族才可使用，后又逐渐成为王公贵族们的日常饮品，秦汉以后逐渐普及到民间（见图 14 – 1）。隋唐之前，喝茶风俗已经盛行全国，茶叶遂成为重要商品，并通过丝绸之路传到世界其他地区。

　　Historically, uses for tea evolved from medicinal to food to a beverage. In the Spring-Autumn/Warring States period, only the nobility could use it, and they mostly used it in sacrifices to ancestors and curing illnesses. Later it gradually became a daily beverage among the aristocrats and nobility. After the Qin-Han, it gradually spread extensively to the common people (see Figure 14 – 1). Prior to the Sui-Tang, tea drinking customs were already prevalent throughout the country, and tea leaves became an important commodity. Moreover. it spread along the Silk Road to the rest of the world.

　　陆羽的《茶经》是我国第一部研究茶道的著作，将普通的茶升格为一种美的文化艺术和技能。到宋代，饮茶的风俗已经相当普及，宋徽宗赵佶也以皇帝之尊，写了一篇《茶论》，人称《大观茶论》，是我国历史上唯一由皇帝御写的茶文。宋代到明清，喝茶成了雅俗共赏的一件乐趣。

　　Lu Yu's *The Classic of Tea* is China's first manuscript researching the *dào* of tea, raising common tea to a kind of beautiful, cultural art and technique. In the Song Dynasty, the social custom of tea drinking was already quite widespread. The Huizong Emperor of the Song,

图 14 -1 撵茶图（南宋·刘松年）
Figure 14 -1 Picture of Working Tea (Southern Song · Liu Songnian)

Zhao Ji, with the full honor of the emperor, wrote a *Treatise on Tea*, which people commonly referred to as *The Daguan Treatise on Tea* ("Daguan" being the reign title for 1107 – 1110 when it was written). It is the only article on tea written by an emperor in Chinese history. From the Song to the Ming-Qing era, drinking tea became a delight that could be enjoyed by scholars and laypeople alike.

中国是茶树的原产地，是世界上最早发现茶树、开始喝茶的国家。唐代陆羽（733—804）的著作《茶经》是中国历史上第一部有关茶文化的专著，其中记载着"茶之为饮，发乎神农氏"（饮用茶是从神农氏开始的），认为是神农氏最早发现茶叶可以饮用。神农氏为了辨别草木的药理作用，曾经亲口品尝百草。有一次他在野外休息时煮水喝，恰巧有几片叶子飘进锅中，水变成棕黄色。神农氏尝了一点，感觉味道清香，从此便发现了茶。这样说来，饮茶的历史距今约有 5000 年左右了。神农氏采草药时遇到毒药，都是用茶来解毒，故早期以茶为药。茶也是主要的祭祀用品。道教把茶看作是养生的"仙药"。今天人们仍然认为茶具有医疗价值。

China is the original source of the tea plant *camellia sinensis*; the earliest country in the world to discover the plant and to start drinking tea. The *Classic of Tea*, the work by Lu Yu (733 – 804) of the Tang Dynasty, is the first text devoted to tea culture in Chinese history, and it records that, "as a drink, tea was discovered by Shennong the Farmer God". So, he believed Shennong was the earliest to discover that tea leaves could be used to make a beverage. Shennong personally sampled all kinds of flora to differentiate the medicinal effects of plants. One time while in the countryside resting and boiling water to drink, it so happened that several leaves floated into the pot, and the water turned a brownish-yellow color. Shennong tasted it and appreciated the flavor and fragrant odor, and from this disovered tea. This history is around 5000 years old. When Shennong in the course of gathering medicinal plants came across a toxic one, he used tea as a detoxifier. Therefore, tea was used as medicine in the early days, and also the main sacrificial materials. In Daoism, tea is regarded as an "immortal medicine" for maintaining good health. Today people still believe tea has medicinal value.

## 2. 茶的种类、功效
### Types of Tea and Its Effects

从茶的制作工艺来分，基本有八种。

绿茶：不需要经过发酵，在我国产量最大。绿茶类名茶最多，例如，江西的庐山云雾、浙江的西湖龙井、安徽的黄山毛峰、河南的信阳毛尖、江苏洞庭山的碧螺春等。

There are basically eight types of tea, differentiated in the ways they are made.

Green tea, which does not need to undergo fermentation, has the largest production in China. The types of famous green teas are numerous, such as Lushan Yunwu of Jiangxi, West Lake Longjing of Zhejiang, Huangshan Maofeng of Anhui, Xinyang Maojian of Henan, and Biluochun of Dongting Mountain in Jiangsu.

红茶：属于全发酵茶（发酵度为100%），水色红亮，干茶色泽黑褐，略带乌黑，所以英语称之为"black tea"。红茶深受欧美人喜爱，是世界上消费量最大的茶类，国际市场上的红茶的贸易量占世界茶叶总贸易量的90%以上。名茶有安徽祁门红茶和云南滇红等。

Black tea (*hóngchá* "red tea") is classified as a completely fermented tea (100% degree of fermentation), a shiny red color in water, black-brown, almost jet black color and luster when dry. Thus, in English it is called "black tea". It is extremely popular in Europe and America. This type of tea has the largest consumption in the world, making up over 90% of the world market in tea leaves. Famous teas include Anhui's Qimen Black Tea and Yunnan's Dian Hong Tea.

乌龙茶：又称青茶，属于半发酵茶（发酵度为10%～70%），是介于不发酵的绿茶和全发酵的红茶之间的一大茶类，冲泡后既有绿茶的清香，又有红茶的醇厚。名茶有武夷岩茶、闽北水仙、凤凰水仙、铁观音和台湾乌龙等。其中福建武夷岩茶中的大红袍被誉为"中国茶王"，是茶中极品；台湾乌龙有"东方美人"之称。

Oolong tea is also called blue-green tea. It belongs to the semi-fermented category (degrees of fermentation between 10%～70%), so it is a large category of tea intermediate between green teas and the completely fermented black teas. After being steeped, it has both the aroma of green tea and the mellow richness of black tea. Famous ones include Wuyi Rock Tea, Shuixian of northern Fujian, Phoenix Shuixian, Tieguanyin and Taiwan Oolong. Among them, Dahongpao (Large Red Dress Tea) among Fujian's Wuyi Rock Teas has been praised as "The King of Chinese Tea", having the best quality. Taiwan Oolong has the appellation, "Beauty of the East".

白茶：是我国茶类中的精品，茶叶多为条状的白色茶叶，满身披毫，如银似雪，因此而得名，咖啡因含量非常低。其名茶不多，主要是产于福建福鼎、政和、建阳的"银针白毫""白牡丹"和"美眉"等。

White tea is a premium product among Chinese teas. The leaves are mostly white strips, covered in hairs, like silver or snow, from where it gets its name. The amount of caffeine is very low. There are a few famous varieties, such as "Silver Needle White Hair", "White Peony" and "Pretty Eyebrow" produced in Fujian's Fuding, Zhenghe, and Jianyang.

黄茶：属于轻微发酵茶（发酵度为10%），特点是黄叶、黄汤，代表品种有君山银针、蒙顶黄芽、温州黄汤等。

Yellow tea belongs to the slightly fermented category (10% degree of fermentation), characterized by yellow leaves and yellow water. Representative varieties include Junshan Silver Needle, Mengding Yellow Sprout, and Wenzhou Yellow Water.

黑茶：是我国特有茶类，制作时先烘干，再经过长时间发酵，然后烘烤。茶叶加工后完全被氧化，呈黑褐色，故名黑茶。冲泡时呈琥珀色，是茶类中咖啡因含量最高的。黑茶有云南普洱茶、四川边茶和湖南益阳等。

Dark tea (*hēichá* "black tea") is a tea type specific to China, made by first drying the leaves in a stove, then undergoing a long period of fermentation, and finally it is roasted. Through this process the leaves are completely oxidized, presenting a black-brown color, thus its name. Upon steeping it, it assumes an amber color. It is the type of tea with the highest amount of caffeine. Famous types are Yunnan's Pu'er, Sichuan's Bian Tea, and Hunan's Yiyang Dark Tea.

花茶：元代时，一些文人雅士在茶叶中放入茉莉花、玫瑰花、菊花等，在茶叶中加入花香。饮用时以绿茶和红茶为主，混合以干花。

Scented tea started in the Yuan Dynasty, when some literati and elegant officials placed jasmine flowers, rose petals, or chrysanthemum petals in their tea, adding a floral aroma to the tea leaves. Based primarily on green and black teas, the teas are mixed with dried flowers.

茯茶：将黑茶蒸后压缩成各种样式，以长方砖形为主，故也称"茯砖茶"，可存储很长时间，方便运输。古代"茶马互市"时流通到西北地区的茶即以茯砖茶为主，西北俗称为"砖茶"。西北人多饮用此茶，尤其在食用牛羊肉以后，砖茶既可以帮助消化，还可以补充维生素。正因为此，高原人才愿意用珍贵的马匹来换取茶叶。流行于西北的砖茶主产地为湖南益阳。

Brick tea: after dark tea is steamed, it is pressed into various shapes, primarily into rectangular bricks, thus it is known as "brick tea". These can be stored for long periods of time, making them convenient for transporting great distances. In the time of the ancient "tea for horses markets", the tea circulated to the northwest was primarily this brick tea. People in the northwest drink this tea a lot, especially after eating beef or mutton. Brick tea is an aid to digestion and can supplement vitamin content. Because of this, people on the plateaus of the northwest traded valuable horses for tea. The brick tea popular in the northwest is primarily made in Yiyang, Hunan.

在茶的发展过程中，一些能够泡制饮品的植物花叶、种子、根茎等，也被称为茶，例如用花瓣泡制的"花茶"，用药草等泡制的"养生茶"，有枸杞茶、决明子茶等。唐代药典《唐本草》中有茶疗的记载。医书上说到，茶有止渴、清神、利尿、治咳、祛痰、明目、益思、除烦去腻、驱困轻身、消炎解毒等功效。

In tea's developmental process, some plants that could be steeped into a beverage, such as flowers, seeds, and roots, were also called "tea", such as the scented teas using steeped flowers, the "good health teas" steeped with medicinal herbs, wolfberry tea, cassia seed tea, etc. The Tang pharmacopeia *Tang Materia Medica* has records of tea therapies. The efficacy of tea mentioned in medical texts includes stopping thirst, clearing the spirit, promoting urination, treating a cough, dispelling phlegm, brightening the eyes, increasing thought, removing trouble and expelling the unctuous, driving out sleepiness and easing the body, reducing a fever, and detoxification.

## 3. 茶具
**Tea Sets**

古人习惯把茶具称为茶器或茗器，指的是煮茶、品茶所要用到的所有工具，有风炉、釜、罗合、夹、碗、巾等24种。今天人们所说的茶具，更多的是按用途来分，包括泡茶用的茶壶、茶壶的垫底器具茶船、盛茶用的茶罐、饮茶用的茶杯、品茶用的闻香杯、茶杯垫底用的杯托。器具不仅要求好用，还要有美感，能承载文化情怀。

唐代以前，茶具和一般的食器没有明显的区分，可以相互混用，例如碗。唐代以后，茶器的制作开始有了审美要求，由早期的古朴、绮丽到清雅，影响至今（见图14-2）。

The ancients called tea sets "tea tools" or "tea implements", referring to all the tools necessary for making and tasting tea, twenty-four in all, including the furnace, kettle, bamboo sieve, pincers, bowls, towels, etc. The tea tools of modern times are mostly differentiated according to their uses, including the tea pot used for steeping tea, tea boat under which the tea pot sits, tea can for filling the tea, the cup for drinking, the tasting cup for sipping, the saucer under which the cup sits, etc. The tools must be useful, but they also must be pleasingly beautiful, able to bear the cultural mood.

Prior to the Tang Dynasty, tea sets and general eating implements were not noticeably different, able to be used for both activities, such as the bowl. After the Tang, the manufacture of tea implements began to aquire an aesthetic, from the beautifully simple and unadorned to the elegant which has its influence till today (see Figure 14-2).

图14-2 清代青花山水人物纹茶具

Figure 14-2  Qinghua Landscape and Design Tea Set (Qing Dynasty)

## 4. 煮茶
## Making Tea

### (1) 概述
### General Remarks

对于煮茶的水，陆羽认为用山泉水最好，江河水次之，井水最差。自古至今，爱喝茶的人都重视泡茶的水,所谓"水为茶之母"。不管是哪里生产的水,好水的标准一致被认为是源头清澈、水味甘甜、品质轻软。

"融雪煮茶"是文学作品里经常描述的煮茶方法。

对于煮茶,陆羽提出了"三沸"说:水煮沸前,先是冒出像鱼眼睛的小气泡,有轻微的响声,称作"一沸";其后,锅的边缘有连珠般的泡往上冒,称作"二沸";最后,水波翻腾,称作"三沸"。至三沸时,应立即提起汤瓶,把开水注入放有茶叶的茶杯中。再继续煮,水老了,味道不好,就不宜饮用了。

As for the water for making tea, Lu Yu believed the best was water from a mountain stream, river water was next best, and well water the worst. From ancient times to the present, tea-lovers have always paid particular attention to the water for steeping tea, as "water is the mother of the tea." Regardless of where the water is from, the standard for good water has always been believed to be clear at the source, sweet, and light in character.

"Melt snow to make tea" is a method for making tea frequently described in literary works.

For making tea, Lu Yu proposed the theory of the "three boils". When boiling water and it emits small bubbles like the eyes of a fish and there is a slight sound, this is called "the first boil". When a series of small bubbles like a string of pearls is emitted around the rim of the pot, this is called "the second boil". When waves of water surge and churn, this is called "the third boil". When the third boil starts, one should immediately pick up the pot and pour the boiling water into the cup with tea leaves. If one continues to boil the water, it gets past its prime and the flavor suffers and it is not suitable for drinking.

(2) 关于煮茶的诗词
*Poems on Making Tea*

晚起<br>白居易(唐朝)<br>Late Rise<br>Bai Juyi (Tang Dynasty)

融雪煎香茗,
调酥煮乳糜。
……

With melted snow I cook the fragrant tea
Seasoning pastry I boil the milk porridge
…

## 雪后煎茶
### 陆游（南宋）
### Making Tea after Snowfall
### Lu You (Southern Song Dynasty)

雪液清甘涨井泉，
自携茶灶就烹煎。
一毫无复关心事，
不枉人间住百年。

Snow melt clear and sweet swells the wells and springs,
Carrying the tea and stove myself I start to heat and cook.
Once I care not one wit for returning to the affairs of heart,
I will live among people not in vain for a hundred years.

## 茶中杂咏·煮茶
### 皮日休（唐朝）
### Various Songs about Tea: Making Tea
### Pi Rixiu (Tang Dynasty)

香泉一合乳
煎作连珠沸。
时看蟹目溅，
乍见鱼鳞起。

声疑松带雨，
饽恐烟生翠。
尚把沥中山，
必无千日醉。

From the fragrant spring I get a cup of water,
Heating makes a string-of-pearls boil.
In time I see splashing crab eyes (small bubbles)
Suddenly appears the fish-scales (large bubbles) rise.

The sound I suspect is the rain among the pines
The foams I fear are smoke produced jade.
I still hold the stream among the mountains

And must not be drunk for three years straight.

(3) 备茶图
*Sketch of Prepairing Tea*

图 14 -3 《备茶图》(辽代墓碑画)
Figure 14 -3 *Preparing Tea* (a Liao Dynasty Tomb Mural)

《备茶图》：辽代墓碑画（见图 14 -3），1993 年出土于河北省张家口市宣化下八里村辽金张氏墓群。壁画中，一名身着汉服、右膝盖上还打着块补丁的女童正低头侧坐在茶碾旁碾茶，旁边的地上摆放着盘子和一块待碾的圆形茶饼；另一名小童则身着一身契丹人的装束，躬腰跪坐，鼓起双腮用力给正在煮茶的风炉吹气；男童身后是另一着契丹服装的成年男侍伸出双手，似乎正要取走风炉上已经煮好茶的茶壶；在其身后的桌子上摆放着一系列壶、盏、瓶、夹、宗、扎等茶道工具与器皿。画面左侧，两名着汉服的成年女侍手捧着盛好茶的茶盏。

*Preparing Tea* (see Figure 14 -3): a Liao Dynasty tomb mural, unearthed in 1993 in the Liao-Jin era Zhang Family Tomb Complex in Lower Bali Village, Xuanhua, Zhangjiakou City, Hebei Province. In the mural, a small girl wearing Chinese clothing with a patch on the right knee sits with a lowered head beside the tea-roller rolling tea, and beside her on the ground is a platter and a tea cake waiting to be rolled; the other child is wearing Khitan clothing and sitting with a bent waist, his two cheeks puffed out as he blows on the furnace; behind the boy is an adult male servant wearing Khitan clothing extending his two hands as if about to pick up from the furnace a tea pot of already made tea; on the table behind him are arranged implements and tools for the tea ceremony, including a series of pots, cups, pitchers, tongs, cases, bars, etc. On the left were two adult women servants in Chinese clothes holding in their hands tea cups filled with tea.

### 5. 品茶
### Tea Tasting

#### (1) 概述
#### *General Remarks*

对于爱喝茶的人来说，喝茶是在品茶，而不仅仅是为了解渴。最常见的喝茶方式是泡茶法，各地区泡茶法不尽相同，但总的来说，能使茶味尽发、茶色显露，就算泡茶成功了。

茶的质量依据味道、颜色、水质判断，甚至茶具也会影响茶的质量。品茶的时候先观汤色，再闻茶香，再慢慢小口啜饮。一口喝干杯中茶，被称为"驴饮"。

To tea-lovers one does not drink tea simply to slake a thirst; rather, one tastes tea. The most common way to taste tea is the steep-tea method. The method is not necessarily the same in each region, but generally speaking, if it can make the tea's flavor come into play to the fullest and reveal the full color of the tea then it counts as having successfully steeped the tea.

The tea's quality is judged on flavor, color and water quality, and even the tea set can influence the quality of the tea. When tasting tea, first observe the color, and then smell it, then drink it slowly. One who drinks a full cup of tea in one gulp is said to be "donkey drinking."

品茶有三乐：一曰独品得神，让心驰骋；二曰对品得趣，和朋友相对品茗，谈心聊天；三曰众品得慧，多人一起品茶，互相沟通启迪，为一乐事，在品茶活动中去品味人生。

The three joys of tea tasting: The first: tasting alone to attain the spirit, it makes one's heart gallop. The second: tasting with a partner to attain interest; drinking tea with a friend and chatting intimately. The third: tasting in a group to attain knowledge; many people tasting together and edifying each other through interaction. In the course of tasting tea activities, one appreciates life itself.

爱茶人感悟："世人若解茶之道，不羡仙人做茶人。"

People who love tea realize: "If a mortal unlocks the way of tea, they do not envy immortals, they'd rather be a tea person."

**残年书事**

魏时敏（明朝）

Writing in My Disabled Years

Wei Shimin (Ming Dynasty)

待到春风二三月，

石炉敲火试新茶。

I'll wait for the spring winds in the 2$^{nd}$ or 3$^{rd}$ month,

And strike a fire in a stone furnace and taste the fresh tea.

(2) 七碗茶歌

*The Song of Seven Cups of Tea*

中国文人七千多首写茶的诗文中，影响最大也最有意味的一首是唐代"初唐四杰"之一卢照邻的嫡系子孙，唐代诗人卢仝（约795—835）的《走笔谢孟谏议寄新茶》（也称《七碗茶歌》）。这首诗是卢仝品尝友人谏议大夫孟简所赠新茶之后的即兴作品。

Among the more than 7000 poems Chinese literati have written about tea, the one with the most influence and the most meaning is "A Note of Thanks to Advisor Meng for Sending Fresh Tea", also known as "The Song of Seven Cups of Tea" by the Tang poet Lu Tong (c. 795 – 835), direct lineal descendant of Lu Zhaolin (637 – 689), one of the Four Great Poets of the Early Tang. The poem is an extemporaneous piece written after tasting the fresh tea his friend Meng Jian, an official in the censorate, sent him.

**七碗茶歌**

卢仝（唐朝）

The Song of Seven Cups of Tea

Lu Tong (Tang Dynasty)

日高丈五睡正浓，军将打门惊周公。

口云谏议送书信，白绢斜封三道印。

开缄宛见谏议面，手阅月团三百片。

闻道新年入山里，蛰虫惊动春风起。

天子须尝阳羡茶，百草不敢先开花。

仁风暗结珠琲瓃，先春抽出黄金芽。

摘鲜焙芳旋封裹，至精至好且不奢。

至尊之馀合王公，何事便到山人家。

柴门反关无俗客，纱帽笼头自煎吃。

碧云引风吹不断，白花浮光凝碗面。
一碗喉吻润，两碗破孤闷。
三碗搜枯肠，唯有文字五千卷。
四碗发轻汗，平生不平事，尽向毛孔散。
五碗肌骨清，六碗通仙灵。
七碗吃不得也，唯觉两腋习习清风生。
蓬莱山，在何处？
玉川子，乘此清风欲归去。
山上群仙司下土，地位清高隔风雨。
安得知百万亿苍生命，堕在巅崖受辛苦！
便为谏议问苍生，到头还得苏息否？

Though the sun is high, my sleepiness is heavy, and then a general knocked at my door and startled me from a dream.

He claims to have been sent by Censor Meng to deliver a letter, and he carries a white silk-wrapped package affixed with three seals.

Perusing the letter is just like seeing Censor Meng's own face, and I opened the package to find three hundred discs of tea.

They say tea farmers ascend the mountain to pick tea in the early spring, and startle awake the sleeping bugs as the spring wind blows.

As the emperor is awaiting a taste of Yangxian Tea, even the grasses do not dare to blossom before the tea bushes.

As the wind rises the tea bushes seem to grow flowers, in fact they are the tender yellow buds grown in early spring.

After toasting the freshly picked tea buds they are packaged, so such fine tea is rarely seen.

The tea leftover from presenting to the emperor is given to princes and dukes, how can there be enough to send to my lowly mountain home?

In my spare room with the wicker gate closed and no guests about, I don a gauze hat and make myself some tea.

Endless whisps of steam rise from the green surface of the tea, fine bubbles float in the tea and a white glow congeals on the cup.

The first cup wets my lips and throat; the second cup dispels my gloom.

The third cup searches through my gut, to find only 5000 chapters of writings.

After the fourth cup I break out in a light sweat, all the unfair things I've encountered in my life are expelled through my pores.

With the fifth cup my body is strong and bones are light, with the sixth cup it is as if

I am conversant with immortal spirits.

The seventh cup is amazing, as I feel a light breeze blowing under my arms.

Where is Penglai, that famous mountain of the immortals?

I, Son of Jade Stream, will ride this clear wind to thee.

Those immortals on the mountain govern the affairs of the world and its people, on high separated from the wind and rain of earthly concern.

Would they know the fates of the myriad commoners who endure such suffering as if hanging on a mountain cliff?

In passing I will ask after the welfare of the common people on behalf of the Censor; can they in the end obtain a bit of rest?

卢仝以神逸飘洒之笔把仅有262字内容的诗歌划分为三个部分——茶的物质层面、茶的精神层面和茶农的苦难场面。开头写谢谏议送来的新茶,至精至好至为稀罕,这该是天子、王公、贵人才有的享受,如何竟到了山野人家,似有受宠若惊之感。中间叙述煮茶和饮茶的感受。由于茶味好,所以一连喝了七碗,喝到第七碗时,觉得两腋生清风,飘飘欲仙,写得极其浪漫。最后,忽然笔锋一转,转入为苍生请命,希望养尊处优的居上位者,在享受这至精好茶时,知道它是无数茶农冒着生命危险,攀悬在山崖峭壁之上采摘来的。诗人期待茶农们的苦日子能有尽头,诗里蕴含着诗人对劳苦人民的深切同情。全诗奇谲特异,句式长短不拘,错落有致,行文挥洒自如,直抒胸臆,一气呵成,成为写茶的经典诗文。

Lu Tong with his elegant, graceful pen divides the poem of merely 262 characters into three parts: the material aspect of the tea, its spiritual aspect, and the difficult circumstances of the tea farmers. It starts with thanking the Advisor for sending the fresh tea, refined, tasty and rare. It must be a pleasure only experienced by kings and noblemen, so how could it come to his remote mountain home? He seems to feel overwhelmed by this favor from a superior. The central part narrates his feelings making and drinking the tea. It tastes so good that he drinks seven cups one after another. By the time he finishes the seventh cup, he feels as if a light breeze blows beneath his arms, raising him up to join the immortals. It is extremely romantic. In the end, he suddenly turns the direction of his writing and switches into the role of a common person asking a favor, hoping those residing up high who enjoy a life of luxury know that this most exquisite of teas was picked by innumerable tea farmers braving life-threatening dangers, scaling to the top of cliffs and precipes. The poet wishes the bitter hard days of the tea farmers are able to come to a close as the poem contains the poet's deep sympathy for the hard-working people. The whole poem is sly and peculiar; the differing length of the lines makes it charming in its irregularity; the style is free and easy, directly speaking the poet's mind in a smooth flow, making it the classic poetic work on tea.

图14-4中的文字就是卢仝"七碗茶歌"的一部分:……书信,白绢斜封三道印。开缄宛见谏议面,首(手)阅月团三百片。闻道新年入山里,蛰虫惊动春风起。天子须尝阳羡茶,百草不敢先开花。仁风暗结珠……

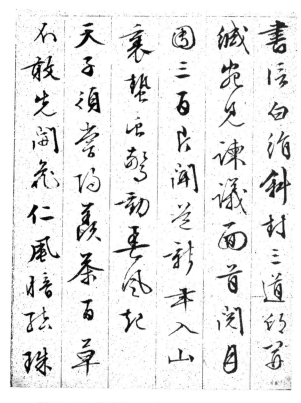

图14-4 茶歌帖(局部)(明朝·文徵明)
Figure 14-4　Tea Song Ties (Part) (Ming·Wen Zhengming)

## 6. 茶道
**Tea Ceremony**

茶道就是把喝茶作为一种修身养性之道。中国茶道的主要内容讲究五美,即茶叶、茶水、火候、茶具、环境,同时配以情绪等条件,以求口味和精神的最高享受。中国茶道以"清、敬、怡、真"为基本精神。

The tea ceremony regards tea drinking as a kind of skill for the cultivation of moral character. The Chinese tea ceremony's primary content pays particular attention to the five beauties: tea leaves, tea water, heat control, tea sets, and the environment, while simultaneously joining them with such conditions as the mood, in order to achieve the highest pleasure in taste and spirit. The basic spirit of the Chinese tea ceremony can be expressed in four characteristics: "purity, respect, pleasure, and truth".

### (1) 清
#### *Purity*

"清"指清洁、清廉、清静。不仅要求事物外表的清洁,更追求心境清寂、宁静、明廉、知耻。崇尚饮用环境的清寂,主张回归自然,在宁静的气氛中喝茶,把喝茶和山泉树林结合起来,理解喝茶的奥妙。

This means "clean", "quiet", "uncorrupted". This not only requires that objects are externally clean, but even more pursues a pure quietude of mood, tranquility, clear incorruptibility, and a sense of shame. Revering the tranquility of the tea-drinking environment, it advocates a return to nature and drinking tea in an atmosphere of tranquility, combining tea drinking with mountains, springs, and forests, and thereby comprehending the profundity of drinking tea.

### (2) 敬
#### *Respect*

"敬"是对他人尊重,对自己谨慎。以诚恳的态度对待一切。

Respect means to honor others, to be prudent with regard to oneself, and to adopt an attitude of sincerity in treating all things.

### (3) 怡
#### *Pleasure*

"怡"是欢乐,是精神的愉悦。精神上的快乐在于不狂妄傲慢,而是变得和蔼有礼貌。

Pleasure is joy, spiritual delight. Happiness in one's spirit lies not in brassy arrogance, but in becoming amiable and polite.

### (4) 真
#### *Truth*

"真"是追求真理和真知。至善至美的东西是真理和真知的结合。即饮茶的真谛,在于启发智慧与良知,使人在日常生活中都能过简单的生活,实现自己的抱负,节俭地、合乎道德地处理日常生活中的事务,从而达到真、善、美的境界。

Truth is the pursuit of truth and real knowledge. The best and most beautiful things are the integration of truth and true knowledge. That is, the essence of tea-drinking lies in stimulating wisdom and conscientiousness, allowing one to be able to lead a simple life in their daily existence, attain their own ambition, deal with life's daily matters with frugality and in line with morality, and through this attain the realm of truth, beauty and the good.

茶叶较早传入日本，宋代日本荣西禅师（1141—1215）写了《吃茶养生记》，是日本第一部茶书。唐宋时期日本社会饮茶风俗已经普遍。

Tea leaves spread to Japan relatively early. The Zen master Eisai (1141 – 1215) wrote *Drinking Tea for Health*, Japan's first book about tea. In the Tang-Song period, tea-drinking customs were already widespread in Japanese society.

(5) 关于茶道的诗
*A Poem on Tea Ceremony*

与元居士青山潭饮茶
灵一僧人（唐朝）

Drinking Tea with Hermit Yuan by the Qing Mountain Pool
Monk Lingyi (Tang Dynasty)

野泉烟火白云间，
坐饮香茶爱此山。
岩下维舟不忍去，
青溪流水暮潺潺。

Beside a wild spring a fire's smoke drifts between white clouds
Sitting to drink fragrant tea, I adore this mountain.
A lonely skiff below the cliffs cannot bear to depart,
The clear stream of flowing water murmurs at dusk.

## 7. 少数民族的茶文化
**Tea Culture Among Ethnic Minorities**

藏族的酥油茶：用茯茶（砖茶）、大茶熬制，茶水煮开后加入牛奶、酥油、盐等。值得一提的是，藏语里茶的发音是"Jia"。《尔雅》里记载，"槚，苦茶"，即槚就是苦茶，藏语里对茶的称呼至今未变，仍称为"jia - 槚"。

Tibetan Butter Tea：Made from steeping brick tea and adding milk, butter and salt after the tea reaches a boil. Worth mentioning is that the Tibetan word for tea is *jia*. The *Erya* records that, "Jiá is bitter tea". The Tibetan word for tea hasn't changed ever since.

苗族的"菜包茶"：用白菜或青菜把茶叶包好，放在火塘的灰中捂熟，再用开水冲泡。

Miao Veggie Wrapped Tea：Made by wrapping tea leaves in cabbage or green leafy vegetables, then placing that in the ashes of an indoor fire pit and covering until cooked, then steeping it in boiled water.

景颇族的"竹筒腌茶":把新鲜茶叶用水蒸煮,在竹帘上揉搓出味道,再装入竹筒内,竹筒内的水分渗出后,用灰泥封上竹筒口,腌制两三个月,可生吃也可以炒制食用。

Jingpo Cured Tea in Bamboo: Steam fresh tea leaves, rub out the flavor on a bamboo mat, then put them in a bamboo shaft; after the liquid has seeped out of the shaft, use plaster to seal the bamboo ends and let cure for two to three months. This can be eaten raw or used in a stir fry.

德昂族的腌茶:把新鲜茶叶放入有灰泥的缸里,塞满后用盖子压上,数月后取出和香菜一起凉拌食用。

De'ang Cured Tea: Put fresh tea leaves in a vat that has plaster; after stuffed full, press down on it with a lid. Take it out after several months and cold toss it with cilantro to eat.

基诺族的凉拌茶:生活在西双版纳景洪县基诺山的基诺族人,习惯食用凉拌茶叶,将黄果叶、酸笋、酸蚂蚁、白生、大蒜、辣椒、盐巴等凉拌在一起,称为"拉拨批皮",即凉拌茶。

Jinuo Cold Tossed Tea: The Jinuo people living on Jinuo Mountain in Jinghong County, Xishuangbanna, have a custom of eating cold tossed tea leaves. Mix together citrus leaves, sour bamboo shoots, sour ants, *báishēng*, garlic, chili pepper and salt. They call it "labopipi", which means "cold-tossed tea".

布朗族的酸茶:布朗族为"濮人"后裔,是最古老的种茶民族之一,至今有食用酸茶的习惯。每年的五六月间,布朗人会把鲜茶叶蒸煮熟放在阴凉处让其发霉,之后装进竹筒埋到土中,数月后取出,制作好的酸茶可直接嚼食。

Bulang Sour Tea: As the descendants of the Pu people (an ancient native ethnic group in Yunnan), the Bulang are among the oldest tea cultivating people in the world. Up to the present, they maintain the custom of eating sour tea. In May or June of every year, Bulang people will steam fresh tea leaves and then place them in a dark, cool location and let them become moldy. Then, they pack them into bamboo tubes and bury them in the earth. Several months later, they dig them out. Sour tea that has been made correctly can be directly eaten as food.

纳西族的烤茶:纳西族最喜欢的茶叫"阿吉勒"烤茶,做法是把茶放入特制的土壤中烘烤至焦黄,然后倒入开水煎煮到浓稠。在茶杯中放入半杯白酒,把煮好的茶水倒入杯中,茶香与酒香就会混合在一起,所以也叫"龙虎斗"。

Naxi Baking Tea: The tea most favored by the Naxi people is "Ajile" roasted tea. It is made by putting the tea in specially made dirt and roasting it until it is brown, then pouring it in hot water and boiling it until it is dense and creamy. After filling half a cup with liquor, the rest of the cup is filled with this tea, allowing the fragrance of the liquor and tea to blend together. It is also called, "Dragon and Tiger do Battle".

怒族的盐巴茶：做法是把小陶罐放在火炭上烤烫，然后把茶放入罐内烤，再倒入开水、盐巴块。

Nu Salt Tea: This is made by placing an earthenware pot on hot coals until it is very hot, then placing the tea in the pot to roast, and later pour it into boiling water with salt.

傈僳族的油盐茶：傈僳人喜喝"华欧腊渣渣"，就是油盐茶，这是一种古老的饮茶方式，制法也是先用小土陶罐把茶烤至焦黄，加入开水，或加入食油、盐巴。

Lisu Oil-salt Tea: Lisu people are fond of drinking "Hua'oulazhazha", or oil-salt tea, an ancient method for drinking tea. It is made by roasting the tea in a small earthenware pot until browned, then pouring it into boiling water; or, mixing it with cooking oil and salt.

爱尼人的土锅茶：西双版纳州勐海县的爱尼人最爱土锅茶。制法是用柴火地锅把山泉水烧开，放入当地著名的"南糯白毫"煮 5 分钟，然后以竹制茶盅盛茶饮用。

Aini Clay-pot Tea: The Aini people of Menghai County, Xishuangbanna Prefecture, love to drink clay-pot tea. It is made by boiling spring water in an earthen pot over firewood, to which they add "Nannuo baihao", which is their famous local variety of tea, and boil it for five minutes. Then, they fill bamboo tea cups with this tea and drink it.

撒尼人的铜壶茶：居住在阿诗玛故乡的撒尼人，喜欢铜壶茶，此茶是用紫铜壶烧山泉水，放茶叶煮沸饮用。

Sani Copper-pot Tea: The Sani people who reside in the ancient homeland of Ashima are fond of copper-pot tea. This tea is made by heating mountain spring water in a pot made of pure copper, and then boiling the tea in it.

傣族的竹筒茶：傣族人喜欢竹筒茶，此茶兼有竹子的清香和茶叶的芳香，甘醇可口。

Dai Bamboo-tube Tea: Dai people like "bamboo-tube tea". This tea has both the fragrance of bamboo and the aroma of tea leaves; sweet and rich, it is very tasty.

少数民族居住地区，尤其是藏族的生活区，大多地处高寒山区，蔬菜缺少，喝茶就起到了代替蔬菜以补充身体所需要的维生素的作用。

Areas where ethnic minorities reside, especially the areas with Tibetan people, are mostly located in high, cold mountains which lack vegetables. Drinking tea serves the purpose of replacing vegetables and supplementing the vitamins needed by the body.

下面这几条谚语形象地描述了人们对茶的喜爱程度。
The following proverbs figuratively describe the level of affection people have for tea.

- 宁可三日无粮,不可一日无茶
- 苞谷粑粑盐巴茶,老婆孩子一火塘
- 早茶一盅,一天威风;
  午茶一盅,劳动轻松;
  晚茶一盅,提神祛痛。
  一日三盅,雷打不动。
- I'd rather have three days without grain than one day without tea.
- Corn cakes and salted tea; wife, child and an indoor fire pit (the necessities of a full life).
- A cup of tea in the morning, to greet the day with might; a cup of tea at noon, and the day's work goes easily; a cup of tea at night, to freshen up and rid oneself of pain. Three cups a day, and thunder will not shake me.

# 六、酒
# Alcohol

## 1. 酒的历史
## The History of Alcohol

史书上记载,大禹时期的仪狄和黄帝时期的杜康是酒的酿造者。仪狄用发酵的糯米酿出了酒,杜康用高粱酿出了最好的酒。据史书记载,杜康把一些高粱种子存储在空心树桩里过冬。第二年春天,芳香的气味从树桩里飘入杜康的鼻孔。之后,杜康发现是发酵的高粱种子发出的诱人香味。这个意外的发现启发他用发酵的高粱种子酿酒。曹操的诗里写着"何以解忧,惟有杜康",杜康成了酒的代名词。

Historical texts record that Yi Di of the period of The Great Yu and Du Kang of the period of the Huang Emperor were the first ones to ferment alcohol. Yi Di used fermented glutinous rice to brew alcohol, and Du Kang made the best alcohol from fermenting sorghum. According to the historical records, Du Kang stored sorghum seeds in a tree stump over the winter. In the spring of the next year, Du Kang discovered that the fermented sorghum seeds produced a captivating aroma. This unexpected discovery inspired him to use fermented sorghum seeds to brew alcohol. Cao Cao's poem writes, "Who can unravel these sorrows of mine, I know of only one man, the God of Wine (Du Kang)", in which the name "Du Kang" has become a synonym for alcohol.

## 2. 酒的种类
### Types of Alcohol

大多数粮食都可以酿酒。

Most types of grain can be used to make alcohol.

### (1) 白酒
#### *Liquor (White Alcohol)*

白酒实际上是蒸馏酒，一般含 40%～60% 酒精，是宴会用餐的正式用酒。

白酒主要分为三类。

酱香型：豪放品质的特香蒸馏酒，香味浓烈。代表性酒是贵州茅台酒。

浓香型：有入口甜、落口绵、回味悠长的特点。代表性酒是四川泸州老窖特曲和宜宾五粮液。

淡香型：酒气清香，入口柔和，甘润爽口。代表性酒是山西汾酒。

Liquor (white alcohol) is distilled alcohol, generally in the 80 to 120 proof range. It is the formal drink used in banquets. There are primarily three types:

Marinated paste type: distinctly aromatic distilled alcohol with bold characteristics and a strong bouquet. A representative of this type would be Maotai, from Guizhou.

Pungent type: with the characteristics of a sweet first taste, silkiness in the mouth and an aftertaste that lingers; representatives include Laojiao Tequ from Luzhou, Sichuan, and Wuliangye from Yibin, Sichuan.

Mild aroma type: the liquor's essence is a fragrance that enters the mouth gently, and has a sweet glossy fresh taste; a representative is Fenjiu from Shanxi.

### (2) 黄酒
#### *Mulled Rice Wine (Yellow Wine)*

黄酒，因其颜色黄亮而得名，也有透明、米色或红棕色，以糯米、黍米和大米为原料，属低度发酵的原汁酒。适于长期贮存，有越陈越香的特点。一般在 8～20 度之间。黄酒除饮用外，还可作为中药的"药引子"。在烹饪菜肴时，它又可作为一种调料，对于鱼、肉等荤腥菜肴有去腥提味的作用。根据其原料、酿造工艺和风味特点的不同，可以划分成以下三种类型。

第一,江南糯米黄酒。产于江南地区,以浙江绍兴黄酒为代表。以糯米为原料,酒质醇厚,色、香、味都高于一般黄酒,存放时间越长越好。主要品种有状元红、加饭酒、花雕酒等。

第二,福建红曲黄酒。以糯米、粳米为原料,以红曲为糖化发酵剂酿制而成。代表品种是福建老酒和龙岩沉缸酒。

第三,山东黍米黄酒。是我国北方黄酒的主要品种,以黍米为原料。

Mulled rice wine (yellow wine) is named for its bright yellow color; there are those that are clear, rice-colored, or even reddish-brown. Made from glutinous rice, millet and husked rice, it is classified as a low-level fermentation stock wine. It is suitable for storing for long periods of time, with the characteristic of becoming more fragrant the older it is. They are generally in the 16 – 40 proof range. In addition to drinking, it is used as a "medicinal primer" in Chinese medicine. In cooking, it can also be used as a flavoring. It has the effect of dispelling fishy odors in fish and meat dishes. They are divided into three categories based on ingredients, fermentation techniques, and characteristic flavors:

First, mulled glutinous rice wine from Jiangnan: Produced in the Jiangnan area (the lower reaches of the Yangtze River), it is represented by the rice wine of Shaoxing in Zhejiang. Made from glutinous rice, the wine's characteristic is mellow and rich, better than average wines in terms of color, aroma, and flavor. The longer it is stored, the better. The primary varieties are Top Scorer Red (*zhuàngyuán hóng*), Added Rice Wine (*jiā fàn jiǔ*) and Flower Carved Wine (*huādiào jiǔ*).

Second, Fujian red dye wine: Made from glutinous rice and Japonica rice, it is fermented using a red dye made from yeast as the glycation compound in the fermentation; representatives are Fujian Laojiu and Chen'gang Wine from Longyan.

Third, Shandong millet wine: This is the primary variety in North China, made from glutinous millet.

## (3) 果酒
### *Fruit Wines*

凡是用水果、浆果为原料直接发酵酿造的酒都可以称为果酒。果酒品种繁多,酒度在15度左右。果酒大都以果实名称命名,如葡萄酒、苹果酒、菠萝酒等。

唐太宗李世民(599—649)十分喜爱果酒,大臣魏征(580—643)擅长酿制葡萄酒,唐太宗曾亲自写诗称赞他酿的酒令人"千日醉不醒",而且"十年味不败"。

Any wine brewed by directly fermenting fruit or berries can be called fruit wine. There are numerous varieties, all around 30 proof. Most are named for the type of fruit used, e. g. grape wine, apple wine, pineapple wine, etc.

Li Shimin (599 – 649), the Taizong Emperor of the Tang Dynasty, was particularly fond of these, and his cabinet minister Wei Zheng (580 – 643) was expert at fermenting grape wine. The Tang Tai-zong personally penned a poem praising the wine Wei made that has the lines, "Never sobering up from a thousand day drunken spree; for ten years the taste can not be defeated."

### (4) 药酒
### *Medicinal Wines*

药酒是在白酒中配各种中药材和糖料浸泡而成。酒可以提高药物的疗效,所以,药酒既是一种饮料酒,又有滋补美容作用。

Made from steeping various medicinal materials and sugars in liquor, the wine can raise the healing efficacy of the medicines. So, medicinal wines are both drinkable and have a nutrious, beautifying effect.

### (5) 啤酒
### *Beer*

啤酒是以大麦为原料,啤酒花为香料,经过发芽、糖化、发酵而制成的一种低酒精含量的原汁酒,通常人们把它当作一种清凉饮料,酒精含量在2～5度之间。啤酒含有大量的二氧化碳和丰富的营养成分,能帮助消化,促进食欲,有清凉舒适之感。啤酒中含有11种维生素和17种氨基酸。1升啤酒经消化后产生的热量,相当于6～7个鸡蛋,或500克瘦肉,或800毫升牛奶,故有"液体面包"之称。

Made from barley and flavored with hops, this type of low-alcohol drink is made by going through a germination stage, glycation stage, and a fermentation stage. Generally, people regard it as a light, refreshing drink. Alcohol content is generally in the 2% to 5% range. It contains a large amount of carbon dioxide and rich nutrional elements. It can help with digestion, increase appetite and leave one with a refreshing, snug feeling. Beer has eleven types of vitamins and 17 types of amino acids. Calories produced from digesting a liter of beer are equivalent to 6 – 7 eggs, a pound of lean meat, or 800 milliliters of milk. Thus, it is called "liquid bread".

## 3. 酒令(喝酒游戏)
## Wine Games (Games Played While Drinking Liquor)

传统的喝酒游戏,即酒令,用来助酒兴。一般是指席间推举一人为令官,余者听令轮流说诗词、联语或压数字等,违令者或负者罚饮,所以又称"行令饮酒",是中国文化独特的一部分。酒令种类多,大致分三类,即雅令、通令、筹令。

Traditionally wine games were used to pique the interest in drinking liquor. Generally, one person at the banquet is chosen as the game's official, and the others listen to his commands and take turns composing a poem, connecting words, or guessing numbers. Those that disobey or fail are fined by being made to drink; thus it is also called "carry out the order drinking wine". It is a unique aspect of Chinese culture. There are lots of variations on these games, but they can be categorized into three types: elegant games, common games, and chips games.

雅令：即文雅的酒令。它要求即兴创作诗词曲文或咏诵古人诗词歌赋，是酒令中智力品位最高、难度最大的一种酒令。

Elegant games: These require impromptu creation of poems, lyrics, or the recitation of ancient poetry. This type of game requires the highest amount of knowledge and taste and it has the highest degree of difficulty.

通令：以划拳、猜数、抽签等方式比输赢。西北地区常见的是划拳，即两个玩家口中大声喊数，手比划对应的数字，通常是从0到10的数字，口中所喊之数与双方手指比划的数字之和一致者赢，输者罚饮。划拳很容易烘托出酒宴中热闹的气氛，西北地区至今流行。

Common games: These use finger guessing, number guessing and drawing lots to determine winner and loser. The finger-guessing game is popular in the the northwest; the two participants each shout out a number between zero and ten and at the same time they put out their hand with a certain number of fingers extended. If the number you shout corresponds to the total number of fingers between the two participants, then you win and the other person drinks. The finger-gussing game easily brings out a lively, bustling atmosphere to a banquet, and it is still commonly played in northwest China.

筹令：是指把酒令写在酒筹之上，抽出酒筹的人依照筹上的酒令规定饮酒。这类酒令在唐代就已经出现，现在不多见。

Chips games: In this game the commands are written on chips (nor mally bamboo sticks) and drawn at random, the person drawing the command must drink according to what is written on the chip. This game was already in circulation during Tang times, but is relatively rare these days.

## 4. 酒礼
### Drinking Etiquette

酒礼即饮酒的礼节，它使饮酒成为一种庄重的活动、一种仪式，"无酒不成宴"。

在中国，喝酒不只是一种乐趣，它与尊重、自我肯定、友谊和保持传统等相关。例如，在婚礼中，新郎、新娘先喝交杯酒，两人交臂喝完自己杯中酒，然后向新人父母敬酒。

The etiquette around drinking alcohol turns it into a dignified activity, like a ceremony, as the saying suggests, "Without wine there is no banquet."

Drinking alcohol in China is not just a pleasure, it is related to respect, self affirmation, friendship and the preservation of tradition. For example, in a wedding, the bride and groom drink the formal exchange of wine cups, finishing their own cups while their arms are linked before then offering drinks to their new in-laws.

今天,喝酒是应酬和交友的重要组成部分,自古以来就是"酒逢知己千杯少"。喝酒时一般遵循的规则是:

先给老人和尊者斟酒,敬酒时自己的酒杯不要高于对方的酒杯。

同一张桌子上有人提议举杯祝酒时,大家都站起来一起举杯,否则视为不礼貌。

如果有人说"干杯"时,饮酒者须喝完自己酒杯中的酒,然后给客人看自己已经喝完。

Today, drinking alcohol is an important element in social interaction and making friends. Since ancient times, as the saying suggests, "Coming across an intimate friend, a thousand cups of wine is a bit too few." Generally, the rules to follow are:

First pour for the elders, and when offering a toast, one's own cup should not be higher than theirs.

When someone at a table raises a cup to make a toast, everyone at the same table should also stand up, otherwise, it will be seen as rude.

When someone says, "Bottoms up!", those that are drinking must finish the alcohol in their cup, then show the guests that they have finished their drink.

## 5. 古人饮酒诗
**Ancient Poetry on Wine**

清明

杜牧(唐朝)

Tomb Sweeping Festival

Du Mu (Tang Dynasty)

清明时节雨纷纷,
路上行人欲断魂。
借问酒家何处有,
牧童遥指杏花村。

During the Qingming Festival, rain falls again and again.
On the road, a traveler's spirit is very dejected.
May I ask, sir, where is there a tavern?
The shepherd boy points his finger at a far off village among apricot blossoms.

## 月下独酌四首·其一
### 李白（唐朝）
### Drinking Alone under the Moon: Part One of Four
### Li Bai (Tang Dynasty)

花间一壶酒，
独酌无相亲。
举杯邀明月，
对影成三人。

A pot of wine among the flowers, a single cup without anyone to share.

I raise my cup and invite the bright moon, and with my shadow we become a party of three.

## 自遣
### 罗隐（唐朝）
### Self Dismissal
### Luo Yin (Tang Dynasty)

得即高歌失即休，
多愁多恨亦悠悠。
今朝有酒今朝醉，
明日愁来明日愁。

Upon getting the chance I raise my voice in song, but if it's lost I simply rest.

Many sorrows, more worries, yet for my part carefree and at ease.

If there's wine this morning, then I'll be drunk this morning.

If tomorrow the worries come, then I'll worry tomorrow.

## 凉州词
### 王翰（唐朝）
### Liangzhou Lyric
### Wang Han (Tang Dynasty)

葡萄美酒夜光杯，
欲饮琵琶马上催。
醉卧沙场君莫笑，
古来征战几人回。

Beautiful grape wine, the night shines in my cup,
I'm about to drink when the *pipa* playing reaches crescendo.
Don't laugh while I lay drunk on the sand,
Since ancient times few people have returned from war.

## 饮中八仙歌
### 杜甫（唐朝）
### Song of the Eight Immortals in the Drink
### Du Fu (Tang Dynasty)

李白斗酒诗百篇，
长安市上酒家眠。
天子呼来不上船，
自称臣是酒中仙。

Li Bai can write a hundred poems after drinking a *dou* of liquor,
And slept in taverns in the capital.
The emperor called him, but he wouldn't get on the boat,
Claiming himself to be an immortal in the wine.

## 自遣
### 郑板桥（清朝）
### Self Dismissal
### Zheng Banqiao (Qing Dynasty)

看月不妨人去尽，
对花只恨酒来迟。

Observing the moon, the people might as well all leave,

Facing the flower, I only regret the wine is brought slowly.

## 6. 古人饮酒轶事
## Anecdotes of Ancients Drinking Alcohol

"元四家"中的黄公望是"酒不醉,不能画"。"书圣"王羲之醉时挥毫而作"绝代所无"的《兰亭集序》,酒醒时"更书数十本,终不能及之"。

Huang Gongwang (1269 – 1354), one of the "Four Masters of the Yuan", is said to have "been unable to paint without being drunk." Wang Xizhi, the "Sage of Calligraphy", when drunk composed the peerless *Orchid Pavilion Preface*. After sobering up, he tried to "emend the text dozens of times, but in the end was unable to match it."

李白写醉僧怀素:"吾师醉后依胡床,须臾扫尽数千张。飘飞骤雨惊飒飒,落花飞雪何茫茫。"怀素酒醉泼墨,留下"神鬼皆惊"的《自叙帖》。草圣张旭"每大醉,呼叫狂走,乃下笔",于是有其"挥毫落纸如云烟"的《古诗四帖》。

Li Bai wrote of the drunken monk Huai Su (737 – 799), "My master leaned on the couch while drunk and in a flash whipped out thousands of pages. Floating and flying, like a rain shower, they whooshed in fright; so many and vast, like falling petals or drifting snow." Huai Su, while drunk, splashed ink and left behind the ethereal "Chatting with Oneself". Zhang Xu, the Sage of the Grass Script, said, "Every time I get really drunk, I'm called to run madly, and only then put down the brush." Thus, he wrote the "Four Ancient Poems", described as "writing clouds and vapor onto the paper."

## 7. 古人饮酒之道
## The Methods and Experiences of the Ancients Drinking Alcohol

饮酒时心境要好:选择合适的时间,如凉月好风,下雨飘雪,花开满庭,新酿初熟,旧地故友,久别重逢时,都是饮酒好时候。中国人无酒不成宴。

选择合适的场合:花前月下,湖上泛舟,山峦之巅,溪水之畔,郊野之中,宅舍酒楼,使人感到幽雅、舒畅的场合。

When drinking, one should be in a good mood. Select an appropriate time, such as under a bright moon with a good breeze, when raining or snowing, when the blossoms open, after a new batch of wine is made, meeting friends at an old haunt, or getting re-aquainted after a long separation. A Chinese feast is impossible without wine.

Select an appropriate venue, such as under the moon beside the flowers, on a boat floating on a lake, at the top of a mountain, beside a stream, in the countryside, in a home or a restaurant; a place that makes one feel serene and happy.

温酒而饮：古人饮酒多温热而饮。其原因，元人贾铭说："凡饮酒宜温，不宜热。"认为喝冷酒对身体不好，喝多了手会颤抖。

西方人喜欢饮葡萄酒，中国人偏爱白酒。

Warm the wine before drinking. The ancients mostly drank warmed wine. The reason is as Jia Ming (ca. 1269 – 1374) says, "In any particular case of drinking wine, it should be warm; it should not be hot." He believed drinking cold wine was bad for your health, because if you drank a lot of it your hands would shake.

Westerners like to drink grape wine, but Chinese people like to drink distilled alcohol.

**思考题**

1. 与西方菜相比，中国菜最显著的特点是什么？
2. 你最喜欢的中国菜是哪个菜系的？有什么特点？
3. 学做一样中国菜。
4. 中国人喝茶追求茶道，西方人喝咖啡的时候有什么讲究吗？
5. 写文章、宴宾客时，为什么酒能助兴？

***Questions***

1. In comparison to Western cuisine, what are the special characteristics of Chinese food?
2. What is your favorite regional cuisine among Chinese food? What are its characteristics?
3. Learn to make a Chinese dish.
4. When Chinese people drink tea, the ideal is the tea ceremony; what particulars do Westerners have about drinking coffee?
5. Why does alcohol liven things up when writing an essay or entertaining guests?

# 第十五章 中国武术
## Chinese Martial Arts

## 一、武术的起源
### The Origin of Martial Arts

武术，南方人称为功夫，民国初期称为国术。早在春秋时期就已出现，《礼记》中提到一种名为"角力"的搏斗法，包括攻击、投掷、控制关节和压点进攻等技巧。

Martial arts, which southerners refer to as "kung-fu", was called a national art form in the Republican Period. Martial arts themselves had already appeared in the Spring-and-Autumn Period. The *Book of Etiquette* mentions something called *juélì* (wrestling) as a way of fighting, which included such skills as attacks, throws, and controlling key joints.

## 二、武术流派的划分
### Classification of Schools of Martial Arts

中国武术有的按地理位置分类，例如，少林派基地在河南省少林寺，武当派基地在湖北省武当山。

Some martial arts are classified geographically, such as the Shaolin School centered in the Shaolin Temple in Henan, or the Wudang School centered in Wudang Mountain in Hubei.

有的是根据不同的训练方法来分类，例如内家拳、外家拳。

内家拳练内功，主练气，即内练一口气。内家拳重柔，柔显于外，强调后发制人、以静制动、主于御人，具有尚意不尚力、四两拨千斤、以柔克刚等特点。代表性拳种有太极拳、形意拳、八卦掌等。

Some are classified according to different methods of training, such as the Internal Boxing and External Boxing.

Internal Boxing trains internal skills, primarily *qì* "vital energy". Internists emphasize flexibility, gaining mastery only after the enemy has struck, using quietude to conquer activity, and defense. It has high regard for intention over power, "using four ounces to push aside a thousand pounds", the use of softness to conquer strength, etc. Representative arts are *Taiji* Boxing, *Xingyi* Boxing, and *Bagua zhang*.

太极拳：动作比较缓慢，把道家、传统医学、体育锻炼的主导思想融合在一起，具有以柔克刚的特点。

形意拳：特点是直拳快击，适合搏斗。

八卦掌：特点是稳步于圈内，随走随变，掌式连续变化。八卦原指八个方位，即北、南、东、西、西北、西南、东北、东南。八卦掌以掌法为主，在行拳时，要求步走圆形，将八个方位全都走到，而不像一般拳术那样，走一条线、走四角等，所以称为"八卦掌"。

*Taiji* Boxing: The actions are relatively slow, combining into one form the main ideas from Daoism, traditional medicine and physical training. It is famous for the principle of using softness to conquer strength.

*Xingyi* Boxing：Famous for quick attacks, it is suitable for fighting.

*Baguazhang*：Characterized by a steady pace within a closed circle, adjusting as one moves, the style of fighting continually evolves. *Bāguà* originally refered to the eight directions: north, south, east, west, northeast, southeast, southwest, northwest. *Baguazhang* emphasizes the use of the hands, so when fighting, it requires that one move one's feet in a circle, covering all of the eight positions. This differs from other styles that fight in a straight line or across four corners.

外家拳练外功，主练筋骨皮，提高击打能力。外家拳重刚，刚显于外，强调先发制人、以动制静、主于搏人。代表拳种有少林拳、长拳等。

武术也注重内外合一，例如内外功结合训练的铁砂掌、铁拳功，可以一掌打碎几块砖等。

External Boxing trains external skills, emphasizing sinew, muscle and skin; it raises one's ability to fight. Externalists value strength made apparent externally. They emphasize gaining the initiative by striking first, using action to control the quiet, and mastering fighting. Representative styles are Shaolin Fist, Long Fist, etc.

The martial arts also focus on the unity of inner and outside world. For example, the iron sand palm and iron fist are combined with internal and external skills which can break several bricks with one hit with the palm etc.

## 三、武术的主要派别
## Main Schools of Martial Arts

### 1. 少林武术
### Shaolin

少林武术起源于河南嵩山少林寺,故其身体训练和心理训练都基于佛教哲学之上。少林武术发展的转折点是在唐初,少林寺十三僧人因帮助唐王李世民讨伐王世充有功,受到唐朝封赏,赐大量庄田银两,扩建少林寺,并特别允许设立常备僧兵,少林武术得以快速发展。这一派的代表性拳种有少林拳、南拳、北腿和咏春拳。

Shaolin martial art was originated in the Shaolin Monastery on Mount Song, Henan Province. Its physical and mental training is based on Buddhist philosophy. The turning point in the growth of Shaolin Martial Arts was in the beginning of the Tang Dynasty. Because thirteen monks from the Shaolin Monastery helped the Tang Emperor Li Shimin suppress the late Sui general Wang Shichong (d. 621), they were bestowed with rewards by the Tang court and granted a large amount of land and silver. They expanded the monastery and were especially granted permission to maintain a monk army. As a result, Shaolin Martial arts rapidly developed. Representative boxing styles of this school include Shaolin Fist, Southern Fist, Northern Foot and *Yongchun* (Singing Spring) Fist.

南拳:以广东省和福建省为中心,流传于长江以南地区。特点是套路短小精悍、手法多变、步法稳健。常伴以声助威,技击性强。南拳讲究桩功,以练坐桩为主,也练打沙袋、铁砂掌、点穴功、童子功等。黄飞鸿擅长的就是南拳。

Southern Fist: Centered in Guangdong and Fujian provinces, it spread throughout the area south of the Yangtze. Its characteristics are movements that are concise and forceful, handwork that is multivaried, and footwork that is stable and steady. Their actions are often accompanied with a shout to boost morale, and it is strong in skilled attack. Southern fist is particular about "stump technique", primarily in the practice of *zuòzhuāng* (sitting like a stump). They also practice hitting sand bags, iron fists, pressure point techniques, and *tóngzǐ* technique. Huang Feihong (1847 – 1924) was expert at precisely this Southern Fist.

咏春拳:注重防卫,较其他派别,强调正面制敌,尽快制服对手。

*Yongchun* (Singing Spring) Fist: This emphasizes defense, and in comparison with other styles stresses confronting the enemy head on and quickly subduing the opponent.

嵩山少林寺（见图 15 - 1）位于河南省郑州市嵩山五乳峰下，因坐落于嵩山腹地少室山的密林之中，故名"少林寺"，属汉传佛教寺院，始建于北魏太和十九年（495年），是孝文帝为印度高僧跋陀修建。历代少林武僧有苦练功夫的传统，于是有了"天下功夫出少林，少林功夫甲天下"之说（见图 15 - 2）。

Shaolin Monastery on Mount Song (see Figure 15 - 1): Located below Wuru Peak on Mount Song, Zhengzhou City, Henan Province. Because it sits in the dense forest of Shaoshi Mountain in the hinterland of Mount Song, it is called Shaolin Monastery. It is a Chinese Buddhist monastery, first built in 495 A. D., by Emperor Xiaowen of the Northern Wei for the Indian monk Buddhabhadra. The military monks over the years have had a tradition of diligently practicing kung-fu, so there is a saying, "The world's kung-fu comes from Shaolin, and the best kung-fu in the world is Shaolin" (see Figure 15 -2).

图 15 -1　嵩山少林寺
Figure 15 -1　Shaolin Monastery on Mount Song

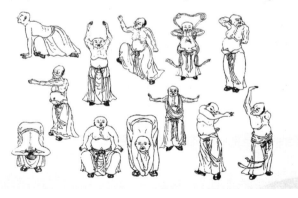

图 15 -2　少林功夫·易筋经十二式
Figure 15 -2　Shaolin Kung-fu; Twelve Forms from the *Classic on Changing the Tendons*

## 2. 武当武术
**Wudang Kung-fu**

武当武术发源于湖北省武当山（见图 15 - 3）。以道教"道法自然"为原则，在道教理论的指导下得以发展。这一派的代表性拳种有太极拳、形意拳、八卦掌（见图 15 - 4）。

Wudang Kung-fu was originated in Wudang Mountain, Hubei Province (see Figure 15 - 3). It developed under the direction of Daoist theory, using the principle of "Dao follows the law of Nature". Representative styles of this school include *Taiji* Boxing, *Xingyi* Boxing and *Bagua zhang* (see Figure 15 - 4).

图 15 - 3　湖北武当山
Figure 15 - 3　Wudang Mountain, Hubei

图 15 - 4　武当派功夫
Figure 15 - 4　Wudang Kung-fu

武当山：道教圣地，位于湖北省十堰市。元末明初，道士张三丰开创武当派。

Wudang Mountain: A holy place in Daoism, located in Shiyan City, Hubei Province. The Daoist master Zhang Sanfeng (b. 1247) started the Wudang School in the late Yuan to early Ming period.

## 3. 峨眉武术
**Emei Kung-fu**

峨眉武术发源于四川省峨眉山（见图15-5）。峨眉拳融合了少林武术和武当武术的优点，集众家之长，形成自己的风格。主要特点是动作小，变化大，以柔克刚，借力打力，以静制动和以动制静并用（见图15-6）。峨眉拳术有僧门、岳门、杜门、赵门四大家和洪门、化门、字门、慧门四小家。

Emei martial art was originated in Emei Mountain, Sichuan Province (see Figure 15-5). Emei boxing mixes the strong points of Shaolin and Wudang boxing, gathering the strengths of the various schools to form its own style. The main characteristics are small movements, large changes, using softness to overcome strength, absorbing power to fight power, using quietude to control action and, at the same time, using action to control quietude (see Figure 15-6). Emei boxing has four great traditions (Sengmen, Yuemen, Dumen, and Zhaomen) and four lesser traditions (Hongmen, Huamen, Zimen, and Huimen).

图15-5 四川峨眉山

Figure 15-5 Emei Mountain, Sichuan

图 15-6 峨眉派功夫
Figure 15-6 Emei Kung-fu

峨眉山：位于四川省乐山市，山上的万佛顶海拔 3099 米，高出峨眉平原 2700 多米。以峨眉山为主的地域性武术派系称为峨眉派。

Emei Mountain: Located in Leshan City, Sichuan Province, the Myriad Buddha Peak at its top is 3099 meters above sea level, rising 2700 meters above the Emei plains. The regional martial arts school based in the Emei area is known as the Emei School.

## 4. 截拳道
### Jeet Kune Do (Way of the Intercepting Fist)

截拳道是李小龙创立的武术派别（见图 15-7），以中国道家思想为指导，融合各国拳术，以咏春拳、拳击及击剑作为技术骨干。"截拳道"的意思是阻击对手来拳的方法，注重"实用"，自由打斗，不遵循传统武术的套路。

Jeet Kune Do was founded by Bruce Lee (1940-1973) (see Figure 15-7). Guided by Chinese Daoist ideas, it takes *Yongchun* (Singing Spring) Fist, boxing and fencing as its technical backbone. Emphasizing "practicality", it practices free fighting, rather than respecting the traditional martial arts' sequence of movements.

图 15-7 李小龙
Figure 15-7　Jeet Kune Do Founder Bruce Lee

近现代中国，武术得到了迅速发展。1999 年，中国功夫成为奥林匹克赛事之一，越来越多的外籍人士开始对中国功夫感兴趣。

In modern times, Chinese martial arts have attained rapid growth. In 1999, Chinese kung-fu became an event in the Olympics, and more and more people from foreign nationalities are interested in Chinese martial arts.

思考题

1. 中国武术和西方竞技的区别是什么？
2. 中国功夫为什么受到人们欢迎？

*Questions*

1. What are the differences between Chinese martial arts and Western athletic competitions?
2. Why has Chinese kung-fu been so popular?

# 第十六章 中国传统节日
## Traditional Chinese Festivals

中国大多数的传统节日与农业生产活动相关，时间的安排上都采用中国传统的农历，即根据日月运行规律计算岁时节令的历法。一年有二十四节气，四季的开始与结束都成为节日，还以月亮的圆缺来确定节日。主要节日有春节（农历的正月初一，公历的元月一日是元旦）、元宵节（农历正月十五）、清明节（公历四月五日前后）、端午节（农历五月初五）、七夕节（农历七月初七）、中秋节（农历八月十五）、重阳节（农历九月初九）、腊八节（农历十二月初八）。

中国传统节日大部分产生于先秦，后来随着佛教的传入也增添了一些节日习俗。

Most traditional Chinese festivals are related to agricultural activities, and their dates are arranged making use of the traditional lunar calendar; i.e., the calendrical system based on the ordered movements of the sun and the moon that calculates the seasons and marks the passage of time. There are 24 solar periods in one year. The beginning as well as the end of each of the four seasons has become a festival, and festival days are also determined based on the fullness of the moon. The main festivals are Spring Festival (first day of the first lunar month), Lantern Festival (fifteenth day of first lunar month), Qingming (Tomb Sweeping) Festival (around April 5th), Dragon Boat Festival (fifth day of fifth lunar month), Qixi (seventh day of seventh lunar month), Mid-Autumn Festival (fifteenth of the eighth lunar month), Double Ninth Festival (ninth day of ninth lunar month), *Laba* Porridge Festival (eighth day of twelfth lunar month).

Most traditional Chinese festivals started in the Pre-Qin period. Later, some festival customs were added after the spread of Buddhism.

## 一、主要的传统节日
## The Main Traditional Festivals

### 1. 春节
### Spring Festival

春节俗称"过年"。年的名称,《尔雅·释天》中说,年者,禾熟之名。谷禾一年一熟,把年当作收获的象征,并引申为岁名。古人过年不叫春节。民国初年,因为要改用公历,为了和传统使用的农历有所区分,公历(阳历)第一天定为"元旦",意即"首日";农历(阴历)正月初一称为"春节",这也是春节名称的开始。过春节从农历正月初一开始,到正月十五(元宵节、上元节)才结束。这是中国最隆重、最盛大的一个传统节日。

The Spring Festival is commonly known as "*Guo Nian*" in Chinese, the name of the New Year. In "*Er-Ya, Shi Tian*", it says "*Nian*" is the name of mature seedlings. The seedlings yield one crop a year, so that Chinese treat the "*Nian*" as the symbol of harvest, and extended to the name of the "year (*suì*)". The ancient people did not call "*Guo Nian*" "the Spring Festival". In the early years of the Republic of China, because they needed to change the calendar to the Gregorian calendar, in order to distinguish it from the traditional lunar calendar, the first day of the Gregorian calendar was called *Yuan Dan*, meaning "the first day", and the first day in lunar calendar is called the "Spring Festival", which is also the beginning of the term "Spring Festival". The Spring Festival starts from the first day of the first month in the lunar calendar until the fifteenth day (the Lantern Festival and the Shangyuan Festival).

传说远古时有一种凶猛的怪兽叫"年",每到除夕就来到村里伤害人畜。后来人们知道了怪兽年害怕红色、火光和炸响的声音。所以,为了把年赶走,人们把红纸对联贴在门边,晚上点燃爆竹和火把,这样,怪兽年就被驱赶走了。第二天早晨,全村人聚集在一起,庆贺取得的胜利,互相说着祝贺、恭喜的话语。从此,每年的除夕,家家都贴红对联,燃放爆竹,以驱赶年,户户灯火通明,一家人围坐在一起,吃喝说笑等待天亮,称之为"守岁"。这一风俗就演变成了中国最隆重的传统节日"过年"。

According to legend, in ancient times there was a ferocious monster named *nián* (year). Every new years eve, it would come around to villages and do damage to people and livestocks. Later, people learned that the monster *nián* feared the color red, flames, and the sound of explosions. So, in order to drive off this *nián*, people put up red colored couplets on their doorways, at night they lit firecrackers and torches, and in this way the monster *nián* was driven away. The morning of the next day, the people of the whole village gathered together and celebrated the victory they achieved, saying to one another, "Congratulations" and such celebratory phrases. After that, every year on New Years Eve, every family attaches red couplets to their doorways, sets off firecrackers and drives away the *nián* (year); every home is brightly lit, and the whole family sits together eating, drinking, talking, and laughing waiting for dawn. This is what is known as "seeing in the new year". This social custom evolved into China's most solemn traditional festival, "celebrating the new year".

春节期间的礼仪习俗相当丰富，主要包括三方面：一是祭祀，祭祀的对象很多，最普遍的是祭灶神和祭祀祖先。二是驱鬼，源于除夕驱赶"年"。贴门神、贴对联、放爆竹、庙里打鬼都是为了驱鬼避邪。现在更多的是辞旧迎新、祈求吉祥的目的。三是社交娱乐，最主要的社交活动就是拜年，亲戚邻里、朋友之间相互拜访探望；再就是各种民间娱乐活动，耍狮子、舞龙灯、扭秧歌、踩高跷等。

Ceremonies and customs in the Spring Festival season are particularly abundant. They generally encompass three aspects: 1) Sacrifices, the objects of which are numerous, but most generally they are sacrifices to the Kitchen God and to ancestors. 2) Driving out ghosts, which originated in the story about driving out *nián*. Putting up Door Gods and couplets, setting off firecrackers, etc., are all about driving out ghosts and avoiding evil spirits, though these days these are even more about bidding farewell to the old and ringing in the new or seeking good luck. 3) Social interaction and entertainments, the most important social interaction being paying a New Year's visit. Relatives, neighbors and friends visit each other. Then there are all the various folk entertainments, such as lion dance, dragon dance, performing Yangge dance, walking on stilts, etc.

(1) 祭灶

### Sacrifice to the Kitchen God

腊月二十三是农历腊月的第二十三天，南方部分地区是腊月二十四，民间称"小年"，是祭灶、扫尘、吃灶糖的日子。

首先是扫尘，就是打扫卫生，一早开始擦窗户、扫屋里灰尘、清洗衣物等，要把家里家外打扫一遍，把家收拾得干干净净，意味着扫除陈旧不好的，迎接来年好运气。

The 23$^{rd}$ day of the twelfth month, though in some places in the south it is the 24$^{th}$ day, is popularly known as the "lesser year", the day for sacrifices to the Kitchen God, cleaning, and eating kitchen god candy.

First, there is cleaning. Early in the day it starts with wiping windows, sweeping up dust, cleaning clothes, etc., and inside and outside the house should be thoroughly cleaned and tidied up. This signifies the sweeping away of old, bad things to welcome good luck in the coming year.

到了晚上，最重要的就是祭灶神，也称"送灶王爷"。灶王爷负责管理家中的饮食，古代民间几乎每家都设有灶神牌位。腊月二十三，灶神要上天向玉皇大帝汇报这一家人一年当中的善恶行为，依据行为的好坏，玉皇大帝就给做好事多的人家赐福，做坏事多的人家降灾。因此人们特别重视，家家户户在这一天都要祭祀灶王爷，献灶糖，甜蜜灶神的嘴，以便让他上天说好话。至今民间一些人家的灶台上还贴着"上天言好事，下地保平安"的对联。

That night, the most important thing is making sacrifices to the Kitchen God, also called "seeing off the Kitchen God". The Kitchen God is responsible for managing the food and drink in the household. Nearly every home in the past had a memorial table set up for the Kitchen God. On the 23$^{rd}$ of the twelfth lunar month, the Kitchen God must ascend to Heaven to report on the household affairs, good or bad, to the Jade Emperor. Based on whether the home's actions are good or bad, the Jade Emperor will bless the families that were good, or deliver disasters on those that were bad. So, people pay particular attention to this, and every family makes sacrifices to the Kitchen God by offering stove candy. The candy sweetens the Kitchen God's mouth so that he will say nice things in Heaven. To this day, over the stoves in some family's homes one finds a couplet that reads, "Ascend to Heaven to say nice things, descend to earth to ensure peace."

(2) 祭祖

### *Sacrifices to Ancestors*

对于重视血缘家族的中国人来说，祭祀祖先是一个重要的活动。明清以后南方各地遍布祠堂，每个大家族都有自己的家庙，即祠堂，祠堂内供奉家族祖先，一宗族一祠堂，有严格的族规，平时由族长管理。每年春节由族长率领全体族人祭拜。各房子孙平时有办理婚、丧、寿、喜等事时，活动都在祠堂内进行。族人商议重要事务，也用祠堂作为开会之地。古代的祠堂发挥着民间小政府的作用。

To Chinese people who pay particular attention to bloodline clan, sacrificing to ancestors is an important activity. After Ming and Qing Dynasties throughout the south there are ancestral halls everywhere. Every large clan had their own household temple, the ancestral hall, in which the clan's ancestors were offered sacrifices. There was an ancestral hall for each family name, with strict clan regulations, generally overseen by the clan elders. Every year, in the Spring Festival, the entire clan would make sacrifices led by the clan elder. The weddings, funerals, birthdays, and other important events of each household's sons and grandsons would be held inside the ancestral hall. The clan would discuss important affairs and use the hall as a meeting place. Ancient ancestral halls played the role of folk governments.

现在，绝大多数祠堂已在"文革"中被拆除，正月初一祭祖的日子里，人们就将祖宗遗像或牌位供在家中正厅，摆上供品，焚香、敬酒，全家一起祭拜，仪式比起古代简单许多。

These days, because the majority of ancestral halls were destroyed during the "Cultural Revolution", people place ancestral images or tablets in their main rooms and on the day for making sacrifices they place objects before them, burn incense, and make a toast and the whole family makes obeisance together. The ceremony is simpler now than in ancient times.

毛氏祠堂（见图16-1）位于湖南省湘潭县韶山冲，是韶山毛氏家族的总祠堂，始建于1758年。建筑系砖木结构，青砖青瓦，建筑面积约700平方米，宗祠大门天头有"毛氏宗祠"四字，毛氏家族的名人后代有中华人民共和国领袖毛泽东主席。

Mao Family Ancestral Hall (see Figure 16-1): located in Shaoshan, Xiangtan County, Hunan Province. This is the main ancestral hall of the Mao Family clan, first built in 1758. Built of brick and lumber, using green tiles and bricks, the structure is 700 sq. meters. The four words "Mao Family Ancestral Hall" hang above the door of the main hall gate. A famous member of this Mao Family clan is the founder of the People's Republic of China, Chairman Mao Zedong.

图 16-1　毛氏祠堂

Figure 16-1　Mao Family Ancestral Hall

### (3) 贴春联
### *Pasting Couplets*

春联也称楹联、对联、对子，起源于古代的桃符，是写着吉祥词语的红色条幅。古代把春联叫桃符，题写在桃木板上，后来改写在纸上，人们有时仍习惯叫桃符。

Spring Festival couplets are called simply couplets, rhyming couplets or antithetical phrases, which originated in the peach wood charms in ancient times. They are red rectangular banners on which are written auspicious phrases. In olden days, Spring Festival couplets were called "peach signs", because they were written on peach tree wood. Later it was changed to using paper, though still today, some people are still accustomed to calling them "peach signs".

长条形对联由左右两幅及一短横幅（横批）组成，长条形两幅贴在门框两边，短横幅贴在门框上方（见图 16 - 2）。春联大多用毛笔黑字写在表示喜气吉祥的红色纸上，也有的用代表好运的金色书写。

Rectangular couplets are composed of long left and right strips and one short horizontal strip. The long strips are pasted on the sides of the gate frame, while the horizontal one is pasted along the top (see Figure 16 - 2). Most are written with black ink on red paper that symbolizes happiness, though there are also those that are written in gold to symbolize good luck.

图 16 - 2　贴在大门上的对联和门神
Figure 16 - 2　Couplet and Door God Pasted on Main Gate

一到腊月，许多地方一些会写书法的人就沿街支桌摆摊为人们写对联（见图 16 - 3）。因为古代读书识字的人少，很多人家里没有会写字的人，所以，士子们就在腊月里为邻里乡亲们服务写对联。现在，读书识字的人多了，但是会写毛笔字的少了。所以，除了使用毛笔书写的对联，很多的是用印刷的对联。

In the twelfth month in many places some people who know how to write calligraphy set up a vendor's stall and write couplets for people (see Figure 16 - 3). In the past, there were not many people who knew how to read and write. Indeed, many families had no one who could do so. So, scholars would provide the service of writing couplets for their neighbors.

图 16 - 3　写春节对联
Figure 16 - 3　Writing Spring Festival Couplets

Nowadays, many people know how to read and write, but there are still very few who can write well with a brush. In addition to hand-written couplets, many more people make use of printed ones.

### 对联作品选
### Selected Couplets

上联：和和顺顺千家乐
下联：月月年年百姓福
横批：国泰民安
First half: Harmony and favor, one thousand families are joyous
Second half: Over the months and years the common folk are lucky
Horizontal: The country at peace, the people contented

上联：一帆风顺吉星到
下联：万事如意福临门
横批：财源广进
First half: Through plain sailing, the star of good luck arrives
Second half: The myriad affairs go as one wishes, blessings overlook the door
Hortizontal: Wealth and resources spread wide and enter

上联：一帆风顺年年好
下联：万事如意步步高
横批：吉星高照

上联：一年四季行好运
下联：八方财宝进家门
横批：家和万事兴

上联：上上下下男男女女老老少少都添一岁
下联：家家户户说说笑笑欢欢喜喜同过新年

上联：大江东去浪淘尽千古英雄问楼外青山山外白云谁比我洪武皇帝
下联：小苑西回莺唤起一庭芳草看池边绿树树边红雨此间有舜日尧天

### (4) 贴年画
**Pasting up New Year Pictures**

除了贴对联，人们在窗户上贴窗花、贴福字，在大门上贴门神、年画。

In addition to couplets, people paste paper flowers on their windows, and the word *fú* for "good luck", and on their gates they put up images of the door god and New Year pictures.

### (5) 放爆竹
**Setting Off Firecrackers**

大年三十晚上，几乎家家户户都要燃放鞭炮。整个春节期间，处处鞭炮声不断，直到春节结束。但是，如今很多城市地区为了环境和安全等原因禁止燃放爆竹。

On the night of the 30$^{th}$ of the twelfth lunar month, nearly every household sets off firecrackers. During the whole season, the sound of firecrackers can be heard everywhere, all the way up to the end of Spring Festival. However, for the sake of environment and safty, many urban areas are for bidden to set off firecrackers.

### (6) 压岁钱
**New Year Money (Restraining Age Money, or Lucky Money)**

春节时拜年的风俗在汉代已经出现，向同族尊长、亲戚、邻里、友人拜年，拜年时给压岁钱。一般由长辈给晚辈，意思是压住年岁，老人们不再增长岁数，可以长寿，同时把长辈对美好生活的希望寄托给晚辈。家里长辈早早准备崭新的钱，把压岁钱装在红包里，在大年三十晚上或者春节期间拜年的时候给晚辈。现在人们在春节期间也普遍互赠红包以为礼物。

The custom of New Year's greetings during the Spring Festival were formed in the Han Dynasty. People pay New Year's greetings and lucky money to the elders from the same family, relatives, neighbors, and friends. Generally given by the older generation to the younger generation, the meaning of lucky money is to restrain one's aging, so the older generation doesn't get any older and they can live a long life. At the same time, they entrust their hopes for a beautiful life to the younger generation. The older generation in a household early on prepares brand new money and wraps it in a red envelope to give to the younger ones on the night of the 30$^{th}$ or when they pay a New Year visit during Spring Festival. Nowadays, people send each other red envelopes during Spring Festival as a kind of gift exchange.

### (7) 除夕（腊月三十）
**Chinese New Year's Eve**

除夕又称大年三十、大年夜等，是农历一年中最后一天的晚上，有除旧迎新的意思。"除夕"中"除"字的本义是"去"，引申为"易"，即交替；"夕"字的本义是

"日暮"，引申为"夜晚"。人们在这一天准备除旧迎新，吃团圆饭。

New Year's Eve, also known as 30<sup>th</sup> of the Big Year, Night of the Big Year, etc, is the night of the last day of the lunar year. The idea on this day is to wipe out the old and ring in the new. The Chinese term for this night is *chúxī*; the first syllable originally means "to remove", and by extension, "to change", i. e., to replace; the second syllable originally means "sunset", and by extension "night". On this day, people prepare to drive out the old and ring in the new while eating a large meal with the whole family.

### (8) 年夜饭
### *New Year's Meal*

年夜饭，就是团圆饭，这几乎是一年当中最重要的一顿饭。

除夕的年夜饭很像美国的感恩节晚餐，是一年当中最丰盛的一餐。

大年三十晚上，中国人传统的春节就拉开了序幕。而且，这一天晚上的年夜饭成了整个春节期间人们最看重的一顿饭，所以，人们不管身处何方，都会想办法在年三十晚上以前回家，目的就是为了和家人聚在一起热热闹闹、开开心心地吃一顿热热乎乎的团圆饭，这是每一个中国家庭一年中最重视的一顿饭。所以，现在到了每年年底，中国交通部门就进入了一年中最繁忙的运输季节——春运。人们背着大包小包往家赶，为的是阖家团圆。

The New Year's Meal is the large meal eaten with the whole family on New Year's Eve. It is basically one of the most important meals of the entire year.

It's a bit like Thanksgiving dinner in the USA, the most sumptuous meal of the year.

The night of the thirtieth day of the twelfth lunar month is the grand opening of the traditional Spring Festival. The meal on this night is regarded as the most important meal of the entire Spring Festival. So, regardless of where they are, people all try by any means to return home for this night. The goal is to gather with the family and to happily, noisily, and warmly eat the reunion supper. Every year at this time, the transportation departments in China enter into their busiest season, the Spring Festival travel season. People carry bags large or small and hurry home, and what they are hurrying home for is the reunion supper.

大年三十这一天，要把腊月二十三送走的灶王爷再接回来。年夜饭开始前要放鞭炮，然后一家人围坐在一起，团圆饭就开吃了。不同的食物有不同的寓意。例如，饺子象征着财富，因为饺子的形状像古代的元宝，现今更多地象征着一家人团团圆圆。吃鱼寓意"年年有余"，因为鱼和"剩余"的"余"发音相同，吃鱼象征着家里来年富余。

During the day of New Year's Eve, the Kitchen God who was sent away on the 23<sup>rd</sup> of the month is welcomed back. Firecrackers are lit before the big meal, then everyone sits together and begins to eat. There are different implications for different foods eaten. For example, dumplings symbolize wealth because their shape resembles ancient ingots of silver or gold. These days, they are more likely to symbolize reuniting. The implication of eating fish is that "every year there will be abundance", because the word for "fish" *yú* is homophonous with the word for abundance. So, eating fish on New Year's Eve implies the family will be in surplus in the coming year.

虽然春节是新年的第一天,但是中国人的传统习俗中,新的一年已经从除夕的这一晚开始了,没有三十晚上的一顿团圆饭,很多人觉得就没有过春节。所以,快过春节的时候,人们都要在三十晚上赶回家去吃这一顿团圆饭,春节也就过得圆满了。

Although Spring Festival starts on the following day, in traditional Chinese customs, New Year really begins on New Year's Eve. If they don't participate in the reunion supper on New Year's Eve, many Chinese people feel like that haven't celebrated the Spring Festival. So, everyone tries to get home before the night of the 30$^{th}$ to eat the reunion supper and properly celebrate the festival.

(9) 关于春节的诗
**A Poem about the Spring Festival**

元日
王安石(北宋)
First Day
Wang Anshi (Northern Song)

爆竹声中一岁除,
春风送暖入屠苏。
千门万户曈曈日,
总把新桃换旧符。

Amid the sounds of firecrackers the old year is sent off,
And the Spring winds warmly enter the holiday wine.
Every home and every family warms to the day
And always exchange the old sign with the new peach sign.

## 2. 元宵节
**The Lantern Festival**

元宵节是春节的最后一天,在农历正月十五日,也叫"灯节",道教称为"上元节"（上元祭天官，中元祭地官，下元祭水官；上元是"三元"中的第一个），过完这一天，春节正式结束。"元"者始也，"正月"也叫"元月"；古人称夜为"宵"，正月十五日这天是新年第一次看到满月，所以正月十五日这天也被称为"元宵节"。

The Lantern Festival is the last day of the Spring Festival, on the fifteenth day of the first lunar month, also called the "Lighting Festival". Daoists refer to it as "Upper Primary Festival" (the first of three festivals celebrating Heaven, Earth, and Water). After this festival, the Spring Festival season is officially concluded. "Yuan" means the beginning, thus "the first month" is also called "the Yuan Month". The fifteenth day of the first month is the first full moon of the new year, so this festival is also known as the "Primary Night Festival".

元宵节的习俗，一是张灯赏灯，一是猜灯谜。还有吃元宵、舞龙狮等活动。元宵节的夜晚，各种各样的灯笼悬挂在大街上供人们欣赏，花灯上贴有谜条，猜中谜底的会有奖品。猜灯谜、吃元宵、赏月成了元宵节的主要内容。

As for the customs of the Lantern Festival, one is to admire the lanterns and another is to guess the lantern riddles. There are also activities such as eating sticky rice dumplings, watching dragon and lion dance, etc. On the night of the Lantern Festival, all kinds of lantern are hung on the street for passersby to appreciate. The colorful lanterns have riddles pasted to them, and if one answers the riddle correctly, one gets a prize. Guessing riddles, eating sticky rice dumplings and appreciating the moon are the primary contents of the Lantern Festival.

元宵节吃元宵的风俗始于宋代，元宵用糯米粉做成，有的实心，有的带馅儿。元宵馅以甜味为主，用糖、芝麻、玫瑰花、桂花、枣泥、豆沙等做馅儿，水煮、油炸或蒸。元宵形状圆圆，含有团团圆圆的意思。南方人称为"汤圆"，北方人叫"元宵"。

The custom of eating sticky rice dumplings on the Lantern Festival began in the Song Dynasty. Made from glutinous rice, some have fillings and some do not. The filling is generally sweet, made from such things as sugar, sesame seeds, rose petals, cassia flowers, jujube paste and bean paste. They are boiled, steamed or deep fried. Round in shape, they imply the idea of circular unity, like the full moon. Southerners call them *tāngyuán* "soup circles", while northerners call them "Yuan Xiao".

到了清代，闹元宵的活动里又多了耍龙灯、舞狮子、踩高跷、划旱船、扭秧歌、打太平鼓等传统民俗表演。

Starting in the Qing Dynasty, activities for celebrating the Lantern Festival included such traditional folk performances as playing dragon lanterns, performing the lion dance, walking on stilts, oaring a boat on dry land, performing the *Yangge* folk dance and beating the drum of

Great Peace.

## 3. 清明节
### Tomb Sweeping Day (Qing Ming Day, or Qingming Festival)

清明节是扫墓祭祖的日子。清明本来是我国特有的二十四节气之一,在春分后两周左右。按《岁时百问》之说,万物生长时,皆清洁而明净,故谓之清明。1935年民国政府规定每年4月5日为清明节,一般在公历每年4月4日、5日、6日三天中的一天。祭祖扫墓、踏青郊游是清明节的主题。

"Qing Ming Day" is the Tomb-sweeping Day. Originally, this was one of the twenty-four solar periods unique to China, about two weeks after the vernal equinox. According to the *Hundred Questions of the Season*, when everything grows, it is the time for everything to become clean and clear. Thus, in Chinese "Qing" means "clear", and "Ming" means "clean". In 1935, the government of the Republic of China established April $5^{th}$ as the "Qing Ming Day". Usually, the Tomb Sweeping Day falls on April $4^{th}$, $5^{th}$, or $6^{th}$. Tomb-sweeping and hiking are the themes on that day.

#### (1) 清明节的习俗
#### Customs of Tomb Sweeping Day

祭祖扫墓。清明节也称扫墓节,扫墓俗称上坟,是去祖先墓地祭拜的日子。扫墓时,人们要携带酒食果品、纸钱等物品到墓地,将食物供祭在亲人墓前,再将纸钱焚化,为坟墓培上新土,折几枝嫩绿的新枝插在坟上,然后行礼祭拜;如今也越来越多地使用鲜花。

Tomb-sweeping. Tomb-sweeping involves going to the clan's cemetery to offer sacrifices. People take food, wine, fruit, and paper money to the cemetery, offer the food as a sacrifice before the graves of their relatives, then burn the paper money, add fresh dirt to the grave mound, break off fresh twigs to insert into the grave mound, and then pay obeisance before the grave. More and more people these days also use fresh flowers.

踏青郊游。清明节,又叫踏青节,在这草木发芽的时节,人们喜欢春游(古代叫踏青),并有荡秋千、踢蹴鞠(cu ju,踢球)、打马球等体育活动。从清明这一天起,气温开始升高,民间开始春耕春种,所以有"清明前后,种瓜点豆"的说法。

Spring hiking. Qing Ming Day is also the season of Spring hiking. In this period when the grass is freshly sprouting, people like to take long walks, and they engage in various physical activities such as playing on swings, kicking a ball, and playing polo. From the Tomb Sweeping Day forward, the weather begins to warm up and folks begin their spring planting season. So, there is a saying, "Around Tomb Sweeping Day, plant the melons and beans."

## （2）清明节的起源
### *Origins of Tomb Sweeping Day*

相传春秋时期，晋国的公子重耳（前697—前628）为逃避迫害而流亡国外。流亡途中找不到吃的，臣下介子推（d. 636 B.C.）从自己的大腿上割下了一块肉，让公子吃了。19年后，重耳做了国君（晋文公），却忘了介子推。介子推便带着母亲到绵山（位于山西省介休市）隐居去了。后来，晋文公想起了介子推的功劳，亲自带人去请他，为了让他出山，晋文公下令大火烧山，以便逼出介子推。火熄后，发现背着老母亲的介子推已坐在一棵老柳树下死去。第二年，晋文公率众臣登山祭奠介子推，发现老柳树死而复活。为了纪念介子推，晋文公下令把这一天定为寒食节，命令每年介子推被烧死的日子都要严禁烟火，吃冷食物。这就是禁火寒食的由来，后来称"寒食节"。因为寒食节和清明的日期非常接近，故古人又往往把寒食的活动延续至清明，把寒食节的后一天定为清明节。后来这两个节日合并成一个节日——清明节。所以，清明时节的另一个习俗是，清明之日不动烟火，只吃凉的食品。到了唐代，唐玄宗下诏允许官员寒食扫墓。五代时，皇帝亲自在寒食节时上坟。自此，两节合并成了清明节，主题转为敬宗祭祖。元明以后，扫墓之风遍及全国，沿袭至今。

According to legend, in the Spring Autumn Period, a prince of the State of Jin, Chong'er (697 – 628 B.C.), fled into exile in a foreign land to escape persecution. While traveling he was unable to find food to eat, so his subject, Jie Zitui (d. 636 B.C.) cut off a piece of flesh from his own leg to feed him. 19 years later, Chong'er became the king of Jin (Wengong of Jin), but forgot about Jie Zitui. Jie Zitui then took his mother to live as a hermit on Mian Mountain (located in Jiexiu county, Shanxi province). After Wengong remembered him, Wengong personally went to the mountain to beseech him to return. In order to force him out of the mountain, Wengong ordered the mountain be set on fire. After the fire died out, they discovered Jie Zitui dead sitting under a willow tree carrying his mother on his back. The next year, Wengong returned with his entourage to ascend the mountain to offer sacrifices when they discovered the willow tree had come back to life. To commemorate Jie Zitui, Wengong ordered that only cold food be eaten on this day. Therefore, he ordered to ban fireworks and only eat cold food on the day that Jie Zitui died. This is the origin of the "Eating Cold Food Day". Because the date of the Eating Cold Food Day and the date of Qing Ming Day are very close, the ancients often extended the activities of eating cold food to Qing Ming day.

Thereupon, Wengong ordered the following day become the Tomb Sweeping day. Later, the two days, one for eating cold food and one for sweeping tombs, were combined. Therefore, another custom of Tomb Sweeping Day is to not operate stoves and only eat cold foods. Until Tang Dynasty, Emperor Xuanzong of the Tang Dynasty issued an order to allow officials to sweep the tomb and eat cold food. Since then, the two days have been merged into one as the "Qing Ming Day". The theme has been changed to worship the ancestors. After the Yuan and Ming Dynasties, the tomb-seeping spread over the whole country, and is used until today.

## 4. 端午节
### Dragon Boat Festival

端午节是在农历五月初五日，又称端阳节。最初是百姓祛病防疫的节日，江南一带有在农历五月初五以赛龙舟的形式举行部落图腾祭祀的习俗，后因诗人屈原在这一天投江自尽，便成了民间纪念屈原的节日。节日习俗主要是赛龙舟、吃粽子、喝雄黄酒、挂艾叶等活动。

The Dragon Boat Festival is on the fifth day of the fifth lunar month. At first, it was a festival for commoners to drive away illnesses and prevent diseases. In the Jiangnan area, there was a custom of racing boats on this day as a tribal totemic sacrifice to ancestors. Later, because the poet Qu Yuan tossed himself into the river to commit suicide, it became a festival to commemorate Qu Yuan. The primary festival customs are racing boats, eating *zongzi* (glutinous rice wrapped in leaves and boiled), drinking realgar wine, and hanging out artemisia.

端午节的来历，人们普遍认为和纪念屈原有关。屈原，春秋时期楚怀王的大臣。在报国无门后，于公元前278年五月初五抱石投汨罗江而死。屈原投江后，楚国百姓哀其不幸，投粽子、咸蛋于江中以饲蛟龙，希望保全屈原躯体，又驾舟江中以觅屈原。以后，每年的农历五月初五，就举办各种活动来纪念屈原。

The origin of the Dragon Boat Festival is generally believed to be related to commemorating Qu Yuan. Qu Yuan was the minister of King Huai of Chu State during the Spring and Autumn Period. After being treated unjustly, he carried some stones and cast in the Miluo river, died on the fifth day of the fifth lunar month in 278 B. C. After Qu Yuan's death, the people of Chu mourned for him. They threw some *zongzi* and salted eggs in the middle of the river to feed the dragon, as they wished the dragon ate the *zongzi* and salted eggs instead of eating Qu Yuan's body. They also rowed a boat to find Qu Yuan. After that, every year on the fifth day of the fifth lunar month, various activities would be held to commemorate Qu Yuan.

## 5. 七夕节
### *Qixi Festival* (Double Seventh Festival)

七夕节是在农历七月初七，公历八月，也叫"乞巧节"。七夕节始于汉代，起源于对自然的崇拜及妇女穿针乞巧，后被赋予了牛郎织女的传说使其成为象征爱情的节日。七夕节今天成了中国的情人节。

*Qixi Festival* is the seventh day of the seventh lunar month (Double Seventh), and it is also the "Beseeching Skills Festival". It started in the Han Dynasty as a nature worship and women's needle-threading festival. Later, having been bestowed with the Cowherd and Weaving Maid legend, it became a festival symbolizing romantic love.

### (1) 牛郎织女的故事
### *The Story of the Cowherd and Weaving Maid*

传说在很久以前,有个孤儿叫牛郎,靠一头老牛种地为生。有一天,天上有个名叫织女的仙女来到人间遇到牛郎,两人相爱,仙女便留在人间和牛郎结婚了。牛郎在地里耕种,织女在家织布,并生了一儿一女,一家人过着幸福的生活。但是,天上的王母娘娘知道后,派人来要抓织女回到天宫。

牛郎在老牛的帮助下,用箩筐装着儿女,挑着追到天上。王母见牛郎追来,就用头上的金钗在织女和牛郎之间划出一道大河,这就是银河。牛郎无法过河,只能和织女隔河相望痛哭。他们的爱情感动了喜鹊,无数喜鹊飞来,用身体搭成一道跨越天河的彩桥,让牛郎织女在天河上相会。最后王母娘娘也被感动,允许牛郎织女每年七月七日见面。因此牛郎和织女见的日子就称为"七夕"。

Long ago there was an orphan cowherd boy who made his living planting fields with one old ox. One day, a fairy weaving girl from heaven came to the mortal world and met the cowherd. The two fell in love, and the weaving girl stayed in the mortal world to marry the cowherd. The cowherd planted the fields while the weaving girl made cloth at home. They had a son and a daughter, and the whole family lived happily together. But, after Wangmu Mother in heaven heard about it, she sent someone to capture the weaving girl and bring her back to the heavenly palace.

With the help of the old ox, the cowherd loaded his kids in two wicker baskets and carried them on a pole on his shoulder as he pursued them into heaven. Wangmu saw the cowherd giving chase, so she used a golden hairpin from her head and carved out a river in the sky, the Milky Way, to separate the weaving girl and cowherd. The cowherd was unable to cross the river, so all they could do was look at each other across the river and cry bitterly. Their love so moved magpies, that a great number of them flew up to make a rainbow bridge across the Milky Way that allowed the two to meet. Finally, Wangmu was also moved, and she permitted the two to meet on the seventh day of the seventh month.

(2) 关于牛郎织女的诗
*A Poem about the Cowherd and Weaving Girl*

鹊桥仙<br>
秦观（北宋）<br>
Immortal of the Magpie Bridge<br>
Qin Guan (Norther Song Dynasty)

纤云弄巧，飞星传恨，银汉迢迢暗渡。
金风玉露一相逢，便胜却人间无数。

柔情似水，佳期如梦，忍顾鹊桥归路。
两情若是久长时，又岂在朝朝暮暮。

Delicate clouds make a flowery sky;
A meteor transmits the sorrowful separation.
The far off Milky Way quietly crossed.
Like golden wind and jade frost they chance to meet.
Far better than innumerable mortal encounters.

Together at last they are as tender as water.
Their short time together as if a dream.
Time to depart they can't bear to see the magpie bridge.
As long as their feelings are unfailing,
Must they crave their love all day and night?

## 6. 中秋节
### Mid Autumn Festival

中秋节是在农历八月十五日，公历的九月或十月，又称团圆节等。中秋节起源于古老的"秋社"，由秋季祭祀土地神而来。唐代成为固定节日，宋代以来盛行不衰。中秋节习俗主要是拜月、赏月、吃月饼。中秋节时亲友之间一般互送月饼，因为这一天月圆，所以人们期望家人也能团圆，有月圆人圆之意。中秋夜便有一家人相聚赏月、祭月、分享月饼的习俗。

The Mid-Autumn Festival is the fifteenth day of the eighth lunar month, September or October in the solar calendar. It is also called the Reunion Festival. The Mid-Autumn Festival originated from the ancient "*qiushe*", and it is the etiquette for the emperor to worship the god of earth in autumn. It became a fixed festival in Tang Dynasty, and prevailed in Song Dynasty. The custom of Mid-Autumn Festival is mainly to worship the moon, admire the moon and eat moon cakes. Friends and relatives exchange moon cakes on this day. Because the moon is full, people on this day hope to have their full family together. On the night of this festival, the family gathers to admire the moon, offer sacrifices to it, and share moon cakes.

### (1) 中秋节"嫦娥奔月"的传说
### The Legend of Chang'e Fleeing to the Moon

民间相传,远古时候,天上有十个太阳,晒焦了庄稼,人民生活很苦。一个名叫后羿的人想帮助大家,他登上昆仑山顶,使出全身力气,拉弓把其中九个太阳射下来,他命令最后一个太阳按时升落。为此,很多人前来拜师习武,一个叫蓬蒙的人也来学习。

According to folk legend, long ago there were ten suns in the sky which burned people's crops making their lives miserable. A person named Hou Yi wanted to help people, so he climbed to the top of Kunlun Mountain, used all his might and shot arrows to take out nine of the suns. He ordered the last sun to rise and fall according to a regular schedule. Many people came to him as disciples to study military ways, among whom was one named Peng Meng.

后羿有个美丽善良的妻子,名叫嫦娥。一天,后羿到昆仑山访友求道,巧遇由此经过的王母娘娘,便向王母求得一包长生不老的药。据说,服下此药,能即刻升天成仙。然而,后羿舍不得撇下妻子,只好暂时把长生不老药交给嫦娥珍藏。嫦娥将药藏进梳妆台的百宝盒里,不料被蓬蒙看见了,他想偷吃长生不老药自己成仙。

Hou Yi had a good and beautiful wife named Chang'e. One day, Hou Yi went to Kunlun Mountain to seek teachings from a friend when he chanced upon meeting Wangmu Mother. He asked Wangmu for an elixir for immortality, and she gave it to him. It was said that once the elixir was taken one would immediately ascend to heaven as an immortal. But Hou Yi couldn't stand the idea of leaving behind his wife, so he temporarily gave it to Chang'e for safekeeping. Chang'e put the elixir in a jewelry case inside her dressing table, not knowing that Peng Meng saw her and wanted to steal the elixir to become an immortal himself.

有一天,后羿带领众人出去打猎,他走后不久,蓬蒙手持宝剑闯入内宅后院,逼着嫦娥交出长生不老药。嫦娥知道自己不是蓬蒙的对手,危急之时她当机立断,转身打开百宝盒,拿出长生不老药一口吞了下去。嫦娥吞下药,身子立时飘离地面、冲出窗口,向天上飞去。由于嫦娥牵挂着丈夫,便飞落到离人间最近的月亮上成了仙。

One day, Hou Yi led a group of people out on a hunt. Not long after he left, Peng Meng, carrying a sword, burst into the back courtyard of their inner chambers and compelled Chang'e to turn over the elixir to him. Chang'e, knowing she was no match for Peng Meng, made a quick decision in the crisis. She turned around, opened the jewelry case, took out the elixir and took it herself. As soon as she took the elixir, her body immediately floated off the ground and out the window toward heaven. Because Chang'e was so worried about her husband, she floated to the moon which was closest to the mortal world and became an immortal there.

傍晚，后羿回到家，侍女们告诉他了白天发生的事。后羿仰望着夜晚的天空，呼唤着爱妻的名字，这时他惊奇地发现，今天的月亮格外皎洁明亮，而且有个晃动的身影很像嫦娥。他拼命朝月亮追去，可是他追三步，月亮退三步，他退三步，月亮进三步，无论怎样也追不到月亮。

That night when Hou Yi returned the servant girl told him what had happened that day. Hou Yi looked up longingly to the night sky and called out the name of his beloved wife. To his surprise he discovered that the moon on this night was particularly clear and bright, and that there was a swaying shadow that looked much like Chang'e. He struggled with all his might to pursue her, but every three steps he advanced, she retreated three steps; and every three steps he retreated, she advanced three steps. No matter what, he couldn't chase down the moon.

后羿非常思念他的妻子，就到嫦娥喜爱的后花园里搭起了香案。放上她平时最爱吃的水果，向远在月宫里的嫦娥祭拜。人们听说嫦娥变成了仙女后，就在月光下摆设香案，向善良的嫦娥祈求吉祥平安。

从此，中秋节拜月的风俗在民间传开了。人们在中秋节的夜晚，还会从水里月亮的倒影中寻找嫦娥的影子。

Hou Yi missed his wife tremendously. He went to the back garden Chang'e so loved and built an incense burner there. He placed the fruit she loved to eat on it and made obeisance to Chang'e in the far off moon palace. After people heard that Chang'e had become an immortal, they set up incense burners under the moonlight and appealed to the good Chang'e for good luck and peace.

From this the custom of praying to the moon spread among the people. On the night of the Mid-Autumn Festival people will look for Chang'e's shadow in the reflection of the moon in water.

## (2) 关于中秋节的诗
### *A Poem about the Mid-Autumn Festival*

**华阳观中八月十五日夜招友玩月**

白居易（唐朝）

Calling for a Friend to Enjoy the Moon on the Mid-Autumn Festival in the Hua Yang Monastery

Bai Juyi (Tang Dynasty)

人道秋中明月好，
欲邀同赏意如何。
华阳洞里秋坛上，
今夜清光此处多。

People say the bright moon at mid-autumn is the best,
I hope to invite like-minded appraisers to discuss it.
On the Autumn altar in the Hua Yang Cave,
There is a lot of clear light here on this night.

## 7. 重阳节
## The Double Ninth Festival

### (1) 概述
### *General Remarks*

重阳节是在农历九月初九日，公历9月或10月。重阳节又叫老人节、登高节。古人把天地万物归为阴阳两类，阴代表幽暗，阳代表光明。奇数为阳，偶数为阴。九是奇数，因此属阳，九月初九，都逢九，二阳相重，故称"重阳"。重阳节有登高、赏菊花、饮菊花酒、插茱萸的习俗。

This is the ninth day of the ninth lunar month, around September or October in the solar calendar. It's also called Old People's Day and Ascend the Heights Day. The ancients classified all things into the categories of *yīn* and *yáng*; the former representing dark and the latter light. Odd numbers were *yáng*, and even numbers were *yīn*. Since nine is an odd number, so this day is *yang*. Both the date and the month are "the ninth", i.e. *yang*, on this day, too, so this is also called the Double *Yang* Festival. Customs on this day are climbing hills, admiring chrysanthemums, drinking chrysanthemum wine and inserting cornel dogwood twigs into their hair.

## (2) 关于重阳节的诗
***A Poem about the Double Ninth Festival***

### 九月九日忆山东兄弟
王维（唐朝）

### Remembering My Brothers on the Double Ninth
Wang Wei (Tang Dynasty)

独在异乡为异客，
每逢佳节倍思亲。
遥知兄弟登高处，
遍插茱萸少一人。

Alone as a strange guest in a strange place,
I am doubly homesick for our dear ones on every festival day.
Though far away I know my brothers have ascended to a high place,
There is one fewer person to insert the dogwood twig.

## 8. 腊八节
***Laba* Rice Porridge Festival**

腊八节，是在农历十二月初八日，公历一月。这一天也是佛祖释迦牟尼成道之日，称为"成道节"。腊八节有吃腊八粥的习俗，腊八粥用大米、小米、糯米、黄豆、红豆、绿豆、红枣、花生、莲子、枸杞子、葡萄干等多种谷物和干果熬煮而成。

*Laba* is the eighth day of the twelfth lunar month, sometime in January in the solar calendar. This is the day Sakyamuni reached enlightenment, so it is also known as "Festival of the Buddha's Teaching". The custom is to eat *laba* rice porridge, made from boiling together rice, millet, glutinous rice, soybean, red bean, mung bean, jujube, peanut, lotus seed, *goji* berry (Chinese wolfberry), raisins and other kinds of grains and dried fruits.

中国的四大传统节日是春节、清明节、端午节、中秋节。

The four most important festivals in China are Spring Festival, Tomb Sweeping Festival, Dragon Boat Festival, and Mid-Autumn Festival.

## 二、中国节日的特征
## Characteristics of Chinese Festivals

中国人的节日，具有浓厚的家庭伦理色彩。几乎所有的节日活动中都有祭祀祖先的内容，祠堂是节日里重要的活动场所。节日的活动中心都以家庭为中心，家人团圆是许多节日永远的主题，所以中国人"每逢佳节倍思亲"。

Chinese people's festivals possess a dense family-ethic coloring. Nearly every festival activity has some component of making sacrifices to ancestors, and the ancestral hall is the site of important festival activities. The household is central in festival activities, and the constant theme of many of them is family reunion. So, Chinese people feel, "doubly homesick for our dear ones on every festival day".

西方狂欢节、感恩节、复活节等大家聚集在一起或在街头游行的时候，中国人毫无疑问地都是聚集在家里。通过这些节日，可以从另一方面理解宗法制度对中国的影响。

In the West, on Carnival, Thanksgiving, or Easter, everyone convenes together or parades on the street. Chinese people always gather in the home. Through these festivals, one can understand from another perspective the influence of the patriarchal system on China.

在家享受天伦之乐，是中国人幸福生活的一个重要标志。同时，节日也是维系中国人亲情关系的重要纽带，走亲访友是中国人节日的又一重要内容。今天，上述节日内容依旧，每到节日，通过中国繁忙的交通，商场里畅销的月饼、粽子、汤圆、烟酒类等商品，甚至街头明显增加的醉酒人数中，都可以感受到这一点。

Enjoying the love of one's family at home is an important, happy marker in Chinese life. At the same time, festivals are also an important bond for maintaining Chinese people's affectionate relationships, so visiting one's friends and relatives is another important aspect of Chinese festivals. Today, as before, one can sense the aforementioned festival activity through the busy traffic, sales of moon cakes, rice dumplings, cigarettes, and liquor, as well as the noticeable increase in intoxicated people during festival days.

**思考题**

1. 西方传统节日主要以宗教节日为主，中国传统节日划分的主要依据是什么？
2. 中国传统节日的内容会随着时代的发展发生变化，你认为春节放鞭炮的习俗应该被废除吗？为什么？

***Questions***

1. Western holidays are primarily centered on religion. On what basis are Chinese festivals delineated?

2. Chinese traditional festivals will develop and change following the times. Do you think the practice of setting off firecrackers during the Spring Festival should be abandoned? Why?

# 第十七章　中国文化的基本精神
## The Basic Spirit of Chinese Culture

中国文化的基本精神是指中国传统文化中那些长期受到人们尊崇并成为生活行动的最高指导原则的思想观念和固有传统。

中国学者张岱年（1909—2004）认为，中国文化精神有四点：①刚健有为；②和与中；③崇德利用；④天人协调。张岂之（1927— ）认为有七点：①人文生成——文明之初的创造精神；②刚柔相济——穷本探源的辩证精神；③究天人之际——天人关系的探索精神；④厚德载物——人格养成的道德人文精神；⑤和而不同——博采众家之长的文化汇通精神；⑥经世致用——以天下为己任的责任精神；⑦生生不息——中华人文精神在近代的丰富与发展。

The basic spirit of Chinese culture refers to those ideas and inherent traditions in traditional Chinese culture that people have revered for a long time and which formed the highest guiding principles for life activities.

The Chinese scholar Zhang Dainian (1909 – 2004) believes there are four parts to the spirit of Chinese culture: 1) robust achievement, 2) harmony and centrality, 3) sublime morality and practical utility, 4) fitting together heaven and human. Zhang Qizhi (b. 1927) believes there are seven points: 1) humanistic generation—the creative spirit of the beginning of civilization, 2) mutual aid of the firm and flexible—the dialectal spirit of the thorough-going exploration of origins, 3) careful study of the boundary between human and heaven—the investigative spirit of the relationship between humans and nature, 4) virtuous leadership—the moral humanistic spirit that cultivates integrity, 5) distinct yet harmonious—the spirit of cultural convergence that broadly selects people's best aspects, 6) experience the world to practical ends—the spirit of responsibility that takes the affairs of the world as one's duty, 7) grow and multiply—the humanistic spirit's abundance and growth in modern times.

法国学者孟德斯鸠（1689—1755）认为，中国没有宗教，而是以道德代替宗教，以礼教作为人民行动的规范。儒家强调的礼的精神是在这些日常生活中唤起一种必须铭刻在人民心中的感情，而且正是因为人人都具有这种感情，才构成了这一帝国的统治精神。① 英国学者罗素（1872—1970）认为，"我们的文化最显著的长处是科学方法，中国人的最显著的长处是对人生之目标的看法"。② 德国学者马克斯·韦伯（1864—1920）认为，西方社会的精神气质是以理性主义为取向的，而中国文化的社会气质则是以传统主义为基本特征的。

上述中西学者的探讨都为我们今天认识不同的中西文化精神提供了有价值的启示。

The French scholar Montesquieu (1689 – 1755) believed China lacked religion and had replaced it with morality, using a code of ethics to regulate human activity. The spirit of propriety championed by Ru-ists "in these daily lives awakens a kind of feeling that is necessarily etched into the hearts of people, and precisely because everyone has this feeling, there is formed this spirit of imperial unity" (*L'Esprit des lois*, 1748). The British scholar Bertrand Russell (1872 – 1970) believed, "The distinctive merit of our civilization... is the scientific method; the distinctive merit of the Chinese is a just conception of the ends of life" (*The Problem of China*, Ch. 11). The German scholar Max Weber (1864 – 1920) believed the spiritual temperament of Western society was oriented by rationalism, while the social temperament of Chinese culture is basically characterized by traditional ideology.

The investigations of the Chinese and Western scholars above all have provided valuable insights for our modern recognition of different cultural spirits between China and the West.

# 一、自强不息
## Constantly Strive to Become Stronger

自强不息一词最早出现在距今两千多年以前的《易经》中："天行健，君子以自强不息。"以天体运行无休无止、永远向上的规律，要求人们积极有为、勇于进取，此后就成为中国人积极人生态度的最集中的体现，是中华民族蓬勃发展的动力。

The phrase "constantly strive to become stronger" first appeared in a text more than two thousand years ago, in the *Book of Changes*, which says, "Heaven is ceaselessly in motion, the enlightened exert themselves constantly." Because of the regular pattern of heavenly bodies' endless movement and eternal advance, people are required to actively show promise, to dare to advance. Later, this principle became the most potent embodiment of the Chinese people's positive attitude toward life, the force for the Chinese people's vigorous development.

自强不息首先是就民族的进步和发展而言。每一个时期，士子的理想中总有一股建

---

① ［法］孟德斯鸠：《论法的精神》，许明龙译，商务印书馆2007年版，第260页。
② ［英］罗素：《中国问题》，秦悦译，学林出版社1996年版，第153页。

功立业的壮志豪情，历史上出现了许许多多的民族英雄。其次是就个人人格的独立和人生价值的实现而言。人们把英勇不屈、坚持正义，遭遇挫折时勇敢面对、奋发图强作为应有的追求。自强不息还有一个最重要的体现，那就是积极追求新的变化，追求社会改革。

In the first place, "constantly strive to become stronger" is used in regard of the ethnic group's advancement and development. In every historical era, within the ideal of the scholar-official was always a heroic aspiration to lay a solid foundation and build ever higher. Second, it is used in regard of the implementation of the individual's independence and value. The people regard heroic unyielding, steadfast righteousness, brave confrontation in times of setbacks, and working energetically for the prosperity of the country as proper pursuits. "Constantly strive to become stronger" has another important manifestation, and that is the positive pursuit of new changes and social reform.

## 二、天人合一
## Oneness of Heaven and Humanity

中国古代的天人合一思想，强调人与自然的统一，人的行为对自然的顺应、协调，以及道德理性与自然理性的一致。根据这种思想，人不能违背自然，不能超越自然界的承受力去改造自然、征服自然，只能在顺从自然规律的条件下去利用自然、调整自然，使之更符合人类的需要，也使自然界的万物都能生长发展。同时，自然界也不是神秘的，而是可以认识、并为人类所用的客观存在。

The ancient Chinese idea of the "oneness of heaven and humanity" emphasizes the unity of nature and mankind, of human activity's conforming to and harmonizing with nature, and the identification of moral rationality and natural rationality. According to this idea, humans cannot violate nature; they cannot exceed the natural world's tolerance to transform nature or conquer nature. Humans can only, under the condition of following natural patterns, exploit nature or adjust nature, to cause it to be better suited to the needs of humanity, and cause the myriad creatures of the natural world to be able to flourish and develop. At the same time, the natural world is not mysterious, but can be known, and has an objective existence that can be exploited by humanity.

天人合一思想在古代具有劝阻皇帝端正行为的作用。凡是出现异常的自然现象，例如洪水、干旱等天灾，皇帝就要反省治理国家的政策是否有失误，是否违背了自然的意愿，要做自我检讨、弥补过错。天人合一思想也用来考核地方官员，如果管辖区发生大的自然灾害，就要审查官员的治理能力，作为奖罚的依据。在皇权专制社会，皇帝的权力无法制约,但是,借助天人合一思想则起到了监督皇帝以及官员的作用。

The idea of the "oneness of heaven and humanity" guided emperors to conduct proper behavior in ancient times. For any occurrence of unusual natural phenomenon, such as natural disasters like floods or draughts, the emperor had to review policies governing the country to see whether there were errors, whether they had violated the wishes of nature. He had to examine himself and make up for any faults. The idea of the "oneness of heaven and humanity" was also used to assess local officials. If an area under his administration suffered a serious natural disaster, then the official's ability to govern was examined. Thus, the idea served as the basis for rewards or punishments. In a society of imperial autocracy, there was no way to restrict the power of the emperor, but the idea of "oneness of heaven and humanity" helped serve the purpose of supervising emperors and officials.

天人合一思想长期实践的结果,是得到天地自然与人的统一,人的精神行为与外在自然的一致,自我身心的平衡与自然环境的平衡的统一,以及由于这些统一而达到的天道与人道的统一,从而实现了圆满和谐的精神追求。但是,天人合一思想过于强调人对自然的迎合,而忽视甚至不敢对自然开发利用,成为中国古代科学技术不发达的一个原因。

The result of the long-time practice of the idea of "oneness of heaven and humanity" was to achieve an integration of the world of nature and humanity, an identification between human spiritual practice and the external world, and unity between the balance of one's own mind-body and the balance of the natural environment. Moreover, because of the unity of the way of heaven and the way of humans that was achieved through these integrations, it thus resulted in putting into practice consummate, harmonious spiritual pursuits. However, the idea of the "oneness of heaven and humanity" over emphasized the need for humanity to cater to nature. The Chinese neglected or avoided the exploitation of nature, which became one of the reasons science and technology did not develop in ancient China.

## 三、以人为本
## Humans Are Principal

中国传统文化全部的核心价值都是围绕着人的社会存在而建立起来的,它不追求宗教的寄托,也不追求纯自然的知识体系,而是专注于人的道德的完善与社会关系的和谐,从而表现出鲜明的重视现世人生的人文传统。

The entirety of the core value of China's traditional culture is established around the idea of human's social existence. This culture does not place its hopes on the pursuit of religion, nor does it pursue a systematic knowledge of pure nature. Rather, it is focused on the perfection of human morality and harmony of social relationships. This is expressed through a humanistic tradition that clearly emphasizes life in the world.

具体表现：一是在人与神之间，坚持以人为本。孔子重视人，重视现世，反对以神为本，"敬鬼神而远之"，认为生命最重要，不需要求助于鬼神。孔子对鬼神采取存疑的态度，既不肯定，也不否定，认为人要重视现世的生活，而不必考虑死后的问题。二是在政治上肯定"民为贵"，孟子提出了"民为贵，社稷次之，君为轻"的观点，将"民"列为首位。

Concrete manifestations of this are twofold. First, there persists the idea that humans hold the primary position over spirits. Confucius placed value on humanity and the present world, and he opposed treating the spirits as the root. He said, "While respecting ghosts and spirits, be distant from them," meaning life is the most important thing, and one need not seek aid in supernatural beings. Confucius adopted a suspicious attitude toward supernatural beings, neither confirming nor denying them. He believed humans must place value on life in the world and not worry about the problem of life after death. Second, in the political sphere, this culture affirms that "the people are important". Mencius raised the idea that, "The people are important, the gods of earth and grain and the state they bless and protect are secondary, and lords are unimportant," which placed "the people" in the primary position.

传统的人文精神冲淡了对宗教的信仰，深远地影响了中国文化。所以，在中国文化中几乎看不到把宗教作为生活的主导，不同于西方的古典文化，是一种神本文化，上帝是最高的信仰，是人们精神的最高寄托。中国文化肯定在天地人之间、在人与神之间，皆以人为中心。

The traditional humanistic spirit diluted religious belief and profoundly influenced Chinese culture. So, one can barely find the idea of religion dominating life in Chinese culture. This is different from ancient culture in the West, which is a spirit-rooted culture. The belief that God is supreme is the highest ideal of the human spirit, in which they invest their trust. Chinese culture asserts that between heaven, earth and humans, between humans and spirits, humans are always regarded as central.

当然，中国的"重人"，并非尊重个人价值和个人的自由发展，而是将个体融入群体，强调人对宗族和国家的义务，构成一种宗法集体主义的人学，与文艺复兴时期开始在西方勃兴的强调人性、以个性解放为旗帜的人文主义分属不同范畴。

Of course, the emphasis on humanity in China is not a respect for the individual and individual's independent growth. Rather, it is that the individual integrates into the group, emphasizing the responsibilities of people to their ancestors and their country, thereby forming a patriarchal collectivist humanism. The blossoming emphasis on individuality in the west that began in the Renaissance, with a humanism that takes individual freedom as its banner, is categorically different.

## 四、中庸尚和
## Doctrine of the Mean and Esteemed Harmony

中国文化重视群体关系,把协调人际关系放在首位,所以"和"成为文化的主流,追求的是"中庸""中和"。

所谓"礼之用,和为贵",孟子主张"天时不如地利,地利不如人和",人和是必备条件。把"和"作为处世、行礼的最高境界,这便是儒家所说的"修身",由此生出中庸、中和的价值原则。

Chinese culture places value on group relationships, prioritizing harmonious interpersonal relationships. As a result, "harmony" and the pursuit of "moderation" and "neutralization" are the cultural norm.

Regarding the idea "Harmony is valued in the implementation of rites", Mencius maintained, "Opportunity is not as important as geography, and geography is not as important as interpersonal harmony." Interpersonal harmony is the necessary condition. What the Ru-ists refer to as "cultivating moral character" is to regard harmony as the highest ideal in handling affairs and enacting rituals. This, then, produced the principles of "Doctrine of the Mean" and "Fair Moderation".

"和"的观念运用于社会、政治、人生各个方面。例如,北京紫禁城的主体建筑是三大殿——太和、保和、中和,名字都突出一个"和"字,表达了国家追求祥和昌盛、长治久安的政治理想,正是中国文化"尚和"精神的体现。

"Harmony" is a concept used in various aspects, such as social, political, and lived experience. For example, the main buildings in Beijing's Forbidden City are the three main halls: the Hall of Supreme Harmony, the Hall of Protecting Harmony, and the Hall of Central Harmony. All three include "harmony" in their name, expressing the political ideal that the country pursues auspiciousness, prosperity, and long-term peace and stability. This is a concrete manifestation of the high esteem in which Chinese culture holds the concept of harmony.

何谓"中庸"? 宋代理学家朱熹解释说:"中者,不偏不倚,无过不及之名;庸,平常也。"

"中"就是事物的"度",就是不偏不倚,既不过度,也不要不及,凡事不走极端。中庸的核心便是思想行为的适度和守常。贵和谐,尚中道,认为和谐是最好的状态,是最高的理想追求。实现和谐的途径,在于保持"中"道。归结到对个体人格的要求,则是为人庄重、谨慎,节制个人的情感、欲望,反对固执一端的偏激片面,以达到处世通达圆融。士子们应该像孔子那样"温良恭俭让",才能做到"文质彬彬,然后君子"。道家也提出"不敢为天下先","知足者富",要不争、无为。

What is the meaning of "Doctrine of the Mean"? The Rationalist School (Neo-Confucian) scholar Zhu Xi (1139 – 1200) explained it saying, "That which is center, neither partial nor biased, is the name for lacking excess and not falling short; the usual is commonplace."

"Center" is the "measure" of objects, it is impartial, and not only not excessive, but also must not fall short. In any particular matter, the "Doctrine of the Mean" is the appropriate and entrenched convention, dictating that one must not take the path of extremes in thought and action. To value harmony and esteem the way of the center is to believe harmony is the best state of affairs, the highest idealistic pursuit. The path of implementing harmony lies in maintaining the way of the "center". To sum up the concept, the individual must conduct oneself with dignity and prudence, control individual emotions, and oppose stubborn one-sided extremity in order to attain sense, reason, and integration with all things. Scholar-officials should be "kindhearted and moderate" like Confucius, and only then can they "being refined, then are gentlemen." Daoists also put forward the ideas of "do not dare to be the first in the world" and "one who knows sufficiency is rich"; i. e., do not strive, let things take their course.

做到"中和",就可以实现人与人之间、人与社会之间、人与自然之间的和谐与平和。在中国的语言中就有了"一团和气""妥协折中""随遇而安""知足常乐""安分守己""适可而止""退后一步天地宽""出头的椽子先烂"等成语和俗语。

If one accomplishes "fair moderation", then one may implement harmony and peace between humans, between the individual and society, and between humans and nature. The Chinese language has a number of idioms and sayings that reflect these ideas, such as, "keep on the right side of everyone," "compromise and take the middle path," "be at home wherever one is," "be satisfied with what one has," "be content with one's lot," "stop before going too far," "take a step back and heaven and earth become wide," "the beam that sticks out rots first," etc.

中庸尚和精神渗透到文学艺术创造中,便形成了中和之美,是对平衡、中和之美的追求。建筑、家居讲究平衡对称;文学表达要"乐而不淫,哀而不伤"(快乐而不过分沉浸其中，悲哀而不过分悲伤）；艺术更多表现的是湖光山色、细雨微风，是月景；书画、古典音乐等，充分体现出追求恬静淡远、柔和的文化品格。

The spirit of "Doctrine of the Mean" and principle of harmony permeated into the creation of literature and art, creating the aesthetic of "fair moderation", or the pursuit of the beauty of balance. In architecture, it is in the balanced symmetry of the home. Literary expression must, "Be joyful, but not excessively so; be deeply felt, but not mawkish". This aesthetic is even more expressed in art depicting beautiful lakes in mountain landscapes, fine mists with light winds, and scenic moons. Painting, calligraphy and classical music fully embody the cultural character of peaceful distance and gentility.

**思考题**

1. 中国文化的基本精神有哪些内容？
2. 什么是"中庸"？中庸如何从文学艺术的审美中体现出来？

## *Questions*

1. What are the contents of the basic spirit of Chinese culture?
2. What is the "Doctrine of the Mean"? How does one experience it through the appreciation of art and literature?

# 第十八章　中国文化的特点
## Characteristics of Chinese Culture

有关中国文化的特点，诸多学者从不同角度来认识和总结。陈独秀总结了三条：①西洋民族以战争为本位，东洋民族以安息为本位；②西洋民族以个人为本位，东洋民族以家族为本位；③西洋民族以法治为本位，以实力为本位，而东洋民族以感情为本位，以虚无为本位。[1] 唐君毅认为，"西方文化之重心在科学宗教，中国文化之重心在道德艺术"[2]。梁漱溟在《中国文化要义》[3] 中总结出中国文化的十四大特点，韦政通在《中国文化概论》[4] 中概括出中国文化的十大特点，冯天瑜等人在《中华文化史》[5] 中归纳出六大特点。

各位学者的总结有所不同，但是大都有着对"务实""人本""重血缘""重道德"等特点的一致认识。

Numerous scholars from different points of view have recognized and summarized the characteristics related to Chinese culture. Chen Duxiu (1879 – 1942) summed them up into three: 1) peoples of the West regard warfare as standard, while peoples of East Asian countries regard rest as standard; 2) people of the West regard the individual as standard, while people of East Asia regard the clan as standard; 3) people of the West regard law and strength as standard, while people of East Asia regard emotions and non-action as standard. Tang Chun-i (1909 – 1978) believed, "the central core of Western culture is science and religion, while the central core of Chinese culture is morality and art." Liang Shuming (1893 – 1988) in his *Essentials of Chinese Culture* sums up fourteen characteristics of Chinese culture. Wei Zhengtong (1927 – 2018) in his *Outline of Chinese Culture* summarizes ten important characteristics of Chinese culture. Feng Tianyu (b.1942) et al. in *Cultural History of China* classifies six important characteristics.

---

[1] 陈独秀：《东西民族根本思想之差异》，引自《回眸〈新青年〉·哲学思潮卷》，河南文艺出版社1997年版，第299、300页。

[2] 唐君毅：《中西文化精神之比较》，载郁龙余《中西文化异同论》，生活·读书·新知三联书店1989年版，第31页。

[3] 梁漱溟：《中国文化要义》，《梁漱溟全集》第3卷，山东人民出版社1990年版，第14—29页。

[4] 韦政通：《中国文化概论》，台湾水牛出版社1973年版。

[5] 冯天瑜、何晓明、周积明：《中华文化史》（上），上海人民出版社2006年版，第134页。

There are differences in these various scholars' summations, yet they generally all recognize such characteristics as "pragmatism", "human-centeredness", "importance of blood relations", "importance of morality", etc.

## 一、重实际、求稳定的农业文化心态
## The Agrarian Cultural Attitude of Valuing Practice and Seeking Stability

中国文化是一种农业文化。黄河、长江滋养的亚洲东部这片肥沃的土地，为中华先民从事精耕细作的农业生产提供了极为优越的条件。几千年来，中国人的主体——农民"日出而作，日落而息，凿井而饮"，世世代代在土地上，年复一年地从事简单再生产。这一特征形成重农、尚农、重实际的务实精神。"一分耕耘，一分收获"的务实精神由农耕生活导致。

Chinese culture is an agrarian culture. This stretch of fertile land in East Asia nurtured by the Yellow and Yangtze Rivers has provided favorable conditions to the Chinese people's intensive agricultural production. Over the centuries, farmers, the largest subset of the Chinese people, "worked when the sun rose, rested when the sun set, and drank when the well was dug." For many generations, year after year they engaged in simple reproduction on the land. As a result, Chinese people valued and honored agriculture and stressed the practical. The pragmatic spirit of the saying, "You get what you put in, you reap what you sow" was brought about by an agricultural livelihood.

中国人很早就认识到农耕是财富的来源，"不耕获，未富也"，意思是不种田是不会富裕的。从汉字"富"的结构上来理解：上半部"宀"是房子的意思，"富"即一口之家有房子可住、有田可耕，就是富了。汉字"福"的结构理解是：一口之家有祖先保佑、有田可耕即有福。人们在农业劳作过程中领悟到一条朴实的真理：利无幸至，力不虚掷，说空话无补于事，实心做事必有所获。

Chinese people early on recognized that farming is the origin of wealth, as expressed in the saying, "If one doesn't sow and reap, there is no wealth." The Chinese character for wealth is commonly understood to be constructed as follows: the top part is a roof, meaning one has a home to live in; under that is a "one" and a "mouth", meaning a single family; below that is a field; so, one family with a roof to live under and a field to cultivate has wealth. The Chinese character for "good fortune" has the one family with a field on the right and ancestors on the left, meaning that a family with a field to cultivate and ancestors to protect them has "good fortune". Through agricultural labor, Chinese people understood a simple truth: "Profit does not arrive purely through good luck, and force is not vainly tossed about; spreading empty talk is of no help in taking care of affairs, but if one handles matters sincerely there will inevitably be something to harvest."

这种农人的务实作风也感染了士人,"大人不华,君子务实"是中国贤哲们一向倡导的精神。正是这种民族性格使中国人发展了实用经验理性,而不太注重纯理论的思索,亚里士多德式的不以实用为目的、只探求自然奥秘的文化人,较少在中国产生。作为农耕民族的中国人,从小农业的简单再生产过程中形成的思维定式和思维方法是注意切实领会。

The farmer's pragmatic style also infected scholars. "The great person is not flowery; the noble person is practical" is the spirit advocated by Chinese worthy and wise. It is precisely this ethnic character that has caused Chinese people to develop a practical, experiential rationalism, rather than emphasize purely theoretical ponderings. The Aristotelian cultured person who does not aim for the practical but only pursues nature's mysteries rarely appears in China. Chinese people, a farming people whose ways of thinking are formed in the process of simple, agricultural reproduction, pay attention to practical comprehension.

农业生产中男耕女织的简单再生产方式使社会缺乏扩大再生产的能力,因而社会运行缓慢迟滞。在这样的生活环境中,很容易滋生永恒意识,认为世界是悠久的、静定的,中国人往往表现出遵守传统的惯性,好常恶变,从而培养了中国人清心寡欲、适可而止、知足常乐的特性。

The simple reproductive method of agricultural production in which men do the cultivating and women do the needlework means socially there is no ability to expand production. Thus, society moves along at a slow pace. In an environment such as this, it is easy to create a consciousness of the eternal, and thereby believe the world is long-lasting and settled. Chinese people usually express respect for a kind of traditional inertia, fond of the usual and disliking change. This has consequently fostered the Chinese people's characteristic of purging one's mind of desires, stopping before going too far, and being satisfied with one's lot.

农业经济也培养了中国人吃苦耐劳、勤俭持家的传统美德,培养了中国人注重实际的务实精神和酷爱和平的性格。

The agricultural economy has also fostered Chinese people's traditional virtues of diligence, ability to endure hardships, and thrift, as well as an emphasis on the practical and a disposition toward peace.

## 二、重血缘、重家族的宗法观念
## Patriarchal Notions of Valuing Blood Relations and the Clan

首先,中国人的社会存在依存于以血缘关系为纽带的家庭和宗族集团。

以家族为本位的宗法观念,是中国人重视集体的根源所在。

中国人十分看重家庭生活,血缘观念强大,非常重视亲族之间的交往礼仪。在宗法制度的影响下,个人被纳入家族中,个人作为集体的一分子而存在。人与人之间最基本的关系是相互依赖,而依赖的可靠程度则由血缘关系的亲疏程度来确定。即"母以子贵""夫荣妻贵""一人得道,鸡犬升天"(一个人有了好运,家里所有的人和物都会得益)等。反之,一人获罪,株连九族。

First, the social existence of Chinese people is dependent upon the family and clan that are linked by blood relationships.

The patriarchal idea that regards the clan as the standard is the source of Chinese value of the collective.

Chinese people really care about family life. Their notion of blood relationships is very strong, and they attach great importance to the communion and ceremony between family members. Under the influence of the patriarchal system, the individual is integrated into the clan and exists as a member of the group. The most basic relationship between people is that of mutual dependence, and the degree of reliability of that dependence is determined by the degree of closeness of the blood relationship. Thus, there are such sayings as, "The mother is important because of the children", "The husband is honored and the wife is important", and "If one person attains enlightenment, even their chickens and dogs ascend to heaven" (meaning if one person has good fortune, every person and thing in the household benefits from it). Conversely, if one person commits a crime, the entire clan is guilty by association.

由对家族的依赖延伸到宗族、乡亲等群体,就是对地域基础所产生的人际关系也十分重视。最亲密的关系从亲戚开始,再到朋友、同学、熟人,乃至同乡,所以,"老乡见老乡,两眼泪汪汪"。海外的华人集中居住区有唐人街,在异地有同乡会。

The extended community, including dependence on fellow countrymen, that is, interpersonal relationships generated on the basis of territory, are also highly valued. The closest relationships begin with family, then extends to friends, classmates, acquaintances, all the way to people of the same home town. Thus, there is the saying, "When two fellow townsmen meet, their eyes fill with tears." There are areas in foreign countries where Chinese people congregate, known as Chinatowns, and in different places there are associations of people from the same home town.

由于血缘关系至上的原则,中国人在建立其他社会关系时也尽可能用血缘关系来比附。如朋友之间的友情亲密到一定程度便可互相以兄弟相称,成为哥们;师徒之间、同时学艺的学友之间的称谓,也完全可以比照家族关系,称为师父、弟子、师祖、师叔、师兄弟、师姐妹之类。总之,在关系网络中,要想表示亲近,就以"自家人"相称,反之,则为外人。

Owing to the supreme principle of blood relationships, when Chinese people establish other social relationships they use blood relations as much as possible to draw a parallel. So, for example, when the amity between friends reaches a certain level, then they may refer to each other using fraternal terms, becoming "brothers". Terms of address between master and disciple or between colleagues in a skilled profession are also spoken of as family relations, resulting in such terms as "master-father", "disciple-son", "master-ancestor" (meaning the founder of a craft or sect), "master-uncle" (meaning the junior fellow student of one's master), "master-brother" (meaning a male fellow disciple), and "master-sister" (meaning a female fellow disciple). In short, within one's web of relationships, if one wants to express closeness, then one uses a matching "member of the family" address.

其次,中国人的群体认同的原则是要求每个人必须遵从他在家庭关系及整个社会结构中被确定的身份,不能有所逾越。每个人应当自觉接受"礼"的规范约束,所谓"君君臣臣父父子子",即是要求"父慈、子孝、兄良、弟悌、夫义、妇听、长惠、幼顺、君仁、臣忠"。总之,人首先是为家庭、为他人、为社会而存在,而非为自己而存在。

在宗法制度的影响下,中国文化强调崇拜祖先,注重家族。文化精神的发展路向是家族——宗族——民族。

Second, the principle of communal identification among Chinese people requires every person to comply with the identity determined by their family relationships and entire social structure. This cannot be transgressed. Every person should consciously accept the standard restrictions of "etiquette". As Confucius put it, "The lord acts as lord, the vassal acts as vassal, the father acts as father, the son acts as son." That is, it requires that "fathers are compassionate, sons are loyal, elder brothers are respectable, younger brothers are brotherly, husbands are just, wives are obedient, elders are benevolent, juniors are compliant, lords are humane and vassals are loyal." In short, a person, first and foremost, exists for family, others, and society, and not simply for the self.

Under the influence of the patriarchal system, Chinese culture emphasizes the adoration of ancestors and pays attention to the clan. The growth trajectory of this cultural spirit is family—clan—nationality.

体现在中国文学中，古典长篇小说中往往写一群或一组人物，而不是集中去写个别的主人公，《水浒》《三国演义》《西游记》都是如此，反映出中国文化重视群体关系、轻视个体的文化心态。西方文化基本上是以个人为中心的，追求个性解放、自我的存在和价值。文学形象上便以具有独特个性的中心人物，即以英雄为主线的叙事模式，例如《红与黑》等。

As reflected in Chinese literature, classic long-form fiction usually writes about a crowd or group of characters, rather than writing about the individual main protagonist. *The Water Margin*, *Romance of the Three Kingdoms*, and *Journey to the West* are all like this in that they reflect Chinese culture's attitude of attaching value to group relationships and contempt on the individual. Western culture is basically centered on the individual and the pursuit of individual liberation, self-existence and value. Among literary figures, there are unique, individual central characters, and narrative methods that take the hero as the main theme, as in *Le Rouge et le Noir*（1830）.

梁漱溟在《中国文化要义》一书中指出：家庭生活是中国人第一重的社会生活，亲戚邻里朋友是中国人第二重的社会生活。这两重社会生活，集中了中国人的要求，框定了中国人的活动范围，规定了其社会的道德条件和政治上的法律制度。中国人最重要的是以血缘为纽带的家庭——宗族生活，宗法制度是中国传统社会的基础，也是中国社会重视伦理、重视道德的根本原因。

In his *Essentials of Chinese Culture* Liang Shuming points out that home life is the most important source of social life for Chinese people; relatives, neighbors, and friends are their second most important source. These two sources have focused Chinese people's needs, delimited Chinese people's activities, and formulated their society's moral conditions and political legal system. What is most important to Chinese people is family-clan life which is linked by blood relationships. The patriarchal system is the basis of Chinese society, and the basic reason Chinese society values ethics and emphasizes morality.

## 三、重伦理、倡道德至上
## Valuing Ethics and Advocating Morality above All Else

许多学者认为可以把中国文化叫作"崇德"型文化。在传统社会中，人们的社会生活是严格按照伦理道德的秩序来进行的，尊卑、长幼、德行成为确定人的地位和建立秩序的要求，服饰举止、人际交往，都严格限制在"礼"的范围内，否则便违背了"伦理"的要求。

Many scholars believe one can refer to Chinese culture as one of "lofty morals". In traditional society, people's social lives were carried out in strict accordance with ethical and moral order. Senior-and-junior, elder-and-younger, and moral integrity came to define a person's position and establish the requirements of order. Apparel, manners, and interpersonal relationships were all tightly restricted within the scope of "etiquette". Otherwise, one risked violating the requirements of "ethics".

在漫长的历史发展中，中华民族建立起了十分成熟的道德价值体系。孔子建立了第一个完整的道德规范体系，他以知、仁、勇三德为主，在此基础上提出礼、孝、悌、忠、恕、恭、宽、敏、惠、温、良、俭、让、诚、敬、慈、刚、毅、直、克己、中庸等一系列德的内容。孟子以仁、义、礼、智为四种基本道德，将它扩展为"五伦"，即君惠臣忠、父慈子孝、兄友弟恭、夫义妇顺、朋友有信。

Over the long course of historical development, the Chinese nationality established a very mature moral value system. Confucius established the first complete system of moral standards. He regarded the three virtues of knowledge, humanity and bravery as primary, and on the basis of this put forward a whole series of moral values, such as, etiquette, filial piety, brotherliness, loyalty, forgiveness, respect, leniency, agility, kindheartedness, tenderness, goodness, frugality, yieldingness, sincerity, careful treatment, kindly love, firmness, resoluteness, worthiness, self-control, and the "Doctrine of the Mean". Mencius took humanity, justice, etiquette, and resourcefulness as the four basic virtues, and expanded them into the "five cardinal relationships", i.e., that lords are benevolent and vassals are loyal, that fathers are caring and sons are filial, that elder brothers are amicable and younger brothers respectful, that husbands are just and wives are obedient, and that friends are trustworthy.

传统的伦理道德更重视个人的"修身"，人际关系中，个人被重重包围在群体之中，因此特别重视家庭成员之间的人伦关系，不同的关系规定不同的责任和义务，例如父慈、子孝、兄友、弟恭等，以及对君臣、夫妻、长幼、朋友等关系的处理原则。其中，"孝"是最基本的原则，孝的内容强调子女对父母的绝对服从，转化为君臣关系，大臣必须绝对服从君主，孝道转化为治国之道，这就是"以孝治天下"。

Traditional ethics and morality attached much importance to "moral cultivation". In interpersonal relationships, the individual was layer upon layer encircled in a community, and because of this, they paid special attention to the relationships between family members. Different relationships had different duties and responsibilities, such as fathers being caring, children being filial, elder brothers amicable, younger brothers respectful, etc. This extended to the relationships between lords and vassals, husbands and wives, elders and juniors, and friends. Among these, "filiality" was the most basic principle, emphasizing the child's absolute obedience to parents. It extended to the relationship between lord and vassal, so vassals must be unconditionally obedient to their lords. The way of filiality transformed into the way of ruling the state. There is a saying that attests to this, "use filiality to rule the world."

一个有道德的人要以爱心来对待同类,这就是"仁"的主要内容。统治者治理国家就要用"仁政",个人的道德修养要以"圣人"为最高的理想境界。一个人只有道德高尚,才能有所作为,只有"修身",才能"齐家、治国、平天下"(只有提高自身修养,才能管理好家庭,治理好国家,让天下太平)。

提高道德水平的必要途径是接受教育,因此,中国各个朝代都重视教育。中国传统的哲学、历史、文学、教育思想与重伦理、倡道德紧密结合。

A moral person had to treat others of the same rank with kindness, which is the principle substance of the virtue of "humanity". Rulers had to rule their country by means of "humane government". An individual's moral self-cultivation had to regard "the sage" as the highest ideal. Only when a person is morally noble can he accomplish anything. Only if you have "cultivated your moral character" can you "manage the household, rule the country, and bring peace to the world".

The required path for raising one's morality level is to receive an education, so every Chinese dynasty attached importance to education. Traditional Chinese philosophy, history, literature and education were tightly integrated with valuing ethics and advocating morality.

## 四、专制主义、民本主义共存
## The Co-existence of Absolutism and People-rooted Ideology (Democracy)

君主集权政体的专制主义与"民为邦本"的民本主义相反相成,彼此既相对抗又互为补充,这是中国农业文明在政治意识上富于特色的表现。

Absolutism, the system of government that concentrates on authority in the sovereign, and people-rooted ideology, which regards the people as the root of the state, contrast and complete each other. They both resist and mutually complement each other. These concepts are the characteristic manifestation of Chinese agricultural civilization in the realm of political consciousness.

中国以自然经济为主的农业社会，是由千百个彼此相似、极端分散而又缺乏商品交换关系的村落和城镇组成。然而，社会需要对外抵抗游牧民族的入侵，对内维持社会安定，就要求建立一个统一的、权威巨大的帝国。要实现国家的大一统，只能依靠政治上和思想上的君主集权主义来完成。自秦汉确立起专制主义的中央集权的君主政体，到清朝历经两千多年，皇帝拥有无上权威，臣民对君主则必须唯命是从。这种君主集权政体自形成之日起，就剥夺了民众的一切权利，并将军事、政治、财政、文化及思想大权全部集中到朝廷和皇帝个人手中。总之，中国的农业社会需要并养育了这样一个君主集权政体。

China's agricultural society, based on the natural economy, is formed of villages and towns that resemble one another yet lack trade relationships. Yet, this society had to fight off the incursions of nomadic peoples. Maintaining internal social stability required the establishing a large, unified, authoritarian empire. To implement national unification politically and ideologicaly, this society had to rely on a centralized monarchy. From the Qin-Han era's institution of a despotic, centralized monarchy up to the Qing Dynasty, it lasted more than 2000 years. The emperor held supreme authority, and his subjects must obediently submit to his rule. Since the day it began, this system of government with power concentrated in the monarch expropriated all rights from the populace and concentrated military, political, financial, cultural and ideological authority in the court and the hands of the emperor. In short, China's agrarian society required and fostered this kind of concentrated monarchical system of government.

农业社会存在和发展的前提，是农业劳动力——农民的安居乐业，这样，农业生产才能稳定有序，国家的国库才能充实，天下才能太平。反之，如果农民失去了起码的生存条件，饥寒交迫的农民就会无所畏惧地起来反抗，统治就会不稳。所以，"民为贵""民为邦本"（人民是国家的根本）的观念很早就已经形成。

The precondition for the existence and development of an agricultural society is the agricultural labor force—peasants living in peace and able to work. Only then can agricultural production be regular and orderly, the state's coffers be filled, and the world be peaceful. Conversely, if the peasants lack basic conditions of existence, then the peasants, beset by hunger and cold, will fear nothing and rise up in resistance, and the regime will become unstable. Therefore, the ideas that "the people are important" and "the people are the root of the state" formed early on.

民本主义与君主专制主义的相互关系是双重的。

一方面，以"爱民""重民"为主的民本思想与专制主义的"贱民""虐民"的暴政思想和绝对君权论是相互对立的。

The relationship between people-rooted ideology and absolutism is two-fold.

On the one hand, the people-rooted ideology based on "loving the people" and "valuing the people" is in mutual opposition to absolutism's despotic ideology and absolute monarchical authority that "cheapens the people" and "oppresses the people".

另一方面,民本主义与君主专制主义又相互补充,构成所谓"明君论"。这种明君因为"爱民""重民",所以,百姓将安定温饱生活的希望寄托于明君。明君既强调"国以民为本",又强调"民以君为主"。

On the other hand, the people-rooted ideology and monarchal absolutism mutually complements each other, creating the so-called "enlightened ruler doctrine". Because this enlightened ruler "loves the people", so the commoners entrust their hopes for a secure and adequate livelihood in the enlightened ruler. The enlightened ruler stresses both "people are the root of the state" and "the people regard the ruler as primary".

总之,民本主义和君主专制主义是矛盾的统一体,他们共同组合为中国农业社会政治思想的主体,而明君统治天下,则是中国民众期盼的理想境界。

In short, the people-rooted ideology and absolute monarchy are a contradictory single entity. Together these ideas formed the mainstream political philosophy of China's agrarian society. From the perspective of the China's populace, they expected an ideal state of an enlightened ruler governing the world.

## 五、绵延韧性、长期存在的生命力
## Vitality from Continuous Tenacity and Long-term Survival

世界上其他古代文明因各种原因大都相继中断,而中国文化则是罕见的古今延续的文化类型。

如埃及文化曾被波斯帝国所灭(公元前525),后又因马其顿亚历山大的占领而被希腊化,因恺撒的占领而罗马化,因阿拉伯人的移入而伊斯兰化,多次出现文化的中断和变异。巴比伦文化也在屡遭中断之后走向毁灭,旧巴比伦王国在公元前16世纪灭亡,新巴比伦王国在公元前538年被波斯帝国所灭,巴比伦城到公元2世纪已成废墟,是现代考古发掘破译了它昔日的辉煌。印度境内的哈拉巴在不到10个世纪的繁荣之后,也因中亚雅利安人的进攻而于公元前18世纪突然毁灭。希腊文化在公元前2世纪被并入罗马的版图,而罗马文化也因以日耳曼为主的蛮族侵入而毁灭变异。

The other ancient civilizations of the world have generally all come to an end for various reasons, yet Chinese culture is the rare cultural form to have continued from ancient times to the present.

For example, Ancient Egyptian culture was extinguished by Persia (525 B. C.), and later because it was occupied by Alexander the Great it was Hellenified, and because it was occupied by Caesar it was Latinized, and later because Arabs moved in it was Islamicized, so that many times there was a cultural disruption and transformation. Babylonian culture trended toward ruin after repeated interruptions. The Old Babylonian Kingdom was destroyed in the 16$^{th}$ Century B. C., and the New Babylonian Kingdom was wiped out by the Persian Empire in 538 B. C.. By the 2$^{nd}$ Century B. C., the city of Babylon was in ruins. Modern archeology excavated and solved the riddle of its ancient glory. The Harappan Civilization on the boundaries of India, after nearly a millennium of prosperity, suddenly perished because of Aryan invasions from Central Asia in the 18$^{th}$ Century B. C.. Ancient Greek culture was incorporated into Roman territory in the 2$^{nd}$ Century B. C., and Roman culture perished or was transformed by primarily Germanic invasions.

上述诸文化形态大都沿着中断——重建的轨迹跳跃式地演进成现代文明，被称为"突破性文化"，例如苏美尔→巴比伦→希腊→罗马。但是，中国文化古今绵延、连续发展，从未中断过，它堪称"连续性文化"的典型。无论是汉族人执政，还是游牧人入主，中华民族都以其强大的同化力和凝聚力维持着一以贯之的文化传统。中国文化的连续性、独特性，丰富了世界文明的内涵。

The aforementioned cultural forms evolved into modern civilization along a leap-frog trajectory of interruption-and-reconstruction. They are known as "break-through cultures", as for example the trajectory of Sumer→Babylon→Greece→Rome. However, Chinese culture has continuously developed from ancient times to the present, and has never been interrupted. It can be said to be the prototypical "continuous culture". Regardless of whether Han people held power or nomadic peoples entered and ruled, the Chinese people, by means of their strong power of assimilation and cohesiveness, have maintained a consistent cultural tradition. Chinese culture's continuity and distinctiveness have enriched world civilization.

这种延绵韧性具体表现在下述三个方面。

第一，同化力，是指外域文化进入中国后，大都逐步中国化，融入中国文化而成为其中一部分。比如佛教文化的传入和中国化。佛教兴起于古印度，在公元1世纪的两汉之际传入中国。传播的结果，一部分变为中国式的佛教（如禅宗），一部分反而消融于宋明理学之中，成为中国文化的一部分。中国佛教实现本土化。

This continuous tenacity is concretely manifest in the following three areas.

First, the ability to assimilate, which refers to the phenomena that after foreign cultures enter China, they generally gradually take on Chinese characteristics, blending into Chinese culture and becoming a part of it, as for example Buddhist culture's transmission to China and sinification. Buddhism arose in ancient India and was transmitted to China in the 1st Century A. D. in the period between the two Han Dynasties. The result of the transmission was that one part became a Chinese style Buddhism (such as Chan, or Zen), and another part melted into the Rationalist (Neo-Confucian) School of the Song and Ming eras, becoming a part of Chinese culture. Buddhism in China achieved localization.

第二，融合力，是指中国文化并非单纯的汉民族文化，而是在中原文化的基础上吸收各民族及不同地域的文化——如楚文化、吴文化、巴蜀文化、西域文化等，形成具有丰富内涵的中华文化。中华各民族文化，例如历史上的匈奴、鲜卑、羯、氐、羌、契丹、女真等民族的文化，都融汇于中国文化的血脉之中。没有这种融合，也就没有中国文化的博大精深。

Second, the ability to amalgamate, which refers to the fact that Chinese culture is not simply pure ethnic Han culture, but rather a culture with a foundation of Central Plains culture that ingests the cultures of each nationality and of different territories, such as the cultures of Chu, Wu, Sichuan, and the Western Territories. In so doing, it forms the abundantly rich Chinese culture. Every ethnic culture in China, such as the historical Xiongnu, Xianbei, Jie, Di, Qiang, Khitan, and Jurchen, have fused into the very blood of Chinese culture. Without this amalgamation, there would not be the current breadth and depth we have in Chinese culture.

第三，凝聚力，是说在漫长的历史年代里，中国文化虽屡次遭到北方游牧民族的军事冲击，游牧民族甚至多次建立起强有力的统治政权，但在文化方面却总是自觉不自觉地被以华夏农耕文化为代表的先进的中原文化所同化。而在这一过程中，中国文化又多方面地吸收了新鲜养料，如游牧民族的骑射技术，边疆地区的物产、技艺，从而增添了新的生命活力。

Third, cohesiveness, which speaks to the fact that through many historical eras China suffered through military attacks from northern nomadic peoples, who even on several occasions established powerful unified governments. Despite that, as regards the culture, the northern nomadic peoples were always, consciously or unconsciously, assimilated by the advanced Central Plains culture, i. e., the Hua-Xia agrarian culture. Through this process, Chinese culture in many respects absorbed fresh nutrients, such as riding and hunting technology of nomadic peoples, and natural resources and skills of border regions, thereby adding new vitality.

**思考题**

1. 为什么中国文化是"崇德"型文化?

2. 请列举几条你在生活中观察到的体现中国文化特点的事例,并说明为什么。例如,因为中国人重视人际关系中的"和",所以提倡做一个"谦谦君子",这一特点形成的原因,是因为在宗法制度的影响下,家族利益高于个人,个人行为要以集体为重,要做到温良恭俭让,以维护和睦的人际关系,只有做到这些,才算是一位君子。

*Questions*

1. Why is Chinese culture a "lofty virtue" type of culture?

2. List several examples manifesting Chinese cultural characteristics that you have observed in your own life, and explain why. For example, because Chinese people put value on "harmony" in interpersonal relationships, they promote being a "modest, self-disciplined gentleman"; this characteristic was formed because, under the influence of the patriarchal system, the family's interests are higher than the individual's, so the individual's behavior must recognize the importance of the group, and one must be warmly respectful and modest, in order to safeguard harmonious interpersonal relationships. Only by acting as such, may one be considered a gentleman.

# 第十九章 中国文化的近代转型及中西文化交会：晚清迄现代
## The Sino-Western Encounter and the Modern Transformation: Late Qing to the Present

鸦片战争以来，中国文化受到了根本性的冲击。中华文化遭遇到前所未有的挑战，正是在与西方资本主义文化的交锋中，中华文化实现了向近代形态的转型。

Since the Opium War, Chinese culture has endured a fundamental shock. Chinese culture met with an unprecedented challenge; that is, in crossing swords with Western capitalist culture, Chinese culture turned toward modernity.

## 一、开眼看世界
## Widen Horizons and View the World

1840 年，英国发动鸦片战争，用大炮轰开了中国紧闭的国门，给中华民族带来深重的灾难和屈辱，但它同时也开启了一扇窗口，使中国人得以看见外部世界。"开眼看世界"成为中华民族从沉睡中觉醒的标志。林则徐（1785—1850）、徐继畬（1795—1873）、魏源（1794—1857）等人，担当了时代的前驱。

In 1840, Great Britain initiated the Opium War, blew open China's doors with large cannons, and brought profound hardship and insult to the Chinese people. Yet, it also opened a window that let the Chinese people see the outside world. The phrase "widen horizons and view the world" came to symbolize China's awakening from a deep sleep. Lin Zexu (1785 – 1850), Xu Jiyu (1795 – 1873), Wei Yuan (1794 – 1857) and others assumed the forward impetus of the age.

1839 年，林则徐以钦差大臣身份，赴广东禁烟。在同洋人直接打交道的过程中，林则徐深感迫切需要了解西方。于是通过报刊掌握西方知识，开始介绍英、美、法、俄等国情形。

In 1839, Lin Zexu went to Guangdong to prohibit opium as an imperially appointed envoy. Over the course of direct negotiations with the foreigners, Lin Zexu deeply felt the urgent necessity of understanding the West. So, he mastered some western knowledge through newspapers and periodicals and began to introduce to China knowledge of the national situation of such places as England, America, France, and Russia.

徐继畬撰写十卷本《瀛寰志略》,配以 42 幅地图,论述地球,介绍亚、欧、非、美、澳洲数十国的情形。

魏源完成的《海国图志》(见图 19-1),是 19 世纪中叶中国乃至东亚内容最丰富的世界知识百科全书。他提出"师夷长技以制夷"的思想,不仅承认西方物质文明相对于中国的先进性,而且明确表现出学习西方、赶超先进的开放襟怀,预示了中国近代文化变迁的基本方向。

Xu Jiyu wrote the ten chapter *Ying Huan Zhilüe* (Outline of the Oceans Encirclement), including 42 maps, which discussed the world, and introduced Asia, Europe, Africa, Americas and Australia, as well as the conditions in dozens of countries.

Wei Yuan finished *Haiguo Tuzhi* (Pictorial Record of Overseas Countries) (see Figure 19-1). It had the richest content of any encyclopedia of world knowledge in mid-19$^{th}$ century China and even all of East Asia. He also put forward the idea of "learn from foreigners in order to control them". It not only conceded that Western material culture was more advanced than China's, it also expressed the open minded need to study the west, to advance, and to overtake it. In this way, it foretold the basic direction of modern China's cultural changes.

图 19-1 魏源和他的《海国图志》
Figure 19-1 Wei Yuan and His *Haiguo Tuzhi*

鸦片战争后救亡图存的时代要求，使"开眼看世界"和"师夷长技以制夷"成为先进中国人共同的思想主题。一百多年来的中国，在国家体制、社会生活、思想意识诸领域都发生了深刻的巨变。

After the Opium War, the requirements of the age to save the country from extinction and to plan for survival made the ideas "widen horizons and view the world" and "learn from the foreigners in order to control them" the joint ideological theme of advanced Chinese people. One hundred years later, China has undergone a profound transformation in the areas of national system, social life, and consciousness.

## 二、文化教育革新
## Innovation in Cultural Education

19 世纪中后期，洋务运动兴起。主要代表人物有奕䜣（1833—1898）、曾国藩（1811—1872）（见图 19-2）、左宗棠（1812—1885）、李鸿章（1823—1901）（见图 19-3）、张之洞（1837—1909）等人。目的在于学习西方，以维护清朝统治。与此同时，近代工商业的发展，直接促成了文化的近代转型。

In the middle and latter parts of the 19$^{th}$ Century, the Self-Strengthening Movement (Westernization Movement) arose, primary representatives of which include Yixin (1833 – 1898), Zeng Guofan (1811 – 1872) (see Figure 19 – 2), Zuo Zongtang (1812 – 1885), Li Hongzhang (1823 – 1901) (see Figure 19 – 3) and Zhang Zhidong (1837 – 1909). Their goals lay in learning from the west in order to defend Qing's rule. Meanwhile, the development of modern business directly spurred the modern cultural transformation.

图 19-2　曾国藩
Figure 19-2　Zeng Guofan

图 19-3 李鸿章
Figure 19-3 Li Hongzhang

## 1. 书院改制与新学堂开办
## Change of Academies and Opening of New Schools

书院改制与新式学堂的设立是近代教育改革的主线。在西学东渐的影响下，洋务派着手兴办新式学堂，为近代化事业造就专门人才。清政府要求各省所有书院改设学堂。1862年开办京师同文馆，很快发展成为一所文理综合性的实用学科专门学堂，其培养目标、课程设置、训练制度，均与旧式书院有所不同，初步具备近代学校的特点。旧的书院改制，新学堂不断开办，外国传教士设立的教会学校，成为近代新式学校教育的开端。

Change of Academies and the establishment of new schools are the main lines of modern education reform. Under the influence of western learning, the self Strengthening Movement (Westernization Movement) set up new schools to train specialized professionals for modernization. The Qing government required all academies in the provinces to change into schools. The School of Combined Learning was established in 1862, and it soon developed into a comprehensive school of combined disciplines of liberal arts and sciences. Its training purposes, curriculum design, and training systems are all different from those of the old academies.

Old academies changed, new schools continuously opened, and church schools were founded by foreign missionaries: they pioneered a new-style, modern education.

## 2. 近代报刊及出版机构兴建
### The Construction of Modern Newspapers and Publication Industry

近代报刊出版业从零起步，迅速发展。从 1860 年到 1890 年，仅耶稣会主办的报刊就多达 70 余种。教会报刊中，影响最大的是《万国公报》，发行量最高时达 54000 份，曾对维新派人士产生重要影响。外国商办报刊也发展起来，而且后来居上，在社会影响方面超过了教会报刊。

外国商办报刊中最著名的是《申报》（见图 19-4）。从 1872 年 4 月 30 日创刊到 1949 年 5 月 27 日停刊，长达 77 年，是中国近代历史上发行最久的报纸。

The modern newspaper and magazine industry started from zero. Between 1860 and 1890, Jesuit organized periodicals numbered more than 70. Among church periodicals with the greatest influence was *A Review of the Times*, which had a circulation at its peak 54000, generating a significant influence on public figures of the reformist faction. Foreign commercial periodicals also expanded, and later even outstripped the former, and in terms of social influence, surpassed church periodicals.

Among the foreign commercial periodicals, the most famous was *Shenbao* (see Figure 19-4). Published from April 30th, 1872 until May 27th, 1949, it had a run of 77 years, the longest running newspaper in Chinese history at the time.

图 19-4 《申报》(1945 年 1 月 31 日)
Figure 19-4  *Shenbao* (Jan 31, 1945)

近代中国人自己主办的报纸，开始于林则徐1839年在广州组织人员编译的《澳门新闻纸》。1868年，伍廷芳（1842—1922）在香港创办《中外新报》，首次采用西方报纸形式编排，不再采用书本形式。1874年2月，改良派思想家王韬（1828—1897）在香港创办《循环日报》。1895年8月，康有为创办的《中外纪闻》在北京出版发行。

The first newspaper supported by Chinese people themselves in early modern times was the *Macau Newspaper*, which Lin Zexu organized staff to edit and translate in Guangzhou in 1839. In 1868, Wu Tingfang (1842 – 1922) started the *Chinese and Foreign Gazette* in Hong Kong, the first to adopt a foreign newspaper format for its layout, rather than the traditional book form. In February 1874, reformist faction thinker Wang Tao (1828 – 1897) started the *Universal Circulating Herald* in Hong Kong. In August 1895, the *Domestic and Foreign News*, launched by Kang Youwei, was published and distributed in Beijing.

1898年6月，在变法高潮中，光绪帝下令准许官民自由办报。中国近代报刊事业出现第一个高潮。

近代出版机构中，历史最久、影响最巨的是商务印书馆和中华书局。

In June 1898, at the height of the reform movement, the Guangxu Emperor issued a decree permitting officials and individuals to freely start newspapers. The early modern Chinese periodical industry set its first high water mark.

Among early modern publishing agencies, the longest-lasting and most influential are the Commercial Press and Zhonghua Shuju.

商务印书馆于1897年创设于上海。初以印刷外商商业文件为主，后重点出版古籍、科学、文艺类书籍，尤其是1903年设置编译所之后，在译介西方文化新知方面发挥了重要作用。

The Commercial Press started in 1897 in Shanghai. At first, it primarily printed foreign businessmen's commercial documents. Later, it re-evaluated and published ancient texts, science, and art works. After the setting up of the translation and edit office in 1903, it played a significant role in translating and introducing Western culture and new knowledge.

中华书局成立于1912年元旦，教科书和儿童读物是中华书局的出书重点。从创办之日到1949年，共出版教科书400余种，居出版界之冠。

Zhonghua Shuju was set up on January 1, 1912. Their focus was textbooks and children's reading materials. From their founding until 1949, they published more than 400 textbooks, the best among the publishing world.

## 三、"维新"与"革命"
## "Reform" and "Revolution"

在中国近代历史上,人们将主张对君主专制制度实行改良、推行君主立宪的政治力量称为"维新派",而将主张彻底推翻专制,建立民主共和国的政治力量称为"革命派"。这两派都要求在制度文化层面上学习西方,但在方式、手段上存在分歧,前者温和,后者激烈。

In China's recent past, people who advocated improvements to the autocratic system and implementing constitutional monarchy were called the "reform party", while those who advocated a thorough toppling of the autocracy and establishing a democratic republic were called the "revolutionary party". Both of the parties, at the level of institutional culture, required learning from the West, but in terms of models and methods, there were deep divisions. The former were moderate, while the latter were spirited.

### 1. 维新
### Reform

维新派领袖康有为(1858—1927)(见图19-5),生长在最早接触西方资本主义文化的广东。他早年接受严格的正统教育,成年后逐渐接受新学,又游历香港,见西方文化制度优越。西方资本主义的社会政治学说和自然科学,中国传统文化中的今文经学,是康有为思想的两大支柱。

The reform party leader was Kang Youwei (1858 - 1927) (see Figure 19 - 5), who was born and raised in Guangdong where the earliest contact with Western capitalist culture took place. He had a strict, traditional education in his early years, but after growing up he gradually accepted the new learning. He also traveled to Hong Kong and observed the advantages of the western system. The two great pillars of Kang Youwei's thinking are western capitalism's socio-political theory and natural science, and Chinese traditional culture's thorough grounding in Ru-ist scholarship.

梁启超(1873—1929)(见图19-6)师从康有为维新变法,倡导新文化运动,支持五四运动,积极宣传康有为的变法思想。

1895年5月,清政府与日本签订丧权辱国的《马关条约》,消息传来,正在北京参加会试的康有为召集各省举人1300余人集会,联名上书光绪帝,力主拒绝和议,恳请变法,变法维新运动由此发端。维新运动作为一场文化启蒙运动,维新派的思想产生了深远的影响。

Liang Qichao (1873 – 1929) (see Figure 19 – 6) studied from Kang Youwei on reform. He advocated a new cultural movement, supported the May Fourth Movement, and actively promoted Kang Youwei's reform thought.

In May 1895, the Qing government signed the humiliating Treaty of Shimonoseki with the Japanese. As the news spread, Kong Youwei, who was in Beijing sitting for the metropolitan exam, called together the 1300 successful provincial examinees, and they jointly signed a petition to the Guangxu Emperor strongly advocating rejecting the treaty and earnestly requesting political reform. With this petition, the political reform movement began. As a cultural enlightenment movement, the Reform Movement's thinking had a profound impact.

图 19 – 5 康有为
Figure 19 – 5 Kang Youwei

图 19 – 6 梁启超
Figure 19 – 6 Liang Qichao

## 2. 革命
**Revolution**

1905 年 8 月,孙中山(1866—1925)在日本东京成立中国同盟会,提出"驱除鞑虏,恢复中华,建立民国,平均地权"的革命纲领,在思想文化战线方面也做了大量工作。他们创办多种报刊,宣传民族主义、民主主义,鼓舞人民对外反对帝国主义对中华民族的殖民掠夺,对内反对满清统治集团的民族歧视和民族压迫政策,呼吁扫除专制政体,建立自由独立的"中华共和国"。

In August 1905, Sun Yat-sen (1866 – 1925) set up the Tongmenghui in Tokyo, Japan, proposing revolutionary program to "expel the Manchu and recover China, establish a republic, and evenly distribute land power". He also did a great deal of work on the ideological culture front. The Tongmenghui set up many kinds of newspapers and periodicals, disseminating national self-determination and democracy, encouraging the people to oppose imperialism's colonial plunder of the Chinese people, and oppose the policies of ethnic discrimination and ethnic suppression on the part of the Manchu Qing ruling clique. They called for sweeping away autocratic government and establishing an independent, free "Republic of China".

孙中山（1866—1925）（见图19－7）贡献给中华民族的最宝贵的文化财富，是他提出的"三民主义"：

第一，民族主义——反对列强侵略，主张各民族平等，承认民族自决权。

第二，民权主义——打倒君主专制，倡行民主政治，立法、司法、行政、考试、监察五权分立。

第三，民生主义——实行耕者有其田，节制私人资本。

图19－7　孙中山
Figure19－7：Sun Yat-sen

Sun Yat-sen (see Figure 19 – 7) contributed the most precious cultural wealth to the Chinese people, his "Three Principles of the People".

First, national self-determination: opposing the Great Powers' incursions, standing for equality of ethnic groups, recognizing the power of ethnic self-determination;

Second, democracy: overthrow the autocratic centralization of power, advocate enacting democracy, and a five part division of powers among legislation, judicial, administrative, examination, and supervision;

And third, principle of the people's livelihood: carry out "land to the tiller" land reform, and restrict private capital.

## 四、"德、赛两先生"
## "Mr. Science and Mr. Democracy"

辛亥革命后,新文化运动兴起。新文化运动高扬科学和民主的旗帜,将中国文化的发展历程推进到一个崭新的阶段。

北京大学成为新文化运动的一个策源地。1915 年 9 月,陈独秀(1879—1942)(见图 19-8)在上海创办《青年》杂志,后更名为《新青年》(见图 19-9),标志着新文化运动的崛起。

After the Xinhai Revolution, the New Culture Movement arose. The New Culture Movement promotes science and democracy, and advances the development of Chinese culture to a brand new stage.

Peking University became one source of the New Culture Movement. In September 1915, Chen Duxiu (1879 – 1942) (see Figure 19 – 8) launched *Youth* magazine in Shanghai, which was later renamed as "New Youth" (see Figure 19 – 9), thus marking the abrupt rise of the New Culture Movement.

图 19-8　陈独秀
Figure 19-8　Chen Duxiu

图 19-9　《新青年》1918 年 1 月第四卷
Figure 19-9　*New Youth* Volume 4, January 1918

陈独秀写文赞颂"德先生"——民主(Democracy)、"赛先生"——科学(Science),"德、赛先生"成为新文化运动两大主题。用民主取代专制,用科学扫荡迷信,新文化运动在众多的领域内掀起了思想解放的浪潮。

Chen Duxiu wrote an essay praising "Mr. Democracy" and "Mr. Science", and the two Mr. s became main themes of the New Culture Movement. The gist was to use democracy to replace autocracy and use science to root out superstition. With this idea, the New Culture Movement lifted the tide of liberated thinking in many fields.

胡适（1891—1962）（见图 19 – 10）等人以白话文取代文言文的"文学改良"，是新文化运动的重要成绩。1920 年，教育部发布训令，要求小学废除文言教科书，以白话文取代古文，此后，白话文作为"国语"被广泛接受并普及开来。

The "literary reform" of Hu Shi (1891 – 1962) (see Figure 19 – 10) and others, which argued for replacing the old literary Classical Chinese with writings in the vernacular, was an important achievement of the New Culture Movement. In 1920, the Ministry of Education issued an order requiring primary schools to abolish Classical Chinese textbooks and to replace the ancient written language with the vernacular. After that, writings in the vernacular were looked upon as the "national language", and began to become widely accepted and widespread.

争你们个人的自由，便是为国家争自由！争你们自己的人格，便是为国家争人格！自由平等的国家不是一群奴才建造得起来的！
——胡适：《介绍自己的思想》（1930）

图 19 – 10　胡适
Figure 19 – 10　Hu Shi

1919 年 5 月 4 日，在北京爆发了抵制卖国条约、抗议屈辱外交的学生游行示威，并迅速发展成为全国性的爱国运动，史称"五四运动"。以此为契机，进步青年们批判传统、建设新中国的热望得到总爆发，将新文化运动推到高潮。新文化运动为后来思想文化的多元化创造了条件，是中国现代化过程中的一座里程丰碑。

On May 4th, 1919, students protested against the traitor diplomacy in Beijing. It quickly developed into a national patriotic movement, known as the "May Fourth Movement."

Taking this as an opportunity, some of the progressive young people criticized the tradition, and their desire to build a new China fully exploded, this pushing this New Cultural Movement into the climax. The New Culture Movement created the conditions for the later pluralism in cultural thinking, an important milestone in the process of modernizing China.

## 五、传统习俗转化
## Transformation of Traditional Customs

19世纪中叶以降,近代工商业的发展为中国人提供了改变生活方式的物质基础。人们的衣、食、住、行、乐均发生着变化。南京临时政府颁布了一系列法令,禁娼、禁烟、禁赌、剪辫、放足、废止清官称呼等。

Since the mid 19th Century, the growth of business and commerce provided the Chinese people with the material basis for changing their lifestyle. People's clothes, food, homes, behavior, and music all changed. The provisional government in Nanjing issued a series of ordinances prohibiting prostitution, opium, and gambling, advocated cutting braids and unbinding feet, and abolished titles of Qing Dynasty officials, etc.

辛亥革命正式废除了妇女缠足的陋习,剪掉了男人头上的辫子。清朝建立后,强迫人们接受满族发式,剃发留辫。因此,辫子便不仅是个发式问题,而成了民族耻辱的标志。清廷被推翻,无数汉人都兴高采烈地剪掉这条奴隶标志的辫子。辛亥革命以后,不剪发不算革命,也不算时髦。西服、西式裙装开始流行。

The October 10 1911 Xinhai Revolution formally eliminated the corrupt practice of foot-binding, and abolished the long braids men wore on their heads. After the Qing Dynasty was established in 1644, the Manchu rulers compelled people to accept Manchu hair styles, which was to shave the front of the head and leave a long braid in the back. Because of this, these braids were not simply a problem of hair style, but had become the symbol of ethnic shame. After the Qing court was overthrown, countless ethnic Han people happily and excitedly cut this symbol of slavery from their heads. After the October 10 Revolution, keeping one's braid was neither revolutionary nor stylish. Suits and western-style skirts became popular.

## 六、中国文化的四次转折
## The Four Shifts in Chinese Culture

一部完整的中国文化史表明,中国文化历来具有坚韧顽强的生存能力和融会更新的发展机制,历经千年不衰。

A complete history of Chinese culture reveals that Chinese culture has a tenacious ability to survive and a growth mechanism for incorporating renewal throughout history, so through thousands of years it did not weaken.

春秋战国之际,中国文化第一次转折的结果是元典并创,贤哲辈出,为中国文化政治体制、社会组织、观念意识都树立了基本范式。两汉时期形成以儒学为核心的大一统帝国文化。这一段落的中国文化,舞台限于东亚大地之内,属于"中国之中国"阶段。

The result of the first shift in Chinese cultural history, which was between the Spring-Autumn and Warring States periods, was the creation of the primary canon, the appearance of numerous worthy and wise people, and the establishment of the basic model of Chinese culture's form of government, social organization, and conceptual awareness. During the Han Dynasties, a unified empire culture with Confucianism as its core was formed. In this stage of Chinese culture, it is only limited to the land of East Asia, so the stage is called "China as China".

魏晋之间,儒学衰落,印度文化进入,中国文化第二次转折,其结果是佛教昌盛,胡汉补强。胡汉互补,儒佛道三教共弘,自此进入"亚洲之中国"阶段。

During the Wei-Jin period, the Ru-ist School declined and Indian culture entered China, marking the second shift in Chinese culture. The result was the prosperity of Buddhism and supplementing and strengthening from Han and non-Han peoples. Han and non-Han people complement each other, and the three religions Confucianism, Buddhism, Taoism are advancing together. From now on, it entered the stage of "Asian China".

唐代中叶,中国文化第三次转折,其结果是儒学复兴,近古文化的各层面形成定式,中国文化吸收佛教文化,创立理学。

In the Mid-Tang, the results of Chinese culture's third shift were the rejuvenation of Ru-ist School, fixing the form of aspects of near-ancient culture, Chinese culture's assimilation of Buddhism, and the creation of the Rationalist School.

从清代中叶以来,中国文化发生了第四次大的转折。中国与西方文化的接触,自汉唐开始,如唐代的景教,元朝的"也里可温",明中叶以来的耶稣会士在华传教。但真正对中国文化产生实质性影响,还是始于清代中叶,自此以来,中国发生了"三千年未有之变局"。这是继印度文化传入中国之后,国外文明对中国文化的又一次碰撞,而这一次的深度、广度都超过前者。中国进入"世界之中国"阶段。中西文明的涵化与融合,至今还是中国文化的一大主题。

Since the mid-Qing, Chinese culture experienced the fourth great transformation.

Contact between Chinese and Western culture began in the Han and Tang, as in the Tang Dynasty's Nestorian Christianity. It continued with Christianity under the Yuan Dynasty, and the evangelization in China by the Jesuits starting in the mid-Ming Dynasty. But real, substantive influence on Chinese culture from the West began in the mid-Qing. Since then China underwent "a turbulent situation not seen in 3000 years". After the Indian culture's influence on Chinese culture, this is once again a foreign civilization colliding with Chinese culture, but the depth and breadth this time far surpass the previous one. The inculcation and fusion of Sino-Western civilization is one main topic of Chinese culture to this day.

## 七、现代的中国
## Modern China

鸦片战争以后中国开始的转折,最为激烈深刻的还是20世纪80年代以后近三四十年来在中国发生的转变,这个转折是震撼世界的,是中国文化史上继春秋战国、魏晋、中唐之后的第四次转折,目前仍然处于这一转折之中。它包括多重转折:

The shift China started after the Opium War has been most acute and profound during the last 30 to 40 years. The transformation in China during this time has shaken the world. It is the fourth shift in Chinese cultural history, following the Sping-Autumn/Warring States, Wei-Jin, and mid-Tang shifts. We are currently in the middle of this fourth shift. It includes many important changes:

一是农业文明向工业文明的转化,二是从国家统制的计划体制向市场体制转变,三是工业文明向后工业文明转化,不可避免地遭遇后现代的种种问题。其深度和广度远远超过历史上任何一次的文化大变革,

One is the change from an agrarian civilization to an industrial civilization; the second is from a government controlled planned organization to a market organization; the third is transformation of industrial civilization to the post-inductrial civilization, and it unavoidably encounters the various problems associated with post-modernity. Its depth and breadth far surpass any cultural revolution of the past.

上述三大转折,不仅提出经济的、社会的课题,也在深层次上提出文化的、精神的课题,要求我们综合古今中外智慧,加以创造性转换,促成可持续发展。

As above, three major turning points not only raise economic and social issues, but also raise cultural and spiritual issues for the underlying reasons. They require us to integrate ancient and modern, Chinese and foreign, wisdom and make creative transformations to promote sustainable development.

中国近代的历史证明，新的文化思潮和新的文化人，无一不是走中西会通之路，既非全盘西化，也不是中国传统文化的陈陈相因。未来的世界既不是西方的世界，也不是东方的世界，而是一个融合共生的新世界；未来的中国文化既不是传统的中国文化，也不是西方或其他文化的移植，而是一种融合共生的新文化。

China's early modern history proves that new cultural tides and new cultural people, all traveling the road which joins China and the West, are neither completely westernized nor stuck in the rut of China's traditional culture. The future of the world is neither a Western world nor an Eastern world, but a jointly amalgamated new world. The future of Chinese culture is neither traditional Chinese culture, nor transplanted Western, or some other, culture, but a jointly amalgamated new culture.

**思考题**

1. 清末新政促成了文化的近代转型，中国人传统的生活习俗发生了哪些变化？
2. 中国文化的转折主要有哪四次？

**Questions**

1. The reform at the end of the Qing facilitated the early modern cultural shift. What changes occurred in the traditional life customs of the Chinese people?
2. What are the four transformations in Chinese culture?

# 附录一　中国历史朝代顺序
## Appendix A　The Order of Chinese Dynasties

中国古代一共出现了 83 个王朝，共有 559 个帝王，包括 397 个"帝"和 162 个"王"。

Ancient China had 83 dynasties, totaling 559 rulers, 397 emperors and 162 kings.

中国历史朝代顺序：夏——商——周［西周、东周（春秋、战国）］——秦——汉（西汉、东汉）——三国时期（魏、蜀、吴）——晋（西晋、东晋）——南北朝［南朝（宋、齐、梁、陈）——北朝（北魏、东魏、西魏、北齐、北周）］——隋——唐——五代（后梁、后唐、后晋、后汉、后周）——十国［前蜀、后蜀、吴、南唐、吴越、闽、楚、南汉、南平（荆南）、北汉］——宋（北宋、南宋）——辽——西夏——金——元——明——清——中华民国——中华人民共和国。

Xia—Shang—Zhou [Western Zhou, Eastern Zhou (Spring-and-Autumn, Warring States)] —Qin—Han (Western Han, Eastern Han) —Three Kingdoms (Wei, Shu, Wu) —Jin (Western Jin, Eastern Jin) — Northern and Southern Dynasties [Southern (Song, Qi, Liang, Chen) —Northern (Northern Wei, Eastern Wei, Western Wei, Northern Qi, Northern Zhou)] — Sui—Tang— Five Dynasties (Later Liang, Later Tang, Later Jin, Later Han, Later Zhou) —Ten Countries [Former Shu, Later Shu, Wu, Southern Tang, Wu-Yue, Min, Chu, Southern Han, Nanping (Jingnan), Northern Han] — Song (Northern Song, Southern Song) —Liao—Xixia—Jin—Yuan—Ming—Qing— Republic of China— People's Republic of China.

# 附录二 中国历史朝代表
## Appendix B  The List of Dynasties in Chinese History

| 朝 代<br>Dynasty | | 起讫年代<br>Years | 都 城<br>Capital | 今 地<br>Modern Location | 建立者<br>Founder |
|---|---|---|---|---|---|
| 夏朝<br>Xia Dynasty | | 约前2070—前1600<br>2070—1600 B.C. | 安邑<br>Anyi | 山西夏县<br>Xia County, Shanxi | 禹<br>Yu |
| 商朝<br>Shang Dynasty | | 约前1600—前1046<br>1600—1046 B.C. | 亳//殷<br>Bo//Yin | 河南商丘<br>Shangqiu, Henan | 汤<br>Tang |
| 周朝<br>Zhou Dynasty | 西周<br>Western Zhou | 约前1046—前771<br>1046—771 B.C. | 镐京<br>Haojing | 陕西西安<br>Xi'an, Shaanxi | 周武王（姬发）<br>King Wen of Zhou, Ji Fa |
| | 东周<br>Eastern Zhou | 前770—前256<br>770—256 B.C. | 洛邑<br>Luoyi | 河南洛阳<br>Luoyang, Henan | 周平王（姬宜臼）<br>King Ping of Zhou, Ji Yijiu |
| | 春秋时期<br>Spring-Autumn Period | 前770—前476<br>770—476 B.C. | | | |
| | 战国时期<br>Warring States Period | 前475—前221<br>475—221 B.C. | | | |
| 秦朝<br>Qin Dynasty | | 前221—前207<br>221—207 B.C. | 咸阳<br>Xianyang | 陕西咸阳<br>Xianyang, Shaanxi | 秦始皇（嬴政）<br>Qinshihuang, Ying Zheng |

续上表

| 朝 代<br>Dynasty | | 起讫年代<br>Years | 都 城<br>Capital | 今 地<br>Modern Location | 建立者<br>Founder |
|---|---|---|---|---|---|
| 汉朝<br>Han<br>Dynasty | 西汉<br>Western Han | 前206—公元8<br>206 B.C.—8 A.D. | 长安<br>Chang'an | 陕西西安<br>Xi'an, Shaanxi | 汉高祖（刘邦）<br>Gaozu, Liu Bang |
| | 新<br>Xin | 9—23 | 长安<br>Chang'an | 陕西西安<br>Xi'an, Shaanxi | 王莽<br>Wang Mang |
| | 东汉<br>Eastern Han | 25—220 | 洛阳<br>Luoyang | 河南洛阳<br>Luoyang, Henan | 汉光武帝（刘秀）<br>Guangwu, Liu Xiu |
| 三国<br>Three Kingdoms | 魏<br>Wei | 220—265 | 洛阳<br>Luoyang | 河南洛阳<br>Luoyang, Henan | 魏文帝（曹丕）<br>Wen, Cao Pi |
| | 蜀汉<br>Shu Han | 221—263 | 成都<br>Chengdu | 四川成都<br>Chengdu, Sichuan | 汉昭烈帝（刘备）<br>Zhaolie, Liu Bei |
| | 吴<br>Wu | 222—280 | 建业<br>Jianye | 江苏南京<br>Nanjing, Jiangsu | 吴大帝（孙权）<br>Da, Sun Quan |
| 晋朝<br>Jin<br>Dynasty | 西晋<br>Western Jin | 265—316 | 洛阳<br>Luoyang | 河南洛阳<br>Luoyang, Henan | 晋武帝（司马炎）<br>Wu, Sima Yan |
| | 东晋<br>Eastern Jin | 317—420 | 建康<br>Jiankang | 江苏南京<br>Nanjing, Jiangsu | 晋元帝（司马睿）<br>Yuan, Sima Rui |
| 五胡十六国 Five Tribes and Sixteen Countries | | 304—439 | | | |
| 南朝<br>Southern<br>Dynasty | 宋 Song | 420—479 | 建康<br>Jiankang | 江苏南京<br>Nanjing, Jiangsu | 宋武帝（刘裕）<br>Wu, Liu Yu |
| | 齐 Qi | 479—502 | 建康<br>Jiankang | 江苏南京<br>Nanjing, Jiangsu | 齐高帝（萧道成）<br>Gao, Xiao Daocheng |
| | 梁 Liang | 502—557 | 建康<br>Jiankang | 江苏南京<br>Nanjing, Jiangsu | 梁武帝（萧衍）<br>Wu, Xiao Yan |
| | 陈 Chen | 557—589 | 建康<br>Jiankang | 江苏南京<br>Nanjing, Jiangsu | 陈武帝（陈霸先）<br>Wu, Chen Baxian |

续上表

| 朝代<br>Dynasty | | 起讫年代<br>Years | 都城<br>Capital | 今地<br>Modern Location | 建立者<br>Founder |
|---|---|---|---|---|---|
| 北朝<br>Northern Dynasty | 北魏<br>Northern Wei | 386—534 | 平城<br>Pingcheng | 山西大同<br>Datong, Shanxi | 魏道武帝<br>（拓跋珪）<br>Daowu, Tuoba Gui |
| | | | 洛阳<br>Luoyang | 河南洛阳<br>Luoyang, Henan | 魏孝文帝<br>（拓跋宏）<br>Xiaowen, Tuoba Hong |
| | 东魏<br>Eastern Wei | 534—550 | 邺<br>Ye | 河北临漳<br>Linzhang, Hebei | 魏孝静帝<br>（元善见）<br>Xiaojing, Yuan Shanjian |
| | 西魏<br>Western Wei | 535—557 | 长安<br>Chang'an | 陕西西安<br>Xi'an, Shaanxi | 魏文帝（元宝炬）<br>Wen, Yuan Baoju |
| | 北齐<br>Northern Qi | 550—577 | 邺<br>Ye | 河北临漳<br>Linzhang, Hebei | 齐文宣帝（高洋）<br>Wenxuan, Gao Yang |
| | 北周<br>Northern Zhou | 557—581 | 长安<br>Chang'an | 陕西西安<br>Xi'an, Shaanxi | 周孝闵帝<br>（宇文觉）<br>Xiaomin, Yuwen Jue |
| 隋朝<br>Sui Dynasty | | 581—618 | 大兴<br>Daxing | 陕西西安<br>Xi'an, Shaanxi | 隋文帝（杨坚）<br>Wen, Yang Jian |
| 唐朝<br>Tang Dynasty | | 618—907 | 长安<br>Chang'an | 陕西西安<br>Xi'an, Shaanxi | 唐高祖（李渊）<br>Gaozu, Li Yuan |

续上表

| 朝代 Dynasty | | 起讫年代 Years | 都城 Capital | 今地 Modern Location | 建立者 Founder |
|---|---|---|---|---|---|
| 五代十国 Five Dynasties and Ten Kingdoms | 后梁 Later Liang | 907—923 | 汴州 Bianzhou | 河南开封 Kaifeng, Henan | 梁太祖（朱全忠）Taizu, Zhu Quanzhong |
| | 后唐 Later Tang | 923—936 | 洛阳 Luoyang | 河南洛阳 Luoyang, Henan | 唐庄宗（李存勖）Zhuangzong, Li Cunxu |
| | 后晋 Later Jin | 936—947 | 汴州 Bianzhou | 河南开封 Kaifeng, Henan | 晋高祖（石敬瑭）Gaozu, Shi Jingtang |
| | 后汉 Later Han | 947—950 | 汴州 Bianzhou | 河南开封 Kaifeng, Henan | 汉高祖（刘知远）Gaozu, Liu Zhiyuan |
| | 后周 Later Zhou | 951—960 | 汴州 Bianzhou | 河南开封 Kaifeng, Henan | 周太祖（郭威）Taizu, Guo Wei |
| | 十国 Ten Kingdoms | 902—979 | | | |
| 宋朝 Song Dynasty | 北宋 Northern Song | 960—1127 | 开封 Kaifeng | 河南开封 Kaifeng, Henan | 宋太祖（赵匡胤）Taizu, Zhao Kuangyin |
| | 南宋 Southern Song | 1127—1279 | 临安 Lin'an | 浙江杭州 Hangzhou, Zhejiang | 宋高宗（赵构）Gaozong, Zhao Gou |
| 辽 Liao | | 916—1125 | 上京 Shangjing | 内蒙古巴林左旗南波罗城 South Polo City, Balin Zuoqi, Inner Mongolia | 辽太祖（耶律阿保机）Taizu, Yelü Abaoji |
| 大理 Dali | | 937—1254 | 羊苴咩城 Yangjumie City | 云南大理 Dali, Yunnan | 太祖（段思平）Taizu, Duan Siping |

续上表

| 朝 代<br>Dynasty | 起讫年代<br>Years | 都 城<br>Capital | 今 地<br>Modern Location | 建立者<br>Founder |
|---|---|---|---|---|
| 西夏<br>Xixia | 1038—1227 | 兴庆府<br>Xingqingfu | 宁夏银川<br>Yinchuan, Ningxia | 景宗（李元昊）<br>Jingzong, Li Yuanhao |
| 金<br>Jin | 1115—1234 | 会宁府<br>Huiningfu | 黑龙江阿城<br>Acheng, Heilongjiang | 金太祖（阿骨打）<br>Taizu, Aguda |
| | | 中都<br>Zhongdu | 北京<br>Beijing | 海陵王（完颜亮）<br>Hailing King, Wanyan Liang |
| | | 开封<br>Kaifeng | 河南开封<br>Kaifeng, Henan | 金宣宗（完颜珣）<br>Xuanzong, Wanyan Xun |
| 元朝<br>Yuan Dynasty | 1271—1368 | 大都<br>Dadu | 北京<br>Beijing | 元世祖（忽必烈）<br>Shizu, Kublai Khan |
| 明朝<br>Ming Dynasty | 1368—1644 | 应天府<br>Yingtianfu | 江苏南京<br>Nanjing, Jiangsu | 明太祖（朱元璋）<br>Taizu, Zhu Yuanzhang |
| | | 北平<br>Beiping | 北京<br>Beijing | 明成祖（朱棣）<br>Chengzu, Zhu Di |
| 清朝<br>Qing Dynasty | 1636—1911 | 盛京<br>Shengjing<br>燕京<br>Yanjing | 辽宁沈阳<br>Shenyang, Liaoning<br>北京<br>Beijing | 清太宗（皇太极）<br>Taizong, Huangtaiji<br>清世祖（福临）<br>Shizu, Fulin |
| 中华民国<br>Republic of China | 1912—1949 | 南京<br>Nanjing | 江苏南京<br>Nanjing, Jiangsu | |
| 中华人民共和国<br>People's Republic of China | 1949— | 北京<br>Beijing | 北京<br>Beijing | |

# 后 记

本书是为母语非汉语的大学生编纂的通识类教材。编纂缘起于（青海师范大学民族师范学院）本科生、国际交流中心留学生的"中国文化"课程。经过几年的教学实践，在普通本科生教案基础上提炼简编而成，涵盖文化各目，既有历史、音乐、教育等偏重于形而上之道的内容，也有医学、建筑、科技、服饰等偏重于形而下之器的内容，还有饮食、节日、旅游等道器兼备的内容。然约而不简，对某些篇章涉及的学术界热门课题，尽量撮其要点，顾及深度，适度析论以引入思考；叙述语言力求精练有趣、通俗易懂，以使内容有可读性；论述力求做到道与器、精神与物质、审美与事功的统一，真实而生动地、全方位地展示中国文化。汉文单行本先行出版，另行出版汉英（即本书）、汉藏双语版。

本书写作之时，合作者就提议请恩师冯天瑜先生为之作序，时闻冯先生已有身疾，不敢叨扰，延至近日出版之际开口，冯先生很快回复。然不知道的是，序言乃冯先生在住院化疗的极度不适中写赠。听师兄详说此情后，心里颇感歉疚，唯有脚踏实地问学做人，方可报答冯先生对后学晚辈的培育支持。

本书得以出版，感谢青海师范大学历史学院（2019年，原人文学院分为历史学院、文学院）的鼎力支持，感谢青海师范大学藏区历史与多民族繁荣发展研究省部共建协同创新中心、青海师范大学高原科学与可持续发展研究院的大力支持。

参与写作人员为高校教师及美国在读博士研究生。高校教师都是有20年以上教龄者，他们皆以认真的态度投入严谨的写作，虽致力精到、努力上乘，然难免瑕疵，若有不足，请读者诸君不吝赐教，敬请指正。

编著者
2018年7月12日

# Epilogue

This book is a general educational textbook for college students whose native language is not Chinese. After several years of teaching practice, the book is compiled based on *Chinese Culture* lessons for undergraduates in Qinghai Normal University and the students in the International Exchange Center. This book covers various cultural topics, including history, music, education, etc., focusing on the spiritual life. It also covers medicine, architecture, technology, clothing, etc., which focuses on material life and includes food, festivals, tourism, etc. However, the content of the book is simple but not brief. For some of the chapters on popular academic topics, the main points are summarized as much as possible, taking into account the depth, and are moderately analyzed to focus on thinking.

The narrative of this book strives to be concise, engaging, and easy to understand. In order to make the content readable, the discussion and analysis strive to ensure uniformity of the spirit and the material, and to present Chinese culture truly and vividly. We first published the Chinese edition, followed by a Chinese-English (i. e. , this book) and a Chinese-Tibetan edition. When this book was written, my collaborators proposed to ask my mentor, Mr. Feng Tianyu, to write a preface for it. However, at that time, I heard about Mr. Feng's illness, so I did not want to disturb him. I asked him until the recent publication, and Mr. Feng quickly replied. However, I did not know that Mr. Feng wrote the preface during the extreme discomfort of chemotherapy in the hospital, and I felt sorry after hearing the details of this situation from my colleague. The only way to repay Mr. Feng's support to us is to have rigorous scholarship and to be an honest person.

This book was made possible thanks to the generous support of the School of History at Qinghai Normal University.

The writers of this book are university faculty and a Ph. D. candidate at a US university. The faculty members have more than 20 years of teaching experience with writing rigorously. Although we are committed to excellence, writing can be inevitably flawed. If there are any mistakes, I appreciate your advice and correction.

Writers

July 12, 2018